Days in the
Lives of
Social Workers

Days in the
Lives of

Social Workers

62 Professionals Tell "Real-Life"
Stories From Social Work Practice

Fifth Edition

Linda May Grobman, Editor

with a Foreword by
Kathryn Conley Wehrmann, Ph.D., LCSW
President, National Association of Social Workers

PRESS

Harrisburg, Pennsylvania

Days in the Lives of Social Workers
62 Professionals Tell "Real-Life" Stories
From Social Work Practice
Fifth Edition

Edited by Linda May Grobman

Published by:

PRESS

Post Office Box 5390, Harrisburg, PA 17110-0390 U.S.A.
717-238-3787 (voice)   717-238-2090 (fax)
http://www.socialworker.com

The editor can be contacted by e-mail at: *lindagrobman@socialworker.com*

Note: The names and identities of social work clients mentioned in this book have been carefully disguised in accordance with professional standards of confidentiality.

Listing of a resource in Appendix A, B, C, or D does not imply endorsement.

Portions of Chapter 37 are reprinted with permission of the New York City Chapter of the National Association of Social Workers. They were published in the May 1996 issue of *CURRENTS* of the New York City Chapter NASW.

Chapter 49: "The opinions or assertions contained herein are the private views of the author and are not to be construed as official or as reflecting the views of the Department of Army or the Department of Defense."

Cover photo credit: Neale Cousland/Bigstock.com

Library of Congress Cataloging-in-Publication Data

Names: Grobman, Linda May, editor.
Title: Days in the lives of social workers : 62 professionals tell "real-life" stories from social work practice / Linda May Grobman, editor ; with a foreword by Kathryn Conley Wehrmann, Ph.D., LCSW, President, National Association of Social Workers.
Description: Fifth edition. | Harrisburg, Pennsylvania : New Social Worker Press, [2019]
Identifiers: LCCN 2019007720 | ISBN 9781929109845
Subjects: LCSH: Social workers–United States. | Social case work–United States.
Classification: LCC HV40.8.U6 D39 2019 | DDC 361.3092/273–dc23
LC record available at https://lccn.loc.gov/2019007720

Days in the Lives of Social Workers
Fifth Edition

Table of Contents

About the Editor

Linda May Grobman, MSW, LSW, ACSW, is the founder, publisher, and editor of *THE NEW SOCIAL WORKER*®, the social work careers magazine, and the co-author of *THE SOCIAL WORKER'S INTERNET HANDBOOK*. She has practiced social work in mental health and medical settings, and is a former interim executive director of the Pennsylvania and Georgia state chapters of the National Association of Social Workers. She received her MSW and BM (Music Therapy) degrees from the University of Georgia, and is a graduate of the Music for Healing and Transition Program. Linda was the 2014 Pennsylvania NASW Social Worker of the Year and is an NASW Social Work Pioneer®.

About the Contributors

Joan M. Abbey, MSW, LMSW, is a research scientist at Eastern Michigan University. She previously was an adjunct lecturer at the University of Michigan School of Social Work and Eastern Michigan University Social Work Department. She serves as a consultant in fiscal, policy, and program evaluation to state and local governments and private agencies. Her publications include *Making Change: The Cost to Michigan's Children* and "We Know Better Than We Do" in the *Michigan Journal of Law Reform*.

Barbara Alexander, LCSW, BCD, is a graduate of the Smith College School for Social Work and the Child and Adolescent Psychotherapy Program of the Chicago Institute for Psychoanalysis. She was President of the Illinois Society for Clinical Social Work for two terms. In 1992, after working for 13 years in child psychiatric settings and 30 years in private practice, she founded and became president of ON GOOD AUTHORITY. She has interviewed more than 200 experts in mental health and psychotherapy for On Good Authority's programs.

Holly Anderson, BSW, works as a social worker on an Unaccompanied Minors Team for a London borough in the UK. She received her BSW from the University of Victoria in British Columbia in 1999.

Ronald M. Arundell, Ed.D., ACSW, LISW, retired in 2009 from positions as Associate Professor of Social Work and Program Director for the BSW program at the College of Mount St. Joseph in Cincinnati, Ohio. He maintained a small private practice specializing in the treatment of adolescent sexual offenders. Dr. Arundell has worked as a clinical social worker with children in residential and psychiatric inpatient settings.

Staci A. Beers, MSW, LSW, is employed at the state level in the victim services field. She received a BS in Criminal Justice/Women's Studies from West Chester University and an MSW from Marywood College School of Social Work.

Yvonne Bergmans, BSW, MSW, RSW, Ph.D., is a suicide interventionist at the Arthur Sommer Rotenberg Chair in Suicide and Depression Studies. Together with her clients, she has created a group intervention for people experiencing recurrent suicide attempts. She is engaged in research and teaching, alongside clinical consultations, risk assessments and individual psychotherapy for those deemed at high risk for suicide.

Amy Blake, MSW, CSW, ACSW, has a private practice in Ferndale, Michigan, where she is also vice-president of A Woman's Prerogative Bookstore. She earned her MSW from the University of Michigan in Ann Arbor. She has received several awards, including the Detroit Chapter, National Organization for Women's Loretta Moore Award for contributions in raising consciousness on issues of concern to women.

Staci Block, MSW, LCSW, is Coordinator of the Reflections and RISE programs of the Bergen County Division of Family Guidance. She is an adjunct professor at William Paterson University. Her expertise involves using action methods in team building, developing peer leaders, and creating interactive training for staff development.

Beth Boyett, MFA, CMSW, is an outpatient therapist at Spectra Behavioral Healthcare Systems in Memphis, Tennessee. Prior to earning her MSSW degree from the University of Tennessee-Knoxville (May 1995), she was an assistant professor of English at Rhodes College (Memphis), Franklin Pierce College (Rindge, New Hampshire), and Visiting Writer-in-Residence at St. Albans School (Washington, DC).

Angela Marie Brinton, BSW, received her degree from Missouri Western State College in 1992. She was previously employed by the State of Missouri in Kansas City.

Asherah Cinnamon, MSW, LCSW, is a sculptor whose art is informed by personal history. She was a national associate and director of the National Coalition Building Institute, East Tennessee Chapter and Maine Chapter. She has received many awards, including the New England United Methodist Award for Excellence in Social Justice Actions. She founded the Second Generation of Maine/ Children of Holocaust Survivors.

Elizabeth J. Clark, Ph.D., ACSW, MPH, is President of the Start Smart Career Center, which helps women navigate nonprofit careers and become leaders. Her previous position of 12 years was CEO of the National Association of Social Workers. Dr. Clark has a background in health care, with a specialization in oncology. Dr. Clark holds bachelor's and master's degrees in social work and a master's in public health from the University of Pittsburgh, as well as a master's degree and doctorate in medical sociology from the University of North Carolina at Chapel Hill.

Kenneth Cohen, BS Social Welfare, is Ombudsman for the Franklin County Children Services in Grove City, Ohio. He has been employed by Franklin County since 1974, previously as an Investigative Social Worker and an Ongoing Social Worker. In his role as Ombudsman, he has worked with a client base approaching 10,000.

Madeline B. Cohen, MSW, CISW, graduated *cum laude* in 1976 from Emory University with a BA in psychology. She went on to the University of Georgia and received her MSW in 1978. She works for the Tucson Jewish Community Center as the Senior Adult Coordinator. Among her professional awards are Outstanding Young Woman of America and Who's Who Among Human Services Professionals.

Cami L. Cooper, MSW, received both her BSW and MSW from Arizona State University, having earned her graduate degree in May 1996. She has been employed as a school social worker since 1993, having previously worked as a case manager for at-risk high school and middle school students and an in-home counselor for pregnant teens. She speaks fluent Spanish and sings in a gospel choir in her spare time.

Michael Crawford, MSW, RSW, has taught welfare theory and family practice in the School of Social Work at the University College of the Cariboo in Kamloops, British Columbia, since 1991. He previously taught at Grant MacEwan Community College in Edmonton, Alberta. His clinical and research interests are in the area of family violence, and he has worked with physically and sexually abusive men for more than 15 years. He received his BSW from the University of Manitoba and his MSW from the University of Calgary.

Catherine Lau Crisp, MSW, is a clinical social worker at the Medical College of Virginia Hospital in Richmond, Virginia. She is a member of the National Association of Social Workers and the National Association of Lesbian and Gay Alcoholism Professionals (NALGAP) and is a co-leader of Bridge Builders: Acting for Justice and Liberation in Richmond.

Stephen P. Cummings, MSW, ACSW, LISW, is a Clinical Associate Professor at the University of Iowa School of Social Work, where he is the Distance Education Administrator.

Judith C. Czarnecki, MSW, LISW, is President/CEO of Family Service of Northwest Ohio, where she has served in various administrative capacities since 1985. Her professional experience also includes direct practice in family service and child protective service settings. She is actively involved in many professional and community organizations, including the Ohio Chapter of NASW, where she was awarded the local Social Worker of the Year Award in 1990 and the State of Ohio Outstanding Service Award in 1989.

Amber Daniels, MSW, is Youth Center Supervisor at Latino Family Services in Detroit, Michigan. She has held various youth development positions and serves on several youth-related task forces and advisory boards in the Detroit area.

Paula David, BA, MSW, RSW, is Coordinator of the Holocaust Resource Project at Baycrest Centre for Geriatric Care in Toronto, Ontario, Canada. She also teaches gerontology at the Ryerson Polytechnic University School of Social Work, Continuing Education Interdisciplinary Studies.

Merle T. Edwards-Orr, Ph.D., LICSW, is the Neonatal Intensive Care Unit social worker at Fletcher Allen Health Care in Burlington, Vermont. He also is an

Adjunct Assistant Professor of social work at the University of VT. He received his MSSW from the University of Tennessee and his Ph.D. from the University of Wisconsin-Madison.

Ann Elliot, LCSW, is a Certified Criminal Justice Specialist, a Certified Domestic Violence Counselor, and a Certified Equine Assisted Psychotherapist. She has been in private practice as a play therapist for more than 15 years. She has worked extensively with trauma and abused victims in individual, family, and group therapy. She works PRN for the local hospital and is the mental health clinician for the county jail.

Brad Forenza, MSW, Ph.D., has been a legislative aide for policy, research, and communications for more than 10 years. He is also an academic whose research foci include child welfare, youth development, and civil society.

Susan Dodd Gaylor, MSW, ACSW, is Area Training Manager for the Virginia Institute for Social Services Training Activities (VISSTA), Piedmont Area Training Center. She also maintains a small private practice in Salem, Virginia. Her previous experience includes working as a child protective services social worker in Washington, DC; Atlanta, Georgia; and Roanoke, Virginia.

Alfreda Paschall Gee, MSW, is a public health social worker for a high-risk maternity clinic in North Carolina. She received her MSW from the University of North Carolina-Chapel Hill and is a member of the National Association of Social Workers, North Carolina Public Health Association, and the North Carolina Association of Public Health Social Workers.

Patricia Gleason-Wynn, Ph.D., LMSW-ACP, is the BSW Director and Assistant Professor in the Department of Social Work at Southwest Texas State University, San Marcos, Texas. She has worked with older adults, particularly in nursing homes, since 1980.

Claire McCullough Godfrey, LCSW, is Crisis Response Team Supervisor in the Victim Services Division of a Texas city police department. She received her MSW from the University of Texas at Austin and BSSW from Texas Christian University.

Gretchen Gross, LICSW, ACSW, NCADC, is a Social Worker II and Staff Counselor at the Division of Reproductive Endocrinology and Infertility at Women's Health Services, Fletcher Allen Health Care in Burlington, Vermont. She is a clinical instructor at the Department of Obstetrics and Gynecology, College of Medicine, University of Vermont, and is a clinical social worker and certified alcohol counselor in private practice in South Burlington.

Carol Hendler, MSW, LCSW-C, LICSW, LCSW, maintains a full-time private practice in Bethesda, MD. While maintaining a part-time private practice, she worked full time in the U.S. Army's Family Advocacy Program, treating child and spouse abuse at both Walter Reed Army Medical Center and at Ft. Meade. She was president of the Metro DC Chapter of the International Society for Traumatic Stress Studies for three years.

Laura Crawford Hofer, MSSW, LCSW, ACSW, BCD, is a counselor at the Counseling Center of Western Connecticut State University in Danbury, CT. After graduating from Harvard University with a bachelor's degree in history, she served as a VISTA volunteer before returning to school at Columbia University for her MSW. She has been a clinical social worker since 1976.

Christian Itin, BSW, MSW, Ph.D., is an Assistant Professor with the Greater Rochester Collaborative MSW Program in Rochester, NY. He is a past program director with both the Colorado and Hurricane Island Outward Bound Schools.

Jerry L. Johnson, Ph.D., is assistant professor at the Grand Valley State University School of Social Work. Before teaching, he spent 13 years as a therapist, administrator, community organizer, and consultant in Detroit, Grand Rapids, and across Michigan.

Judith J. Lacerte, MSW, LISW, G.S., is a home health services team leader at the Department of Health and Environmental Control in Anderson, South Carolina. She is certified by the SC Department of Mental Health as a geriatric specialist and received special training in geriatrics at the University of North Carolina, Center for Aging Research and Education Services. She was the South Carolina Public Health Social Worker of the Year in 1995.

Daniel Liechty, Ph.D., D.Min., LSW, formerly psychosocial coordinator with a hospital-based hospice program, is on the social work faculty of Illinois State University at Normal, Illinois. He is a member of the National Association of Social Workers, the Academy of Certified Social Workers, the Association for Death Education and Counseling, and the Ernest Becker Foundation. He is a graduate of the Bryn Mawr College Graduate School of Social Work and Social Research.

Carol M. Line, BS, ACSW, is in private practice as a social worker and physical therapist. She practiced as a school social worker with the Eastern Upper Peninsula Intermediate School District in Northern Michigan for nine years.

Kim R. Lorber, MSW, CSW, is a social worker at a nursing home in Bronx, New York City. She is enrolled in the DSW program at Wurzweiler School of Social Work, Yeshiva University, and is conducting research on AIDS/HIV issues for women, lesbians, couples of mixed-HIV status, and HIV-positive paid professionals working with HIV-positive individuals.

Gary Lounsberry, MSW, MPH, Ph.D., LCSW, is Associate Professor and Coordinator of the Human Services Program at Florida Gulf Coast University. He received his Ph.D. and Master of Public Health from the University of Pittsburgh, and his MSW from the University of Michigan. He has a variety of clinical and administrative experience, including more than 20 years with the U.S. Public Health Service. He is a retired Health Services Director (equivalent to a Naval Captain) from the Commissioned Corps, U.S. Public Health Services.

Peggy McFarland, Ph.D., MSW, is the co-founder of Senior Management Services, a firm that has provided elder care management and direction since 1990. She is a licensed clinical social worker, earning her MSW from Marywood College and a Ph.D in social work from the University of Maryland at Baltimore. She is a professor of social work at Elizabethtown College.

Toni Murphy, MSSW, CCSW, is in part-time private practice in Raleigh, North Carolina. She specializes in counseling services for families of children with special needs, adolescents with special needs, and adults with disability-related issues. She was previously employed as the Director of Social Services for a nonprofit agency in the Southwest that provided services for children and adults with developmental disabilities. She was nominated for an adjunct faculty position at the University of Texas School of Social Work as a result of her educational supervision of graduate students.

Doris Nelson, LMSW, received her Master of Social Work degree from the University of South Carolina in 2003. She is a Disabled Veterans Outreach Program Specialist at the Georgia Department of Labor. She received an honorable discharge from the United States Army.

Rachel Odo, LCSW, is a clinical social worker with a specialty in acute, chronic, and life-threatening illness. She works as a consultant lecturing and presenting workshops on a range of topics for healthcare professionals, patients, and caregivers, and has served as a moderator in the online support program at CancerCare, Inc.

Lisa Orloff, ACSW, is a forensic social worker at the Legal Aid Society, Capital Defense Unit, in Brooklyn, New York, where she previously worked in the Criminal Defense Division. Before her employment at Legal Aid, she worked in several settings with crime victims, including a domestic violence shelter and a rape crisis center. She received her MSW from Florida State University in 1992.

Julia Ostropolsky, LCSW, came to the United States as a 17-year-old refugee from the USSR, often serving as interpreter for her parents and grandparents. She received her MSW from the Washington University School of Social Work. Before opening her own agency, she worked as a Qualified Mental Retardation Specialist, Service Coordinator, and Mental Health Social Worker. She is Executive Director of Bi-Lingual International Assistant Services, a nonprofit organization offering counseling and case management services to Bosnian-, Russian-, Spanish-, and Chinese-speaking New American elderly and disabled.

David Pérez, MSW, is the Social Work and Diversity Services Manager at Long Branch Free Public Library in New Jersey.

Andrew J. Peters, CSW, MSW, is Project Director at Pride for Youth Project, Long Island Crisis Center.

David C. Prichard, Ph.D, is Associate Professor of Social Work and Associate Dean of Assessment in the College of Health Professions at the University of New England in Portland, Maine. His practice experience includes clinical treatment and supervision, specializing in work with survivors of primary and secondary trauma. He received his Ph.D. in 1996 from Virginia Commonwealth University in Richmond, where he resided for 10 years.

Ogden W. Rogers, Ph.D., CICSW, ACSW, was formerly a clinical social worker in emergency medicine at the Johns Hopkins Hospital, Baltimore, Maryland. He is Associate Dean, College of Education and Professional Studies, and Professor of Social Work at The University of Wisconsin-River Falls. He is engaged in consultation and research on issues of disaster mental health, refugee assistance, and international humanitarian law.

Glenda Dewberry Rooney, MSW, Ph.D., is Associate Professor in the Department of Social Work, Augsburg College, in Minneapolis, Minnesota. She has practice and administrative experience in academic and human service organizations, including an employee assistance program. In 1994, she completed a study that examined the concerns of employed women and the service provisions of employee assistance programs.

Vicki B. Root, Ed.D., MSW, is Associate Professor and Director of the MSW program at Salisbury University. She was formerly Assistant Professor and Director of the social work program at Messiah College in Grantham, Pennsylvania, and has served as Special Needs Assistant for the Lutheran Camping Corporation in Arendtsville, PA.

Diane Rullo-Cooney, MSW, LCSW, CADC, is a social worker in private practice with Rullo Psych Associates in Hazlet, New Jersey. She is also an adjunct professor at Rutgers University in New Brunswick, New Jersey, and has completed coursework toward a doctorate in social welfare at Fordham University.

Fred Sacklow, CSW, R, is a social worker with the New York City Board of Education. He also maintains a private psychotherapy practice in Queens, New York.

Gerhard J. Schwab, Ph.D., MSW, teaches social work at the University of Guam. He received a Ph.D. in social work and psychology from the University of Michigan. He has practiced social work in Austria (his home country), Papua New Guinea, Michigan, and Guam.

Michael Shernoff, MSW, CSW, ACSW, was in full-time private practice primarily with gay men, and taught "Social Work with Today's Lesbians and Gay Men" as an adjunct faculty member at Hunter College Graduate School of Social Work. He edited and co-edited several books, and wrote more than 50 articles, all on psychosocial issues of HIV/AIDS and mental health for gay men. He was also the online mental health expert for The Body, the world's largest HIV/AIDS Web site. In addition, he served on the boards of the National Social Work AIDS Network (NSWAN) and the National Lesbian/Gay Health Foundation.

Kenneth G. Smith, MSW, LCSW, received his BA in Social Welfare from Old Dominion University and MSW from the University of Tennessee-Knoxville. He is Partial Hospitalization Coordinator at St. Anthony's Hospital in St. Petersburg, Florida and has experience as an inpatient therapist, program chief, and chief social worker in a psychiatric hospital; private practitioner; and community mental health clinician. He earned a Diplomate in clinical social work in 1994.

Sara Staver, LMSW, is an instructor and coordinator at for the social work program at Briar Cliff University in Iowa. She earned her BSW from Buena Vista University in Iowa and MSW from the University of Iowa School of Social Work. Sara has dedicated several years to working with individuals experiencing co-occurring mental health and substance use conditions. She holds a certification for Drug and Alcohol Counseling in Iowa.

Juliet Sternberg, LMSW, is founder and practice director at Hope Veterinary Clinic. She obtained her MSW degree from Fordham University in 2002. Prior to launching Hope Veterinary Clinic, Juliet had 10 years of experience in mental health and geriatric case management and counseling. She founded Hope Veterinary Clinic in 2002 with her veterinarian partner, Kristine Young.

Stephanie Taylor, MSW, is Program Director for the Salvation Army Anti-Trafficking Services, in Orange County, CA.

Roxana Torrico, MSW, is a Program Manager for the Youth Services Division of the Child Welfare League of America (CWLA). She provides direction and technical assistance specific to the development and knowledge regarding the intersection of foster care and homelessness. Prior to joining CWLA, she worked as a foster care social worker at Arlington County (VA) Department of Human Services. Ms. Torrico received her MSW from Virginia Commonwealth University.

Ronnita J. Waters, BSSW, MSW, LCSW-QS, is now a Program Operations Administrator with the Center for Family and Child Enrichment, Inc.

John D. Weaver, LCSW, ACSW, BCD, is a Casework Supervisor and Disaster Response Team Coordinator for Northampton County Mental Health and a part-time therapist for Concern Professional Services, both in Bethlehem, PA. He also has a private consulting group practice, Eye of the Storm, Inc. He volunteers with the American Red Cross and has received its Clara Barton Honor Award for Meritorious Volunteer Leadership. He is the author of several articles, chapters, and books, including *Disasters: Mental Health Interventions.*

Foreword

||||||||||||||||||||||||||||||||||||||||||

by Kathryn Conley Wehrmann, Ph.D., LCSW

There are few things more professionally satisfying than having a respected social work colleague ask if you would write the foreword to a new edition of her book. This is especially true when you know how dear the book is to her and you know how dedicated she is to the profession. Linda Grobman, through her efforts to produce this new edition of *Days in the Lives of Social Workers* and her ongoing efforts in editing *The New Social Worker,* demonstrates how intimately acquainted she is with our profession. As I sat down to write, many thoughts came to mind.

The first thing that occurred to me was, how I wish there had been a book like *Days in the Lives of Social Workers* when I was trying to decide what direction to go in with my professional life. Through trial and error and the grace of mentors and role models, including a beloved aunt and uncle who were both social workers, I worked it out. But, I just can't help imagining what it would have been like if I had had a book like this to read and "try on" different professional settings. What if everyone with love for working with people and a passion for social justice had a book like this to read and think about the diverse wealth of possibilities within social work as they chart an educational course to a professional future? I think it would be wonderful if *Days in the Lives of Social Workers* could find its way into our middle schools and high schools, in addition to our colleges and universities, so students might become aware earlier of social work as a profession they could join. The book also serves as an incredible resource for those who might be considering a change in career and for social workers who are thinking about changing their practice while remaining in the profession.

The more I thought about the book and what it contributes, I realized that it paints a "word picture" of what social work is as a profession. This is not an easy thing to do, given how multifaceted

17

social work is and given the many settings in which it is practiced. This book presents the mosaic that is social work—a mosaic of multiple "tiles" held together with the core values of service, social justice, dignity and worth of the person, the importance of human relationships, integrity, and competence, all applied "within the context and the complexity of the human experience," as stated in the NASW *Code of Ethics*. The mosaic that is social work has grown ever larger as practitioners have generated new fields of practice and innovations within already existing fields and because of the profession's demonstrated capacity to meet human needs from its earliest origins in the English Poor Laws to the diversity of contemporary practice.

Our varying practice contexts and the complexity of human experience make it difficult to succinctly explain what it is that social workers do, especially if you are trying to make a case to a policymaker about the value that social workers bring to professional settings. *Days in the Lives of Social Workers* provides immense help in making such explanations possible. This is especially helpful as social work continues to evolve and move into newer frontiers, such as police social work, environmental social work, library social work, and veterinary social work. Linda has also included chapters on social work practice that is becoming increasingly more necessary in our society, including work on suicide prevention and intervention, human trafficking, and intervening with opioid users.

Linda has continued her professional commitment in this new edition by adding "Days" that reflect the ever-evolving profession of social work. There are so many more possibilities as professional social workers break new ground in bringing their knowledge and skill to bear. More "tiles" will be added to the mosaic with each reflecting the commitment of a profession to supporting human potential.

Firmly rooted in hope, social work is the profession of possibility and reinvention. We social workers do the work and we continually demonstrate how instrumental we are in speaking truth to power, advocating for others, creating innovative programs, and negotiating consequential agreements at the highest levels. We are a profession working to demonstrate how what we do contributes at every level of society, in all the old familiar places, as well as many new ones. Our profession is especially needed in a political climate where social justice efforts at the macro level are absolutely critical. I am pleased that Linda included a chapter about policy practice in a legislator's office.

As I am writing this, I have just reviewed a public service announcement (PSA) created by NASW for Social Work Month 2019. The theme of the PSA is imagining a world without social workers and what wouldn't happen, and how people would be affected. Maybe we have a winning combination here with *Days in the Lives of Social Workers* that shows us all what our important, diverse, and vibrant profession brings to the world and what would happen if we did not have social workers.

Thank you, Linda Grobman! This book is an inspiration to social workers-to-be and a tribute to practicing social workers. Choosing social work means having a career that can take you through a lifetime of meaning for yourself and of being meaningful to others. It does not get better than that, and here are 62 "days" to prove it.

Kathryn Conley Wehrmann, Ph.D., LCSW
NASW President, 2017-2020
Illinois State University School of Social Work
February 2019

Acknowledgments

||||||||||||||||||||||||||||||||||||||||||||||||||||||||||||||||||||||||||||||||||||||||||||||

DAYS IN THE LIVES OF SOCIAL WORKERS evolved from an idea to a reality as manuscripts poured into my mailbox from social workers near and far. My excitement grew as each story revealed the vital roles social workers play in people's lives, as well as the role the profession plays in social workers' lives.

I was especially struck by the many social workers who said, "I love my job," and the sense of excitement conveyed in their stories. This book was possible only with the participation of the social workers who took time out of their busy days to write about what happens during those days, and I thank them for the work they do and for their contributions to this book.

Thanks also go to chapters of the National Association of Social Workers that published the original call for manuscripts in their newsletters and to the SOCWORK, BPD, SW-FIELDWORK, AASWG (now IASWG), FEMSW-L, AGE-SW, IASWR, and AAS email lists for providing a means for getting the word out about this project over the years, as well as to the social workers who accepted my personal invitation to share their stories.

I want to thank the many social work educators and students who have read and used the previous editions, and who have taken the time to give me their input. Their comments helped shape the new content in each subsequent edition.

I am appreciative of Judy Margo, Barbara Trainin Blank, Marjorie Bicknell, and Adam Grobman, all of whom contributed to editing of various editions.

Thank you to NASW President Kathryn Conley Wehrmann for her support of this book and for writing the foreword for this edition, and for the inspiration for the book cover.

I am especially grateful to my partner in life, Gary Grobman, for his meticulous proofreading, editorial input, updates to the appendices, and support of this and all of my endeavors.

LMG

Introduction to the 5th Edition

IIIIIIIIIIIIIIIIIIIIIIIIIIIIIIIIIIIIIIIIIIIIIIIIIIIIIIIIIIIIIIIIIIIIIIIIIIIIIIIIIIIIIIIIIIIIIIIIIIIIIIIIIIIIIIIIIIIIIIIIIIIIIIIIIIIIIIIIIIIIII

If variety is the "spice" of life, then social work is one of the "hottest" careers around. Variety is one aspect of social work practice that makes it exciting for so many members of the profession. It's also one of the reasons so many people don't fully understand exactly what social workers do.

A story was told at a social work conference I attended. The speaker related the difficulties he had in explaining to his mother what he did professionally. After years (maybe even decades) in the social work profession, he became a professor at a university. His mother was relieved—when her friends asked what her son did for a living, she simply said, "He teaches."

It is sometimes difficult to articulate exactly what one does as a social worker, and the profession is sometimes misunderstood. So, when I set out to publish a book about social work, I wanted to convey a sense of not only what professional social workers do, but what their lives are like on a day-to-day basis.

This book is about real life social workers. It says, "I'm a social worker. Spend a day with me and see what it's like." It takes a firsthand, close-up look at the roles social workers play every day in places from hospitals and prisons to universities and public libraries and police departments. It celebrates the joys and rewards of social work, and it presents a realistic view of the challenges of being a social worker. In it, real life social workers describe their days—not necessarily "typical" days, since most say there is no such thing, but days that are representative of the essence of their work.

The first edition of this book, published in 1996, included 41 unique narratives that captured the broad scope of the work that social workers do. With each subsequent edition, the experiences represented have been even more varied. The sections on health care; children, youth, and families; and international social work were expanded. The chapter on disaster mental health was updated in the third edition, as its author recounted his involvement in disaster relief after the September 11th terrorist attacks.

After the third edition, the need for social workers continued to grow into even more diverse areas. We continued to see social workers involved in the aftermath of such disasters as hurricanes, mass shootings, and others. Bullying and bullying-related suicide are issues that were and continue to be in the forefront, and social workers need to be and ARE in the forefront helping to alleviate and prevent an epidemic from occurring. Cyberbullying and the effects of social media, both positive and negative, are concerns. Military social work is a growing field, as is gerontological social work. Newspapers have reported the use of social work services in department stores, police departments, and public libraries. Social workers can be found almost anywhere.

I added several new chapters to the fourth edition. These chapters presented social workers who have started their own businesses, are geriatric care managers, work with bullies and those who have been bullied, and a leader in our profession who was the CEO of a major organization, the National Association of Social Workers (NASW).

Technology continues to grow as an integral part of our society. No longer simply an "add-on," knowledge of the latest technology has become an issue of cultural competence for social workers. In fact, in 2018, NASW published a new edition of the *Code of Ethics* addressing ethics related to technology use. Also, the *NASW, ASWB, CSWE, & CSWA Standards for Technology in Social Work Practice* came out in 2017, addressing similar issues.

In response to the enormous and ongoing development of new technologies and their implications for the social work profession, I added an appendix to the fourth edition to introduce readers to social work-related uses of social media, blogs, and other technology. In addition, a chapter on working with online support groups is included in this (fifth) edition.

So, what else could possibly be added in the fifth edition? Several emerging areas of practice have been added, including police social work, library social work, and veterinary social work in the area of pet loss. I have added chapters on suicide prevention and intervention, adoption social work, policy practice in a legislative office, human trafficking, and working with opioid users.

You will notice that some chapters have a note indicating that they originally appeared in other books. There are four books in the *Days in the Lives of Social Workers* series. First came *Days in the Lives of Social Workers,* which you are reading now in its fifth edition.

When I decided to revise it, I received so many new chapters that needed to be read, that I published a second volume, *More Days in the Lives of Social Workers,* focusing primarily on macro social work. Later, I collaborated with two colleagues, Dara Bergel Bourassa on *Days in the Lives of Gerontological Social Workers,* and Jennifer Clements on *Riding the Mutual Aid Bus and Other Adventures in Group Work.* All four books follow the day-in-the-life narrative format.

Two chapters on group work, originally published in *Riding the Mutual Aid Bus and Other Adventures in Group Work,* were added to this edition. Groups are a powerful source of mutual aid, and all social workers would do well to be prepared for group work. In the fifth edition, a new appendix lists government websites that can be useful in social work practice. I have also updated and expanded the other appendices.

Whether you are about to receive your social work degree (or are thinking about it), are already a social worker, know a social worker, or just want to know more about the profession, reading *Days in the Lives of Social Workers* is sure to clear up any misconceptions you may have and will certainly broaden your view of what a social worker can do. Maybe it will help you decide which area of social work to specialize in, to articulate why social work is important to you, or to explain to your mother what it is that you do.

As you read *Days in the Lives of Social Workers,* you will discover that the career possibilities in social work are virtually endless. You will read about social workers who are employed by state and federal governments, social workers in private practice, social workers in different countries, social workers working for communities, and on and on. In each chapter, you will find something different, while you will also notice that many of the same core social work skills are used across settings.

This book is divided into 15 parts, each focusing on a specific population or type of setting. Although not every social work specialty is covered specifically, there is much rich material from which social workers in any setting can learn. Within some specialties, such as mental health, you will read about several subspecialties, because there are many very different settings and roles in which social workers work with these populations. I have grouped the chapters of this book into what seem like neat categories, but in reality, many of these stories could easily fit into more than one.

You may notice, as you read this book, that social workers refer to people in various ways. Some call the people with whom they work clients, while others write about patients, consumers, customers, members, and participants. These terms reflect different philosophies, as well as the ever-changing language of our culture and our profession. In some cases, they reflect the language of a particular area of practice or the preferences of particular populations of people who receive social workers' services. This is an important issue to think about as you consider a career in social work (if that is your goal). What is the most respectful manner in which you can address people? Does it change depending on the setting or situation? Does it change across time or geographic lines? Does it change on an individual basis?

My hope is that you will use this book as a starting point—an introduction to the variety of roles social workers play every day. Use it as you would the opportunity to literally follow and observe 62 different social workers for a day. Soak up as much as you can from each experience, decide what you would like to explore further, and then take it from there!

You will find some questions at the end of each chapter. I decided to call these "Think About It," because the questions are designed to serve as a starting point for further thought about the material that has been presented in each chapter. Certainly, many other questions will come to mind as you read about each social worker's day. Use the questions provided and your own additional questions to "think about it" further with classmates, co-workers, or on your own as you explore the variety of roles in social work.

You may find that you want to do some more reading or research on a particular area of social work practice. Use the appendices in the back of the book to find organizations, websites, and other resources on the areas of social work that interest you the most.

Once you have identified your areas of interest, do a Google search, look on social media sites, contact local agencies to get more information, or do some volunteer work. In other words, explore in every way possible!

So, enjoy, learn, and explore through the "days" presented in the pages that follow. Then you can create your *own* unique days in social work—days that I trust will be filled with much success and many rewards.

Linda May Grobman, MSW, LSW, ACSW
April 2019

Prologue: The Who, What, When, Where, Why, and How of Social Work

‖‖

by Linda May Grobman, MSW, LSW, ACSW

WHO?

Social workers are women and men.
    Social workers are young and old.

We are every race and every religion.

We have varying political views.
    And different life experiences.

Social workers are professional people with BSW and MSW degrees (and their CSWE-accredited equivalents), and Ph.D.s and DSWs, too.

WHAT?

Social work is helping people.
    Social work is helping communities and organizations.
And groups and families.

It is assessing, planning, counseling, consulting, writing, thinking, advocating, and much more.
    It's providing comfort and providing options.
Making things happen and making a difference.
    Sometimes, it's exhausting and exasperating.

It can lead to burnout and compassion fatigue and secondary trauma.
It can make us wish we had gone into an easier field at times.

And then we go to a conference or a beach or a movie or read a book or listen to some great music or do some other self-caring things

and we feel reinvigorated afterwards.
And we're ready to begin again.

Social work is rewarding.

It's fulfilling…when we see the smile of a child or our advocacy efforts become law.

It's important.
What we do—what you do—is important.

It's more than a job.
It's a helping profession.

Some call it a calling.

WHEN?

Social work is 9-5.
It is 24/7/365.
It is in the morning, afternoon, and the middle of the night.
It is anytime a person or a community needs our help.

WHERE?

Social work is in hospitals.
It's in schools.
Nursing homes, community centers, court houses.
On computer screens.

Social work is in mental health centers.
In senior centers.
It is in board rooms and in bathrooms.
In libraries. On the street.

It's in adoption and foster care.
In people's homes and in the workplace.

In Congress.
    In the military.

In an office and in a car.
    In the community.

Social work is anyplace a person or group needs a social worker to be.

WHY?

Social workers do it because they want to help.
    We want to help.
We want to help individuals and families who come to us.
    We want to make the world a better place.

We want a world without the isms—racism, sexism, ageism, ableism, classism, heterosexism, anti-Semitism, too many isms to name— that shape so much of the world around us.

We do it because we are angry when we hear about Ferguson, Missouri, and Trayvon Martin and when we know that there are 47,000 suicides a year in the U.S. alone and that there is still stigma about mental illness and getting treatment for it.

We do it for Charleston, Pittsburgh, Orlando, Sandy Hook, Parkland.

We want to see a world where children aren't bullied because they're gay or because they are different. Where children can go to school and feel safe.

And we don't want to—we can't—sit on the sidelines and watch these things continue to go on in our world and that of our future generations.

Because we want to see social justice.

We do it because along with the challenges, there are rewards.

We want to see people living productive and healthy and happy lives.

We want positive change on the micro, mezzo, and macro levels.

Social workers do it because we care.
    Because we have a passion.

What is your passion?
    Follow that, and you will know why you do it.

HOW?

Social workers help people by talking.
    Or with music, or storytelling, or art.

Social workers work in different ways using different techniques.
    Using theories as eclectic as the social workers themselves.

With empathy.
    With warmth and genuineness.

And compassion.
    And passion.

With gentleness or with "toughness."
    And ethically.

    SO…whoever, whatever, whenever, wherever, whyever, and however YOU do social work, THAT IS SOCIAL WORK.

(NOTE: This prologue is adapted from Linda May Grobman's acceptance speech as Pennsylvania NASW Social Worker of the Year, 2014.)

PART 1:
HEALTH CARE

Chapter 1
Social Work in the ER

llllllllllllllllllllllllllllllllllllllllllllllllllllllllllllllllllllllllll

by Ogden W. Rogers, Ph.D., ACSW

In early December, the air is gray and cold. What starts as a modest breeze off the harbor gets funneled by the faces of multi-story buildings on Monument Street, whipped into a biting blast that always seems to be in one's face. As I walk the blocks from the parking garage, I pass underneath the canyons of the Johns Hopkins Hospital. Towering above me stand many floors of surgery, therapy, and patients. Thousands of people bustle about in a brisk pace that insiders call "a Hopkins Walk." I am headed to the end of the block, the corner of Monument and Wolfe Streets. Of this huge medical complex, this is the basement. This is the Hopkins Emergency, and I'm the social worker on the 10 a.m. to 7 p.m. shift.

There are five ambulance doors, and by this time in the morning, four of them are already filled with the orange and white "cracker boxes" of the BCFD (Baltimore City Fire Department). I walk toward the big electric street doors of the department, emblazoned with the logo of the lofty Hopkins "Dome," and the very clear words, "DO NOT PUSH." I smile inwardly as I think about how later tonight, I'll be giving 4th year meds a lecture on ethics and the emergency room. I will ask them to stand outside with me, read those words, and consider all the possible messages they imply.

The waiting room is packed, as usual. Despite all the efforts of bright paint on modern architecture, it still has the ambiance of a bus station. There are about 80 sullen, tired, and mostly black people, hunkered in coats and plastic chairs. Around them whiz physicians, residents, nurses, med students, and me, mostly white,

33

and mostly looking like they are always in a hurry. I know that some of these people will be sitting here, still waiting, when my shift ends.

I throw my coat in a corner of the closet that is my office and see the notes that have piled waiting for me this morning.

A nurse has donated some clothes for a "clothes closet" I have set up for our homeless patients (who are not an uncommon population, but tend to be treated at times with less than a full measure of respect). I stack them according to blouses, shirts, pants. I secretly hope she will see these clothes walk out a few days from now on the frame of some now-nameless person. I hope it will decrease the distance between them.

Sleeping in the holding area is a young man with no apparent medical problem who says he is seventeen—a runaway from San Diego. I tell him I'm here to help. He has had breakfast, and I am arranging an early lunch while I try to offer him opportunities to tell his story. It is a detailed and confused tale, and the few bits of fact that emerge don't add up. I make some phone calls and find out that none of the addresses in San Diego exist. I go back and forth a few times, getting a new piece of information with each visit. Seeking some resources for possible referral, it seems this young man has already spent some time telling slightly different stories at both the city Department of Social Services and Traveler's Aid. Confronted with this information, and a continued offer of assistance, he indicates he's not really from San Diego, but is an undocumented immigrant from Jamaica. He asks for bus fare to the Consulate in Washington, D.C., forty miles away. I am incredulous, as the accent he has sounds pretty American to me. We have a nurse in the unit from Kingston, and I ask her to help me interview the young man. It becomes quickly apparent that he's lying again, and he gets angry. I tell him I figure he's probably in a pretty tight spot, and I'd like to help him.... I don't need the whole truth, but he's gotta come close enough so that I can find his best way out of this emergency room. He stares at me angrily. Silent.

The klaxon goes off and a garbled radio voice says we have five minutes to two incoming medical emergencies via ambulance. I tell the angry fellow to enjoy lunch, and I'll be back in an hour. Before I even get back to my office, one of the cases is coming through the ER doors on its way to Critical Care Bay One. Shortly after, Bay Two is also filled with activity. I have flagged down the paramedics from both units to get what little I can on addresses, names, and any family who may have been present. I have donned gloves and go through the critical care rooms, picking up the cut-off clothes and searching for identifying materials. I find a purse in Bay 1, a wallet in Bay 2. The wallet in Bay 2 tells me a lot about a Mr. Tolliver. He's a barber, a mason, a husband, and he's been to this ER many times in the past three years with heart problems. There is a well worn photograph of him and a woman when they were both much younger and happier.

Through the elbows and tubes and paddles, I can look into both bays. I can see that both patients are elderly and unconscious. I set up the family rooms for relatives—quiet places where anxious, waiting people can be located. A small elderly woman and her adult daughter come looking for the patient in Bay 2. I inquire if she is Mrs. Tolliver. I offer the orientation and support that this crisis usually calls for. I prepare them for a "medical episode." The little woman's coat smells of mothballs and the faintest hint of stale cigar. They are quiet, trembling, and tragic.

The patient in Bay 1 recovers from the brink of death in 30 minutes, and is stable enough to be sent upstairs to a cardiac care unit. Bay 2 appears to be DOA and the resuscitation effort seems to go on forever. It is "early in the month"—a euphemism that means the ER is staffed with new residents and interns, and they need the practice trying to keep people alive. I guess it's better they practice on somebody who's pretty much dead than somebody who's pretty much alive. I am never easy with this decision.

After well over an hour, Weaver, the medical resident "calls it." I will help him break the news. I help a nurse with the quiet task of tidying up the body. Weaver is on the phone and smiling. His patient has died, but the blood gases and electrolytes induced during the resuscitation effort are the mimics of viability. "Harvard Lytes, man, we got Harvard Lytes!" Weaver says to me. I reach and touch his arm in the enthusiasm. "That's great, Martin," I say. "You are very good at what you do. Now, you need to take a moment, switch gears, and go with me to the family room to tell this patient's wife that her husband is dead." Weaver stiffens and I continue my hold on his elbow. My grasp has shifted from one of celebration to one of support. "Uh... yeah, yeah. Let's go do it. Uh, what was this guy's name?"

In the family room, Mr. Tolliver's survivors sit quietly. I have been in and out in the past hour and have kept them informed. They are prepared to hear that he has died, but until it is said, there is always a prayer upon hope. I have done this with Weaver before, many times. His style is to hem and haw, and when he's really uncomfortable, he starts to go into intricate detail and use medical jargon. He's getting better. Today, he skips the jargon and offers only a moderate amount of highlight about the rescue effort. I offer a brief clarification to the family that both prods him and allows for a moment to catch his mental breath. He enters back into the conversation simply: "I'm sorry, Mrs. Tolliver, we did everything we could, but your husband's heart just gave out. He's gone."

"Johnnie's dead?" she asks quietly.

"Yes ma'am," Weaver replies.

I ask the wife and daughter if they'd like to go back with me to the treatment room to see him and they numbly agree. I look over my shoulder and find that Weaver has gone. He has done his job with Bay 2. He goes back to work with the living. I will go with Mrs. Tolliver and her daughter to face their loss.

Back in Holding, the sullen young man looks a little less sullen, perhaps now a bit resigned. I figure he figures he's run out of time and stories. He's not been hassled by anybody in the last hour, and he got a meal, so maybe, just maybe, this worker will play it square with him. The story that emerges this time is vague enough in the details that it has more of the ring of truth to it. He's from Philadelphia, and has gotten into some trouble with "associates," to whom he sold some crack. He left Philly in a hurry. The car he stole broke down, and he was lucky to get it off I-95 and not attract attention from the Toll Authority police. He has a grandmother in D.C. and he's trying to get to her house. I tell him this one "sounds like it could just be a phone call away," if he gives me the grandmother's telephone number. He hedges for a bit, and then says that he burned her before, and he's not sure she will help. I tell him why don't we give it a try, it's just phone calls.

The klaxon goes off again and some disembodied dispatcher's voice reports that we have 12 minutes to prepare for a pediatric chopper incoming from the Eastern Shore. The peds nurses start preparing a bay. A resident calls up to peds-neuro to get a team on the way down to the ER. Over the radio, a medic starts firing a report. On board is a little girl, apparently run over as somebody backed out of a driveway. One can hear the medic coming in over the static with numbers and facts about her condition that reveal she is strong, but hovering. There is attention in his voice. Somewhere over the Chesapeake Bay, he is focused on this bleeding child, and yet he knows it is just a matter of time and space before what was a situation on a driveway becomes a medical episode in the trauma center. All the people and scenery shift around except for the little girl in front of him.

Back in Holding, I am talking to the seventeen-year-old's grand-mother. At first she is angry that I am bothering her about this grandson who has-no-respect-and-he-lies-and-he-cheats-and-he-steals. Then she catches her breath and she wants to know why he's in-the-hospital, and is-he-hurt and is-he-gonna-be-okay? I take a moment to reassure her about his present medical condition without elaborating on his potential social or legal status. I want to put them together on the phone. I ask if she can talk with him for a little bit, and she agrees. I cover the mouth piece as I hand him the phone. "Be nice to this old lady," I warn. "She cares more about you than anybody in Baltimore does."

The child from the Eastern Shore is now an unconscious case in Bay 3. Except for the thin red trickle from her right ear, and faint bruise above her right eye, she seems an otherwise unmarred 4-year-old. She is the center of an ever-expanding audience that is the hallmark of a pediatric critical care case. The room fills up with interns and residents and nurses from trauma teams that all own some piece of her recovery: Neuro, Internal Medicine, PICU, Surgery. The Peds trauma team is involved in all the work of initial assessment, and consults take place, being fired over shoulders. She is a well of attention, absorbing eyes and hands and thoughts about her vital signs.

Many of these people are "players," but many more are just "watchers." They have an "interest in the case," as a strategy develops to put this broken little girl back together. Those in the outermost rings crane their necks to see. They momentarily join into brief conversations with another spectator who is not central to the action. This is a teaching university hospital, and this is one of its pick-up classrooms. I watch a young surgical resident, who is backed into a far corner, and make a mental note about him. He is standing on a chair so that he can see. His hands are gloved and hold each other.

The beautiful child who looked "like a keeper," begins to "go sour," and what seemed mostly a head trauma goes into a full court surgical press. Before this is over, the floor will fill with blood and fluids, trash and terse words will fly freely, and a young woman will cut open and reach into the child's chest and squeeze her un-moving heart, hoping to make it move. When the collective hope is exhausted, someone in Attending's clothes says softly, firmly:

"Thank you, everyone. We're done here." There is a quiet embarrassment, and the once densely packed room becomes almost instantly empty. I turn to prepare a family room.

On my way back through the waiting room, I am flagged down by the sullen teenager, who is now not sullen, but smiling and waving and looks as if he has become my best friend. "Hey man! I'm outta here," he says. "My moms n' pops is on the way."

"You got a ride," I say.

"I got a ride." he smiles back.

"You be straight with that old lady," I wave my finger at him. "She loves you."

"Thanks, man," he says. "I owe you."

I ask him to tell me where he left the car he took from Philadelphia, and without a beat he gives me a corner about six blocks away. I shake his hand and walk back to the critical care bays.

Bay 3 has been cleaned, and is empty except for two figures. I look in from an adjoining room. Beneath the white-green hospital light, the dead child lies under stark white sheets; all the tubes and machines are gone. The young surgical resident I had noted earlier is the only person in attendance. He has bathed the little girl's face, and is trying to pack her leaking right ear with some nasal gauze. He is silent, and there are tears on his face. The packing will not stay put and keeps spilling out of the dead child's ear. He keeps trying to push it back in and keeps failing. He repeats this process over and over and seems stuck at the task. His hands have the slightest tremble. I move noiselessly up to the young resident and add a hand to his packing. In a moment, it is secure. I offer my hand, "It's Doctor Menedez, isn't it?" "Yes," he grips me back tightly, still fixed upon the little girl's face, "Reuben."

"Let's get some coffee, Reuben," I say, "I need a cup."

"Yeah. Thanks," he nods.

I am called a while later to the triage desk. A large, soft black man who is well known to me is standing across from the nurse. She has a slightly exasperated smile and she makes a motion of introduction with her hand. He has apple butter cheeks and a blank stare. He wears a racing cap.

"I don't feel so good. I don't feel so good—uh hum, uh hum," he quietly drones.

"I don't feel so good. I don't feel so good—uh hum."

"Turn off the machines. Turn off the machines—uh hum, uh hum."

"Turn off the machines. Turn off the machines—uh hum."

I know this man as Willy. I smile and offer my hand, which he takes limply. "Okay Willy, let's look around," I say, and we start to walk around the intermediate care unit. We peek in at the Asthma Room. We look into Holding. I make some reassuring observations about the environment around us, and nod at the people who pass by. People who know me and Willy make smiles and nod back. It becomes clear after five minutes that any machines of any concern are all turned off. Willy's shoulders relax and I walk him out onto the street. He will come back in two weeks after his Prolixin clinic appointment and we will do this inspection again.

Morrison, the sector "cage officer," has swung by, looking for this nurse he wants to date. He gives me a wink and says I must be Willy's best friend. I wink back at Morrison and tell him I'm everybody's best friend. We hang out together at the triage desk and shoot the breeze for a while. All the time, Morrison has an ear cocked to his radio.

The cage car officer patrols the entire Eastern District. He responds to sectors where officers have made an arrest, and transports the arrested person to the district lockup for booking. Morrison moonlights as a police officer in the ER, and over time I have come to know him as a go-between for myself and some of the other sector officers. When issues of domestic abuse arise, the police and I have needs from each other, and Morrison has helped me make small breaks into the blue line. About every other month or so, I go on a "ride-along" for a shift with somebody in the district. I use the time to get tested by the officer at the wheel, and make some points about how we can help each other in those sticky situations. Afterwards, we will go to the Police Union Club and have too many beers. There have been some times now when I have been called from my office to go to some address in the neighborhood and help the officer on the scene. I feel good that these relationships are working.

"Hey Morrison," I punch lightly at his shoulder, "If you promise not to ask where I got it, I'll give you a present." Morrison thinks for a moment and then bites, "Okay, what?"

"There's a green Jeep Cherokee with Pennsylvania plates near the corner of Broadway and Eastern Avenue. It's outta gas and it might be hot from Philadelphia. I'm psychic."

"Cool," says Morrison, and he bends down to his radio.

After hours, the little girl's mother has arrived. As I escort her to the family room, she asks me if the child is all right. When I hesitate, and tell her that I am going to get Dr. Silvertson to come and talk to her, she knows her daughter is dead and she begins to wail and fling about, beating me on the chest. I wrap her with one arm, while waving off security guys with the other. We shuffle into the quiet of the family room to face some facts.

Sometime later, when she has composed herself and had a conversation with the physician in charge, we go into the quiet of Bay 3 and spend some time with the dead girl's body. The mother strokes the little girl's forehead. "She looks like an angel now," she says quietly, "in heaven." I nod and hold her other hand. She wants to know if I want to see some pictures of the little girl from her wallet. At this moment nothing is more important to me, and we share the photographs.

When we are done, I send the child's body off to the morgue, and I place the mother in the care of her people, who traveled hours away from this ER, back to the rural place where they came from, knowing their lives are changed forever. I am starting to get tired, and I hope there are no more child deaths tonight. I then quash the thought with my own magical prohibition about such desires, as they tend to backfire upon me. It's a struggle with magic, I always face, here in the ER. I sit behind the only electric doors in this neighborhood that look constantly onto poverty, death, and tragedy. I am buoyed at times by the human strength that emerges. The humor, courage, and compassion that creeps into those spaces in-between. I am always tugged by my wishes and hopes, against the hard facts of life in East Baltimore. I find a constant struggle between wishes and reality. I go get another cup of coffee, and as I sit looking out onto the ambulance dock, I see this little home-less guy shuffle out of the hospital, wearing a shirt I stacked in the "clothes closet" this morning.

I laugh to myself as I see this bit of serendipity walking down the street. No matter the costs of tragedy, there are little moments of quiet heroics, as well. The ER is a place of disorder, and the worker who works best is the one who can go with the flow. Sometimes hours of boredom are punctuated by minutes of terrific activity.

One has to think fast on one's feet. Up in the rest of "the house," life has more order. Workers get to schedule appointments. Even in the intensive care units, where death is a common visitor, there is a greater sense of control. One is deeper in the hospital; one is on the hospital's turf. The ER is more like a beach, where the sea and the land meet, changing each other over and over. To do social work in the ER takes the heart and mind of a surfer; each new person off the street is another wave to meet well.

It is six o'clock, and the fourth year meds are in a pile at the triage desk, waiting for me. Soon, they will be starting their rotation in the ER, and I get three hours in this week to talk ethics, the state of welfare, and social services in the emergency room. They are dressed in street clothes and these little white jackets that some call "clerk coats." Some have developed an officious defensiveness, while others just look lost and bewildered. I meet each one of them well, handing them a donut. I start off by making a joke that this is one of "two places that's open 24 hours a day and has cops: Dunkin' Donuts and the ER." We laugh for a moment, and then get ready for a little conversation.

"To understand emergency medicine, you have to understand the street," I say, motioning for them to follow me onto the sidewalk outside, where we can look up and face the leviathan of the hospital. "Now... look at these doors and consider what they say: DO NOT PUSH...."

Think About It

1. What skills did the social worker need to develop a rapport with the 17-year-old from Philadelphia?

2. Imagine telling family members that their loved one has died as a result of a tragic accident. How would you feel in this role?

3. Watch a medical show on television. Think about what the social worker's role would be in the situations presented.

4. How important are the relationships the ER social worker has with doctors, nurses, police, and other professionals in this setting?

Chapter 2

Technology in Social Work: Moderating Online Support Groups for Cancer Patients

||||||||||||||||||||||||||||||||||||||||||||||||||||||||||||||||||||||||||||||||||||||||||||||||||||

by Rachel Odo, LCSW

I began my social work training as a second career. I loved working with groups of people, and I was (and remain!) passionate about life and thinking about what makes life important for each of us—how we, as human beings, learn to live fully and well, even in the face of an acute, chronic, or life-threatening illness. While working on staff at a comprehensive cancer center in New York City, I rotated through different treatment areas, working with in-patient, out-patient and post-treatment teams. There, I honed my group work skills, developing and leading face-to-face psychoeducational support groups for patients, caregivers, nursing staff, and medical residents. The power of group process and the deeply healing role of forging connections in our lives—especially when faced with an experience like illness and treatment, which can otherwise be alienating and isolating—came into clear focus as I ran these weekly and monthly groups. And, although I loved hospital work—the fast pace, the intellectual stimulation, the camaraderie of working with dedicated and caring interdisciplinary teams—I needed to transition to a more flexible, part-time career. As I was considering the transition, I searched for a way to maintain my group work practice, and in the end, I found it online.

I left the hospital setting to begin work in a social service agency dedicated to meeting the needs of cancer patients and their family caregivers. Because I am a part-time online support group moderator, I telecommute, which means that I rarely go into an actual office. The bulk of my working hours are spent at a computer at a desk in my home. I can run my groups from anywhere. When traveling for work, for example, there are no disruptions in my groups, because I can get online from any location. I can also fit my group work into my schedule, at times that are most convenient for me. I tend to "think" better and more clearly at night, so I often work then when things in my own home are quiet! The downside to the untraditional schedule is that, when crises within a group do arise, I do not automatically have a colleague or supervisor to turn to for discussion. Newer social workers might find it more comfortable to work during regular business hours, when they can seek supervision as needed. Working online, for telecommuters at least, also has the drawback of being professionally less "connected." I am not at an office seeing my colleagues on a regular basis, so it is important for me to put effort into maintaining relationships with my professional contacts and friends in the field.

The online groups that I run are actively moderated, with clinical social workers providing psychoeducation and supportive counseling, as well as helping to facilitate group discussion and to manage the space in ways that are therapeutic for everyone involved. However, they are not "live." When they are in session, they are run as asynchronous groups, open continuously, so that members can read and post at any time of the day or night. This works well with groups whose members come from all over the country (and sometimes beyond). Group members know that responses are not posted in "real time." They are assessed via e-mail, prior to the group and throughout the session, to be sure that there is a good fit between their needs and the kind of support that this type of online group can realistically provide.

These groups are organized by disease type and/or situation. I've run groups for gynecologic cancer patients, ovarian cancer patients, colorectal cancer patients, men with cancer, women with cancer, pancreatic cancer caregivers, general (mixed) caregivers, and the bereaved.

Members participate by reading the messages that others post and then responding, either directly or simply by sharing their own thoughts, questions, concerns, and issues. I never meet my group members in person. I never even speak with them by phone. I know them strictly through their writing in the group and, for those who do reach out directly for one reason or another, via e-mail contact. The written word is our singular mode of communication. As a social worker, I've learned to interpret narrative text in much the same way that I might interpret speech patterns and body language, appearance and eye contact, tone of voice, and spoken word when working face-to-face.

As I sit at my desk this evening, writing, in the same space where I sit to run my groups, I am thinking about what it means to communicate through the written word in this age of social media. And, I am thinking about the day-to-day experience of clinical practice through text-based relationships. Some days, I sit down and log on, quickly scan my e-mail folder to be sure that no one has written me "offline" with a particular issue, then head over to the group space itself, notice the number of new posts in each group, and settle in to read. Perhaps someone is writing about her anxiety in anticipation of an upcoming scan to determine whether or not a course of chemotherapy is working, and other members of the group have already posted in response, sharing words of support and setting down some of their own fears and worries about treatment or recurrence. In another group, a member may be talking about how hard it is to plan for the future when her husband's disease is so unpredictable. Should she encourage her daughter to move her wedding date up so her father can be there? "But when? When is the right moment? How do I know whether or not he'll be too sick to make it? Or make it at all?" Another member may be facing a transition from active treatment to hospice care and writing about what it means to watch her husband go from being a "big, healthy, strong man" to "skin and bones and pain with hardly any time awake and none of it good." A homebound member of another group, who would have almost no social network if it weren't for an online group like ours, might share a link to a video he's taken of his new kitten, a gift from his far away son. Still someone else may be posting inspirational quotes or jokes to help everyone "make it through the day."

I will sit with all of this, let it percolate for a bit, and then, a day or two later, having gone through this daily ritual of sitting and reading and absorbing, I will sit down once again, only this time, after logging on and reading the latest posts, I will begin to write.

I will write to everyone who has written since my last post, and I will answer queries that haven't already been answered by other group members. I will support healthy coping strategies, point out similarities and differences, teach about emotions and moods, help people grieve their losses and changes. I will share my enjoyment of the kitten, "laugh" at the jokes, encourage the mutual aid and support that flows from post to post, member to member, and help to negotiate the conflicts that sometimes arise. I will speak to the strengths that the group members share. I will write and write and write, and then I will read and re-read what I've written. Checking my "facts" and listening to how the words sound, I wonder whether they will convey what I want to say. I won't know immediately. I won't know until members have posted in response, so I choose my words and phrases carefully, perhaps even more carefully than I did when I was speaking them aloud in a face-to-face setting where I could see, at a glance, how my comments were being received and make subtle changes in the moment. I will post my thoughts to the group and hope that they will resonate, as I hope that some of what I'm saying here resonates with you.

My days are filled with reading and thinking and writing. An average group of this type may include 15 to 30 members posting about 20 to 50 messages each week. Very active groups may post upwards of 80 to 100 messages weekly, and quieter groups can go for weeks at a time with just a handful of new posts. As the moderator, I craft a new post once or twice a week on average. These weekly posts may run anywhere from a few hundred to 1,500 words or more and take anywhere from 15 to 90 minutes to properly craft. When there are larger issues in the space—a recurrence, a death, a new diagnosis, other bad news—I may be more "present" through more frequent, though generally shorter, posts for a period of time. When new members enter the space, I respond within a day to welcome them. On average, I spend about two to three hours each week with each group that I run.

Like any support group leader, I work to make a direct therapeutic connection with each member while simultaneously fostering and nurturing the connections that members make with one another. When we are face-to-face, visual and aural cues and responses are some of the main ways that we do this. Online, we lose the aural cues and have to modify our understanding of the visual. For example, every time I post, I address each member of the group by name. The visual cue of using their names and carving out a separate "space" for each individual within the frame of my posts not only reinforces members' sense of belonging in the space, but also helps others "put names to stories" in more meaningful ways as I synthesize multiple posts by each member and highlight the core issues they are raising.

With text-based relationships, writing style itself becomes a powerful tool. It can be used to better understand individual members (how formal is it, what kind of vocabulary is used, what kinds of punctuation, does a person use emoticons?), and it can be used to clarify roles or encourage a positive countertransference by adjusting one's own style according to the message—more formality in a strongly educational post for instance, or mirroring the style of a group member in a supportive response. In the text-based counseling relationship, text as narrative and text as transitional object become particularly powerful. This is storytelling made concrete. One group member put it this way as she opened a lengthy, emotional post: "This will be a long update, as I am using it to kind of consolidate where I am at mentally. On the one hand I feel weird exposing so much about where I am at mentally.... But it helps me, so I do it." Here, the written narrative itself becomes a crucial healing factor.

For other members, what they gain from the group might look more like this: "The reason I joined this group is because I had reached the limits of my ability to cope with my sister's behavior toward me. I have been visiting her and giving her moral support since she had a gall bladder attack and removal last February. She has always been difficult to deal with, but the pancreatic cancer diagnosis and subsequent surgery, colon injury, and chemo have really made her angry and hostile toward the world in general and toward me in particular. Had I not joined this group and received the support, wisdom, and kind words of Rachel and my fellow travelers, I would have abandoned M some time ago, which I really did not want to do. Since joining the group, I've learned to make changes in my own behavior toward M, and I have also learned important information about drugs and side effects and antidotes that others here may know about and which I am able to at least suggest to M and her medical team from time to time. I also try to show support toward others on this board as we journey together, and sometimes I just blow off steam if I need to. No one is judging. Today, my relationship with my sister is better, and I am hoping we will continue to progress."

The therapeutic potential of the online support group is tremendous. For social workers who like to read and to express themselves through writing, online modalities can be incredibly powerful and highly rewarding. Working in this way has not only broadened my ability to reach people through the sheer impact of technology, but enhanced and deepened my clinical skills in every setting.

Think About It

1. What skills are crucial for an online support group moderator?
2. How are therapeutic relationships nurtured online?
3. Visit *http://www.cancercare.org/* to read cancer survivors' stories online for yourself. What is your response?

(Note: This chapter was originally published in Riding the Mutual Aid Bus and Other Adventures in Group Work.*)*

Chapter 3
Social Work in the Neonatal Intensive Care Unit

||||||||||||||||||||||||||||||||||||||||||||||||||||||||||||||||||||||||||||||||||||||||||||||||

by Merle T. Edwards-Orr, Ph.D., LICSW

I t was January in Vermont. It was cold. It was Monday. That meant I had two pagers to carry on this day at the University Hospital where I work. I had attached to my right side pocket my usual pager so the Neonatal Intensive Care Unit (NICU) could track me down. On my left side, I carried the pager for the Emergency Room, as I do every other Monday. I felt rather like a gunslinger in a '50s western.

All by itself, the NICU had been keeping me busy. Two sets of twins and one single, not a one of them over 2 pounds, had been admitted to the unit over the last week. This along with the usual run of babies with pneumonia, birth defects, and less serious prematurity. In case I had forgotten those five new little ones over the weekend, there were the five Supplemental Security Income (SSI) applications lying on my desk to greet me as I opened my office door.

Since all children born under 1,200 grams, or about 2.5 pounds, are automatically eligible for SSI, I fill out a fair number of these forms. Since they are relatively simple forms, as Federal forms go, I can knock out one, including the supporting paperwork, in about 10 or 15 minutes. I have found it takes me about twice that to teach a parent to fill one out, so I figure I might as well just do it. But that logic presupposes that I won't find myself staring at five of them first thing one gray January morning. It did not look like it was going to be a great day.

In truth, I quite like my job. I love working around babies. I also like that critically ill babies equally befall the rich and the poor, the wicked and the virtuous, and the smart and the stupid. So I get to see a range of people.

I find being the only social worker in my unit a touch lonely. I look forward to my morning coffee time with my social work colleagues as a chance to talk about our own children, complain about the trials of working in healthcare, and share information about the hospital and what's new in the professional world. So, armed with my computer-generated list of all babies in the NICU, I gathered up my coffee cup and crossed over the parking lot to the main building and the employee cafeteria.

I was about halfway there when my pager sounded. "Which one?" was my first thought. I am not frightened of the ER like some of my colleagues, but it still represents the unknown more than the NICU pager does. In this case, it was the NICU. The relative known. I responded and a pediatric intern told me she wanted to send young Heather Suitor back to her local hospital, Westlake, in far Upstate New York. This was a good idea, because it meant the child no longer needed NICU care, she would be closer to home, and our very high census would decrease by one.

Reverse or "back" transports, as returns of babies to local hospitals are known, are a microcosm of the administrative and protocol end of the health care system. No one doubts that it is best for babies to be near their parents. Equally, no one wants babies to receive inadequate care. Putting those two principles into practice can be a complicated task.

When I heard the resident say that the team was planning to transport young Miss Suitor to Westlake Hospital, I sighed and began to check whether the process was being followed and whether it even could be followed, since it was Martin Luther King Day and I was not sure the administrative staff at Westlake was even working. "I'll call Dr. D. at Westlake and make sure I ask him about the administrative staff when I do," said the intern, annoyed by my reminders that red tape is there (and babies end up hanging around ERs and parents get huge bills as a result of transfers that don't respect that red tape).

"Give me a holler when you hear, but I'm on my way up and I'll see where we are on this," I said by way of a sign-off.

When I arrived at the NICU, the father of one of our new micro-preemies greeted me. Roger Innis was somebody's fantasy of back-woods Vermont: laconic and honest with just a touch of deference, which you could tell made him angry. Now he found himself and his 1.5 pound baby in the land of high-tech in what was, to him, the big city. He was not unintelligent (nor unadaptable, as the weeks would reveal when by discharge, he could talk supplemental oxygen needs and feeding schedules with the best of them) but was way out of his element and was needing to talk to me about two items.

First, it was Monday and he was broke and did I remember the $25 check and hospital meal card I usually brought on Monday. I hadn't, which I regretted, since I knew how much it hurt his pride to ask and how much he needed it. Second, he needed to tell me that the baby's maternal grandmother had been admitted to their local hospital with cancer and was not expected to live much longer. That meant he would be on his own up at the hospital for a while during the time his wife tended to her mother's needs. At the same time, the baby had taken a turn for the worse, and the doctors were making no promises about the outcome. He just, in his at once laconic and roundabout way, needed to talk. So, we talked. About the baby, about his mother-in-law. About his relationships with his family (not good) and with Sarah's family (on-and-off). About his not drinking and how hard that was. About what a big town this felt like to him. About how he wanted a job so he could support his new family. I didn't say much. There wasn't much to say. He just needed to know someone was noticing him and his worries. After a while, I told him I would bring by that check. He nodded sort of mournfully but strode off to find a way to kill the time, since looking in an isolette at your tiny baby is not a full-time job.

Back to Suitor. In the minutes between phone calls and talks with medical staff, I filled out some SSI applications. Name (got to make sure I don't get the twins mixed up). Condition (I almost could write "prematurity at 27 weeks gestation with a birth weight of 750 grams" for all of them). Demographics about the doctors and hospital. A little bit on tests. A couple of releases and that was about it. Not very hard, but five times was decidedly tedious. By the time I had gotten through one set of twins, the transfer looked ready.

The final step was to call Heather's mother to confirm this is what she wanted to happen and give her the arrival times. Yes, she was indeed pleased that we were sending her daughter back to Westlake. That way she would have a chance to visit.

"So travel is a problem?" I asked.

"Oh, yes, my husband uses the car for work and I need to be with my two older kids, anyway. I haven't gotten to see Heather in two weeks, since just after she was born," Ms. Suitor replied.

"Have you talked to Medicaid to see if they will help with the transportation costs and maybe even give you a ride?"

"Can they do that? How does that work?"

"I will write a letter of medical necessity and fax it to Medicaid in your county, and then you can get transportation help."

"But what about caring for my older kids?" she asked.

"Have the folks from Public Health checked in with you? They should have, and they often help with that kind of thing."

"No," said the mother.

"Let me give Jean a call at Public Health in your county, and she'll check back with you about child care. Also, have you checked with any of your kids' aunts or grandparents to see if they'd help?" I asked.

"Oh, I couldn't impose," was the predictable response.

"Whatever you feel is right in your family, but this is a real crisis and Heather needs you. Families are often happy to pitch in at these times," I suggested.

This was a routine conversation, helping people locate and sort out resources. Only it was happening about 10 days too late. It had been Christmas and I had been off a fair amount, plus the unit had been very full. As a result, if you weren't in my face, like Roger Innis, you didn't get attention. We sometimes forget the importance of the routine. Here was a family that really needed "Resources 101" but hadn't gotten it yet, and time with their baby had been lost. The baby was out the door by a little after noon. Not perfect, but all told, not bad work.

I grabbed a bite of lunch where I read my several days' mail and generally tried to make sense of my life. Lunch tends to be my quiet time. A chance to read an article and generally chill out. If possible, I give my wife a call (she is also a social worker, in private practice) and remind myself of my life outside the hospital walls.

Just as I wrapped up my lunch remains, my pager went off, this time from surgical ICU. *Why SICU?* I wondered. Not my outfit any longer. But, as a dutiful soldier, I called. They had a 19-year-old woman who was very sick with pre-eclampsia (a very dangerous disease of late pregnancy) who was almost certain to lose her baby at 22 weeks into her pregnancy. My colleague who handled Labor and Delivery was only half time and had left at noon, so that meant this conversation fell to me.

My job was to discuss with the mother and whatever family she had with her what to expect from the delivery. Did they want to hold the baby after she was stillborn? Did they want to name her? Did they want a funeral or the hospital-provided cremation? These were issues they had to begin to think about and be as ready as one can be at the time. This is a particularly grueling and yet satisfying part of my job. Grueling because people who are losing their babies are always profoundly sad. Satisfying because it is one of those times when a social worker knows that he (in my case) is really doing some good. Losing your baby is overwhelming, but a chance to talk and be sad and get information is an important gift another person can provide.

Another beep on the pager. *Did I know about the Lonergans?* asked Sue from the NICU. Well, I knew something. What did she mean exactly? It seems Sue had just gotten off the phone with Jane Lonergan, baby John's mother, and she was making veiled suicidal comments. No, I didn't know about that specifically. I knew that Jane had a history of depression but that she had been doing well over the last several years. I had hoped she wouldn't fall into a new depression sparked by the post-partum period. I'd better give her a call.

She wasn't there (or wasn't answering). I called Nancy Jones, the public health nurse for her area. As it turned out, Nancy had just seen Jane this morning, and she was worried. Yes, Jane had made veiled suicidal statements, but had denied real suicidal intent. Nancy knew Jane far better than I did. What did she think? Well, Nancy noted she was not a mental health professional, but she felt that Jane, while not immediately suicidal, clearly had it on her mind. We discussed psychiatric resources available in her area, and they were fairly sparse. I noted that we had psychologists available to provide mental health supports to families and children and maybe I should try to get them to see Jane. Nancy liked that idea, so I tried Jane again.

She answered this time. I made small talk and made sure she was updated on her baby's condition, but quickly got to the point of my concerns. Jane was embarrassed but agreed that she had wondered from time to time whether she wasn't just causing trouble being around. We discussed this for a while with my agreeing that, while she had suicidal thoughts, she was probably not an immediate risk. She agreed that she did not plan to kill herself, and she knew who to call if she felt a strong urge to do so. She also agreed to see our psychologist when she came over to see John tomorrow. I paged Louise, the psychologist, who agreed she could see Jane. I then just hoped my assessment was right and Jane was telling the truth.

Off to Surgical ICU. Janelle Houseman was there in her bed, with her boyfriend, Mitch, at her bedside. Janelle looked very sick and spoke with difficulty. Mitch was exhausted and scared but trying hard to be strong. They talked about their lives, their hopes for the baby, how they had learned things were going wrong, their expectation that the baby would be born dead or die upon birth, but their hope for the best. I am often struck by how powerfully people struggle to understand and overcome a situation they had never dreamed would happen. Here was a young couple that would survive. They would hurt, but they would find a way to come out the other end whole.

The day was winding down. This all had happened between miscellaneous phone calls, SSI applications, pages from the pharmacy for permission to approve Social Work Department payment for prescriptions, and the rest of the little stuff that no one remembers but takes up minutes and hours in a day. No meetings today. That was unusual.

And charting. I needed to make sure each of these major contacts had a note in the chart, so other team members were aware of my observations. This takes time, but it is a commonplace thought in medical settings that "if it isn't documented, it didn't happen."

It was well past dark when I returned to my office to finish the day's paperwork, pass the ER pager (it had been quiet today) on to the next day's worker, and head home. Not a bad day. Some sense of accomplishment. Certainly some frustrations. Plenty to look forward to for tomorrow.

Think About It

1. In the NICU, the infant is the patient. Who is the social worker's client—the infant, the family, someone else, or a combination of the above?

2.   What are the different roles the social worker in this chapter plays throughout the day?

3.   Do you agree with the social worker's decision to fill out the SSI forms himself, or would it be better to help the parents do this themselves?

4.   Why is paperwork important in this story?

5.   The social worker in this story uses a pager. What benefits do pagers offer over more modern technology? What benefits would switching to a smartphone or other device offer?

Chapter 4
Social Work in an Infertility Clinic

||||||||||||||||||||||||||||||||||||||||||||||||||||||||||||||||||||||||||||||||||||||||||||||||||||||||||||||||||||||||||||||||||||||||||

by Gretchen Gross, LICSW, ACSW, NCADC

L ife in a medical clinic setting is vastly different from my initial experiences as a hospital-based social worker. In those days, working in the Emergency Room, with the Burn/Shock/Trauma team, in a chemical dependency treatment center, or with the inpatient gynecological oncology service meant that I was married to my beeper, and needed to be a jack of all trades, able to go from a family meeting set up to decide on possible organ donation to a discharge planning session. Compared to those days, my current position as a counselor in a University-affiliated outpatient medical clinic provides me with much more autonomy and control over my professional life, my case load, and diversity of population and services offered.

Each day, I see a variety of couples and individuals who are referred to me by physicians, midwives, and the other practitioners who provide reproductive services to our patients. My office is in the Department of OB/GYN, and I provide services in the same manner that I do at my private practice. I schedule my own clients, attend weekly in-vitro fertilization (IVF) team meetings, present at Resident Didactics (meaning I train OB/GYN residents and fellows in the psychosocial aspects of reproductive medicine and women's health care), and present at department Grand Rounds. I consult with physicians on troublesome cases, and treat or refer clients as needed.

Since working in this medical subspecialty, my clinical repertoire has grown significantly, providing me with a diverse experience of reproductive medicine, which I find to be stimulating. Although I meet with infertility patients, I also provide counseling services for depressed women; women who are having postpartum depression; pregnant women with a history of bulimia or sexual abuse; women and couples who experience sexual dysfunction, multiple miscarriages, or fetal losses; and those who are considering treatment alternatives, such as adoption or stopping treatment and leading a "childfree" life.

I perform clinical/psychosocial assessments on couples who, for any number of medical reasons, have been diagnosed with some form of infertility, and are proceeding with reproductive technologies in hopes of becoming pregnant. I meet with every couple considering in-vitro fertilization (IVF), therapeutic donor insemination (TDI—with an anonymous or known donor), and donor egg procedures (both known and anonymous donors) through our clinic. A couple must have this assessment as a part of their pretreatment work-up to assess their marital and individual stability; their coping skills and support networks; their understanding of the psychological, financial, and time demands placed on them during treatment; and their comprehension of their chances of becoming pregnant. Depending on the treatment needed, there can be up to a 75% failure rate, which each person must understand prior to starting treatment.

These procedures, though offering hope for genetic offspring and the experience of pregnancy, often challenge a couple's ethical beliefs about levels of medical intervention. Each couple should consider this before starting treatment. If a Catholic couple is considering IVF, and they have found significant strength in their religion, how do they expect that proceeding with IVF (not sanctioned by the Catholic Church) might affect their religious belief, practice, and participation? In some sense, I slow couples down a bit, to engage them in decision-making processes that are ethically and spiritually compatible. It is far more advantageous to encourage these patients to make a slow and thoughtful decision, rather than to allow them to rush into decisions on procedures that might directly contradict their religious or ethical beliefs.

Infertility treatment has a significant potential to highlight and exacerbate any previous relational difficulties and individual pathologies, rather than to initiate problems. Because of the duration and type of emotional and physical stress, treatment fans the slow-burning embers more often than starts a new fire for couples. For example, if the male partner has a history of an anxiety disorder and is finding that as treatment progresses, he is experiencing more frequent and severe panic attacks, he needs to be identified and treated. His anxiety will affect various levels of treatment, from semen collection and quality of the ejaculate to marital communication and functioning during and after treatment. Now, consider that the wife might begin to blame him for bringing this up if it slows down the process or prevents them from starting treatment immediately. He might blame himself for their infertility, or she might punish him for asking for help. Couples in infertility treatment will experience more marital and intrapsychic stress than they had anticipated. Their ability to communicate this to friends, family, and staff, as well as to each other, is paramount to diminishing their sense of isolation.

The assessment sessions provide patients with a forum to begin to discuss some of these concerns, myths, fears, and expectations while learning that they are not alone in the infertility experience. Current statistics estimate that 15-30% of American couples will experience some level of infertility. However, because of the intimate nature of infertility, few people share their diagnosis, and fewer receive social support for infertility. Many couples will come to sessions fearful that they are abnormal, because they are shying away from malls and grocery stores where there are likely to be more children and families. Simply normalizing the couple's experience of this process, validating their experiences, and providing them with a safe place to talk about their anger, frustrations, and sense of being out of control can help significantly.

Another facet of this position involves helping couples come to terms with ending treatment, to living without children in the case of their not going on to adoption. Because there are so many treatment options, with more developing rapidly, it is difficult for a couple to say "we are through with treatment." However, that can be as therapeutically appropriate as continuing with treatment, which might exhaust them and their resources. The counselor may be one of the first people to raise this option as an acceptable and healthy choice. Helping couples explore their definitions of "family," their expectations of their relationship without children, and to make some sense out of their experience is central to good infertility practice.

I have found work in this subspecialty very exciting, stimulating, and demanding. It requires a significant level of medical knowledge of each procedure (couples do not need the added stress of "teaching" their counselor about their treatment process, expected outcomes, surgeries involved, and so on), an awareness of the possible impacts of fertility drugs on mood states, an ability to work as a member of a multi-disciplinary team where you may be the only mental health professional, and a significant working knowledge of differential diagnosis. Work in infertility is similar to, but not the same as, working with a chronically ill population, in which there is an experience of waxing and waning treatment, changes in mood and affect depending on the phase of treatment, and an understanding of the effects of the process on a marriage and other significant relationships.

Further, in such a cutting edge medical setting, the ethical dilemmas that arise continue to challenge all members of an infertility treatment team. Clinical social workers must constantly check in on themselves to assess their own potential for projection and overlap on the issues and treatment of each couple. Infertility counseling brings the future into the present. Dilemmas and opportunities that most of your social work colleagues consider "science fiction" will repeatedly present in your office!

For example, a young man diagnosed with cancer banks sperm prior to surgical, chemical, and radiation treatments. His prognosis is good, and the couple feels that they can consider fertility issues at a later date, when he is well. That patient dies of complications, and his wife presents six months after his death wishing to be inseminated with his sperm, in hopes of getting pregnant. You are asked to meet with her, to assess whether she is making a rational decision at this time. The clinic team members are unsure about their participation in this process, as it challenges several of them ethically. When you meet with this woman, she is clearly in acute grief, still emotionally numb, and expresses some levels of guilt about the relationship. She tells you that just prior to his death, she and her husband had separated because he had learned of an affair she had started while he was in treatment for cancer.

Difficult ethical questions are now raised, such as: *Would this man, if he were alive, choose to have a child with this woman? What are the legal considerations? Did this man include his frozen sperm in his will? Do his parents and family know about her interest? Would she tell them? What is the woman's level of emotional stability?* Although a composite of many cases of which I am aware, this is not an unusual situation. Medically, physicians are now able to extract sperm from a man in a coma. Is this ethical? Is this legal if the man is unable to give consent? Is this rape? What rights does the wife have to having offspring by her comatose husband? Though again futuristic, these cases have been raised a number of times in hospitals and infertility clinics.

On a more familiar level, couples undergoing IVF can easily freeze embryos not returned to the woman's uterus for later use. Are both partners equally interested in this possibility? Do they consider that these embryos may become a bone of contention should the marriage dissolve? It is difficult but necessary to raise these subjects with this couple prior to their IVF attempt. Knowing when and where to refer to collaterals—whether to a lawyer familiar with reproductive law or to a psychiatrist who can help a patient come off a medication (or start on one) in the best interest of a healthy treatment process and possible pregnancy—is so important when working with infertility.

Though I have always worked in and around the medical setting, this is the most challenging and stimulating arena yet. I must always learn more, to keep up with developments and changes in many areas. I must always challenge my own ethical standards. Can I work with a couple who have recently conceived quadruplets through IVF and are now interested in terminating two fetuses? How do my own feelings affect my work with this population? I rely on my team members, specifically the IVF Nurse Coordinator and Research Nurse, who always have an open door for conversation. These developments happen much more quickly than we generally anticipate. Being able to talk over our own issues, concerns, and ethics is imperative to maintaining a level of self-awareness and effectiveness in this field.

One drawback to this field is that I miss working with other clinical social workers (most clinics have one staff counselor), and therefore, I relish membership in supervision and professional groups. Specific professional memberships of great importance are somewhat limited to the American Society of Reproductive Medicine (ASRM) and the ASRM Mental Health Professional Group, which is made up of clinical social workers, psychologists, psychiatrists, and ethicists who specifically meet to address the changing demands of these positions.

Finally, awareness of one's own reproductive expectations, abilities, and interests is essential to working in this field. If you are experiencing infertility and are in treatment or have been recently, and have not been in counseling yourself, I strongly suggest that this would be a challenging and difficult arena in which to work. Similarly, being a counselor who has children or is pregnant and is sitting daily with patients who are expressing anger at "the fertile world" provides its own set of challenges.

We must ask ourselves, "What is the value of parenthood in this society? Do I understand my own biases one way or the other? Can I be effective in helping to minimize the splitting between the 'haves' and the 'have nots' in a society where 'family' is defined by the number of children in a relationship?" Questions such as these cycle and recycle and can help one become a more effective and compassionate care provider.

One final word. If you are interested in this area of subspecialty, please be sure you are aware of the myths of infertility, which continue to circulate. Be sure to get an extensive background in the medical side of treatment, so your patients do not have to spend session time describing IVF, and become expert in grief and mourning. Without these as a minimum requirement, you are more likely to be unhelpful than helpful to your clients.

Think About It

1. What are some signs that infertility social work might not be a good career choice for a particular social worker?

2. What are some ethical issues involved in infertility treatment?

3. Do you think a sensitivity to religion is important in this field of social work? Explain.

Chapter 5
Working with Pregnant Women in Public Health

IIIIIIIIIIIIIIIIIIIIIIIIIIIIIIIIIIIIIIIIIIIIIIIIIIIIIIIIIIIIIIIIIIIIIIIIIIIIIIIIIIIIIIIIIIIIIIIIIIIIIIIIIIIIIIIIIIIIIIIIIIIIIIIIIII

by Alfreda Paschall Gee, MSW

I work with pregnant women. That is an easy, safe, and accurate assessment of my job that works well in most settings. It immediately distances me from the "I take children from their parents at my own whim" stereotype that I used to live with a few years ago. My work is public health oriented, pro-active, and yes, even appreciated by various, though not all, schools of thought.

I work in a small city that grows with tourism, the movie industry, and other light industries. It grows in poverty for far too many, with seasonal laborers, and the very young giving birth too soon. Sound familiar?

I am paid by the county from funds I generate by billing Medicaid for the contacts I make with patients in the maternity clinics. I follow each patient from the time I meet her until roughly two months after her pregnancy ends, regardless of the pregnancy outcome. I work in two settings: the local hospital's OB/GYN clinic, and a newly-formed private OB/GYN office.

The job has specific requirements set out by state guidelines, but affords a good deal of autonomy and professional judgment. There are four social workers involved in the maternity team, and we work with nurses and are supervised by a nurse. This has provided challenges in the true sense of the word. It has worked very well, and we have been able to carve out our own areas of expertise. It is also helpful, as our team becomes a part of the larger medical community, which includes other disciplines, such as doctors and administrators.

My friend Barbara and I coined the phrase that we are "born again social workers." It is a term we use with care and affection. And yet, we use it more some days than others. Below, I have included some excerpts from a few of my days as a "born again" public health social worker.

Tuesday: Dr. McIntyre, a second year OB resident, calls from the ER about a patient who was just taken to the Birthplace to be monitored. Facts: Nova is 36 years old, has four kids, weighs 350+ pounds (can't be weighed on scales), had two previous C-sections, was gestational diabetic last two pregnancies, and her last delivery was 15 months ago. She has no car, no phone, and lives 15 miles south of the hospital. Husband is "away working." Closest relative is her critically ill father, for whom she is the primary caretaker. Nova's main support is a cousin who lives 18 miles west of the hospital. Nova learned three days ago that she is seven weeks pregnant, and she has two appointments Thursday: one at the OB clinic and one at the abortion clinic, and a decision to make about which one she keeps. She is tearful, but calm and ready to talk. Dr. McIntyre introduces me to her, saying, "Ms. Gee is a social worker. She can help." (NOTE: Gasp!)

I let Nova know what I have been told, let her fill in some details, and check to see if I was accurately informed. I do my best listening, offer referrals, if not solutions, and encourage her to take some time to think. The decision about the pregnancy needs to be made soon, and we agree it is her first priority. We discuss some ways that she has used in the past to make hard decisions, and I teach her one of my own techniques that has worked at times. She agrees to call me or see me Thursday, or sooner as needed. (NOTE: Procured a box of tissues for Nova, as tangible evidence for myself that I was helpful. It is Nova who has the tough job.)

Tuesday afternoon: Sharon, 29, stops by the clinic to show me her 6-month-old baby boy. She's still breastfeeding, still in her apartment, and still clean. She still sees John, who "hasn't hurt me since the baby came," and still has little contact with her family. "I quit going to the [drug treatment] program, but I'm doing fine." (NOTE: Build on the obvious positives. Bite your tongue against sharing what your instincts tell you. She came for a reason. Water that seed you planted with her 10 months ago.)

Tuesday later: Julia is 14 years old, second pregnancy, with one miscarriage earlier in the year. She is tired of living at home, does not like her mother's boyfriend, and wants to live with the father of her baby. "He's 19 or 20 and he makes good money" with no obvious employer. Julia is suspended from school, again. Her mother works swing shift at the sewing mill, and "sits for some old lady sometimes." Julia always comes to clinic alone, goes to *Baby Talk* class for teens, loves the health educator, and considers herself a group leader.

Today, in clinic, Julia is upset that her boyfriend has been turned in to the D.A. for having sex with her (a minor). She suspects the hospital staff made the report. She is not as concerned that her test of cure for syphilis is still reactive, which she has never told her mother about.

We review all the literature on sexually transmitted diseases and prevention. I discuss the idea of abstinence, which makes her smile. I'm not sure if this is because she considers it stupid, or if it's an option she does not think she can choose. I encourage her to talk to her mother.

I tell Julia that I made the report to the D.A.'s office, which nearly ends the meeting then and there. I give the position of my legal obligation, but I doubt if she hears much of it. She leaves the pamphlets on STDs on my desk. (NOTE: Hope she will continue her prenatal care. Get help from the health educator, whom she trusts.)

Wednesday: Charted all the stuff from yesterday. Wrote "creative" job plans and goals for next year. Followed up on that call to the D.A.'s office. Asked Cyndi for help about Julia. Prepared referrals for the Child Service Coordinators and presented cases. Spent time with Cathie about her patient who is HIV positive.

Thursday: Nova chose the OB Clinic, and says she feels "it's the right thing for me." Her husband came "back to town from working off somewhere." Her cousin will move in to provide help with her father and kids and will bring a car. Nova is less tearful. "I'm not used to having others do for me." (NOTE: We'll work on that.)

Sharon's boyfriend was in the newspaper in the Police Blotter for assault and battery. They didn't print the victim's name. Maybe she'll call. Maybe she's upstairs in the hospital. I won't have time to go by her house today. Maybe she'll call.

Signed Toni up again today. Keyetta is only eight months old; this is a different father of baby and "this one is really special." Toni is off her meds, if she ever used them. She is vague. She only fed Keyetta juice today ("She likes juice!"); and left her in the stroller for the entire three hours except to change her diaper (which I provided) and when I held Keyetta to model for Toni "one neat way to help Keyetta go to sleep." (NOTE: Keyetta is beautiful and very alert. She liked *Simple Gifts* and I think Toni had heard it before.)

Saw six other folks, including a frustrated mother about her daughter who is in need of homebound school. I made phone calls about this year's Fall meeting with the school staff. Instigated to trash a friend's office for her 40th birthday.

Friday: Barbara and I kiss our desks today. (A ritual of "born again social workers.") Her patient, whose two children have been in foster care, has been granted custody, and Barbara did not have to testify. I am reminded that I have not set foot in a court room in five years, and we both rejoice that a good decision was reached. Her patient has worked hard and is ready.

Home visit to Julia's house. The first good sign is that she lets me in the house. She says, "I talked to my mom." The investigation prompted her and her mother to talk. She chooses not to share the content of that conversation with me, but doesn't say anything about moving out, either. Julia says little, but asks, "Will Cyndi be having *Baby Talk* on Tuesday?" I tell her I am sure she will and give her a bus ticket to get there.

Voicemail message from Sharon: It was not her this time. John is in jail, but she expects he'll be out soon. "Can we talk Monday?" (NOTE: I know this could mean anything. Hope it means she's ready to leave, and don't even think she wants a way to get him out of it. But she called, and it was not her, and that seed is still growing.)

Think About It

1. Why are rituals important to Alfreda Gee and her co-worker?

2. What rituals might you create for yourself as a social worker?

3. Sometimes, social workers have a legal and/or ethical obligation to report a person's behavior to authorities (as in the case of Julia's boyfriend). This can conflict with the ethical obligation to maintain confidentiality, and it can result in loss of the client's trust in the social worker. Think about or discuss this dilemma in terms of possible courses of action and consequences.

Chapter 6

Managing in Managed Care

IIIIIIIIIIIIIIIIIIIIIIIIIIIIIIIIIIIIIIIIIIIIIIIIIIIIIIIIIIIIIIIIIIIIIIIIIIIIIIIIIIIIIIIIIIIIIIIIIIIIIII

by David C. Prichard, Ph.D.

I park my car in the black asphalt parking lot and stroll at a brisk pace into the newly constructed managed health care office building just off the highway. It is one of many mirrored glass and red brick buildings prevalent in the corporate business park of the posh West End of the city. I take the steps, two at a time, to the second floor, and punch in the security code to gain entrance to the very large office space that, with padded blue partitions, has been divided into four pods of eight cubicles. As clinical supervisor of one pod, I am responsible for the clinical supervision of eight clinical case managers.

It is 8 a.m. sharp, and already there is the gentle trill of the phones, the buzz of voices taking calls. I check in briefly with the crisis worker in a corner pod. She's on the phone. A tap on her shoulder and an inquisitive look provides me with the smile and a thumbs down that tells me I have no emergencies from the previous night. Strolling past the receptionist, I'm informed that there is a call on hold for me, and I am handed a stack of 15 phone messages taken by crisis workers the previous night, apparently routine calls, or so I hope. I rifle through these as I walk briskly to my cubicle in the far corner of the rectangular room. The ivy in the window provides a splash of green; the ficus floor plant has shed its few remaining leaves, its brown branches stark and accusatory.

The shorthand of the receptionist makes sense to me, though it would appear to be a foreign language to one not familiar with the cryptic lingo of the managed care industry. I translate quickly in my head. Smith needs five sessions to terminate; Waklowski needs two sessions for initial intake; Barrow needs authorization for two clients in need of psychological testing; Meldrum needs inpatient evaluation for a suicidal client; Milton is appealing a denial for authorization for inpatient detoxification...the messages go on. Seeing nothing out of the ordinary, I put the messages at the bottom of a stack of 18 messages left over from late yesterday. I will need to get these taken care of immediately. On a typical day, I will receive 40 phone messages, on top of the calls that I pick up while at my desk.

I settle in, tip back in my padded chair, prop my feet on the desk, and begin to sift through the 50+ client charts stacked in several piles on my cubicle table top. The medical records coordinator will stroll by at 10 a.m. and 2 p.m. to drop off records that need review. Providers have mailed in treatment plans, updates, and discharge summaries that will need to be reviewed to determine the medical necessity of mental health treatment. In the case of initial treatment plans, I ascertain whether or not the client has been provided a diagnosis that is covered by his or her particular insurance policy. The diagnosis must be supported by specific symptoms, and the therapist needs to be very specific in presenting a plan for reducing the symptomatology reported by the client. Finally, I need to be certain that the provider has included outcomes measures that will indicate the success of treatment and suggest when treatment may be appropriately terminated.

I boot up the computer, gazing out the window as it warms up. I will spend much of the day here, fielding calls from mental health providers seeking authorization to provide treatment for clients. My job is controversial. There are those who believe that managed care is simply another example of corporate America discovering a means to increase profits for shareholders of insurance companies, at the expense of individuals seeking mental health treatment. To a large extent, I agree. The corporate administrators who run the company appear to be much more concerned about the financial health of the company than the mental health of the clients, or policy holders. I do believe, however, that there are excesses in the system that need to be managed. I recall disturbing cases of fraud and unethical treatment—the case, for example, of a psychiatrist billing Medicaid for weekly sessions for a client who had died two years previously. And the case of the psychoanalyst who, after two years of treatment with a client diagnosed with an adjustment disorder, requested 1,700 additional sessions. I feel conflicted, torn between opposing the profit-driven corporate greed that drives the managed health care industry, and supporting the need to screen out unethical, inefficient, ineffective treatment, that at its best does no harm to clients, and at its worst creates considerably more distress and fosters unhealthy dependence.

I reflect back to my work in community mental health and the indignation I experienced by decisions made by managed care. As did many social workers, I rebelled at the thought of an outside person "dictating" to me how to provide the most effective treatment for my client. And, indeed, with some companies, it did feel as though the managed care case managers were more intent on cutting sessions and reducing costs than providing ethical, effective treatment. I recall a woman who I evaluated for inpatient hospitalization. She was floridly psychotic and experiencing command hallucinations—voices telling her to run her car into the side of a bridge. The managed care company refused to authorize the voluntary inpatient treatment, and encouraged her to drive to the community mental health center to be evaluated for treatment. Their refusal to authorize treatment for a voluntary client disempowered her, and could easily have resulted in the injury or death of herself and others. The latent function of their negligence resulted in the necessity of an involuntary hospitalization, with the state of Virginia paying the bill rather than the managed care company—another example, I felt, of corporate greed taking advantage of a governmental loophole to line the pockets of company stockholders at the expense of taxpayers.

Sighing, I turn back to the computer, lean into the screen, and dive into my stack of client charts, many containing requests by providers for authorization for initial assessments. The first request is typical. The provider is requesting two initial sessions for an assessment and to develop a treatment plan. The client is a 25-year-old single mother whose husband abandoned the family a month ago. Since that time, she has experienced significant weight loss, is unable to concentrate at work, and reports that she has spells of uncontrollable crying throughout the day. She is not reported to be suicidal, but appears hopeless, overwhelmed, and states that her life is worthless. The precipitant is clear, symptoms well-defined, and the provider suggests a course of action that includes crisis-oriented treatment. The situational symptoms suggest an adjustment disorder, which is covered by the client's insurance policy, and I suspect the client will benefit from the solution-focused treatment proposed by the provider. It has taken me two minutes to review the chart, enter authorization for treatment and a short note into the computer, and send the chart back to medical records to be processed and the authorization mailed.

With 10 phone calls interspersed among the reviews, in two hours I have processed 20 charts, all of them requests for initial authorizations for treatment. I have pulled aside three charts that I will present at the team staffing at 10 a.m. The team I supervise meets with the agency medical and clinical directors once a week for two hours to staff more difficult cases. Today, we will also be addressing concerns regarding two providers. One provider appears to have a proclivity toward diagnosing clients with dissociative identity disorder (DID), and is requesting $20,000/month inpatient treatment for a highly functional client; the other relies on hypnosis and past life regression to treat incest survivors. The issue in the former case is whether the provider is properly diagnosing clients and is providing cost-effective and efficient treatment; in the latter case, with what research-informed treatment modalities are considered appropriate.

While most providers appear to be very competent and ethical, there are those few that take up much of our time and energy as we seek to provide the most effective and efficient treatment to clients. The meeting is interesting. The clinical director has done her homework and we spend much of the two hours reviewing DID and the current research on effective treatment for incest survivors. We strategize how best to educate and communicate with these providers. While we do not want to be accused of dictating treatment, we also have an ethical responsibility to insure that clients are receiving competent, effective, and efficient treatment by qualified, competent mental health professionals. There are no easy answers.

Lunch arrives quickly, and I eat at my desk while reviewing the weekly training manual on brief and solution-focused treatment. Tomorrow, I will be meeting with a group of 38 providers in the region to whom I provide clinical case management. I know that it will be a difficult two hours. Providers are struggling to adapt to the managed care system, and there is a great deal of resentment, born largely from resistance to change, fear of the unknown, perceived loss of clinical control, and loss of income. There is a sense among providers that managed care equates to forced unethical, restricted treatment. Later in the week, I will be meeting with the entire clinical staff of a community mental health center to discuss their concerns around managed care, and to provide training on how to provide ethical treatment in a managed health care environment. The presentation will focus on the ethics of managed care and the fundamentals of solution-focused treatment, which is the language of most managed care companies. I will draw largely on my experience in community mental health, private, and managed care practice.

On Fridays, I spend the day in the clinic on the first floor. My specialty is in crisis intervention and trauma, and therefore, I select cases in which clients have clear precipitating events that have led to the presenting symptoms. My treatment is crisis-oriented and focused on reducing the immediate symptoms of the trauma. The deeper work may come later. For now, my work is to help clients regain their equilibrium after a particularly traumatizing life event. The focus will be on normalizing the reactions being experienced by exposure to a difficult, "abnormal" life event and in working with clients to find effective coping mechanisms to adjust to changing life circumstances. It is not unusual for me to see clients in intensive treatment several times per week over a few weeks. Once major symptoms have subsided, and the client appears to be back at previous levels of functioning, we will decide mutually on termination.

I spend much of my afternoon on the phone with providers, discussing cases. Although many providers appear to view me as someone whose job it is to restrict treatment, I see my role as one of collaborator, providing free, collegial, peer supervision. I receive a call from Heather. While many providers are hostile and demanding when they call, questioning the ethics of anyone who could work for managed care, Heather appears friendly, communicative, and direct. We have developed a mutually respectful, professional relationship, and when she calls, I trust Heather to be forthright and honest. For that reason, our call is short. Heather is requesting eight additional sessions for her client who is experiencing trauma reactions from a rape that occurred three weeks ago. The request is clearly reasonable, the treatment appropriate, and most importantly, I have come to trust her professional judgment and integrity. She specializes in and works well with trauma survivors. Continued treatment is authorized. We spend a few minutes talking about plant care—she has no trouble with ficus, and offers several suggestions for determining proper light and water.

I am relieved when 5 o'clock arrives. I feel as though I've been on the phone and computer all day, yet there remain many charts and unanswered phone messages scattered on my desk. These will need to wait until tomorrow. I gather the charts to return to medical records, where they will be double-locked to insure confidentiality. Turning off my computer screen, I water and mist the ivy plants on my window sill. The plants are healthy, of the sort that flourish well with little care and regular doses of water. The ficus on the floor has given up; although I have bought several, I never seem able to coax them to survive, much less flourish—too much water, I suspect, and death by over-attention!

As I head home, driving down the azalea-lined boulevard, I reflect on my last call with Heather. Interesting discussion on plants, I muse. Indoor plant enthusiasts need to acknowledge their limitations with plant care; so too do mental health practitioners need to know their clinical limitations, areas of expertise, and they should practice within these bounds. In a nutshell, that is at the core of my work as a managed care clinical supervisor—assuring that the most qualified, experienced, competent, efficient, and effective practitioners are providing treatment to clients who are, indeed, in need of medically necessary care.

Think About It

1. Why is this job controversial?

2. What dangers/problems might exist in transmitting information via computers?

Chapter 7
Social Work in the Commissioned Corps

ıllıllıllıllıllıllıllıllıllıllıllıllıllıllıllıllıllıllıllıllıllıllıllıllıllıllıllıllıllıllıllıllıllıllıllıllıllıllıllı

by Gary Lounsberry, MSW, MPH, Ph.D., LCSW

E very morning as I am putting on my uniform, I begin to speculate just what this day may bring. There are rarely two days alike as a social worker in the Commissioned Corps of the United States Public Health Service. With our historical link to the maritime hospitals and the U.S. ports of entry, the USPHS uniforms are in the style of naval officers. Most days, we wear the khaki work uniform, reserving those dress blues and whites for more ceremonial occasions. Today, it is definitely khaki because I know I will have field work to do. Before I leave, my wife and I develop alternative plans for the evening depending on who arrives home first. On the way out the door, I plug in the crock-pot containing my secret chili ingredients for tonight's employees' club dinner.

My current assignment, or billet, is as a mental health consultant in an Indian Health Service Unit in Northeastern Oklahoma. I have been here two years, and this is my second assignment since receiving my commission six years ago. Officers change assignments approximately every four years, which may require a move to a new facility. I enjoy the opportunity to experience different parts of the world with different cultures, and the moves are certainly made easier when the Corps pays all the moving expenses.

My home office is at a regional Indian Health Service hospital with inpatient medical services, a busy outpatient department with dental and pharmacy, an eight-bed substance abuse unit, two psychiatric beds, and a "swing-unit" for short-term skilled nursing services. In addition, headquartered at the hospital are

71

public health nursing services, public health education, and the sanitation engineering department. The Service Unit also includes four outpatient clinics in the three surrounding counties and two school clinics at tribal boarding schools.

This morning, I am swinging by the bakery on the way to the hospital, because I am having a staffing meeting with tribal outreach workers. We start at 8 a.m., so coffee and doughnuts are in order for the outreach workers who will have already driven 60 miles or more. I have about a two-mile drive into the pleasant community of 10,000 where the hospital is located. Right up the hill from the hospital is a state college where I either teach a course or do field supervision each semester.

The hospital is pleasant and interesting. It is almost 20 years old now, but it was leading edge when it was built and still looks very contemporary. It was designed by a Native American architect and is filled with local art and design. The Indian Health Service has been a pioneer in the applications of technology in health care delivery, and the hospital includes features that are just starting to appear in other hospitals. There are lots of windows and an open, spacious feeling.

Just as I reach the conference room with the doughnuts, the public health nurse arrives with the coffee. Every two weeks, we meet as a staffing committee with the tribal Community Health Representatives (CHRs) from the three different tribal areas in the service unit. This meeting is part patient staffing, part social support, and part in-service training. All of us are in continuous communication by phone, fax, radiophone, and email referring and coordinating services for all our clients in the five-county area, but these face-to-face meetings help us resolve complex situations, and we enjoy the personal interaction. We have an agenda with specific clients to discuss, so we will have the current information at hand. Then we allow time for a general update and discussion about what is going on in the local areas.

The CHRs live and work in the local tribal communities and do most of the outreach and follow-up care. Most of the CHRs have worked in health care for many years. I rely on them to assess how people are doing at home and to be the direct case managers for people in their areas. I agree to meet one of the CHRs later in the day for a home visit in preparation for a child custody hearing in tribal court.

The meeting ends at about 10:30 a.m. The CHRs fan out to various parts of the hospital and outpatient departments to check on patients from their areas, pick up prescriptions and medical equipment, make appointments, and transport discharged patients home.

I head to the inpatient unit to join the physicians and nurses for morning rounds on all the patients admitted from the previous day. One of the physicians asks me to evaluate a female patient who was admitted for an acute attack of rheumatoid arthritis and then started having hallucinations during the night.

Immediately after rounds, I interview the referred patient and her husband. After the interviews, discussion with the unit nurse, and review of the chart, I conclude that the hallucinations are most likely a result of the large dose of the new steroid that was given for her arthritis symptoms. I record my evaluation using the S-O-A-P format in the automated medical record system with a red flag to the referring physician. This instantaneously brings the report to the physician's attention as soon as he looks at his computer screen, wherever he may be in the hospital.

It is now a little past noon, and I head to the staff dining room for lunch. I see some of the staff from the substance abuse unit and join them. We check the numbers of people in the substance abuse unit and discuss what I should emphasize in the family dynamics group I will lead this afternoon. We discuss a workshop announcement that we all received and decide that we will attend that in two weeks.

After lunch, I head to my office area for a scheduled appointment. The social work suite, with its own waiting area, is located at the intersection of the hallways to the outpatient and inpatient areas, and just a fire door away from the emergency room. We are at the nerve center of the hospital, and at times it seems that there is a crisis in every section. Today, it is a little calmer and the pace is steady but not frantic.

My appointment is with a 20-year-old man who had his first schizophrenic break about a year ago when he left home to attend college in another state. Fortunately, there was an Indian Health Service clinic close to that college and the young man quickly received treatment. After a short hospitalization, he has transferred to the local state college and is doing quite well on medication and supportive therapy. I see him every two weeks, and he sees our consulting psychiatrist about every two months. We discuss his plans for the summer and his success in finding summer employ-ment. There are no problems, and I will see him again in two weeks.

Next, I head to the substance abuse unit to lead that family dy-namics group. The group is meant to be both educational and the entry into family therapy. Clients will be referred to the aftercare program, in which there will be opportunities for outpatient fam-ily therapy. Today I am introducing the concepts of Adult Children of Alcoholics and co-dependency. Almost all of the unit's clients are children of alcoholics, and the concepts quickly resonate with their experiences. There is no trouble getting this group to talk and share, and I have to call time after an hour, so we can decide some topics for the next session.

I have to make a beeline for the door, because I have about a 30-minute drive to that meeting with the CHR for a home visit. At the staff exit, I enter into the staff messaging system the fact that I am out on a field visit. This flashes into the social work suite and at the reception areas, so they know I am out of the hospital. I drive my assigned government vehicle for all on-duty business. The vehicle assigned to me is a full-sized SUV. It is a little hard on gas, but it has the wheel clearance I need for all the back roads and the capacity to haul people and equipment that I also frequently need. It is equipped with a two-way radio to the hospital communication center, and I carry a cell phone.

I drive to the more rural community that is the headquarters for tribal government to meet with the CHR and the family members she has convinced to come along. The CHR has enlisted the aid of the grandmother and aunt of the little girl whose welfare is of concern to the tribe. I swing by the tribally-owned service station, where the CHR is waiting in her car. Everyone gets into my vehicle and off we go.

The CHR is the navigator. We drive back into the country on progressively more primitive roads until I have the four-wheel drive engaged and we are heading over a hill on a rocky path. Most of the local Indian population live in villages or tribal housing develop-ments, while many retain old family country property as weekend or hunting retreats. In this case, family has allowed relatives to occupy a rural cabin because they do not have anywhere else to live. Down in a little gully is a log cabin with some rustic additions. The occupants are on the porch waiting for us. They have heard that Suburban coming and the family network told them we are on the way.

Mom and Dad smell of alcohol and seem to be a little intoxicated, but they are courteous and seem to be expecting our visit.
The mother and father of the little girl are in their twenties. The
mother's mother and her older sister are in our party, and the CHR
is an older cousin of the father. The family confers in their native
language while I talk with the little girl with the assistance of a doll
I brought along. The little girl is reported to be seven years old, but
she is small for that age and has some of the physical characteristics of fetal alcohol syndrome. She also appears developmentally
delayed. The girl does not seem to be afraid and soon goes to sit
on her grandmother's lap.

After conferring briefly, the CHR and I review an intervention
plan with everyone. Mom and Dad will enter the 30-day residential
substance abuse treatment program operated by the tribe. The
daughter will stay nearby with the grandmother and receive a
comprehensive physical and behavioral evaluation to determine
possible educational and developmental services. The CHR will take
the lead on case managing services for the parents, and I will be the
lead for the daughter's services. All parties agree to the plan and
we all get into the vehicle to return to the Tribal Complex. Parents
and daughter were prepared to leave and have clothes packed.

The CHR calls ahead to alert the tribal court that we are coming
in to sign treatment and custody papers. I call my wife to report
that I will be running a little late, and she says she will get the chili
and meet me at the hospital. We arrive at the tribal court, where
the judge and residential treatment counselor are waiting for us.
I provide my assessment and recommendations to the judge, and
the judge asks all others present whether they agree with the
plan. There is consensus, and the judge signs the orders requiring
residential treatment and granting temporary custody of the child
to her grandmother. Everyone shakes hands. The CHR and I make
plans to confer by telephone in two days to coordinate further
services.

I drive back to the hospital, where my wife has already arrived
at the hospital multipurpose room for the employees' club monthly
potluck dinner. My wife works for the credit union serving the
hospital and knows all the hospital employees as well as I do. It
is an interesting group of people from all over the nation and the
world. About 80% are of Indian ancestry, but not necessarily born
in the local area. There is a mix of Commissioned Officers, Federal
Civil Service, and tribal employees, along with their partners and
families. Many of the health professionals are relatively recent

graduates. We all enjoy being together socially and on the job. Once a month, we have a potluck supper where we each bring our own variation on chili or some favorite dish from our home areas. From the hospital-based social events, we are invited to tribal and local community events in the surrounding area.

Reflecting on the day, I am reminded of how much I appreciate the variety of experiences and opportunities to apply a wide range of social work skills afforded by this position. Within a broadly defined position description, I have a great deal of latitude in how I structure and carry out my duties. I know that should I feel the need for new challenges, I can initiate new services in my current position, or seek a transfer within the whole range of the Commissioned Corps. This range includes all the programs in the Department of Health and Human Services, including the National Institutes of Health and the Centers for Disease Control. In addition, there are assignments in the Coast Guard, Federal Bureau of Prisons, U.S. Embassies, United Nations programs, and others. There are opportunities for paid training and education, including attendance at uniformed services graduate programs like the Uniformed Services University of the Health Sciences.

U.S.P.H.S. Commissioned Corps officers are paid on the military officers pay scale with first commission usually at the Lieutenant level for the MSW-prepared applicant. Career officers have the potential of reaching high military rank in a 30-year career. Most career social workers retire at the O-5 or O-6 levels (Commander or Captain in Naval equivalents). However, some social workers have achieved Flag rank—Admiral—by moving into major national administrative and policy positions.

Think About It

1. What do you think it would be like working as a uniformed social worker in a cross-cultural setting?

2. What are the pros and cons of a position in which you change assignments and possibly geographic locations every four years?

3. Why do you think the general public is unaware of the U.S. Public Health Service and its myriad programs?

Chapter 8

Private Practice with Urban Gay Men: With a Subspecialty in HIV/AIDS

||||||||||||||||||||||||||||||||||||||||||||||||||||||||||||||||||||||||||||||||||||||||||||||||||||||||||||||||||||||||||||||||

by Michael Shernoff, MSW, CSW, ACSW

My first client of the day, B, is a 50-year-old fireman whose partner of 27 years died almost a year ago of cancer. Neither he nor his partner were infected with HIV. He is stumbling through life adjusting to being a widower and trying to learn how to do for himself all of those things that he once counted on his partner to do for him. I spend the session empathizing with and validating his feelings while simultaneously trying to keep my feelings in check, even though it has been more than four years since I buried my own beloved partner after his death from a series of AIDS-related lymphomas. I jot a note to remind myself to bring the intensity of the feelings stirred up by this session into my own supervision and therapy later in the week.

My second client is L, a youthful HIV-positive man who is also grieving the loss of his partner, C, from AIDS less than a year ago. Additionally, L is dealing with a flare up of Chronic Active Hepatitis B, for which he is preparing to undergo a liver biopsy. During the session, he is in tears, lamenting that while his family and friends provide support, he does not have the special attentions of a partner "to do for me all that I did for C during his various hospitalizations." My heart goes out to him, as I have thought those same things at various times since Lee died.

The third man I see is M, who is also HIV-positive and though never having experienced any physical symptoms of HIV disease, the level of virus in his blood stream is detectable and increasing. So far, he has chosen not to take any medication, but he feels that the time is approaching when he will need to begin some form of therapy. Our sessions are filled with his discussing all of his feelings about how his condition is progressing and the uncertainties associated with taking the powerful new medications. After M, I go to the gym for an hour and a half to help do something purely physical that takes my mind off of my work.

The landscape of my life, personal history, memories, and dreams is littered with the corpses and ghosts of loved ones, clients, colleagues, and fellow members of my community who have died in this plague. Being a middle-aged HIV-positive gay man living and working in Manhattan's Chelsea neighborhood, literally one of the ground zeros of the AIDS epidemic in North America, there is no way it could be any different. Since the early 1980s, when the AIDS plague began to spread within the gay community, I have been surrounded by illness, death, and grief. My best friend and colleague in my private practice, Luis, died of AIDS in 1989. Six men in my apartment building have died of AIDS over the years, as have more than 100 of my clients. I've had to become matter-of-fact about how the body inevitably fails us, and most of the time I don't worry about what happens when we die. I try to stay focused on how to live life well and how to help my clients live well.

This is nothing like what I expected I would be doing when I was training to be a therapist. I had certain young and hopeful ideas about the potential of human beings, within a normal life span, to grow in self-awareness. But by the mid-1980s, I suddenly found myself with a clientele made up largely of gay men who were either symptomatic with AIDS or anticipating the onset of symptoms, many of them under the age of 40.

Beginning in 1983 as a volunteer at the Gay Men's Health Crisis (GMHC), the world's oldest and largest community-based AIDS service organization, I have worked with dozens of gay men with AIDS, and supervised a team of volunteers caring for the then desperately ill and dying. At that time, GMHC was sounding the alarm that this illness was going to become an epidemic in the gay community. Even those of us working with AIDS clients every day could not wrap our minds around how this illness was devastating our community. As an action-oriented person, the hardest thing for me was knowing that despite my most creative and skillful clinical maneuvers, I was not going to change the essential fact that these men were dying. Since the onset of the AIDS plague, I have been learning how to do this work while simultaneously being immersed in providing both patient care and training to other professionals.

Today is a special day, as it will be the final session of a support group I have been leading for more than six years for the social workers on the AIDS team at St. Luke's Roosevelt Hospital Center in Manhattan. When I was first hired to run this group, these professionals were in a constant state of crisis because of the staggering number of client deaths they regularly experienced.

Despite the excellent supervision they received, the hospital and department were in an enormous period of change and transition that left none of the social workers feeling well enough supported professionally or secure about being able to maintain their jobs. With the advent of triple combination anti-retroviral therapies available, client deaths became increasingly rare, even among the inner city injection drug-using population that made up the majority of the individuals on their caseloads. While the various fiscal cutbacks still create a climate of job uncertainty for these skilled and dedicated social workers, they have become a cohesive team and have learned how to weather the varieties of personal and professionally demanding situations that are a routine part of HIV social work. While we have discussed that there will always be some need for an ongoing support group, most of the members and I have come to the general consensus that the group has really run its course. Riding the subway back to my office, I review the work this group has done and my role in helping them provide services to some of Manhattan's most disadvantaged and difficult-to-serve individuals. I allow myself to feel proud of the part I have played in facilitating the process and the crucial work these wonderful people have engaged in for the previous years.

The first session after returning from the hospital is a lunch time appointment with a male couple. R and T, who have been together seven years, are a mixed HIV antibody status couple with R being the person with AIDS and T being his HIV-negative partner. When I first began working with them, R was critically ill and most of our sessions focused on helping them adjust to R's deterioration, share their feelings about what they were going through, begin their mourning individually and as a couple, and plan for greater levels of caring for each of them. At one point, I referred them to a group at GMHC for couples in which one or both partners have HIV. Their regular attendance in this group provided them with an enormous amount of support, both from the two social workers leading the group and from the other couples who were also struggling to learn to survive and thrive as best they could with one or both partners suffering from this life threatening illness.

Now the picture is entirely different. R has regained his health entirely as a result of the triple combination therapy referred to as HAART (highly active anti-retroviral therapy). He has returned to work full time and is as robust, strong, and energetic as he has felt in many years. This resurgence of his health has had some unexpected side effects, primarily the destabilization of his partnership with T. As he began to grow stronger and accept the fact that he was not going to die soon, he recognized that though he felt strongly for T, he did not want to spend the rest of his life coupled with him. T is understandably hurt, but also recognizes that had R not gotten ill so early in their relationship, they might not have developed into anything more than a passing affair. The work at this point consists of encouraging them each to honestly express to one another their feelings about the relationship and its likely ending. Amidst the tears, pain, and fears, there is a lot of genuine love and acceptance that this upcoming transition will inevitably and likely be in both of their best interests.

Next, my session with S is especially trying. S is a 29-year-old superstar hair stylist who is making enormous amounts of money. At the time of his last HIV test, he was still uninfected despite repeatedly having unprotected anal intercourse while high on amphetamines. He has not been able to cease or reduce his drug binges and only attends AA or NA for three or four meetings. During sessions, he confesses his most recent lapse and vows that it will be the last time. Therapy has helped him see that though he is not physiologically dependent on the drugs, he behaves like an addict and is frequently behaving in highly impulsive and self destructive ways. Even the recent deaths of two of his close friends from overdoses of a "recreational" drug they all were doing has not motivated him to enter a drug treatment program.

S enters the session looking pale, wasted, and obviously recovering from the effects of "partying" on drugs. Before I even say anything to him, he reports that he has partied again. "I'm not surprised. You really look like sh–. Do you know that you look like you have AIDS?" I say to him.

"Do I really look that bad?" he responds.

"I'm not exaggerating at all, and I'm surprised that your clients aren't reacting to how bad you look."

"Actually, my bookings are down."

With that, I proceed to remind him that I do not feel I am helping him any longer. In fact, I believe that our sessions are enabling him by allowing him to think he is doing something to help himself when, in fact, he is not. He just nods in agreement. When I tell him this will be our last session unless he either goes into a rehab, or commits to staying drug free and going to at least one 12-step meeting a day, he just looks at me.

"S, I can't just sit here and watch you kill yourself with the drugs and unsafe sex. You need an intensive drug treatment program before we can do the work in therapy that you need. If I continue to work with you, I will be an accomplice to your death."

"You really think that if I don't stop I'll be dead?"

"Remember F and V," I remind him.

The session ends with my telling him that the only way I will be willing to see him again is if he wants my help in getting into a rehab or he has been clean and dry and working a program for at least six months.

I have four other sessions with people whose issues do not directly relate to HIV or AIDS. Colleagues and friends often ask me how it is that I've been able to work in AIDS for so long, dealing with all the pain and suffering endemic to this patient population. Others ask whether it's overwhelming to have intimately known and worked with so many people who have died or who are dying. I have had to struggle to learn that I am indeed doing something by simply sitting with clients, caring about them, and encouraging them to share any and all of their feelings about what is happening to them. Of course, I am unable to change the outcome of their illness. Accepting this reality, more than anything else, has taught me how to tolerate discomfort.

The discomfort I experience is about many things. Often it arises from a genuine empathetic connection with clients who are honestly experiencing feelings about their loss of health, career, lover, and their own imminent death. Once I have grown to care about a person, I feel all the accompanying discomfort about losing that person. Sometimes there is simply the uneasiness of being close to a person who is very ill or who is dying, simply because this reminds me of the fragility of my own good health. Before the onset of AIDS, active alcoholism, drug addiction, and Hepatitis B were the only life-threatening illnesses likely to kill my patients.

My first professional experience with AIDS was in 1981, when a psychotherapy client began exhibiting symptoms of what we now know is HIV illness. At that time, AIDS was unknown, but shortly thereafter, the syndrome was labeled Gay Related Immune Deficiency (GRID). It soon became clear to me that the men who were sick with this new disease had lived no differently than I had for many years. I assumed that if these people were getting sick, there was an excellent chance that the same thing could or would probably happen to me.

Beginning in the earliest days of the epidemic, there was the problem of burnout: everyone I knew, it seemed, was on death's doorstep. The first few deaths of my clients were terribly traumatic. Even as I grieved and went to the funerals and memorial services, I grew angry and frustrated that my clients' lives had been cut short. Then, after so many deaths, I went through a period of numbness and couldn't grieve for anyone. As treatments began to improve, the crisis and siege mentality of the work began to abate.

Therapy work with people with HIV and AIDS can seem banal as we discuss everything from wills to bowel movements. It may not seem as if much is going on as I sit with clients in their hospital rooms talking about their medical treatments, or just murmur soothing words as they endure intense physical pain. My simple questions to clients with dementia may not penetrate their mental fog. But I truly believe that just being there and caring about them is extremely healing.

There are different stages of therapy with clients who have AIDS. Clients who have just found out, or are just dealing with their positive HIV status, I encourage to talk about their fears, their regrets, their anger. I tell them about long-term survivors and nonprogressors—people like me who have HIV but don't become symptomatic. When it seems clinically appropriate to do so, there have been clients with whom I identify myself as a long-term survivor to give them some living embodiment of hope.

This work has changed me profoundly. It has caused me to lose the illusion of my own mortality that so many of us hold on to irrationally. The work has helped me tolerate enormous amounts of uncertainty and discomfort, both in clinical and personal situations. Most of all, it has humbled me. I feel proud to have been among the first social workers in the world who were there working with individuals and families affected by AIDS.

Think About It

1. How would you cope with working with this population?

2. When might self-disclosure of the social worker's positive HIV status be appropriate? Inappropriate?

3. How have attitudes toward people with AIDS changed since the 1980s?

4. How has treatment for HIV/AIDS changed?

PART 2:
SCHOOL SOCIAL WORK

Chapter 9
Elementary School Social Work

||||||||||||||||||||||||||||||||||||||||||||||||||||||||||||||||||||||||||||||||||||||||||||||||||||||||||||||||||||||||||

by Cami L. Cooper, MSW

My first experience as a school social worker was my undergraduate internship in an alternative high school. I often refer to that experience as "social work boot camp." As a result, I aspired to become a school social worker. I am now employed full-time at Washington Elementary School in Phoenix, AZ. Some of my colleagues are envious of the three-month summer vacation, but I am quick to inform them that it is well-earned.

School social work has other advantages, besides the generous vacation time. The working hours (I work 7:30 a.m. to 2:30 p.m. Monday through Friday) are also excellent and allow for time to engage in activities outside of work. The typical working day is also an advantage, if you enjoy being continually challenged and never repeating the same day twice. But, in my opinion, the kids are the greatest advantage. There is nothing in the world more precious than a small child delivering an "I love you" note to your desk at the end of a tiring day.

School social work also has its disadvantages. They may include having to work at more than one school and having a tremendous caseload. The job description is limiting and does not permit for in-depth therapeutic interaction with students or families. Also, you are often the only social worker present on a school campus. It can be somewhat isolating not to have someone close at hand who shares the same background and knowledge. However, I meet once a month with the other social workers in the school district, which helps eliminate feeling completely isolated.

With such a big caseload (I average around 120 students), the most important characteristic a school social worker can possess is organization. It is virtually impossible to be effective and get the job done in a chaotic and disorganized work environment. Good time management skills are also important, if one is to manage several different activities at one time. Creativity is also a valuable personal characteristic, particularly for elementary school social workers. Persons with artistic abilities can put them to use to create group and classroom activities for the students. But I believe the most important characteristic a school social worker should have is genuine love for children. They are the foundation of the job.

The salary is competitive with those for other social work positions. The National Association of Social Workers features a specialty section of school social workers and often provides excellent workshops and networking opportunities designed specifically for school social workers.

No two days are ever exactly the same in school social work. The following is a step-by-step account of a typical day in my life as an elementary school social worker. This is actually a composite of several days, which will give you the general idea of what I do.

7:15 a.m. I arrive on campus just in time to assist a teacher in pulling apart two students on the playground who are engaged in a minor physical altercation over a basketball. Since I am already heading in the direction, I offer to escort the two students to the office. After writing up two quick disciplinary referrals for the Assistant Principal, I check the mail that has accumulated in my mailbox: several student referrals from teachers, a request from another teacher to conduct a home visit on a chronically absent student, a note from the principal reminding me of an important meeting with a parent later in the day, and a videotape I ordered from a catalog on conflict resolution, which I intend to use for group.

7:45 a.m. I am stopped by three teachers on my way to the office. One wants a phone number to a local homeless shelter for a family and the other two want to discuss difficult students in their classrooms. I encourage each teacher to complete a Social Work Referral form and place it in my box, and I promise to review them as soon as possible.

8:00 a.m. I open the door to my office/group room just in time to catch the phone. A parent on the other end asks if I would be willing to write a brief statement regarding his child for a local psychiatrist. I agree and listen to my voicemail after I hang up. The first message is a confirmation of a guest speaker who has agreed to share with the sixth grade classrooms about his career in professional sports. As the second message plays, reminding me of a meeting later in the day with a parent, a student enters my office, crying. I ask her what is wrong. She tells me that her parents got into a fight over the weekend, and her dad went to jail. We discuss her feelings regarding the incident, and I sit with her as she continues to weep. When she feels ready to return to class, I send her off with a written pass to the teacher.

8:30 a.m. I quickly locate the parent permission slips for the students signed up to go to School Bell. I leave my office, locking the door behind me, and walk to several classrooms, retrieving students. We all pile into my compact car, seatbelts fastened, and drive ten minutes to the Phoenix Urban League office. The students skip up the stairs and down the hallway to the special room filled with new clothes. The students take their seats at the tiny tables, digging into the bins of crayons and paper. The volunteers assist the students one by one, trying on brand new clothing. Each child leaves with a giant bag filled with new shirts, pants, shoes, and underclothes. I wave thank-you to the kind volunteers and we pile back into the car. Back at school, I escort the proud students back to their classrooms and return to my office.

9:30 a.m. I listen to the new message on my voicemail. After the message ends, I pick up the phone and dial the principal's office to verify that the time she suggested to conduct home visits works with my schedule. I open the filing cabinet and pull out a folder of group activities, quickly sorting through the papers until I find the one I want. I return to the office to make copies of today's group activity. On the way back, another teacher stops me to say that the behavior modification point system I arranged for one of her students appears to be working. I arrive back in my office in time to unlock the door and let the students coming to group file in and take their seats on the couches arranged in a circle.

9:45 a.m. We begin group by rating our week (five is high, one is low) and each student shares one good event and one bad event that occurred over the past week. I introduce the day's topic, peer pressure, and distribute the worksheets. After completing the worksheets, several students volunteer to role play situations dealing with peer pressure. A brief discussion is generated from this activity. I initiate the close of group by asking each member to summarize what he or she learned from today's session. On the way out the door, they each choose a prize from the prize bag.

10:45 a.m. I sit down at my desk to document the events that took place in the group session. The phone rings, and someone in the office informs me that a parent has arrived requesting my assistance. I walk up to the office and escort the parent back to my office. After some informal conversation, the young woman begins to cry and shares some of the struggles she is facing as a single parent. When she is ready to leave, I assemble a small food package from the supply of canned goods I keep in a cupboard. I encourage her to attend the free parenting classes I arranged to have offered on campus and give her one of my business cards.

11:30 a.m. I quickly gulp down a sandwich and some fruit juice just before heading out to the playground. When I arrive, the person completing her duty shift hands me the two-way radio and jokingly wishes me luck. I stand under a shade tree. A girl on my caseload joins me under the tree and informs me that her family was evicted over the weekend and that she may be moving back to California with her grandparents. I tell her how sorry I am to hear the news and we discuss the impact of the changes on her life and her feelings toward the situation. I blow the whistle shortly after she turns to leave, and signal for the students to return to their classrooms. On the way, two students get into a fight. I pull them apart and escort them to the front office. After completing the disciplinary referral forms, I lead the two boys into the back conference room and conduct a brief mediation. They discover the altercation was actually the result of miscommunication and resolve the conflict by shaking hands. I make a brief note of this on the referral forms and return to my office.

12:30 p.m. I enter my office and find the necessary paperwork for home visits and return to the principal's office. No one answers the door at the first home. At the second home, the mother answers the door but does not invite us in. We discuss her child's poor attendance through a tattered screen door. She explains that her child has had a severe case of head lice but will be back in school tomorrow. We thank her and return to the car. I make a brief note in the Home Visit Log as we head back to the school.

1:00 p.m. I return to my office and sit down at my desk to prepare for the upcoming lesson on substance misuse I will be teaching to a second grade class. A few minutes later, the three sixth grade students recruited to be the puppeteers for the program arrive, and we briefly go over the lesson.

1:30 p.m. The three student puppeteers and I walk to the second grade classroom. We are greeted at the door with hugs and applause. As the sixth graders are setting up for the puppet show, I review last week's lesson with the class. I read today's lesson, as the puppeteers bring the story to life. We distribute the worksheets to the children and discuss the important parts of the story. When the lesson is finished, the puppeteers pack up their supplies and we return to my office. They return to their classrooms just as the final bell of the day is ringing.

2:30 p.m. I make a quick call to the front office for someone to make an announcement reminding the teachers on the Social Work Advisory Committee that there will be a brief meeting in the group room.

2:45 p.m. Eight teachers arrive. I distribute a brief agenda and commence the meeting. We discuss some of the challenges I have been facing. The teachers offer some helpful feedback and suggestions. For example, the sponsor of the Student Council offers to recruit some of her students to assist me in organizing a canned food drive to replenish the campus food pantry. Another teacher suggests I make a brief presentation during each staff meeting to describe the various services I provide, for those on the faculty who are still somewhat unfamiliar with the role of a school social worker. I thank them for their support and helpful suggestions. After a brief discussion, the meeting is adjourned.

3:30 p.m. I pack my things and prepare to leave for the day. I stop by the office to run some copies of worksheets to be used in a classroom lesson I will be teaching first thing in the morning. As I pull out of the parking lot, I honk my horn and wave at several students playing on the basketball courts. Today was a good day. I wonder what tomorrow will bring.

Think About It

1. What are some important skills for a school social worker?

2. Do you think this would be an enjoyable job? Explain your answer.

3. What are some challenges that might arise for someone who works as the only social worker in a setting?

Chapter 10
An Inner-City High School

||||||||||||||||||||||||||||||||||||||||||||||||||||||||||||||||||||||||||||||||||||||||||

by Fred Sacklow, CSW, R

Raphael calls first thing in the morning. I'm surprised, and I sense that this can't be good news. He says that he won't be coming to school today. I was expecting to see him today as one of the usual 15 students or so that I see in a combination of individual or group counseling on a daily basis. Raphael says that his grandparents hit him. His grandmother even used a broomstick. Now he is at his girlfriend's house waiting for the City child welfare caseworker to call, because his girlfriend's father reported the incident. I gather the necessary information from Raphael and let him know that I will call his grandmother and the caseworker and try to help him sort this out. We make an appointment to see each other tomorrow at school. I can't help but have strong feelings about this situation. Raphael has already been "kicked out" by his mother and now this. He is hurt and depressed and has a poor hold on his anger. Such impulsiveness and rebellion against "adult" authority is typical at this time for many teens, but it can be too much for some family systems to bear. The school social worker often has to intervene in the student-family system. Such conflict often makes it hard for students to learn and, in Raphael's case, increases his depression, which often gives rise to hopelessness and suicidal thoughts.

Since I work in a vocational high school that teaches aircraft mechanics, most of the students I see are boys. They come from all over the city and represent all nationalities and cultures. My present caseload is about 70 students, although it can go up to 100 students a week. My first discussion today is with Gina. She is a refreshingly sweet girl who is very lively. But she tells me she has not eaten since a day and a half ago. Yet she insists she is not hungry. She has her chewing gum and plans to live on that until she gets home in about six hours. My instant reaction is to want to feed her. But, of course, she would resist this vehemently. I would also like to give her a parental type lecture about getting a good breakfast and the importance of a well-balanced meal, but she already knows this. Gina also likes to wear only black, with dog collars around her neck. If people don't like it, she says it's too bad. Since Gina is only a freshman and our relationship is new, all I can do right now is to try to get her to trust me and feel comfortable with me.

I wonder if Gina has some kind of serious eating disorder. She also has strange likes and dislikes when it comes to foods. She seems of average weight for her size and has no medical problems. I wonder how food may get translated into adolescent identity issues for a young girl trying to find her place in the world.

Not only do many of the kids I see have personal or family issues they struggle with, but many like Raphael and Gina also have learning problems. Both are in "special education" programs. Raphael is in a Resource Room. He goes there once a day for small group tutoring and remediation. Gina is in a more restrictive setting because of her learning disabilities. She is functionally grouped with similar students who share the same special education teachers. Both students recently received their report cards, and each failed two subjects.

Gina says she can't pay attention, because the boys bother her. I have had to intervene with certain boys who never seem to run out of questions for Gina as to why she is so different. They all wear the same baggy jeans and name brand tops and so look like each other, so why can't she dress like the other girls? They also wonder how she can like heavy metal music when everyone knows that rap music is "in."

Raphael says it was the teacher's fault that he failed. He doesn't know how to teach and plus the teacher doesn't like him. Many students seem to share the same explanations for why they fail. Dealing with students' frustrations and disappointments when it comes to their education is a big role for the school social worker. The students have a history of failure and some have become so hopeless and discouraged that they drop out of school. These students need to be motivated and supported and sometimes even led to a goal.

It so happens that today, Gina's mother is coming in to speak to one of the teachers. I make arrangements to see her as well. She comes in with her son, Gina's older brother. The mother is pleasant and verbal. I bring up Gina's eating habits. Her mother is very concerned about this and pleads with Gina often to eat better. She says that Gina is in psychotherapy where this is also being addressed. Her mother says that Gina misses her father a lot. Her parents are divorced and he does not keep in contact with her. I also learn that Gina's brother has just split with his wife, someone with whom Gina was very close. After they leave, I reflect on the difference between school social work and psychotherapy. My goals here are much more practical, it seems. Help the student get his or her high school diploma and then move on. Help them plan for the future, be it the military or college or a job. Many may need referrals to other agencies and institutions for continued training and assistance.

Danny knocks on my door and comes in with two students I do not know. They hover in the doorway as Danny sits down and then asks when he is supposed to see me. I am surprised, because I make it clear to all students at the beginning of the term when our appointment is. I refresh his memory and then give him a pass so he can let his teacher know why he is leaving class. Danny, like all my students, is mandated for counseling. When evaluated by the School Based Support Team, it was determined that counseling could aid his adjustment to school and better his chances for success. Counseling was indicated on his Individualized Education Plan (IEP). This is a plan that is developed for all students in special education. This does not mean that students are volunteers for counseling or that they know why they are given the service in the first place. Some students take to it with apparent ease and have issues they want to discuss. Others come because they feel that at least it is better than being in class, and still others are more ambivalent and may say "go away." Danny is being resistant these days. He feels he doesn't need counseling any more. He can handle his own problems. This wasn't the case just a few short weeks ago, when he was having trouble with his sister and needed to talk about it. Sometimes confronting this teen resistance and ambivalence can be very frustrating. Don't they see that I just want to help? Am I the enemy or what? If you try too hard, you push the teen away, and if you don't try at all, it seems as if goals are not being met. You have to walk a fine line.

I get a call from the Special Education dean. Robert has been talking constantly in class and throwing balls of paper. They want me to talk to him. I meet with Robert, who is initially quiet and does not look at me. We have known each other a while now. He is a junior this year. It is surprising to watch these young people grow up. It is sometimes remarkable the changes that can be seen when you first see a student when he is 14 or 15 years old and then when he is saying goodbye to you at around 18, 19, and sometimes even 20 years old. Robert is growing up and changing, too. He is becoming more aggressive and less likely to take any disrespect (as the kids are fond of saying) from others. He tells me that he is unhappy being in special education. He feels that he is not progressing, and now he is worried about his future. We discuss the possibility of his taking classes in the mainstream. Many students are in special education but still take so-called "regular" classes. Robert is not confident that he could compete with those kids. I tell him that we will see how he does this term and we will look at mainstreaming options for him next year. Robert is labeled "emotionally disturbed." This usually means that the student is intelligent and has at least an average IQ but that his behavior is sometimes beyond his control.

I decide to go to my mailbox to see if the form that Raphael's caseworker said she was going to fax me is there. I only have a few minutes, because the bell will ring soon. Then I expect to have a group of four students. Sometimes it seems that I never left high school myself. I am so geared to the bell. My only break is the forty minutes I get for lunch each day, and sometimes even that is taken up by a student or parent meeting. There is nothing in my mailbox, but I pass many kids wearing hats in the hallway. They are not supposed to wear hats. It is not part of the dress code. Do I confront them or mind my own business? Should I enforce the rules or just try to work with the kids I am responsible for?

Which social work hat to wear is the question. Working in a school puts you in multiple roles. Many students cut a class, sometimes consistently. They question whether they really need to know earth science. Why should they go to art when they say they can't draw? Some even refuse to go to gym. They are not coordinated or good at basketball or maybe just plain scared. These students need a dose of reality, so they know what to expect and can understand the consequences for breaking the rules. The school social worker has to help a student take greater self responsibility, even as he or she assists them in improving their coping skills and maturity levels.

The bell rings and in walk four students for a group session. It is a new group, although some of the students know each other from class or other groups that I have run with them. It is hard to keep a steady group going. Kids' schedules change and then they have to be seen at a different time. The fifth member of this group had to be taken out, because his teacher objected to my seeing him during his class. This happens sometimes. A competition occurs between a class and counseling. I try to explain the service to the teacher in question and we talk of compromises. I usually end up being accommodating since, after all, this is a school. It does have a price in group continuity and cohesiveness.

Mario tells the group that he does not feel good today. His girlfriend broke up with him two days ago. He only knew her for about three months but was sure he wanted to marry her. He can't sleep and has trouble concentrating on his class work. One boy tells him that he should just forget about her—there are plenty of other girls—but Mario is not so sure. He went out last night and got drunk. He doesn't remember how or when he got home. Mario has a history of excessive drinking. Andrew tells him that he is crazy. *Doesn't he know what alcohol will do to him?* he asks. The discussion continues and the bell rings. If only the problem ended there. I give Mario some literature on alcohol and teen relationships. We agree to continue to talk next period privately.

The school social worker is often confronted by students with very self-destructive behaviors. Mario needs immediate and intense intervention. He has already been hospitalized for depression and is on medication. Teen relationship issues can often push vulnerable teens to the edge. Mario is in need of friends. Hopefully, the group can help. Here, the students can talk to and hear each other in a safe environment, and although they sometimes ignore each other, they very often support each other as well.

The last period is finally over. I have about forty-five minutes to finish the paperwork for the day. The attendance for each student has to be recorded. I have two counseling reports to finish, because tomorrow there are two Educational Planning Conferences I will attend. These conferences occur after the School Based Support Team finishes its testing and is ready to sit down with a student's parents to review the results, as well as to determine the most appropriate placement. We also discuss counseling issues at that time and whether or not the service is being utilized by the student and if it should be continued or not.

Many school social workers perform social intakes and evaluations on students as part of their team duties. This helps the team formulate a broader idea about the student's psychosocial functioning and lends itself to determining the student's proper placement and service needs. This is especially critical when the student is first referred for testing. My job is to provide the mandated counseling, not a full social assessment. The team members, the psychologist, and the educational evaluator are often the people social workers interact with most in their professional capacities. These relationships can be rewarding and also conflictual. For the last two years, I have found myself in the middle of two professionals who are at war with each other. It is difficult to remain neutral, but I try to be supportive to both in my own way. A typical day may find me giving advice to one about the other.

It's finally three o'clock. Now I just have to brave the traffic home. I think of the ways I can relieve some stress. At least the sun is shining. Before I leave, I think I will call the teacher's union hotline. We have no new contract, and with the City finances getting worse every day, I wonder what kind of contract and salary increase we will get and when.

School social work is certainly about kids and not money. Many colleagues I know have to work part-time jobs to make ends meet. We often have to work in less than adequate settings with less than adequate supplies. Helping kids grow, develop, and learn is the name of the game. Sacrifice seems to come with the territory.

Think About It

1. How do the school social worker's goals differ from those of a social worker doing psychotherapy with the same clients?

2. Do you think high schools should have dress codes? Should the social worker be required to enforce them? How can a student's dress help the social worker in assessing the student?

3. How are the challenges of working as a high school social worker different from those of the elementary school social worker in the previous chapter?

Chapter 11
Social Work in a Rural School District

||||||||||||||||||||||||||||||||||||||||||||||||||||||||||||||||||||||||||||||||||||||||||||||||||||||||||||||||||||||||||||||||

by Carol M. Line, BS, ACSW

I had always been a city dweller. For forty years, I thought that no one could or should live anywhere but in an urban area, and Detroit was my choice. After receiving my MSW, I immediately went to work as the director of a day program for mentally challenged adults. Within two years, I had a new job supervising the development of community placements for institutionalized clients. Both of these jobs demanded many working hours and generated a great deal of stress. My husband, also a social worker, worked for the then governor of Michigan, William Milliken, staffing his urban affairs office. His job was also pressure-filled and time-consuming.

We both decided that, although we both loved social work, we would very much like to "smell the flowers" as we practiced our profession. We longed to be able to live in a pristine environment, without the stresses of pollution, traffic, crime, and competition for space and services. So, we made a decision to do the unthinkable—leave our very prestigious jobs and try a new lifestyle in a rural area of Michigan.

One of the first jobs that became available was in the Upper Peninsula, about as rural an area as one can get. Some would even call it a wilderness area. The job was with an intermediate school district (ISD), a regional body that served a three-county geographic area, covered 4,000 square miles, including several inhabited islands, and had more deer than people. There were 13 local school districts within the ISD. The smallest of these districts had less than 10 children; the largest had 3,500. At the time I began working for the ISD, there were only three social workers covering the entire school district, and they were all relatively new. Most of the residents of this area had never seen a school social worker, and the schools had little or no idea about what school social workers were supposed to do.

My first challenge came when I realized that the people who lived in this area were very independent and proud. They had been used to working their land, bartering for their needs with their neighbors, and surviving as a result of their own efforts. They all lived like one big, extended family and helped each other without being asked. It was very difficult for them to request or to accept help from "outsiders." They did not feel comfortable with governmental systems or people who had not been born and raised in the area. Winning their trust and confidence was my first major goal.

Even though the school was the focal point for community life, families in trouble tended to distrust school staff and school authorities. As a result, I found it more fruitful to meet with families in their own homes, rather than at the schools themselves. This necessitated a lot of driving, in all weather conditions and on all kinds of roads. Some of the home visits were *memorable*, to say the least.

Directions to homes were given by landmarks, not by miles or road names. One went to a home based on: "It is the first white house on the right, after the dairy farm. If you go up the hill, you have gone too far. There is a blue pickup in the driveway." I became very good at following these kinds of directions, and when someone gave me a direction with an actual road name in it, I continued to ask for landmarks, because there was no guarantee that the road sign would still be standing after the latest storm.

I used to think that urban slums were the worst housing I had ever seen. I still think that, because even though the homes I visited in the U.P. were often very poorly constructed and had minimal amenities, their occupants never had to worry about whether the gas or electricity would be turned off or the toilet would be clogged. They could always use kerosene lamps, wood burning stoves, and outhouses. In the city, when the landlord fails to fix these basic systems, one often goes cold and hungry. Here, there are always options.

My first home visit one day took me to a small structure with no windows. I knocked on the door and was met with a cheerful: "Come in!" I noted, when I looked for the doorknob, that THERE WAS NONE, just a big hole where the knob should have been. So, I gave the door a push, figuring that it would open smoothly. To my surprise, the unhinged door fell inward, hitting the floor with a thud. You might say I made a grand entrance.

Other home visits also presented surprises. I once was greeted by a flock of "watch geese" who snapped and hissed and chased me back to my car in record time. In other homes, I met up with a variety of dogs, goats, and sheep, all wandering around the yard, waiting for a fresh face to harass. Mind you, these animals were not deliberately set out to deny access to visiting social workers. They were simply living at the residence and had the ultimate freedom, the ability to wander at will. I learned very quickly to wear clothing that was easily washed, boots that could be hosed down, and to bring nothing that I could not do without, in the event it was eaten.

Small towns present unusual problems relative to confidentiality. Since everyone knows everyone else and is probably related to them in some way, it is not unlikely that one would be accosted in the grocery store by a well meaning neighbor or relative wanting to know how so-and-so is doing. I developed a number of pat responses to this question, all the way from: "I am sorry but I cannot talk about my clients," to "You will have to ask their parents," to "Isn't the weather awful today?" Although this dilemma followed me constantly, I was not annoyed, because I really believed that the people who lived here were interested in their community, and not merely interested in the latest gossip.

At times, however, it was scary how fast word got around. One night, my friend became lost in the woods while preparing his deer blind. It was quite late by the time he was found. The next morning, at 9 a.m., the local bank teller asked me how my friend was doing after his adventure the previous night. I once had a UPS delivery person leave a package for me in my agency vehicle, which was parked outside a local school. How the driver knew that I was the ISD employee who was inside the building at the time is beyond me! Several of us drove the school car at different times, but somehow he knew that it was *me* who drove it on that day. We have a better communication system here than the Internet will ever be, but it certainly makes confidentiality a challenging issue.

There are many factors that allowed me to work effectively with the rural population in my area. The first of these was a social work education that taught a systems approach to social work practice. There were many occasions when I was called upon to work with individuals, groups of parents, staff or administrators, agencies, and communities. Without a problem-focused approach to social work practice, I would have been unable to do the job. The flexibility to be able to flow from one skill to another is critical to working in an area where YOU ARE THE ONLY SOCIAL WORKER. Social workers who are stuck in casework or group work or community practice and do not have the ability to move into different systems effectively are very handicapped in this setting.

The other major necessity in school social work practice in rural areas is that one has to become a trusted member of the community. This means respecting local values and traditions, and being a part of the community during non-working hours. There are times when advocacy is necessary and runs in the face of local practices, but if one has gained the confidence and trust of the community, it will accept your intervention, even though it may not agree with it. I remember having to report a beloved teacher to protective services because she punished a child who had decorated the bathroom with toilet paper by wrapping him in toilet paper and parading him through the halls.

The school district wished that I hadn't reported the incident but understood that I had certain responsibilities in my job that I could not avoid. I learned to pick my battles but do what was ethically responsible, even if it meant the entire community would know.

It was extremely important to be able to efficiently network with other agencies in the area. We were all on a first-name basis, and when I called an agency with a concern or a question, I was always treated like royalty. One's reputation is extremely important in rural school social work because word of mouth is the method most often used to evaluate people. If the word passed about you is that you are professional and competent, but also understanding, compassionate, and respectful of the community in which you practice, you will be given the best that other agencies and professionals have available to give. How you handle your personal and professional life is a major component in how successfully you can practice rural school social work. You are very visible.

The difficulties that hampered my professional performance most were the lack of other professional social workers from whom to learn and the ability to obtain continuing education without great commitments of travel time and money. At one time, we tried to form a peer review group consisting of the six professional social workers in the area. We found that we were all in need of new input, and without it we were just trading old, stale material. This meant making continuing education a major priority. Some of the individuals were not committed to that end. For this reason, the group disbanded and those of us who could, made the long journeys to new professional learning opportunities. Those who could not or did not want to make this commitment remained in a static position relative to their professional knowledge and practice.

Practicing rural school social work has been, for me, a good professional decision. I have become very close to the population I serve, and I feel as though I am a respected member of the community. This has enhanced my ability to practice without sacrificing ethics or values. Being nonjudgmental about the differences between my personal beliefs and those of the community is a priority, but then, it is in any social work practice. It is just more important in rural school social work, because EVERYONE KNOWS your personal beliefs.

My husband and I have indeed "smelled the flowers" for more than twenty years now and have never regretted our decision to leave the urban area. We have felt personally and professionally satisfied and have learned that people everywhere are just people and need to be respected for the individuals that they are.

Think About It

1. What are some special challenges involved in working in a rural area?

2. How would you feel about reporting the unethical, illegal, or inappropriate behavior of another professional (such as the teacher)? How would you handle such a situation?

PART 3: CHILDREN, YOUTH, AND FAMILIES

Chapter 12
Urban Child Protective Services

||||||||||||||||||||||||||||||||||||||||||||||||||||||||||||||||||||||||||||||||||||||||||||||||||||||||||||||||||||||

by Susan Dodd Gaylor, MSW, ACSW

I was experiencing one of the "goods"—and I knew it was one of those that would last a long time—and I took the time to savor it.

I learned early in my career as an inner-city social worker working in child protective services that I would see more than my share of the bad that life has to offer. I learned to work in an environment of broken families, extreme poverty, violence, and rampant substance use—where there was little quality of life for those who existed there. There is no way to work in this environment if you don't have the "goods." The "goods" are what make working in an inner-city environment rewarding—the things you carry with you for when the going is tough. You have to be able to recognize a "good." It may be a child's smile or a caller who says, "It has only been a month, but I'm still clean!" The inner-city environment is tough; but the rewards are many—if you recognize them. You can truly be an instrument of change in this place. My advice to someone who wants to work in the inner-city or to work anywhere in child protective services is an always and a never—ALWAYS recognize and hold onto the "goods" and NEVER lose your sense of humor!

There were baby clothes and toys scattered all over the room—we had walked into a baby shower! Minutes earlier, I had placed a baby in the arms of the man and woman who became her new parents in that instant. Definitely one of the "goods!"

As the baby began a new life with adoptive parents, I thought about the baby's birth mother, Karen—now an adult "street person."

Karen came into the state foster care system as a teenager. She was mentally ill, had mild brain damage, and had suffered severe physical and sexual abuse. I worked with Karen—sometimes on a daily basis—and I constantly fought for funding to insure that Karen received the care and help that she needed. But funding was scarce and Karen ran away every time she was placed in a new program. Karen was a chronic runaway, often months at a time. With the help of a benevolent police detective, I retrieved Karen many times from other cities, other states. She always questioned how we were able to find her, and never suspected that it was from the return address that she always (inadvertently?) put on letters she mailed to me.

Placing the baby in the adoptive home would have been a great way to end a day; however, on the way back to the city, the beeper signaled that my on-call weekend had begun.

One-year-old Tanika had been taken to a local hospital with third-degree burns from the middle of her back down to the backs of her knees. She had been transferred to a regional burn center. These types of burns are indicative of a child being dipped in scalding water, and this was in direct contradiction to her father's story of the child having accidentally injured herself. Tanika's father was known to our agency and had a history of substance use disorder and psychiatric problems. He was also a suspected drug dealer and had a long history of violence. Her mother was in jail on drug and prostitution charges. Tanika was safe at the hospital, but there were two other small children in the home.

I was asked to accompany another social worker to remove the two other children for placement in foster care. Police officers accompanied us to the home, which was located in a federal housing project. When we arrived, we found 2-year-old Renata and 4-year-old James alone with their elderly grandmother, who was in poor health and could not care for the children. As we were preparing to leave with the children, we heard loud crashing noises. The father had crashed through the back door of the house and was screaming curses. He grabbed James, who appeared terrified of his father; and the police officers wrestled the child away from him. As he grabbed me and threw me against a wall, Laura picked up Renata and ran for the agency vehicle. As the police subdued the father, I took a screaming James to the car. Following our agency procedures, we took the children for pre-placement physicals, which had to occur through the emergency room of a large, public hospital. When you sit with children for hours in emergency rooms, it teaches you to be very creative! We played games with them and kept them comfortable. They were very dirty and hungry, but were in general good health. At the end of our time together, James looked at me and asked, "Do you have any little boys at home?" I did not back then, and when I told him "no," he said in a hopeful voice, "I could go home with you and be your little boy!" It still amazes me how many times children said that to me over the years. I did as I always did—I hoped he wouldn't see the tears well up in my eyes as I explained to him about the foster home picked especially for him because he is such a special little boy.

As we were finishing another "good"—talking with James' and Renata's new foster parent, a spiritually strong woman devoted to children and to bettering her community—the beeper went off again.

The car clock read 9:45 p.m. when our agency vehicle followed four police cars onto a street known as "Crack Alley." The neighborhood had earned this name because of the abandoned houses turned "crack houses," the ever-present drug deals, and the violence that is part of that package. Our report stated that two children were being kept in one of the "crack houses." I was accompanied by Liz, a brand new social worker, who was making her first "beeper call." She stared at the dark house and said, "We're not actually going to go in there, are we?" Actually, Liz didn't go too far into the house. She was so overwhelmed by what she saw inside that she and a rookie police officer (also making his first call) repeatedly bumped into each other attempting to be the one closest to the door! The floors were covered with old clothes, trash, and debris piled waist high—barely enough for tiny paths through the house. There was no electricity, so there was no heat (this was a cold November night), but more importantly, there were NO LIGHTS!

The dark made this an extremely dangerous place. Initially, it was impossible to determine how many people were in the house and what weapons might pose a threat. The police searched everyone who could be found. Ever the social worker—trying to establish rapport—I found myself (amidst this utter chaos) going up to the person who appeared to be in charge in this house (at least he was the biggest, meanest-looking person there), introducing myself, shaking his hand, explaining what we were doing there, and asking for his help in this situation. The man appeared so stunned by my gesture that he actually began showing us around inside the house. With only the aid of police flashlights to navigate the tiny paths through the debris, we discovered that there was no running water (no bathroom facilities) and there was human waste strewn about the house. Old food in the refrigerator laid under mold that grew out of the refrigerator and up the wall.

The man led us to where 8-year-old William and 2-year-old Darius were asleep on an old couch under a pile of clothes. The children seemed sluggish and were difficult to awaken—I knew it was important to get them to a hospital as soon as possible. As we started to leave with the children, Liz finally found her voice and yelled, "There's a crowd outside!" There was a hostile crowd of about 50 people outside the house. Everything happened very fast—shielded by the police officers, we carried the children, literally through a gauntlet to the agency vehicle. Liz clutched the 2-year-old in the car and kept repeating, "I'll never get used to this," as we made a speedy exit from the neighborhood. It turns out Liz was right—she never did get used to it, and she left the agency several months later. We took the two unwashed, malnourished little boys to the public hospital, where lab tests revealed traces of drugs in their blood. We stayed overnight at the hospital with the little boys, because there had to be someone with them to offer security and comfort.

As this day was ending and a new day beginning, 8-year-old William asked me, "Do you have a little boy at home?"

Think About It

1. Why do you think Liz "never got used to" this kind of work?
2. Do you think you could do this kind of work? Why, or why not?

Chapter 13
Social Workercise and the Adoption Social Worker

IIIIIIIIIIIIIIIIIIIIIIIIIIIIIIIIIIIIIIIIIIIIIIIIIIIIIIIIIIIIIIIIIIIIIIIIIIIIIIIIIIIIIIIIIIIIIIIIIIIIIIIIIIIIIIIIIIIIIIIIIIIIIIIIIIIIIIIIIIIIIIIIIIII

by Ronnita J. Waters, LCSW-QS

It is Monday morning, 7:23 a.m. to be exact, and I am already out the door. I am so excited and happy, because I have two adoption finalizations today for three kids. I am also excited because I have a home visit tonight to introduce a prospective adoptive family to one of my kids, Joey, by phone. I leave earlier than my usual time in an effort to beat the traffic to my office 45 minutes away. I am excited to get to the office to knock some paperwork out of the way, so I can spend the remainder of my day having client contact, including three home visits. I have some court documents to print, sign, and submit to my supervisor before my 1:30 p.m. adoption hearings. So I will drive past the courthouse to my office, and I finally arrive at the office at 8:35.

As I arrive, my alarm goes off. I have a 9 a.m. conference call to update all parties (Joey's guardian ad litem, DCF attorney, Joey's caregivers, Joey's attorney ad litem, and Joey's therapist) on the family's decision after reviewing the disclosure file. My supervisor isn't in the office yet—only five other case managers, a supervisor, and the clerical staff are present this early. This is great, because now I have the community printer to myself. I start on my sched-uled paperwork, which today includes updating a child study for a child for whom I have been searching for a forever family for two years, correcting a status report for court on the adoption process for a sibling group of eight, printing the adoption home study on an aunt applying to adopt her fourth child from her sister (I typed the home study up last night from my Thursday interview notes), putting together the adoption package that goes with her home study, and entering the two siblings I was assigned on Wednesday into the state adoption recruitment website.

The conference call, as I knew it would, goes longer than planned, so I decide to check my emails...only 63 new emails from Friday at 8 p.m. to Monday at 9:30 a.m. The call ends with all parties in agreement to supervise contact by phone or in person, until further recommendation of the therapist. My supervisor and I pretty much co-train all parties on our agency's adoption matching and finalization process in one conference call. This includes references to the federal Multi-Ethnic Placement Act requirements, state dependency statutes, and the state administrative code. I haven't gone to law school, but my paralegal certificate gets its fair share of work. I was able to respond to all my necessary emails, so this call has multiple positives in my book.

I get to my final print (the home study), and the office has bloomed into the majority of our case management workforce, including my intern. I have the social work intern use our checklist to pull together the adoption package, while I start entering the first sibling into the statewide recruitment system. I decide I'll enter one sibling and let the intern review my entry to create the entry for the second sibling. I use my remaining time to follow up on service provider requests and to make corrections to the few court and adoption documents my supervisor returned to my attention. Working on papers doesn't stop my phones from ringing or my emails from dinging, so I stop and respond to those, too. This stop-and-go switching from papers to phones to emails is a daily routine. I call it "social workercise."

Although I plan to leave at 12:30 for my 30-minute drive to court, my intern and I don't get on the elevator until 1 p.m. after my stop-and-go routine and putting the last-minute touches on the adoption package. We leave the package and other corrected documents with my supervisor for review and head out. I remember my adoption finalization folders as I step on the elevator and rush back to get them out of my desk. When I get to the parking lot, I give the social work intern the courtroom number, so he can meet me to observe the adoption finalizations.

Thank God I packed water, fruits, and nuts today. I snack and drive and return to aimless thoughts and various car karaoke moments as the radio seems in tune with my mood today. I have three missed calls, and two are on one of the cases I am finalizing today. I walk into the courthouse holding on tightly to my adoption finalization folders. The folders have various adoption forms and information on adoption resources for the adoptive families and their "new" children. I greet the security guards and go through the metal detector.

I check my phone, and one of the families adopting today has called for the second time, but has left no voice message. I call them back, and they confirm the details of the hearing. They acknowledge that they confirmed yesterday, but they are so excited they want to verify again whether they should call in or if I will call them. I explain that the court will call them and verify that they have the notary present. I don't have a folder for them, but I will put it in the mail tomorrow. They are appearing by phone, because they reside outside of the state. They are adopting Trice, a sibling in the first case I received as an adoption worker.

I flew to their home and placed Trice when she was five years old, more than a year ago. The process for new placements without concern usually takes 90 days. With this case, we also had to wait out an adoption application appeal process. The child's previous caregiver applied to adopt, so the competing applications had to be reviewed by a committee. After the committee made its recommendation and the department decided not to approve the previous caregiver, the previous caregiver appealed the decision. We awaited an administrative hearing to be set. Once it was set and done (it lasted two days), we awaited the administrative order, and then the appeal time for that order. The family and I are so excited to finally have this adoption hearing set.

The other finalization today is a family completing their second adoption, and this time it is a sibling group of two. I did their first adoption a year ago, with Trice's sister, Lisa. I plan to keep in touch, because Trice and Lisa's biological brother remains in foster care awaiting a family, and I want to ensure these siblings don't lose contact.

I get to the courtroom waiting area, and my intern is waiting with the family and the adoption attorney, everyone dressed in some type of purple. I greet everyone with hugs. One of the children taps me and asks, "Where is your purple?" I unbutton my jacket and proudly show my purple satin ruffled shirt. The kids beam smiles. Lisa chose our dress code today—purple is her favorite color. She saw another family do some dress coordination on her adoption day and asked her mom if this time their family could do some matching. We all excitedly complied. The adoption attorney states, "We're next." I've worked with him on many adoptions over the years, but I am not sure if he knows it is me, since he calls my co-worker my name all the time.

The adoptive mom, Mrs. Smith, jokes with me: "Well they about to be all mines now, don't you bring me no more." The whole group, including me, laughs. The bailiff looks at me and in a deep voice says, "You noising up my hallway again, young lady." He has known me since I was a social work intern eight years ago at 20 years old. He gives me a smile and a wink. I know he is joking, but I smile and apologize out of habit.

The bailiff signals to the adoption attorney, who says, "It's show time." I lock eyes with Mrs. Smith, and tears have already formed in the pockets of her eyes. Her adult daughter rubs her back, and the tears are now running down her face. Lisa falls into her usual role and quickly wipes her mom's face. I love seeing Lisa after her adoption. Seeing how she grew to be comfortable with emotions and so protective of her mother ensures me this was the right family for her. I know Mrs. Smith's tears are tears of relief. I also know she isn't comfortable with them but can't stop them. I feel my eyes burning. Mrs. Smith looks at me and jokes, "My eyes hot. They sweating."

We walk into the courtroom. I let the family enter first—about 15 attendees. When I get to the front of the courtroom, the judge is already asking for the adoption worker. I announce myself, and then the adoption attorney leads the family introductions. The judge does some fact reviewing, and the adoption attorney confirms. He asks Mrs. Smith to share why she wants the judge to grant her petition for adoption. I look straight up to the ceiling, because I know I will not be able to hold back these tears. Mrs. Smith tells the court how much she and her family love the children. Now there is not a dry eye in the room. The children are not old enough to require their consent, but they are of age to understand this process. I know they understand it, because I worked with them regarding adoption, starting soon after their parents' parental rights were terminated. The adoption attorney asks if the children want to share why they want Mrs. Smith to adopt them. The youngest shakes his head no. The older sister tearfully says, "Because she is our mommy, and me and my brother love her."

Now it's my turn, and the adoption attorney asks if I signed the consent for this adoption. "Yes." He asks if I completed the adoption home study recommending that Mrs. Smith adopt these siblings. "Yes," I answer. He then asks, "And why did you recommend Mrs. Smith to adopt these beautiful children?" I do my look to the ceiling to hold my tears, breathe, and state, "I saw what Mrs. Smith did for Lisa and knew these children needed only her to get them to an emotionally safe place. I believe this forever home and family is the best for the children." The judge says, "I agree, so I am granting this petition for Mrs. Smith to adopt these two beautiful children." She announces each child's new legal name, and we all cheer. We do some quick pictures in the courtroom and with the judge. Mrs. Smith says she'll wait for me outside, and I turn back to do the other adoption by phone.

On my way out of the courtroom, I give Mrs. Smith and her newest two children each a folder, explaining to her the tuition waivers and adoption tax credit information inside of her folder. I encourage her to join a foster and adoptive parent group and to keep an eye out for chances to advocate for the tax credit to continue. I exchange see-you-later hugs. Mrs. Smith invites me to lunch, but I explain I have to head down south for home visits. She gives me a hug and thanks me for everything. I thank her for being the best mommy for my kids.

I rush to my car in hopes of beating the traffic and getting to my 3:30 p.m. home visit with Joey on time. I give my intern a few moments to debrief, as I switch into comfortable flat shoes and put my "court shoes and jacket" in my trunk for my next court date (Wednesday).

I finish my day at 8:30 p.m., when I walk out of my last home visit. I have a new to-do list from each home visit, but I am happy because tonight every child I visited appeared safe and with caregivers who were ensuring the health of the children's well-being. Joey's call with the prospective adoptive family is moving him toward permanency. A 16-year-old child who said she didn't want to be adopted agreed to participate in an adoption recruitment event. And I did an adoption placement and subsidy agreement for a sibling group of four with their godfather. Safety, permanency, and well-being are the core objectives in child welfare, and in five hours, I made progress in all three areas for six children who do not have legal parents. I love my career!

When things don't go well, I call it "The Journey," as I believe the destination will prove the twists and turns are necessary. Of course, life has various twists and turns. Life in "foster care" adoption is no different. For example, I arrived home at 9:15 p.m. and I was able to sleep in using my flexible schedule. But at 10 a.m., my 16-year-old from last night's home visit was calling me. She was in a heated argument with her caregiver. While I was speaking with

114 *Days in the Lives of Social Workers*

the caregiver, the child packed a bag and left the home, stating she would not be returning. Now I have a missing child. A week and a half into their telephone contact, Joey and the prospective adoptive family had a spat, and the family wants to stop the process and consider another child. The day after the three children were adopted, one of my co-workers went on medical leave, so I have my cases PLUS I am covering half of her cases until her return or a new person is hired.

My organization skills are put to the test, but they are sharpened at the same time. I learn my self-care has a direct effect on my engagement skills and rapport building.

In the end, I still love my career!

Think About It

1. What are the core objectives in child welfare, and how would you ensure them as an adoption social worker?

2. What are the possible pros and cons of "social workercise"?

3. What are some factors you would consider when recommending which family should adopt Trice?

4. How is a home study different from a home visit?

5. Trice, Lisa, and their biological brother are being adopted by different families. How would you explain to the adoptive families why sibling contact is important post adoption?

Chapter 14
Child Welfare Ombudsman

llllllllllllllllllllllllllllllllllllllllllllllllllllllllllllllllllllllllllllllllllllllllllllllll

by Kenneth Cohen, BSW

Building Fourteen, the administration building, is unlocked, coffee is started, and I can already hear my phone ringing. It's twenty minutes before eight—twenty minutes before I intend to answer it. I know there is someone on the other end seeking justice—revenge for something a social worker or supervisor has or has not done. On adrenaline alone, this unknown caller has risen hours before regular routine—unaccustomed to how low the sun can be on the Eastern horizon. Today's light is still soft. Except for the persistent, clamoring phone, the air is still. Awakening song birds reinforce how early it is. The quiet glides me through morning's minutia. I'm not answering that phone until eight—this time is mine!

In what has now become one fluid routine, doors, file cabinets, and lights are beckoned to perform. Life comes to my outer office. In 90 minutes, it will house one of my students and my assistant. It will be filled with the noise of printers hammering out pages, keyboards clicking away in response to conversations with other expectant customers over the phone—for now, it's still. My briefcase finally reaches its second home. With the push of a plastic button, a reassuring flurry of tiny, electric, mechanical sounds begins. Like the impatient and persistent caller, it's all getting ready.

The phone begins to ring again as I leave the room for more preparatory trivia. I unlock the back door, anticipating the morning's first cigarette, now tepid coffee, and what the day portends. Letters to be sent out to complainants explaining why Agency staff have done the things they have, final disposition on a case into its 60th day, and retrieving information from administrators who feel their right to work with families, the way they see fit, is sacred. The cigarette gone, the cup almost empty, the phone waiting to be answered, it is time to begin.

One minute after eight and again the caller reaches for a sympathetic ear. Headset on, fingers at the keys of my electronic memory, a blank screen, the rhapsody begins, the caller hits pay dirt. She's reached someone in the administration building, someone with the capacity to make change. I don't attempt to alter the image as she tells me about her two children in a foster home.

She saw her kids at a visit last night, and she thought they looked ill. She feels guilty, although she doesn't come out and tell me that. She is paying more attention to their appearance and affect now than she did when they were home. She feels guilty about them being taken away—away to a stranger's house—but she doesn't come out and tell me that. She feels guilty and she can't escape the pain. The social worker offers her no receptive tone, no reassuring words. She says the social worker stopped returning her calls, suggesting the social worker is sick of hearing from her. I suggest too many responsibilities, with too little time to tend to them, is the answer, but I know there is truth to what my caller says. The social worker is sick of talking to her. Someone who answered the Agency's 24-hour hotline, where you can call in allegations of child abuse and neglect, told her she had to talk with her social worker, but her social worker won't return her calls. My caller tells me the disinterested voice on the other end of that line told her, "You can call the ombudsman. He's there to fix things."

"Help me," my caller pleads, but I know before I start that time is the answer. She will have to grow used to the quiet in her life. She's never had such quiet before. Another computer screen reveals my caller as a second generation "Agency Brat," with involvement in Children Services ever since she reached adolescence, five years ago. The social worker was assigned to the case only six weeks ago, and has less than a year under his belt. My caller tells me she has tried to talk with the supervisor, who tells her she has to talk to the social worker. Everyone wants mother to talk to the social worker, but mother says the worker ain't talking. I can hear the slight relief talking to me has given her. Perhaps she'll get some peace. Perhaps she'll get too comfortable.

The lower light on my telephone begins to flash. A secretary has "parked" another call on the line. Another set of expectations in line, waiting. After collecting some data, explaining the procedure I'll follow to resolve the mother's concerns, I'm on to my second caller.

The school principal can't understand why the social worker hasn't removed the children of a mother who can't keep the children from repeatedly getting head lice. Her angry words meld together to form a recognizable tone that causes me to wait. I have learned to let it come without response or judgment. Like the tears from the loss of a loved one, she needs to let it out. When the time is right and some of her tension is gone, I offer several explanations in soft and thoughtful tones. I tell her how the social worker's supervisor needs an opportunity to hear what she has to say. I tell her the supervisor needs an opportunity to address these concerns before I'll intervene. I invite my caller to call back if there is no response to her call, or the response is unsatisfactory. She tells me it's nice just to have someone who listens without judging, who hears what you're saying without signaling you're running out of time. She says she'll call the worker's supervisor. For now, it's okay.

As I finish my first caller's characterization, a yearning for nicotine and caffeine reemerges. I finish typing the brief narrative and data that turns my first caller's plea into a complaint. The computer prints a copy for the social worker, supervisor, associate director, and region director and sends our request for response within five business days to its destination. Before the phone can sound another alarm, I slink through the back door of my smoke-free building. Before the third puff is exhaled, a secretary leans out telling me there is someone calling from a pay phone who has an "emergency." A final drag and I'm off.

An hour has passed, and my student is busy screening someone else's emergency. This is an opportunity to assemble a response to the adoptive couple. They are sick and tired of being accused of abusing their sexually abusive teen boy. The technology allows me to fill in a template as an opening to my written response. "Dear...I am writing in response to the contact made with my office on... concern for the Agency's misbehavior was voiced." The letter goes on to explain how the Agency is mandated to respond to allegations and how no one is protected from this intrusive process. I suggest she consider allowing a protective service case opening. The Agency's involvement could assist in getting services for their troubled teen, and ongoing involvement would allow a familiarity that could help avoid repeated visits from an Intake investigator.

I'm on a roll, 60 words per minute, when the executive director's assistant asks me to come to the executive's office. The anxiety of being summoned to his office 10 months earlier returns. I freshen my coffee, walk toward his door, and the recollection of turning gray while he told me my 22-year career with Children Services was ending, overwhelms me. I was numbed. I remember that feeling in my stomach. You read about it all the time—it's the subject of fiction and fact, and you're glad it's not your stomach. Well, here it was for me, as he threw these words at me. Half of my life was spent in child welfare. I sleep, eat, and breathe these issues. I advocate for the innocents. I will never forget him telling me he had to show others he was willing to make sacrifices in the Executive Office. How dare he do this to me.

Later, the County Commissioner's office made a deal to keep the Office of the Ombudsman alive. They found some bucks to keep a few pet projects going. They like having someone to send disgruntled constituents to. They like knowing there is someone there to listen and respond. I'm still here, the office is busier than ever—almost 1,500 calls last year—but the anxiety of being summoned in this way now shares my space. It sits in one of my chairs, always, like an uninvited guest.

I enter his dark wood decor and he invites me to sit. He tells me of a situation in which a woman claims we allowed her birth daughter to find her. Thirty-two years back, the woman relinquished her child for adoption. She signed no consent to have her child know where and who she was. She's angry, and the executive wants to know what, where, who, and when. I commit to query staff who were involved, imagining the wording that will go into this complaint. I leave his office with a small sigh of relief.

Letters—callers—a staffing to determine the best resolution for a foster parent who suffered $10,000 in damages to her home from a fire a foster child started—all blend together to speed the day closer to an end. A call from my wife becomes an oasis with a friendly voice. The first activity of the day in which nothing is asked of me. The respite ends too soon, as the day grows old.

My best writing is done in the morning hours, so I reserve the afternoons for reviewing case documents, if time allows. This afternoon's prize is a 40-page investigation. The handwritten record of activities is barely legible. My complainants are grandparents who have been accused of molesting their grandson. The investigator concluded they had done what they were accused of. Having found significant omissions in the work, I draft a memo to the director of Intake requesting consideration for another finding. I ask him to respond within five working days.

It goes on like this until it's time to close shop. I back up the digital files that have collected the day's activity, clean the coffee pot, and lock the back door.

While on auto-pilot, I relish the activity that has allowed me to have an impact. I remember cases, too rare, in which I was able to shape the way this huge child protection agency deals with people. I recall having created a safety net for some, and how antagonistic a dolt I appear to others. I envision the Agency as a large ship, cruising steadily in an ocean to its unknown destination. Every once in a while, I am able to alter its course, ever so slightly, in a direction that offers children a better way. Every now and then, I am able to make it a better world for the innocents.

Those recollections fuel the desire to keep at it, to try and make the difference. This is the best child protection agency and the first ombudsman exclusive to a child welfare agency in the state—maybe in the country. I help make it happen.

Think About It

1. What is an ombudsman?

2. What role does technology play in this job?

3. How stressful do you think it would be to work in a job in which, by definition, your clients are likely to be angry about their situations and the treatment they are receiving from your organization?

Chapter 15
A Neighborhood Youth Center

||||||||||||||||||||||||||||||||||||||||||||||||||||||||||||||||||||||||||||||||||||||||||||||||||||||

by Amber Daniels, MSW

7 a.m. Wake up from a fitful sleep. I'm ready to loosen up with a run. Ring, ring. "Amber, David's school is closed because the power is out. I can't come to work."

Mary runs the day treatment program for adolescent drop outs, Survival School. She picks them up in the van and then starts the program. I have to find a van driver and a program facilitator.

"I'm going to use today to find David a new day care. He got kicked out of his old one last week. They said he was being too violent." David is a special needs child. He's been kicked out of four other day care programs.

"Okay, Mary, thanks for calling." I get another van driver to come in two hours early. Today it works out. My morning run is preserved. My morning run is necessary. My morning run is sacred.

One and a half hours later, I arrive at Latino Family Services. The receptionist informs me we are having an impromptu management team meeting. In ten minutes. Cancel your appointments with clients; the executive director has important things to discuss.

It's not fair to imply that my director is placing her needs over those of the clients. I am the supervisor of a youth center in Southwest Detroit and I also happen to have an MSW. I love the client interaction, seeing them in a group or one-on-one setting. Therefore, I have given myself the privilege and difficulty of trying to manage a department of a middle-sized human services agency, while still trying to maintain a small caseload. The agency is in a low-income neighborhood with historically high crime rates and low pay, so not many social workers want to work here. That means we are in short supply, so seeing clients is a necessity. But so are the administrative tasks. Today the administrative tasks win.

Latino Family Services is a "neighborhood" human service organization. Most of the Latinos in Detroit city live in a 5-census track area, the small southwestern corner. We work toward meeting the advocacy and mental health needs of the broad Latino community that is located here. We employ approximately 45 folks, mostly from the community. We serve approximately 2,000-3,000 clients a month through outpatient substance use treatment; HIV/AIDS counseling, testing and outreach; English as a Second Language classes; developmental disabilities case management; senior outreach; and youth programming. The Youth Center serves approximately 70 youth a day in afterschool programs and through our Survival School.

My job consists mostly of managing the staff, interns, and volunteers, and supervising the programming. I also maintain a small caseload of adolescents in need of individual therapy. I have about 12 staff during the school year and 20 during the summer. We also have between 20 and 40 interns and volunteers from the University of Michigan and Wayne State University. The staff and volunteers are very diverse. They range in age from 15-65, their educational level varies from GED to Master's level, and their socioeconomic background varies from working poor to upper middle class.

The most challenging part of the work is managing the staff. I'm young (28), and my mistakes far outweigh my successes at this point. Many decisions are educated guesses. That makes guiding other people somewhat of a challenge.

"So, the thing is that when we went to pick up Michael and Manuel today, the next door neighbor told us that they were going to be evicted by the end of the week." Michael and Manuel's mom is slightly impaired and has difficulty keeping the family out of financial difficulty. Their gas and water has been shut off for months. Manuel is on probation. Neither of the boys has consistently been to school since they were in kindergarten. They are now 15 and 16 years old.

"Well, I suppose the only thing we can do is just ask Michael and Manuel how they are doing. Make sure mom knows about our next parent group meeting."

"But shouldn't we do something? The family is going to be homeless." But what can we do? Mom hasn't told us about her financial difficulties herself.

"Just keep picking them up every day and offering consistent services. That is all we have to offer."

After the management team meeting, I head out for a city-wide meeting. I have been working in youth development for four years in Detroit, so I know many folks at other youth service agencies.

As I walk in, I wonder to myself if I am somehow invisible or have some sort of obvious ailment. I feel faceless, without identity.

"Hey, hi, how are you?" I walk up to the first person I recognize. She struggles between faint knowledge of who I am and ignoring my presence altogether. She chooses to acknowledge me.

"Blessed. I have been trying to get to your parent involvement meetings." She knows where she knows me from.

"I know, I appreciate your efforts. This initiative requires so many meetings. I've been at four already this week."

I put on my nametag and I can see her relief as she finally has access to my name.

Conversation remains polite, as she introduces me to her colleagues. It is genuine and warm. We serve on a volunteer council that is attempting to reform the public school system. It is hard work, long term, but good in quality, and has created many strong, honest relationships.

It is uncomfortable, meetings like this. People I know very well will sit down and chat. But acquaintances either pretend they don't know me or that they barely know me. At least until some good friend validates my existence. It is a phenomenon I'm not resentful of. This is something I probably perpetuate. I sometimes feel safer in the role of inside outsider, knowing it is much easier to watch than participate. Lonely, sometimes ineffective. But easier.

The instant distrust that says, "What gives you the right to be here?" or the anxiety, "You're not going to *teach* me or *help* me are you?" or the out and out hate, "What are you doing here, white girl?" All those unspoken questions are exhausting for me. It has to be tiring for everyone else, as well. I understand that I represent my race, gender, socioeconomic status, and profession, regardless of people's best efforts not to stereotype. It is just exhausting to always be surprised back into reality. The surprise gets me every time.

I make more than double what some of my staff make. A portion of that differential is because I have two advanced degrees. But I have those degrees in part because of the many privileges that come with being from a middle-class suburban white family that is able to value education. Some of it is my own ambition and dedication. And some of it is just luck. Given my background, I often feel honored to be allowed into the intimate spaces of other cultures.

Yes, it's lonely because the insight I have gained forces me out of the community I come from. Yet, I don't really belong with the people I work with. Sometimes I'm able to find other double dwellers. And for a moment or two, it is a relief to speak the same language. Could be called something like suburban urbanesque. When we speak it together, it feels wonderful to not have to be an advocate or to have to be careful of offending someone. We share and, for a moment, it is wonderful to belong. And I vaguely understand how communities isolate from each other in an attempt to buffer themselves.

After the meeting, back at L.F.S., I settle myself in for a long day. The maintenance man is on vacation, so I need to stay until 7:00 to lock up the building when the afterschool program is over. We run programs from 9:00 a.m. until 7:00 p.m. It's not every day that I need to stay all day long, but my schedule must be flexible enough to be able to fill in, should someone call in sick.

I walk into another office to talk to my intern. She's graduating and she's having many mixed feelings about leaving. In the middle of the discussion, as if to prove her point that it's a crazy place to leave, another staff member comes in.

"Amber, you have to deal with John. I can't get him to do anything. I'm about to lose it."

"Send him in."

John comes in with his whole posture screaming that he's on the defense. He is wearing his best gangster garb, name brand coat, stocking cap, baggy jeans, headphones on his ears.

"Why do you have on your headphones?"

"Don't ask me to give them up, man. Can't nobody take them from me. You'd have to kill me first. Nobody." The tears are creeping up in his eyes. He's bursting at the seams. A time bomb, one staff said.

We talk more about the headphones, his desire to go back to school, his refusal to look at alternatives to violent outbursts and substance abuse.

"John, I'm worried you are going to die."

Jerks the hat down, purses his lips in a stoic gangster grimace, knits his eyebrows. "So what man, so what?" His hands gesture in a calculated fashion, scooping the air with pointed fingers. "Everybody gotta die sometime."

The little boy is just below the surface, pounding to get out. He screams without words, "Grab me, it's a big hole and I'm slipping." His out loud words go on, "My homeys keep dying and that didn't change anything. So what?"

"John, didn't it change your life?"

Silence. "Yeah, right."

John came to us wanting to be an artist and go back to school after being kicked out of three of them. He designed and painted two murals for the agency, and he spoke at a conference about his turn-around.

But with more intensive counseling, staff has discovered a badly beaten past. Everyone in his life has either abandoned or tried to kill him. Asking him to dip below the carefully crafted, albeit fragile exterior of flat affect has resurrected an unfathomable rage. He's beating up "crackheads and neighborhood drunks."

"I don't care what happens. I gotta do what I gotta do when they get up in my face and start talking about my mom...or my sister...or take my bike. I just got to go to a school where I don't know anyone. I just need to start again."

The Survival School youth leave and the staff depressurizes.

"Has anyone seen my keys?"

"Did you ask Don Herman?" Don Herman has a long-standing tradition of hiding stray keys and denying any knowledge of their whereabouts.

"Don Herman?"

"I don't know anything, but I saw some keys in the trash can...." He laughs and shrugs his shoulders.

"Argh." The owner has again been foiled by Don Herman's key retrieval antics.

"You shouldn't leave your keys just lying around. You never know who might pick them up."

Although sometimes to the detriment of the kids, the Youth Center staff has a frisky sense of humor. They pull pranks, laugh at themselves, and bring each other goofy gifts. They pick play fights with one another as the youth gleefully join in.

At 3:15, we get an all-call telling staff to leave the building by 4:00 because the roads are covered in snow. We were just about to leave to pick up the elementary school children to bring them to the program. The coordinator of the elementary school program and I hop in my little car to make sure they can find alternative transportation. The van driver takes home the kids who have already arrived at the agency.

It's 10 degrees outside and as my car swerves into a spot near the school, we see that some of the children are already waiting for us.

"What are you doing here, Ms. Amber...isn't there *Latino* today? You sent us a letter. Didn't you send us a letter?" We've already been closed for a week because of heavy snow.

My staff member ducks into the building to talk to the principal and call parents.

"Okay, who can walk?" I check to make sure everyone has on thick coats and gloves.

"Is there ever going to be *Latino* again?"

"I hope so...be careful."

I'm left with three 8-year-old girls. My staff member waits at the school with the others while I take the girls home. We squeeze into my little Civic.

"How was your snow week?"

"Cold. I froze my fingers off." Pause "We just got our heat turned back on the other day." I swallow hard. It has been subzero temperatures for a week.

"Yeah, us too—our heat was off for two or three days."

"How did you stay warm?"

"Went to my grandma's."

"Not me. We just waited for them to turn it back on. It was only a couple of days." It's a wonder they still have fingers.

Their streets are completely unplowed. Even though they've declared a snow emergency, many cars are still under a foot of snow.

The girls are giggling about their pets.

"My pit bull ripped the head off my best Christmas gift—my big teddy bear."

"Well, it better not have been your chihuahua."

"Did you have a nice Christmas?"

"It was okay. Most gifts were old and opened. But I got a nice basketball and clothes from *Latino*." I wonder about the wisdom of being able to outdo their parents so they can have Christmas gifts.

All these difficult discussions don't appear to affect their energy. They laugh and play the whole way home. As I pull up to their old and broken houses, their mothers, brothers, and families greet them worriedly at the door.

"See you tomorrow, Amber. Thanks."

I, however, am left to contemplate the contrasting scenario they've left me with. Childhood discussions of pets and toys, adult thoughts on staying warm and getting what they need. The young people who grow up here in our program need to be children. But they are required to be adults from the day they are born.

Working with the littlest children is often the best and hardest part. Their innocent questions, their poking and prodding for attention. Their desire for gifts and treasures of any kind. I had to equally divide up a few handfuls of glittering confetti the other day. I wish I could fulfill everyone's wishes with a bit of shiny paper.

With the little guys, it's also hard to know how much to focus on their brokenness, how much on their strengths. The other day, I had the 5- to 8-year-olds paint pictures of their families. It was a tougher project than I thought: only one of eight could draw parents, only three could draw siblings. The children were lost when it came to figuring out who or what was in their "family." But they all needed support for the work they had done...whether they drew mom, dad, a blank field, or three rocks. Their pictures were a far cry from the mom, dad, and two children with a dog, but it was their understanding of family and it was important to them that I validate what they created.

After I return to L.F.S., I take a few minutes to open my mail. There are endless stacks of healthy-people propaganda. I invest daily in the hope that there will be some news of new money: a grant granted, new requests for proposals, unrestricted generous gifts to urban youth who just need a chance.

No such luck today—a few meeting notices, some drug-free pamphlets, and a fabulous new nonprofit management training for only $500 a person. And a packet containing a small glossy booklet in black and white. The end product of a teen summer project. 20 poems and pictures.

Coughing back tears, I read the bleak hopeful pain-become-words of these nine African American Detroit young people. The project is sponsored by a poet we worked with last year. I am struck by their insightful grasp of the local found-art installment, their self-strong discussion of their home. I hope fervently that they get a chance to keep giving voice to their all-too-often ignored world.

At the end of the day, a 14-year-old young man comes into my office in search of the canceled after school program. I know him well. We've been involved together in leadership development projects for the last two years. He comes to us just to "see how we are." He tells me he's going to court in the morning because his parents have declared him incorrigible. After some discussion, I realize he's trying to tell me that his dad has threatened him and beat him up. It is a startling realization for me. I almost missed it. We call the runaway shelter, and they request that he go to the police.

We're driving down the Boulevard at 9:00 p.m. We reminisce about other youth leaders. I want to talk about different times.

"Remember David...how is David?"

"David...he's fine. Annoying, but fine." Quiet laugh. Sobering pause. "He's annoying because he's got a right to be annoying. (Pause.) He's been through some stuff." The Christmas lights are gorgeous.

"I like that." I don't know how else to respond to his gentle wisdom.

At the police station, they don't believe he's been beaten up by his father. They call his parents and send him back home.

He calls me after he gets home, whispering into the receiver, "Could you come to court with me and just sit?"

"I can't hear you."

"I know, I'm trying to be quiet...on the low down. I'm home."

"Are you safe for now?"

"Yeah, whatever...I'll see you at court. 8:15, right?"

Think About It

1. Why is cultural competence important in this job?

2. What is your reaction to Amber's discussion of herself as a "double dweller"—a white middle-class person working in a low-income, mostly Latino neighborhood?

Chapter 16
Play Therapy and Bullying

IIIIIIIIIIIIIIIIIIIIIIIIIIIIIIIIIIIIIIIIIIIIIIIIIIIIIIIIIIIIIIIIIIIIIIIIIIIIIIIIIIIIIIIII

by Ann Elliot, LCSW

About a year ago, I bought a house and transformed it into a play therapy facility. Each playroom has nurturing toys, such as dolls, kitchen play sets, and doctor kits. Each playroom also has anger-venting toys, such as dinosaurs, army men, swords, and armor. Each one additionally has its own built-in sandboxes, costumes, games, and lots of other fun toys to facilitate many modes of expressive therapy. When we opened our doors, I was very excited about how spacious our new office was. Now, I am thinking, "We are so cramped!" I am now contemplating expanding and making more office space. I already have two other therapists here and two more who want to learn more about play therapy and children's issues. When am I going to find time to train them, and where will I find a room to put them in?

On Tuesday morning at 8:30, I unlock my office to see what adventures the day holds. On this particular day, I find 25 messages on the answering machine inquiring about appointments. I check my email. Fifty-two emails since 9:30 last night, which is when I finally got around to replying to all of yesterday's questions and requests. I have a two-page waiting list, and I can't seem to even fit in a lunch break. I look up at the sign on my door, which says, "Good Morning! Let the stress begin." I chuckle to myself as I look at the schedule. My first patient is a 10-year-old boy to whom I am scheduled to help teach stress management techniques! I have been seeing him for about two months now, because he threatened to kill himself and then blow up the school (in that order). I hear him come in, as he is yelling at his mother that he wants to go home, because he doesn't feel well.

As I enter the waiting room, he quickly turns to me and hollers, "...And I ain't going to breathe no more!"

"Oh, good!" I say cheerfully, "You remembered the first thing you need to do when you get angry."

He, as he often does, heads for the playroom.

"Wonderful! You're eager to get started today!"

He stops and starts to puff up, "I just want to play, NOT talk to you!"

"That's great, Johnny, because I want to teach you things that will help you get to play more," I casually state.

We have gone over many aspects in the eight prior sessions concerning Johnny's bullying issues. He has a long history (in his 10 short years) of hitting and kicking other children, as well as verbally abusing the authorities in his life. I involved his mom initially, but it quickly became clear I needed to work with her on communication and parenting skills before we tried to do family therapy. Johnny and I have already gone over the goals of bullying, and he has decided he does it mostly for attention and power. His favorite bullying techniques involve making fun of people and threatening them. His "homework" for a couple of sessions was to try to do the opposite of his favorite techniques. Instead of making fun of people, he was to try to compliment them. Instead of threatening people, he was to invite them to do something fun with him. His conclusion from this homework was to "just not say nothing" (which his teachers reported as the greatest couple of weeks of their lives in terms of dealing with Johnny). He did acknowledge in one session, ever so briefly, that he possibly learned his current anger style from his step-dad. His mom now has an ex parte to protect both of them from him.

I tried to introduce relaxation techniques earlier, and I received a lot of resistance from him, because, "That is stupid, and only sissies do that stuff."

In a previous session, I told him we were going to learn from the polar bear, who loves to lie on the mountain, soak in the warm sunshine, and breathe in the fresh air (to which he informed me he would shoot the bear). Today, I bring out a balloon and "dare" him to slowly count to three, blow up the balloon, and see how big it gets in one breath. Then, I instruct him to slowly count to four and try to catch all the air the balloon releases with his mouth, but without letting his lips touch the balloon. If he obtains more air in his lungs than he put in the balloon, he can go to the "next level," which is to do it without the balloon. If he does this correctly three times, he will "win" and get to play for the rest of the session. He quickly accepts this dare, but struggles with the task and whines that he can't do it. With quite a lot of encouragement, he tries until he completes the task. He boasts about winning and getting to play for the rest of the session. However, as he plays, I ask his mom to join us, and I ask him if he can teach her what he learned, so he can help her do it. After that is done, their homework is to do this together once a day until I see them again. Mom agrees, and Johnny agrees. They agree on a time to do it, which is just before bedtime. I'll see next week if they have been able to spend some fun time together and accomplish their goal.

My next clients are waiting for me in the waiting room. They are two sisters, seven and nine years old, and they have been sexually abused by their mom's paramour. They are now in the custody of the state, and mom has gone into rehab. The paramour has been arrested. The girls are being victimized, as well. At school, two neighbor boys made fun of them after the allegations were made public. Today, I decide to see them together to role-play numerous situations in which they can practice previously discussed skills for people who find themselves being bullied. Their favorite one is thinking three good thoughts about themselves, and then confidently walking away. It is a very fun session, because both girls are natural actresses. After all, they have been acting most of their lives to survive. Now they are enjoying how they choose to act and react.

My next session is with a teenager who assaulted another classmate who he had reported for bullying him. Now he has been expelled from school. The person he felt bullied him was not expelled. This is our fourth session. Previously, I discussed with him his "hot thoughts," and asked him to record them weekly. We are now trying out some "cool thoughts" and ways to "change channels" when he is focused on a "bad station" in his mind. We also go over the goals of bullies, to remind him it is not always all about him.

My next hour, I am supposed to be at a meeting with the county juvenile office and the Department of Family Services to have a "family support team meeting." We were to discuss the progress of a family I have been working with for more than two years. I gather my stuff before being stopped by my colleague. He hands me a note from the victim's crime unit. There is a date-rape victim who may be suicidal, and she needs to see a female therapist as soon as possible. I call back and leave a message saying I will see the client at 6:00 p.m. (This is the time I usually use to return all my calls.) After hearing some of the details of the case, I hang up and head to the juvenile office. I am met at the front door by Officer Crawford, who has a subpoena for me to be in court next Tuesday at 9:00 a.m. My look must say a lot, because his response is, "Don't kill the messenger." We laugh. He walks me out to my car and warns that "stress kills." I thank him for stating the obvious and finally head to the juvenile office. There, I am greeted by four attorneys, two caseworkers, three family members, and two juvenile office staff. I insist on sitting on the floor (because there are no chairs left), and after all, I am used to it because "all I do is play all day and sit on the floor." The meeting goes fairly well, because surprisingly, almost everyone agrees on the goals at hand. I am to continue to work with the children. Mom and dad are to try and continue to show up to the scheduled appointments and commitments. It seems to go longer than usual and I have to excuse myself, because it is time for me to go to jail.

No, I didn't go off and assault someone. About six months ago, I agreed to be our county jail's "mental clinician," and I contracted to do three hours a week of work. I do suicide assessment, as well as assess the need for psychiatric medication. But one of the first things I did (in hopes of cutting down on this need) was to start group therapy for the inmates. When I first started, I had very few show up. Today, they ask me if I need to break up the male group because it is so big. I decide to go ahead with one group each (one female and one male), not just because I am trying to make it back in time for my new patient, but because I know the participants and believe it will be a profitable session.

In our groups, we have been discussing learned behaviors in reference to anger management. Most of the participants say they learned their coping skills (or lack of) from their parents. Today, I ask them: *How many of the techniques you currently use did you use in grade school?* Most acknowledge they still yell, threaten, and use physical force to get what they want. We examine the cost of that behavior. The next question I am curious about is: *How many of you would consider yourselves bullies or victims of bullies?* I am not surprised when the majority of the male inmates state that they were bullies (and still are). Several say they were both, and after being a victim they decided never to be that again. That is when they became the bully. The last part of my session with them is to teach meditation and breathing. The comments I hear are, "That is stupid and only ____ do that stuff." I smile and am reminded of my interaction with Johnny earlier in the day. I play the CD, and some actually participate. One man who has been in the group for a while comments on how breathing has helped him from wanting to assault another inmate and also a prison guard.

I think, "Wow. Can you talk to Johnny?"

I make it back to the new victim, and I am able to stabilize her through a family suicide prevention plan. She tells me that she was a victim of bullying as a child and has never felt that she could speak up and get help. She says she doesn't like herself, so her homework is to think daily of ten things she has to be thankful for and what she likes about herself. She also has so much anxiety that she has been having panic attacks. By the end of our session, I give her a tape on breathing and relaxation techniques, and she has come up with four of her ten things to be thankful for. I say "good-bye" and schedule an appointment to see her in a couple of days.

As I sit at my desk, I stare at 21 more emails and 15 more phone messages. I look at tomorrow's schedule, which is the first day of an 18-hour course I offer on anger management and batterer prevention. Most of the participants are court ordered. Most will come in thinking: *I don't need this class; everyone else does.* I smile and take a deep breath in. I imagine myself blowing up the balloon, changing my channels in my mind, and reminding myself of all the blessings I have to be thankful for today. The biggest blessing that comes to mind is that I love my job and can't wait to do it all over again tomorrow.

Think About It:

1. What would be different and what would be similar in working with children who bully and adults who bully?

2. What do individuals need in order not to bully?

3. What are some factors that tend to allow people to be victims of bullies?

Chapter 17

Social Work and the Arts: A Theatre-Based Prevention/Intervention Program

|||||||||||||||||||||||||||||||||||||||||||||||||||||||||||||||||||||||||||||||||||||||||||||||||||||||||||||||||||||||||||||||||||||

by Staci Block, MSW, LCSW

I direct the audience's attention to the stage. "Let's watch." These volunteer high school age teenagers, who are cast members in an improvisational theatre program sponsored by Bergen County Division of Family Guidance, are performing at a school assembly program on today's requested topic, cyber-bullying. The cast members have already "warmed up" the audience with an interactive improvisational theatrical activity, and the audience feels connected to what is about to take place.

We get to the school about 40 minutes before the show begins. I have picked them up at our meeting spot, at our call time of 8:20 a.m., in our county vehicle. One of the cast members asks if she can sit in the front with me; I remind her that she needs to sit amongst the other cast members, as it is important for them to work as a team. We are expecting five cast members today, and right now we only have three. One of the two missing cast members already emailed me to let me know that he was going to be five minutes late. We wait, as that is within our "grace period."

Had they all arrived on time, they would have earned a credit toward a "Perfect-Pick Up." Three shows in a row, where everyone arrives by the call time, earns a cast member who was at any of those three shows an extra "absence" that can be used to miss one of the required, three-hour, weekly rehearsals. They start the school year with 12 absences that can be used for anything that they would like, including if they need to miss rehearsal for not feeling well, to study for a test, or for an emergency. I would like to think that this helps them to prepare for the real world where, when at a job, they only get a certain number of vacation and sick days, and they have to manage their time so they have it available to them when needed.

The late-arriving cast member joins us at 8:25 a.m. One of the scheduled cast members is still missing, and the teens in the van are checking their group chat for a sign from her. Grace period is over, and we need to arrive at the school with enough time to check in at the main office, secure our visitor passes, get comfortable in the performance space, go through a sound check if there are going to be microphones, and figure out the spacing for the show. I make a note to reach out to the missing cast member when I am back in the office to see if she is okay and to ask what happened. Unfortunately, she loses four absences for not communicating and not getting a replacement for herself. I hope this cast member does not run out of absences, or she will not be able to be in our program any more.

I remind myself that our system allows the cast members to earn absences by doing extra shows, helping me out in the office, or using other incentives that I have set in place for them to assure that they are learning from their mistakes. Cast members are empowered to make their own choices to ensure they are going to stay in this program if they really want to be here.

After making sure that the four cast members are buckled up, we begin to talk about the upcoming show. I had planned the show for the expected five, so in my head, I am starting to reorganize the show. It's a good thing that I can think quickly on my feet! We discuss who is going to play which role, keeping in mind to vary the roles that they are assigned, so the teens learn to play different parts.

We are almost at the school, and one of the cast members realizes that he has forgotten to wear his shirt with the group's logo on it. I remind the group of the rule—he can't perform without his shirt, and he is welcome to watch the show from the audience. This show will not count for one of his required shows in this cycle, and he is going to need to do another one to meet the minimum requirements. Again, the scenario needs to be adjusted for the show, knowing that only three cast members will be performing. I ask the group for ideas to make it work, and we quickly brainstorm suggestions and choose a solution. I am mentally exhausted, yet ironically excited at the same time.

Once they know who they are in the scene and what needs to happen, we "block" out the scenario, so the actors know from where and when they are entering and exiting. The dialogue is not rehearsed. The scenario is enacted for the audience, and when there is a point of conflict, I yell "FREEZE." The actors stop, and we begin to process with the audience while the actors remain in role. They share from their character's perspective what they are thinking and how they are feeling. I facilitate an interactive discussion between the audience members and the teens on stage. I encourage the audience members to ask questions, make suggestions, and offer alternate ways of handling the situation for problem-solving purposes. This provides the audience with a space to hear each other and be educated and entertained at the same time. I remind the audience that the teens are acting and that the parts they play don't necessarily reflect how they are in their real lives. The actors "de-role" by sharing their names, ages, grades, towns, schools, how long they have been with the program, and anything they would like to share about the performance that just took place.

As a piece of my recruiting efforts, I inform the audience that if anyone is interested in being part of the program, they can come up to any one of us to get a brochure with our contact information. Quite often, audience members can relate to the scenarios and want to share their personal stories with us after the show. I listen, and if I think further exploration is needed, I refer them to the appropriate school personnel.

We drive back to the meeting spot, where the cast members are met by their rides. On the way, we "process" the show and do our compliment ritual, in which we all give a compliment to ourselves, acknowledging something that went well for us during the show. Then, in turn, we each give a compliment to everyone else who was part of the show, highlighting a strength upon which we hope to build. When everyone has gone through this process, we discuss some of the things that we still need to improve and commit to do that during one of our upcoming rehearsals.

The performances can take place for a variety of audiences, including middle and high school assemblies, client programs, community events, parent groups, conferences, and college classes. We have a list of more than 150 topics on which we can perform. These include parent/teen conflicts, vaping, peer pressure, prejudice, dating abuse, stress management, mental health issues, suicide prevention, homelessness, and many others.

When I am not facilitating the performances, I am preparing for our weekly, 3-hour rehearsals. A few days before the next rehearsal, I send a "log question" to the cast members, through Google Classroom. The question can be anything from giving feedback regarding one of the performances or rehearsals, to an issue with which the group is currently struggling, to situations from their personal lives having to do with a topic for an upcoming performance. Their responses help me to tailor the next rehearsal, where we use the time to do a variety of things. We focus on getting the cast members to know each other better while increasing the trust level amongst the group. I teach the cast members a variety of improvisational techniques that are used during the shows.

At a typical rehearsal, one would likely see the following: cast members gather around and set up the room, writing things that need to be taken care of on the board. A group star is selected who runs the "group business" for the night. This is done on a rotating basis, so their leadership skills develop. The group star calls out, "Group spit, cell phone check, and hair flick!" Gum is thrown away, phone ringers are turned off, and they make sure we can see their expressive faces, without their hair getting in the way.

Next, I lead some kind of "focus game" and then implement a "check-in," which is an action-oriented activity that helps the cast members share something about their week, in a creative way. Check-ins can be done in small groups, as a whole group, in pairs, or by individuals. This activity helps to ground the cast members to the rehearsal process and also promotes skill-building, spontaneity development, fostering connections amongst group members, and warming up the group to further action.

Following the check-in, group members might work on their improvisational skills through theatre games or drills. Perhaps there is an upcoming performance about a topic on which the group members need to focus. Scenes may be discussed or improvised, so cast members scheduled to perform in that show will reap the benefits of the ideas and suggestions of the entire group.

We conduct group business, and the group goes over commitments, "missed cues," "applause," the "hot stuff" for the night, "re-runs" from the week before, the "new releases," and group issues concerning one of the "foundation stones" of our program. These include focus, responsibility, commitment, cohesiveness, group spirit, trust, confidentiality, communication, cooperation, empowerment, professionalism, leadership, respect, acting, and self-growth. Other issues that the group addresses include transportation logistics, as well as making sure that the cast members are keeping up with their performance cycle commitments. Sometimes guest speakers are brought in to share their expertise on an upcoming topic.

We all take turns bringing in snacks for break time. During the "performance review" time, cast members who were at a particular performance that week are encouraged to share what they learned about themselves, the topic, the audience, or anything else that is pertinent. At the closing circle, everyone goes around and reviews what needs to happen between that night and the next time the group sees each other.

My time at work is filled with many supportive tasks for running this program. I ask the cast members to let me know what their conflicts are for the next month, and then I have to organize which cast members are going to be doing which show. Although this is a logistical nightmare, it has to be done for there to be a balance of meeting the needs of the cast members and the performance venues. I schedule an average of three shows a month and work closely with the people who are booking us to think about the size of the audience, the nature of the topics, the kinds of scenarios they want us to do, and the performance space where we will be. I conduct new member orientations, prepare for our summer program, and organize annual reunions, so cast members from the past 29 years can reconnect with each other and once again spend time improvising their life.

I feel fortunate that I have found a career where I can combine my social work, education, prevention, and theatre arts background at a job that gets my creative juices flowing and never feels like work.

Think About It

1. What creative ideas do you have for recruiting teens for the program described in this chapter?

2. Even though this is not a "therapy" program, because the teens are volunteering their time to do outreach work, what do you see as the "therapeutic" benefits to the cast members?

3. What are some of the therapeutic benefits for the audience members?

4. One of the weekly rehearsals each month is called "Ensemble Night" and focuses more on building the "ensemble" instead of working on "skills." What ideas do you have for "Ensemble Night" activities that can further develop the trust and cohesion of the group members?

Chapter 18

Working with Gay and Lesbian Youth

||||||||||||||||||||||||||||||||||||||||||||||||||||||||||||||||||||||||||||||||||||||||||||||||||||||||||||||||||||||||||||||||||||||

by Andrew J. Peters, CSW, MSW, BA

I work at a small, not-for-profit, community-based organization that operates a project for lesbian and gay youth. Since I began working at this agency as a second-year graduate school intern, I have risen up in the ranks to Project Director, in charge of a small staff of social workers, health educators, adolescent peer educators, and social work interns.

What I like most about my job is that I have the ability to combine administrative work (program development, grant writing, supervision) with direct client services—individual, family, and group counseling. I would not give up the latter for anything in the world! Each week, I look forward the most to the times when I meet with the kids, either individually, through my weekly group, or at our Friday night Drop-in Center program called "The Coffeehouse."

I knew that I wanted to do this work even before I started graduate school to become a social worker. As a young gay man, I felt a desire to help young people who were struggling to come out. I knew that coming out to myself and others was a painful struggle—the most difficult thing that I had ever done in my life. At the same time, I was lucky—having a largely supportive family and group of friends who helped me through this time. I knew that there were many teenagers who did not or would not have it so easy. I learned from the social work literature about the high rates of suicide, substance use disorders, and HIV among lesbian and gay youth. In school, I devoured any books or articles I could find about lesbian and gay adolescents, keeping my copies of journal articles neatly organized in a filing cabinet.

My personal experience and research provided a foundation for understanding and helping young people through the complicated process of coming out. But it is the experience of actually working with these young people that teaches me new lessons practically every week. It is very easy from reading the literature and analyzing the tremendous stigma attached to being gay to view lesbian and gay adolescents as passive victims, coping with isolation, violence, and rejection from family members and peers. I find it also important to acknowledge that growing up gay can be a very positive experience for many young people. Amidst the self-doubt, confusion, and sometimes anguish, there exists exceptional resilience, excitement, and creativity in the youth with whom I work. These are the qualities that keep me motivated for doing this work—the opportunities in the face of very difficult circumstances.

My biggest day of the week is Friday, when my work starts at 1:00 p.m. and ends at ten or eleven at night. Arriving at the office, my first task is to sort through an overflowing mail box, full of envelopes, intra-agency memos, and phone messages. After prioritizing the heap, I return a couple of calls—a request for a sensitivity training for high school faculty and a call from a psychologist looking for referrals for his 15-year-old client who has recently come out as gay.

My intercom buzzes and a counselor tells me she has a young man on our hotline who is interested in joining my Wednesday night support group. She wonders if I am available to talk to him about the group. I pick up my phone and speak with a 16-year-old young man who just came out to his mother last night. He is feeling relieved about having "finally" told her and happy that she told him she still loves him. He wants to meet other teenagers who are gay and get some help with figuring out how to tell his dad. I tell him about the group—six to eight teenagers between 15 and 18 years old who are each gay, bisexual, or questioning. The group helps members work on problems around coming out, and I tell him that it is important that he comes into the group as both a person needing help and a person able to provide help to others. I ask him if he has time to answer some questions for my group screening. In addition to identifying information, I ask him about his mental health history, risk factors like suicide and substance use, and his coming out experience. I deem him appropriate for the group, so I give him the time and location of the meetings.

After the call, I am joined in my office by my Drop-in Center Co-ordinator. In addition to overseeing the "Coffeehouse" program, she carries a caseload of youth and families. She is looking for last minute guidance around working with a young woman and her mother. Her appointment is in 30 minutes, and she has been telling me about her anxiety around engaging the mother, who has pronounced her 18-year-old lesbian daughter an "abomination." I validate her fears, sharing my past experience working with a fundamentalist Christian mother and her gay son. I talk about what seemed to work for me—validating the mother's sense of disappointment and loss and searching for the strengths in her relationship with her son. We talk about how to engage the mother while supporting the daughter's brave decision to come out and be honest with the people around her. Armed with a little more confidence, she leaves the office to face this difficult pair.

At two o'clock, it is time to meet with my executive director to discuss grant-getting leads. We have put together a list of private foundations that support services to lesbian and gay youth. We go over the application guidelines and create a timeline for applying to a small array of local and national groups. My executive director will help me construct a budget for these proposals, and I will write the need statement, organizational history, and description of services to be funded. During my history at this agency, we have been fortunate to secure both public and private support for this work. State grants comprise the bulk of my project's budget, and annual grants from private foundations allow us to provide services like client transportation and a summer recreation group.

At three o'clock, I am meeting with one of my interns, reviewing her weekly process recording and talking about her work with a young gay man who is also hearing impaired. We talk about the dual stigma of growing up gay and growing up deaf. We brainstorm ways to communicate better with this young man. I attend to her own feelings about working with this client, listening to how she has joined with him in his frequent sense of hopelessness, feeling as if he will never "fit in." I offer some suggestions around validating these feelings at this beginning stage of their work together. I caution her about moving too quickly into problem solving, challenging her to make greater use of silence and reflecting his feelings.

One hour later, I have my staff together for our weekly meeting. We start out with "Appreciations," giving each staff member an opportunity to thank co-workers for something they have done during the week. After an initial awkward silence, several thoughts are shared, appreciating each other for helping with various projects or taking the time to listen to each other. We cover a packed agenda, starting with plans to collaborate with a local hospital to provide HIV testing and counseling to our program participants. The social worker reports back from a conference he attended on harm reduction counseling. We talk about a new group that the social work interns are starting and share leads on recruiting group members. The Drop-in Center Coordinator gives an update on upcoming programs at the Coffeehouse—a speaker from the local chapter of Parents and Friends of Lesbians and Gays (PFLAG) is coming next week, two young people have volunteered to DJ for our monthly Club Night, and we will be having an Open Mic/Poetry Reading Night.

Last, we move into my favorite part of the agenda—the "Participant Round-Up," where we share significant news about Drop-in Center participants. We review an incident from last week when three young women were smoking pot in the parking lot. I share that one young participant contacted me during the week to tell me that his mother had died. We talk about how to approach this young man, offering support but trying not to draw attention to his grief, per his wishes. We engage in a lengthy discussion about how to socialize into the Drop-in Center group a socially awkward young man who has recently started attending. I suggest that we try to wean him away from spending all of his time with staff members when he could be socializing with people his own age.

At the end of the meeting, staff members are scrambling to get things together for the opening of the Coffeehouse. While they busily collect their things to trek over to the site in a nearby town, I have a brief quiet moment when I can microwave a bowl of lentil soup that one of the agency's volunteers has graciously brought in for me. Used to working through most of my breaks, I find myself reading mail and studying my appointment book while I drink the soup.

I make the drive over to the Coffeehouse and carry my briefcase and an assortment of items up the stairs to a narrow hallway. My arms are full with a box of cookies, light bulbs, and copies of flyers to post on our community awareness bulletin board. Even though the place has not officially opened, there are already a half dozen young people wandering around the site, helping staff move tables and chairs, and anxiously awaiting the arrival of others. I brightly greet each of them, happy to see them after spending most of the week in front of my computer, in meetings with adults, or on the phone.

I am particularly happy to see Richard, an 18-year-old man who seems to pop in and out of our program. Richard is a handsome young man, short and slight of frame, who dropped out of school a year ago and has been working from time to time as a drag queen at a local gay nightclub. He has been participating at the Drop-in Center almost as long as I have been working there, but there are times when I don't see him for months. I tell him that I'm glad to see him and ask him what he's been doing. He tells me that he got a new job working at a fast food restaurant and says that he sometimes has to work Friday nights. I ask him if he ever followed through with the suggestions that I gave him for G.E.D. programs. He says "Not yet," and looks a little annoyed. I resist giving him a lecture about the importance of getting a high school diploma, but tell him that I would love to help him get back into school if he is interested in returning.

I settle into an office that staff members use for counseling and groups. Well worn by the dozens of young people who use it each week, the room has a pair of small couches, some comfortable chairs, and a tiny desk that we rarely use. This will be my headquarters for most of the evening—meeting with three clients back to back before I have the opportunity to join the rest of the gang in our large meeting room.

My first client is a 19-year-old named Carl with whom I just started working. A recent immigrant to the U.S., Carl has a limited command of English, but this handicap hardly subdues him from telling me the details of his week. I break up his excited telling of a new boy he met at a nightclub last weekend to clarify what he is saying. Carl is living in an emergency shelter for youth, on the waiting list for a longer-term placement in an independent living home for boys. He came to this country about six months ago, escaping his father, who threatened to kill him after he revealed that he is gay. Carl enjoys the freedom of living in the U.S., explaining how difficult it was to live as a young gay man in his country. It is strange for me to imagine suburban New York as a liberating place for young gay people to live, but his tales of persecution and violence from his home country help put things in perspective.

He is barely out of my office when Jeanette arrives, a 20-year-old young woman who also has had instability in her living situation. Jeanette is a bright young woman who seems to have become considerably more comfortable with me since we started working together six months ago. Originally coming into my program homeless, she presented an array of concrete needs—finding shelter, applying for Medicaid, getting a full-time job. She also revealed a complicated history of physical and sexual abuse by family members. Presently, neither parent appears to want to have anything to do with her. Her mother recently told her that she was not welcome in her house if she "continues" being a lesbian. We have just started talking about her deep despair and rage at her father and mother. Hardened by three years of living on the edge of homelessness at various friends' homes, Jeanette is guarded when talking about these feelings. We have also slowly started talking about her own stereotypes about lesbians and gay men, a conversation that began when I reflected on her frequent criticism of "butch" lesbians. This exploration of the young person's internalized homophobia is an almost universal component of working with lesbian and gay kids.

I have a short break before Barbara arrives. She has been late for her last two appointments, having difficulty tearing herself away from her friends at the Coffeehouse. She bounces into the office about ten minutes late. Sixteen years old, Barbara is a tall, somewhat awkward-looking girl. She came out as bisexual nine months ago and is presently dating a young man. Full of nervous energy, she smiles and laughs a lot, enjoying her frequent success at making me laugh at her funny faces and jokes. We have been using her poetry as a way to explore her feelings around being bisexual and the recent death of her mother. Each week, Barbara proudly produces a new poem and we read it together. The poems express her fears about not being accepted by others and her worries about important people in her life disappearing, like her mother.

Once settled in, it is difficult to get Barbara out of the office at the end of our appointment, but I slowly coax her back to the Coffeehouse room. Now I have a moment to breathe before venturing out to see how things are going in the big room. I scribble a few notes about my sessions on a pad.

Loud pop music, laughter, and voices fill the large room of about forty young people. At least a dozen others have gone out to the parking lot to smoke cigarettes and hang out in this quieter space. I check in with the other staff—most are engaged in conversation with the kids. The Drop-in Center Coordinator filters through the crowd with a clipboard trying to take a census. Several of our regulars say hello to me as I enter the room. I have to work on establishing a rapport with the new kids and the shyer ones. There's a 15-year-old boy who nervously runs by me every time we are in the same space. I always make a point of saying hello to him, hoping one day to have the breakthrough of his returning my greeting. Jesse, a stout 18-year-old boy, rushes over to me and dramatically breathes out, "I have to talk to you!" Before I can even suggest that we go somewhere more private, he rattles off his latest dilemma—he has a crush on his best friend and can't tell if his feelings are returned.

I help the staff gather the group to watch our Peer Educators perform their monthly educational skit on a small stage at the end of the room. Under the direction of our health educator, they have put together an improvisational piece about getting tested for HIV. Assembling a group of about fifty kids and quieting them down (it takes five of us to do it!), we sit and stand in the audience as the youth on stage depict a story about a young woman deciding to get the test.

Afterwards, a pair of peer educators facilitate a short discussion about their performance, asking how people felt watching it and if they have any questions about testing. One young man complains that he is sick of hearing about AIDS and already knows everything he needs to know about it. Another young woman tells the group that she has a close friend who is HIV-positive and thinks it is important that others realize it can happen to them. Proud of the peer educators' progress in putting together skits, I clap loudly during their second round of applause. I go over to congratulate the group, beaming at their success.

The remainder of the evening passes quickly—following up with a former client who was in crisis last week because his father angrily confronted him about being gay, a brief consultation with a staff member who just finished screening a young woman with a drug abuse history, hanging out with a group of kids who each came into the program separately but have since become close friends. Looking at my watch, it's now eleven o'clock. The Coffeehouse will close in a half hour, but I have the freedom to go home early, leaving my staff in charge of closing up. My good-byes stretch out all the way to the parking lot, where some kids are still hanging out, furtively smoking cigarettes and joking around.

I experience a sense of satisfaction, thinking about how the Coffeehouse provides a safe place for so many young people to gather and make friends. They may be going home at the end of the night to families who demand that they hide being gay and returning to schools where they are targets of taunts and verbal intimidation, but they have at least one place where they know they can be who they are.

Think About It

1. What are some important tasks that are accomplished in the weekly staff meeting?

2. What are some goals that can be met through the use of peer education?

3. How is working with gay and lesbian youth different from working with other youth? How is it the same?

Chapter 19
Employee Assistance Programs

||||||||||||||||||||||||||||||||||||||||||||||||||||||||||||||||||||||||||||||||||||||||||||||||||||||||||||||||||||||

by Glenda Dewberry Rooney, MSW, Ph.D.

Employee assistance programs (EAPs) are often described as humanizing the workplace, because they are a mechanism for providing human services to employees and their family members. Employee assistance is a short-term, cost-effective intervention strategy considered to be of benefit to the employee and the employer. A program may be sponsored by an employer or a union. Perhaps the most important contribution of the employee assistance program is that it serves as an alternative to the termination of an employee who is experiencing problems that alter productivity. Services are also available to employee family members. The following hypothetical account is a composite of some of my own experiences as a former EAP professional and those of my colleagues currently in the field.

Let's say that I work for a family service agency that is a member of a national network of employee assistance program contract providers. I am a licensed clinical social worker, a certified employee assistance professional, and a certified chemical dependency counselor. There are many other health and helping professionals involved in occupational settings. While there are other corporate social work roles, most social workers in occupational settings work in employee assistance programs.

I consider myself a workplace expert. My primary role is to help employees take their personal problems out of the workplace and into the employee assistance program. Hopefully, this occurs before their job performance becomes impaired.

Being an employee assistance social worker is quite different from my previous position as a clinical social worker in a mental health organization. My job involved seeing clients in my office over a longer period of time. The specialized nature of that work meant that I was rarely involved in other service activities. By comparison, as an employee assistance professional, emphasis is on the immediate problem, in particular, concerns that have an impact on job performance. The position also involves a number of roles and functions, both in and out of the office. On any given day, I deal with an array of organizational and employee concerns. The range of social work roles I engage in include being a counselor, mediator, broker, advocate, and organizer. I also function as a trainer, information specialist, account manager, and contract negotiator.

To help you understand the role and function of the employee assistance professional, I invite you to follow me through a day of work (actually a composite of EAP experiences). While the day begins in the office, my work in the afternoon is out of the office. I begin the day at 8 a.m., meeting with a family who has self-referred. Their specific concern according to Intake is parent/child conflict—specifically, a teenager who is involved with friends the parents consider to be unsuitable. The contact with the EAP was initiated by Mariana, the teenager's mother. The primary concern of both parents is that hanging out with certain groups of youth will lead to involvement with drugs. They trust their daughter, but they feel that the other youth lack appropriate parental supervision. This is a typical family issue that is presented to the EAP.

The next office appointment is with Paul, an African-American male who has been referred by the supervisor for inability to get along with co-workers. This is a difficult situation, because the supervisor did not indicate that Paul's job performance was an issue. Although EAP professionals emphasize using the program as a supervisory tool, utilization for non-performance related issues or as a form of punishment is inappropriate.

This situation is particularly problematic to me for several reasons. First, the referral appears to single out one individual, and I do not have the benefit of observing group dynamics. Paul can provide me with his perspective; I will also need to discuss the matter with the supervisor. Second, "inability to get along with co-workers" is quite vague. Third, it is unclear what outcome the supervisor expects from my contact with Paul.

And finally, the situation is troublesome, because I have noticed an increase in the number of African-American and Hispanic employees being referred by supervisors for similar reasons. This fact suggests to me that an overriding concern may be organizational, in which case the intervention strategy may involve Paul and the work group.

Matters related to diversity are still common, even in those organizations that actively seek and support a diverse workforce. Tensions tend to emerge from the fact that while the organization may embrace diversity, there is the unspoken expectation that the employee who is different will not act differently.

In this situation, I will need to help Paul find ways of coping, so job performance does not become an issue. I will also mediate between the employee, the work group, and the supervisor. If the situation warrants, one of my co-workers or I may offer to provide diversity training for the organization.

The final appointment for me in the office is a chemical dependency assessment. John has been referred by the supervisor for poor job performance. According to his supervisor, John has been absent from work 15 days over the past three months and has been found several times asleep on the job, smelling of alcohol. The assessment involves a standardized questionnaire that explores chemical use.

During the assessment, John admits to smoking marijuana and drinking beer. He asserts that he does not smoke or drink while at work and does not see job performance as an issue. In the course of our discussion, he gives several reasons for being absent from work. He also reluctantly admits that his drinking may at times interfere with his work.

The supervisor has indicated in the referral and has told John that he is on the verge of losing his job because of poor performance. The referral is an opportunity for John to use the employee assistance program as a resource. John has the option to not use the EAP, at which point the supervisor may take action based on his performance, which may include termination.

Although substance use may be the focus, the supervisor's main concern is job performance. John's contact with me is a coerced choice. In this initial contact, it is important that I acknowledge this fact and that he and I reach an agreement about our work together.

The assessment with John will explore his substance use and the extent to which his use impairs his ability to function on the job. After the assessment in my office, John has the option of accepting a referral for an additional assessment and treatment at an outpatient facility. In addition, it is important that he and I work out a plan that will enable him to maintain an acceptable level of productivity at work, and also reduce the number of times he is absent.

Helping employees with substance use disorders was at one time the primary focus of human services programs in the workplace. The employee assistance program evolved from the Occupational Alcoholism Programs (OAPs). One of the things you may have noticed about my schedule is that contemporary EAP services are responsive to a broader array of issues.

Much of the afternoon will be spent conducting training for managers and supervisors about how to manage employee situations. I stress to the group that they should not become involved in the personal affairs of employees, as this involvement tends to complicate and confuse the situation. Part of the session with managers and supervisors is devoted to identifying performance issues—for example, excessive absenteeism, work slow down or stoppage, arriving late or leaving early, excessive personal phone calls while at work, or emotional issues. I also help supervisors become aware of the stressors experienced by employees. Most of all, I want them to understand and utilize the EAP as a resource, and as an alternative to terminating employment.

Later in the week, I will hold employee orientation sessions for employees at the same organization. These sessions are a form of outreach, in that the focus is on ensuring that employees are aware of the EAP.

Before I leave the office, I have several phone calls to make. A portion of my job involves information and referral, follow-up evaluations, and locating provider services for employees in other states. This function requires that I stay abreast of community resources in the local community and also those resources available through the provider network.

The first call is to a local child care resource center to obtain information about affordable day care for an employee who is a single parent. I also call an EAP network provider in Connecticut to refer an employee who needs assistance for an elderly parent there. The final call is to a couple I referred to a local agency for marital counseling. I want to follow up on their success with accessing services provided by the agency. As I am walking out the door, Intake puts a call through to me from an individual who is seeking vocational/career counseling. Because the caller is anxious not to miss or be late for work, the appointment is made for 7:30 a.m. the following day. At 6 p.m. today, I will return to the office to meet with a couple experiencing marital conflict.

Following me through this hypothetical day has hopefully given you a glimpse of employee assistance work. I used a number of social work skills. I have found that assessment skills are very important at both the individual and organizational levels. Knowledge of effective, short-term models of practice is important, as is an understanding of the dynamics of relationship building and working with involuntary clients. Remember, John and Paul did not seek help from the employee assistance program on their own—they were referred by their supervisors.

It is also important to adhere to the ethics required of a social worker and to balance the needs of both the employer and the employee. An EAP professional is the neutral party whose job it is to help the employee and the supervisor stay focused on and resolve issues surrounding productivity and job performance. Equally important is understanding that the workplace may also be a source of stress and strain for employees and that all performance issues may not be solely related to employee personal problems.

Over the course of the week, I am scheduled to conduct a series of informational/educational seminars related to work and family balance, parenting, strategies regarding the management and reduction of stress, and elder care. My colleagues and I also distribute informational materials in the workplace.

Another aspect of employee assistance is critical incident stress debriefing. My most recent session was the result of an employee being assaulted at the worksite. When a situation of this type occurs, assistance is needed not only by the individual affected, but also by co-workers who fear for their own safety.

One challenge for employee assistance professionals involves helping organizations understand and deal with issues that will accompany a more feminized and diverse workforce. Work and family balance and quality, affordable child care will remain prominent issues. The demand for elder care assistance is expected to increase. Health conditions, AIDS in particular, and problems associated with an aging population may be expected to be central concerns. Because of their proximity to employees and their concerns, employee assistance professionals may be strategically positioned to articulate these concerns and influence organizational benefit policies.

Think About It

1. What is the primary goal in EAP work?
2. What concerns might employees have about confidentiality? How would you address these concerns?

Chapter 20
Social Work Goes to Summer Camp

IIIIIIIIIIIIIIIIIIIIIIIIIIIIIIIIIIIIIIIIIIIIIIIIIIIIIIIIIIIIIIIIIIIIIIIIIIIIIIIIIIIIIIIIIIIIIIIIIIIIIIIIIIIIIIIIIIIIIIIIIIIIIIIIIIIIIIIII

by Vicki B. Root, D.Ed., MSW

I awaken on a clear, crisp, cool morning in midsummer. Is it really time to get up? I would like to burrow down into the blankets for just a bit longer listening to the sound of the birds chirping, leaves rustling, and a woodpecker practicing his craft. However pleasant this feels, I know that in less than an hour the morning bell will ring, signaling a stroll to the dining hall for breakfast and the start of a busy, yet fulfilling day.

I am at summer camp, living in a cabin in the woods with a babbling stream running past the front porch, and little separating me from the outdoors but sheets of plywood painted forest green. I am the social worker at a church camp, nestled in the mountains and orchards of Pennsylvania. I have lived at camp for the past five summers, made possible by a 9-month teaching position in a BSW program that affords me the summer to practice social work in this unique setting. Each week, 100 to 150 campers from grades one through twelve spend the week in residence enjoying many program options. My days begin and end in the peacefulness and tranquility that serve not only to restore my inner soul, but also rejuvenate me for the busy pace of teaching social work to eager students most of the year.

I rouse myself out of bed to prepare for the day, and am reminded of the simplistic living that is a hallmark of camp. Do I really get paid for all this peace and restoration? In the ten weeks I spend at camp, I prepare no meals, wash no dishes, barely drive my car, and am far from a television. Computers, admittedly, have found their way into the offices, but Internet access is hit or miss, at best. While that may sound too rustic for some, it is a welcome respite as I am able to spend some time each day reading, writing, and reflecting on the wonders of nature.

I dress in the "uniform" of the summer—shorts, a t-shirt, and sneakers, and take a moment to sit on the porch, feel the sun through the trees, and mentally prepare myself for the day to come. I think about the current campers and potential situations that may arise during the day. I wonder what particular problems the staff members are addressing in their personal lives or in the communal living situation they are navigating. It is midway through the season, so my knowledge of group formation tells me I can expect more interpersonal problems as they move through the stages of group development. As I look toward the evening's schedule, I am excited for the possibility of an all-camp recreational activity, where I can observe the entire staff and groups of campers in social interaction, a perfect time to gather informal information that is valuable when potential problems erupt between campers, or if a staff member needs help with camper discipline.

There's the bell—it's time for breakfast. As I walk the short distance from my cabin to the dining hall, I savor the few minutes of solitude in the quiet, serene camp, soon to be flooded with children's excited chatter, their faces fresh from sleep and the (cold) shower. Most are dressed in fresh clothes packed lovingly by their parents, while others test the limits of the counselors' patience by insisting on wearing the same clothes for the third day. The first sounds are beginning to pierce the air. Laughter, running feet (followed by a stern "walk" by a counselor), calling to each other morning greetings—all welcome sounds that tell me it is time to begin another day.

Breakfast is barely served when a counselor brings a child to me. I only have to look at the child's face, see the sad expression, and my experience tells me I have a case of homesickness. As I hear the counselor's version of the night's sleeplessness, crying, and attempts to comfort, the child seems mollified by the fact that I am holding her hand and gently stroking her hair in a nurturing gesture that does wonders for alleviating the sharp pangs of missing home and family. I forfeit my own breakfast (I'll have something later) and take the child for a walk outside to the nearest bench, out of range of the hustle and bustle of the dining hall, and listen to her story. I validate her feelings, and she begins to focus on the day ahead and is easily distracted, becoming engrossed in talking about the skit her group is preparing for "skit night." In a short time, we return to the dining hall and resume the breakfast ritual. Her prognosis is good. She does not display signs of severe homesickness that can result in a call to Mom, Dad, or Grandma to come and take the child home, with the assurance of "maybe next year."

As the morning moves on, I prepare for a meeting with a counselor to discuss a behavior problem with a camper. I look through the files to determine whether the camper was here in previous years, and if there were any particular behaviors exhibited. I also check with the nurse to find out if there are any medical issues noted in the chart, and whether the child is medicated. One of the reasons I am at camp in the capacity of a social worker is the increased use of psychotropic medications by campers. Ten years ago, only a few campers brought medication for psychological disorders, usually Ritalin. Now, psychotropic medication at camp has increased almost 80%, and more heavy duty drugs such as those prescribed for severe depression and bipolar disorder are finding their way into campers' knapsacks. Staff counselors are typically college students in a variety of academic majors and are not trained or experienced with the behaviors and psychological issues children bring to camp. A large part of my summer is spent consulting with staff about how to work with behaviors they see in their campers and reassuring the staff they are not the cause of the behaviors. My background as a school social worker, the bulk of my years of practice, well prepared me for the types of issues I confront at camp. Even though this is not a camp designed for special needs, children bring a plethora of problems with them, and often camp provides the safe environment where issues tend to surface.

It is almost lunchtime, and the meeting with the counselor has resulted in his feeling support and validation for the way he is handling the child's behavior. He knows I am accessible and therefore goes back to his cabin group with a renewed sense of capability, having heard some possible options for how to handle the annoying behaviors of his camper who has Attention Deficit Disorder.

"Vicki, phone call in the office." The camp director comes to find me in the athletic field where I am observing a group of campers and their counselor. It's not easy to be paged for a phone call, since someone has to physically come and find me. Phone calls do not happen often, and I am curious to uncover this mystery.

We reach the office and I am told a parent is on the phone to report that her child's grandmother has suddenly died, and she needs to come and pick up the child in a few hours. The call has been referred to me for advice on how to prepare the child for this devastating news. I speak to the mother and after finding out some background information, we come up with a plan that is comfortable to the mother as to how I will approach the child, what information I will share, and how we will make this as gentle as possible. In these situations, one of the important factors is to try to lessen the connection between the event and the child's camp experience, so the child retains fond memories of camp rather than relate it with a negative occurrence.

This is not my last death issue today. Sometime later, a counselor shares the news that a camper has disclosed that her mother died two days before camp started. This is incredible! Why wasn't I told? I am supposed to be apprised of any pertinent information that may result in psychological distress of any campers or staff during the course of the week. More importantly, is this child leaving for a funeral? How is she processing her feelings? A myriad of other questions come to mind as I am absorbing this news. I call the nurse, who remembers the child's father dropping her off, saying he may need to pick her up early, but not elaborating. Further discussion with the counselor determines that the child told another cabin mate she would be leaving for the funeral as soon as Dad called. Until the confidante told the counselor, the child had shown no signs of emotion. And who thinks there is no place for social work in a summer camp?

After recovering from the shock of that incident, and skipping lunch (who's hungry?), I continue my day by spending time at the pool (ah, the perks of a summer camp program). I go to the pool as many afternoons as possible, although I can't say I am able to enjoy soaking up sun or cool off in the spring-fed pool. All the campers and staff visit the pool during their scheduled "pool time," and I have found over the years it provides an opportunity to informally meet and begin establishing relationships with the campers, which provides a basis should any formal work become necessary during the week. I often find the pool to be the center of the camping experience for children. They seem to be more open to talking, and through their love of swimming, or in some cases, fear, they tend to become less inhibited. I almost invariably establish connections that carry over to all aspects of camp programming.

All too soon (in the campers' perspective) it is "rest time" and the camp becomes quiet in the late afternoon sun. I decide rest is a good idea and take my current reading material to the hammock outside my cabin.

I guess I fell asleep. If not for the shrill call of the bird, I may have slept through dinner!

Perhaps I will get through one meal today with no interruptions!

Dinner proceeds without crisis, and I spend time in the office writing notes on the day's activities. Soon it will be time for the evening game of Capture the Flag, and luckily my position does not require me to play rough and tumble physical games with the campers. I unobtrusively observe the game and make mental notes of any potential problem situations. The time is also helpful in monitoring staff interaction, which allows me to be proactive if I see a situation in which encouragement to use a different tactic with a child is appropriate.

The game is enjoyed by all; evident by the joyful cries and reluctance to quit when time is called. As the sun goes down, the campers (and staff) are tired and ready to fall into their cots and dream of the fun the next day will bring. Now free of my official duty, I can relax and reflect on the day. I decide this night to take a walk around the vast grounds of the camp on a trail I know well. I am not frightened or daunted by the night's darkness. Rather, I long for the coolness the night is bringing and the brilliant starry sky that is only visible, I believe, from this particular place on earth.

Think About It

1. How is confidentiality important in a summer camp program?

2. What roles, other than those discussed in the story, might a social worker in a summer camp perform?

3. What are some reasons social work practice is effective in summer camp programs?

PART 4:
MENTAL HEALTH
AND DEVELOPMENTAL
DISABILITIES

Chapter 21
Involuntary Admission: A New Worker's Introduction to the "603"

||||||||||||||||||||||||||||||||||||||||||||||||||||||||||||||||||||||||||||||||||||||||||||||||||||||||||||||||||||||||||||||||||||||

by Beth Boyett, MFA, CMSW

I had scarcely learned the term "603" when, on the second day of my final field placement, I found myself hurtling down a hospital alley in a security van, trying to calm the first adult I had ever seen in therapy, all the while garnering sympathetic stares by four burly security guards who kept my client pinned to the van's bench.

The attending psychiatrist's last words to me as Jesse was being carried out of the therapy room—two guards at her feet, one guard on each arm—a strange, yet stunningly graceful ballet—"You made the right call. No doubt about it."

But, as I made my way behind my struggling, 100-pound patient, now being ported in pig-on-a-spit fashion—as if she were a wild beast carried off to slaughter—I doubted plenty.

How could this *be right?* Yet, I had tried every option available to me. The client had presented intoxicated, still swigging rum from an Icee cup, all attitude, yet plaintive.

"You got to help me," she said.

"You got to help *me*," I said. "We can't have a session when you're drinking. Let's schedule some time tomorrow."

"Don't matter. I got a piece in my truck, and I'm gonna blow my f—ing head off. F—therapy!" She slumped down on the therapy room's couch and gave me a curious smile. "I'm gonna do it," she said again, softly this time.

161

I had witnessed some great histrionic performances with former adolescent clients, but her resolve frightened me: she supposedly had the means and she had a definite plan. She was drunk. She had driven herself to the appointment, so she was a danger of harming self, not to mention other motorists, if she were to insist on leaving. I decided to set some limits, yet give her the choices. I asked for some phone numbers of friends or relatives to call to pick her up.

I was surprised when she lifted her head and recited five names and numbers, as if it were rote to her. Five calls later, three people had refused to help her, and two lines had been disconnected. I had, however, gotten her to give me the keys to her truck—perhaps the only confident decision I had made all day.

"I want to call my mama," she said.

I handed her the phone.

I watched her transform from a hard-talking, 33-year-old woman to a child in mere seconds. The salutation was a torrent of whines:

"Hey, it's Jesse. I messed up again and—" She began to wail. "I don't want a damn thing from you! Just—hey!" She let the phone drop beside the chair. "My own mama won't help me. My own *mama...*"

She looked up at me. "I got to go. Ain't no more use trying."

I wanted to slow her down a bit, see if I could learn more and buy time to figure out how to insure she wouldn't harm herself or put anyone else in danger. I was in way over my head. The kids at the residential treatment center where I had interned the previous year were monitored 24 hours a day, so when I left them at night, I knew they were protected as well as anyone could be. But this was a strong-willed adult who had a history of threatening others at gunpoint, and I was scared but simultaneously intrigued. According to the intake form, Jesse had requested counseling because she had been raped four months previously; that was all I knew. I decided to play it safe.

"Jesse, since I think we're going to be here past five (it was now 4:55, and everyone in the office was due to leave), I need to let my supervisor know we'll need this room for a while longer."

Jesse slumped down on the couch and closed her eyes, either passing out or ignoring me.

I left the door ajar and stepped next door to let the secretary know to notify the psychiatrist on call that I might need him and to please check in with me when he arrived from the hospital.

I went back in and pulled my chair a little closer to the couch.

"So, Jesse, you've been trying?"

"I been trying all my life since the day I was born!" Her eyes snapped open. "And I ain't gonna try no more!"

In rapid fire, she spoke of a family lost to her, a series of abusive men, three instances of rape, the constant struggle to avoid killing herself with a gun she either kept at her bedside at home or in her truck.

"That truck's paid for. Don't nobody love me, and I don't love nobody but my truck, my gun, and my drink, you know?"

I didn't know. I didn't know anything. Dumbly, I nodded, and just let her talk. *I'm not supposed to know,* I reasoned with myself, *I just have to make sure she does not harm herself. How could I have known my first adult client was going to come in drunk and talking suicide? How can one prepare for this? One can't.* I recalled the oft-repeated advice by instructors at the University of Tennessee School of Social Work, "Start where the client is!" *The client is DRUNK, damn it, and I'd like to be at this point!* My sarcastic inner monologue kept me sane a few more seconds. Then I heard myself say, "This is the first time we've met, so I need to ask you something. What are you hoping to get from therapy?"

"Not a damn thing." She snorted.

"You sure went through a lot of trouble to get here today. Didn't you want something?"

She locked eyes with me a few seconds. I knew I was failing miserably. "I'm so tired. I'm so damned tired of this sh–. I know I'm going to do it. I done it once already. Only, I didn't do it right." She pulled at her collar, and showed me a long, violet scar at the base of her throat. "I just want to do it right."

"So, you're telling me you plan to injure or kill yourself, and maybe you're telling me so that I'll stop you?"

"I'm tired," she said, and closed her eyes again.

There was a rap at the door—my mentor, my savior. I glanced back at Jesse, who appeared to have passed out again. Tom, my mentor, was still in his white coat, and I felt oddly comforted by its brightness, imagined it could cut through the darkness of my ignorance.

"I screwed up," I greeted him.

The elder, Tom, peered around me. "Is she dead?" he asked, mocking my serious tone.

"No."

"Then you didn't screw up. What's her name?"

"Jesse."

I was angry now. Didn't Tom realize I didn't know what I was doing?

Tom squatted beside the couch. "Jesse, I'm Dr. C—, and I need to ask you a question."

Jesse opened her eyes and scowled.

"I don't need no f—ing doctor. I hate the bastards."

Tom grinned broadly. "Then I'll make this as quick as possible. I want you to tell me something. Is it true you told Beth you were thinking about killing yourself and that you have a gun in your truck?"

"I ain't thinking 'bout, I'm *gonna*," she whispered.

Tom cocked his ear closer to her. "You're gonna what? Tell me."

"I ain't telling you sh–!" She sprang to her feet, and was suddenly in my face. "Gimme my damn keys!"

Tom stepped in front of me, and Jesse backed up.

"Will you sign yourself in or let us arrange for someone to pick you up? You need some time to let the whiskey wear off. Then we can talk." He managed to keep a pleasant, yet firm tone of voice.

"Gimme my keys!" She raised a fist to him, but he just stepped back.

"Is there anybody we can call for you?"

Jesse shook her head.

"Go call the emergency number on her chart," he told me. As I dialed, they shadowed each other, Tom blocking the door.

"It's Jesse's answering machine." I put the phone down.

"Jesse, I'm going to sign you in at the hospital for observation until I am sure you are sober. Then we'll talk." Tom eased around the door. "Jack, 603."

An older guard from downstairs entered. "Miss, I'll just see that you get over to the hospital safely." He offered her his arm as if to escort her.

"I ain't going!"

"Yes, you are," Tom said quietly and he took her other arm. Three other guards entered the room, and she began screaming at me:

"I trusted you, bitch!"

Within seconds, four security men, Jesse, and I were moving in a huddle toward the elevator.

"You don't have to go with them!" Tom called after me.

But I did. She was my first adult client; this was our first therapy session, and if I had made this decision to detain her, I had to see and be responsible for it. I had to know what happened after attempts toward reason failed and blurred into the irony of "the unreasonable," being forced into restraints in order to prevent her from harming herself.

"I trusted you," she said to me as we pulled up to the hospital.

You'll live and perhaps trust me again, I thought, but held my words; this was *her* pain; she needed the last word.

When Jesse refused to leave the van, the guards pulled her hands from the armrest and carried her through the door.

"We'll send the doc out to you. It's pretty tight in there!" One of the guards called to me. Even after they were through the door, I could hear Jesse's curses.

A more experienced therapist could have prevented such drastic measures, I berated myself as I waited in the alley. I had no concept of what lay beyond the door in front of me.

An intern clad in seafoam scrubs burst through the door, took one look at me, and grabbed my arm. "Looks like your first 603," he said as he propelled me down a brightly lighted hall. "You brought us a wild one. She almost bit one of the techs! Looks like she did some crack with her vodka, and God knows what else. It'll take awhile for her to sober up, and then we'll assess the suicidal intent." We stopped at a security door, and he punched numbers into a key pad. "Exclusive club you've joined." He smiled. "We'll make sure she's safe. The place looks bad, but the staff's good."

He led me to a cinder-block room the size of a closet. Jesse lay on a stretcher, trussed up and florid. When she saw me, she began struggling.

"What kind of therapist are you?" she screamed.

I wondered myself, but became momentarily distracted by a pale line moving down the wall. I watched it travel all the way down until it faintly tapped the floor's cotton matting.

"The last guy just peed," the intern said. "We had to hustle him out to make room for her. Housekeeping will be by in a minute to clean it up."

He talked as if it all made sense, and without commenting or understanding, I followed him to the entry desk to complete the paperwork—all that was required was a signature under Tom's—*my* signature—indicating that Jesse was a "harm to self." It was, on the surface, such an ordinary action, like signing for an overnight letter. I made my mark, stepped back, and that was that.

As I made my way out, Jesse said, "Hey, Bitch!" She forced up one fettered wrist, giving me the finger. Then she smiled a strange smile, as if indicating we shared some funny secret. I felt strangely victorious as we locked eyes, and that repulsed me. *Had I enjoyed being a part of this mad dash toward "sanity"?* No. But I knew that she was not likely to kill herself this night, and maybe there was a chance to begin again tomorrow.

When I returned to the office, the older security guard led me over to Jesse's truck. He pointed to the handgun, lying in full view, on the front seat. On the driver's side, there were pills and prescription bottles scattered about.

"I reckon we done her and somebody else a favor," he said, and left me, truck-side, staring at the mess, contemplating the myriad of messes that fuel and sustain human suffering.

The fact was, there was no *right* choice that day or any day. Six hours later, Jesse would be transported by ambulance to a public mental hospital, where she would remain, against her will, for five days. As I had no privileges at the public hospital, and since I was not yet her primary therapist, I was not permitted to call her or to receive any information about her progress.

Much to my surprise, upon discharge from the hospital, she returned to my office and requested that we resume individual outpatient therapy. Jesse and I were to work together for seven months, and our last meeting was no less surprising than our first.

At our last meeting, I waited to see if Jesse would talk about her decision regarding my recommendation that she enter a drug and alcohol program (as she had recently acknowledged that she wanted to stop using). She began to tell me about her intake appointment with the director of the drug and alcohol prevention center:

"I asked that woman what would she do if I ever said I was low and I was gonna kill myself: would she put me in the dirtiest, meanest, crazy bin in the state?" Jesse snorted and took a long drag of her cigarette. "And that woman, she said to me, 'If it was the only other option between having you alive or dead, then yes!' And I said, 'Well then, I reckon you'll do.' "

I suppose my bewildered look prompted her to add, "You was the only one who stopped me. All them other times, I'd tell 'em I wouldn't promise not to do it, and they'd pack me off home in a cab or even call the cops on me. They sure never rode with me! It's easy to send somebody off when you don't have to see that place, but you seen it! You keep on bein' a bitch when you have to, Beth!"

The decision to admit a client involuntarily is not an easy one. Jesse is the only suicidal client with whom I have worked who refused inpatient admission. Through her sacrifice, she taught me plenty. As Jesse once put it, "You can get over mad, but you can't get over dead."

You make the hard decision when you have to.

Think About It

1. How do you feel about working with involuntary clients?

2. How do you feel about working with clients who present a danger to themselves or others?

Chapter 22
A Day in My Life as a Suicide Interventionist

IIIIIIIIIIIIIIIIIIIIIIIIIIIIIIIIIIIIIIIIIIIIIIIIIIIIIIIIIIIIIIIIIIIIIIIIIIIIIIIIIIIIIIIIIIIIIIIIIIIIIIIIII

by Yvonne Bergmans, BSW, MSW, RSW, Ph.D.

T he dog nudges my shoulder. I groan, roll over, and look at the clock through bleary eyes. Ugh! "It's 4:30 in the morning. GO LIE DOWN!" I growl in my most sleep deprived stern voice. We both roll over and restlessly try to nap with one eye open until it's time to get up. No luck. I'm up before 6:00 and head downstairs to make coffee. Waiting for the water to boil, I check my phone and see that I have a text. My client Julia messaged at 4:30 a.m. (good dog!) stating, "Thanks for everything. It's not your fault. I can't do this anymore." As I dial the number, I feel my face flush, my heart thump, and multiple thoughts running through my head. *Oh no! Have I missed her? Has she gone on to hurt herself, or worse, tried to end her life?* At the same time, the conflicting refrain admonishes the client: *You know I don't sleep with my phone!* No answer, so I leave a message, "It's Yvonne. Please text or call in the next 15 minutes, or I will need to call for help." Now I pace, waiting for the "ting!" that will tell me that Julia is alive.

My day has officially begun. "Will one of my clients die by suicide today?" is a persistent backdrop to my work as a suicide interventionist. It's not often that I get these kinds of calls in the middle of the night, and when I do, they are not to be ignored. Whether it is despairing thoughts in a dark, lonely night of sleeplessness; a plan to deal with the deep pain for which the only perceived solution is to "end it"; the impulsive moment arising after having coped with voices or thoughts by using substances; or the startling awakening after a flashback/nightmare—someone's risk has increased in that moment. The great news is, they reached out.

Fifteen long second-by-second minutes pass. No response. I call my colleagues at the hospital to see if Julia is there. Negative. I get the address and call police. The last thing I want to do is call 911, and still, I can't take the risk of not doing so. I'd prefer a gentle "wellness" check by the mobile team. However, they're not on at this hour of the morning. Calling 911 is a crap shoot in terms of how my client will be spoken to or treated. I give the dispatcher the details of my concern, and they tell me someone will be sent out right away. It is now out of my hands, and I know that I will surreptitiously cast an eye to my phone every chance I get.

I arrive at my office before 8:00 a.m. and open my emails. Since I left yesterday, 30 new messages have arrived. Delete requests beginning with, "Dear Esteemed Author/Researcher. We invite you to submit...." I have three papers sitting in my "get to it" pile and data worth at least another three papers that I continuously tell myself I'll get to this month. I've been saying this for a very long time now. I open client-related notes first. A couple tell me they won't be at group today for varying reasons. I respond to each, validating their choice to take care of themselves, wishing them well at an interview, "humanizing" the immense challenges they're facing, and ending with a reminder to "keep safe" and looking forward to seeing them at the next session.

Next is the person who writes me each day as part of his accountability check in an externalized "report" of the feelings he experienced, moments of control he recognized, and choices he made to keep himself safer. I respond, validating the choices he made, humanizing the feelings he experienced given the situation, hypothesizing an expansion of the number and names of feelings that might have also been operating, challenging and suggesting a reframe to a thought he may have had, and reminding him that he is worth being part of the human race and we care.

I read the next emails from colleagues. One is informing me of whether one of my clients has presented to the hospital. Another updates me on a current situation that might escalate a person's risk, and another requests a risk assessment/consult for someone on the inpatient unit.

My phone rings. It's my colleague Sophie, who is bereft of ideas of what to do next with a high-risk client named Kevin. She is scared for the client and feeling helpless and frustrated, especially given the recognition that by virtue of repeated presentations to the Emergency Department (ED), she knows if she sends Kevin back to the ED, it will be another experience of the "same old, same old"—assess for immediate risk, identify as "chronic borderline presentation" (for whom admission is not helpful), discharge (leaving the client feeling rejected, abandoned, and thinking he is unworthy of help). We commiserate on the failures of our system and the lack of recognition that multiple presentations in a week are an indication that something is seriously wrong. We hypothesize what client-centered intervention focused on the needs of the client beyond "assess and dispose" might look like in the ED setting. Sigh. Neither of us has the power to make changes in the systemic attitudes toward people experiencing recurrent suicide attempts. I feel bad for Sophie.

She implores me to see Kevin to identify any strategies or interventions that might have been missed by her team. She asks me to consider Kevin for our next cycle of group and meet with her team to develop a care plan for Kevin. I look through my calendar and see that I can see him at the end of the week, during what most people would call a lunch hour. Sophie gives heartfelt thanks, and I sigh inwardly, knowing that we can't do this work alone, and still, sometimes it's very lonely work.

Just as I begin to respond to the email requesting the consult on the inpatient unit, the phone rings again. It's a resident working in the ED asking if I can come and see "a 35-year-old female borderline patient presenting with superficial self harm and vague threats of suicide" who presented last night and the ED believes can be discharged today. I ask if said 35-year-old female borderline patient has a name. Anna. I ask if the resident is aware of the intent of the "superficial" self harm—to die, to end pain, to externalize the internal "something" for which Anna has no words? The resident is not sure but will ask. Nonetheless, will I come to see the patient this morning? "I'm sorry, I have a group this morning. I can see her after group." The resident thanks me profusely, sounding "extra nice."

It's 9 a.m., and my student arrives spot on time. We go over any impressions, insights, concerns, questions, and thoughts she may have had since yesterday. Maggie is concerned about one of her psychotherapy clients' safety and wants to know how to approach the session later today. We review and plan. She identifies that she now feels more confident.

It's now time to head over to the hospital a block away to set up the room for one of our three weekly 20-week groups that consist of 8-10 people each with a history of recurrent suicide attempts. I rush to print the minutes from last week before we go. Of course, there's a paper jam! Swear, admit my own technocidality as I'm ripping paper out of the machine, gather the handouts, and we're off. Despite having requested the team arrive 15 minutes prior to group so I can give any updates, one co-facilitator had to squeeze in a client for a meds review. Another is stuck in transit. All of our co-facilitators are volunteers who are either students, people with lived experience who are graduates of the intervention, or professionals who have squeezed this group into their regular clinical day. I feel grateful and beholden to them, leaving me hesitant to make too many demands for fear they will withdraw their time. This would leave me in a position of not being able to run the group in what I feel is a safe manner (that is, without another regulated professional in the room), or not being able to offer the group at all. And I know I have a wait list for the next cycle due to begin within the next few months.

The group goes well with the not unusual ups, downs, tears, laughter, and challenges. It's an exhausting and exhilarating hour and a half. The team does a quick debrief regarding concerns, follow-ups, noticeable movements forward, and insights. We agree to table some issues for our supervision with all of the group facilitators in a couple of days.

I go down to the ED for the consult requested earlier. Anna was discharged and told to call me. The ED was backlogged and needed the bed, and she "seemed safe enough to go." Triaging for discharge based on least at-risk is perhaps contributing to the frustration my early morning colleague was experiencing. Chances of Anna cold-calling me are slim to none. Permission was not obtained from her for me to reach out to her. Silent frustration abounds. I say "thank you."

This afternoon, I see three people from our Urgent Care Program for individual therapy. Each has been deemed at high risk of harm to self and has been recently discharged from one of our mental health care programs. I am theoretically only to follow them for up to 12 weeks. One we will be able to transfer to longer-term follow-up, thanks to our urgent care triage nurse. The next one has now stabilized and assures me he has had no thoughts of suicide for the past two and a half months. He is still intermittently self-injuring to deal with the intensity of feelings in the context of a history of trauma and would like to get back to graduate school next semester. The third is someone I've been seeing weekly for a year and a half, and she still scares the daylights out of me at least two out of four sessions that I see her. Her psychiatrist feels the same way, so we have joined forces to tell management there is no way we are letting her go...oh, and yes, we do realize her 12 weeks are up.

It's theoretically the end of our paid working day. My student Maggie and I meet to review what she has observed and learned, and to process any potentially traumatizing/concerning material she may have experienced or witnessed.

In the midst of this, I receive a call. Julia, the client who texted me in the wee hours of the morning, was found unconscious. She is currently in our medical ED and is stable. I give silent thanks and say I'll drop by in the morning on my way to work. I give Maggie the update, as she knows the client from discussions in our group supervision sessions. The sigh of relief is audible.

I finish my response to the email request for consult on the inpatient unit, indicating I'll start my day over there tomorrow. A request to do a workshop in two months at a community organization has crossed my email. I agree to do it, trying to ascertain where I can put down the reminder to myself, so it doesn't come as a big surprise two days before the event. Ughhh, notes. Guess I'll need to listen to voicemails in the morning.

Off to see my shiatsu/acupuncturist now. Hope I'm not late.

Think About It

1. What are your clinical, ethical, and personal thoughts and feelings about people who have repeatedly attempted to end their lives? How would you manage those in the context of your practice?

2. What are your thoughts when someone tells you, "I need to end my life. I'm done."

3. As a social worker in a multi-disciplinary hierarchical institution, how would you choose to advocate for a client for whom you see risk increasing, knowing there are no beds on any inpatient unit and the emergency room will require a 5- to 6-hour wait for "non-urgent" cases?

Chapter 23
Partial Hospitalization

IIIIIIIIIIIIIIIIIIIIIIIIIIIIIIIIIIIIIIIIIIIIIIIIIIIIIIIIIIIIIIIIIIIIIIIIIIIIIIIIIII

by Kenneth G. Smith, MSW, LCSW

I am an experienced clinical social worker who enjoys doing accelerated therapy work with clients over a succinct period of time. Inpatient psychiatric hospital work—which I did for several years—has limited appeal to me now, especially with ever-decreasing lengths of stays and quicker patient turnover. I am not now attracted to being in private practice, something I've also done in the past. I am stimulated by doing groups, and though I have skills in psychodynamically-oriented therapy, I am most comfortable in the cognitive-behavioral arena.

Is there a place for someone like me in today's clinical social work? You bet, and I have found it! It's called Partial Hospitalization, which is a fancy word for day treatment.

The partial hospitalization model is based on the fact that numerous mental health clients do not need 24-hour, locked inpatient treatment, but do need more than the traditional one-hour-per-week outpatient appointment. The partial hospitalization mode of treatment began to take shape in the 1960s, when a small group of clinicians in the northeast United States became frustrated at what they saw as a lack of alternatives for mental health clients. These clinicians believed that psychiatric clients could recover more quickly if they could pursue their treatment in concert with their existing community and family ties. With the increase of community mental health and deinstitutionalization movements in the 1970s, partial hospitalization programs began to build their strength and effectiveness on core values of group therapy, psychological rehabilitation, and the use of therapeutic milieus. The discovery of new psychiatric medications, which reduced client hospital stays, also helped. By the 1980s, partial hospitalization programs were widespread, particularly as third-party payors began to realize the cost effectiveness of day treatment, as opposed to 24-hour inpatient care.

I am the coordinator and primary therapist for a Partial Hospitalization Program (PHP) in St. Petersburg, Florida. The program is housed at a mid-sized, not-for-profit medical hospital. The basic requirements for someone in my position are being licensed in my state and having at least five years' post-graduate clinical experience.

Since I wear both administrative and therapy hats, a typical workday begins with my assessing the upcoming day in both areas. My staff—consisting of psychiatric nurses and mental health technicians—meets each morning to receive assignments from me. Within their core job descriptions, each day is varied as to specifically what duties my staff may perform. For example, the nurse could focus on technical obligations (charting, taking orders from physicians, checking clients' vital signs), or clinical work (doing assessments and leading groups), depending on where the greater need exists that day. The staff and I then work on facilitating any admissions or discharges planned for that day, and work on updating clients' treatment plans. A treatment plan is a formal document found in the client's chart, detailing the client's problems, specific goals for each problem, discharge criteria, and expected length of stay in PHP. When the staff meeting ends, I make my own appraisal as to what kind of interface I may need to have with peers, supervisors, physicians, or persons outside the hospital during that day.

Clinically, with staff input, I ask myself several questions in pondering clients' needs for the day: Who is presenting for treatment today? How are they progressing (or not) in treatment? What might be some leftover issues from the previous day's therapy? What patterns of group dynamics are surfacing? What mental health topics do my clients need to focus on today? This assessment phase usually takes about an hour.

I typically lead two morning groups of an hour and fifteen minutes each. The first is the community meeting, which has a several-fold purpose: (a) for clients to report to each other how they are feeling and functioning, (b) for clients to share victories and struggles they have experienced since the last group they attended, (c) for clients to set daily, specific treatment goals, and (d) for clients to give each other support, feedback, or confrontation. I view my primary therapeutic role in the community as creating a warm, accepting milieu where clients feel safe enough to describe honestly what they are experiencing. Most, if not all, of my clients need to learn how to be honest with themselves and others. Some have been taught that their feelings and thoughts don't matter. Others have been locked in a pattern of shaming relationships, devoid of honesty. For the aforementioned reasons, I consider the morning community meeting to be the most crucial group of the day for clients. In essence, I believe the community meeting most accurately reflects the reality of the client's current life.

After a break, clients attend the psychoeducational group. During this group, I lecture on various mental health topics of interest to them. I have compiled lectures on more than 30 different topics. Examples include family dynamics, communication skills, anxiety and anger management, overcoming depression, and self-esteem. Addiction topics such as relapse prevention, 12-step work, and co-dependency education are taught if I have clients who have those needs. I strongly encourage clients to take notes during the lecture, and to ask questions. Handouts accompany many of the lectures, and I sometimes give written assignments to be completed during group. Psychoeducation is the group that I most enjoy doing, because if I hadn't become a social worker, I probably would have chosen teaching as a career!

I am an energetic speaker who likes to use humor. When appropriate (and I, like other therapists, must be careful about this), I will share vignettes from my life as they pertain to the topic. Therefore, this group allows me to integrate facets of my interests and personality with my clients. Clients seem to benefit from the practical, life-skill based information they receive.

The next scheduled event of the day is lunch, which is provided to PHP clients at no charge. At first glance, it's tempting to view lunch time as a trivial part of the program. However, I find this time of the day to be clinically important, as I can learn much about clients by observing their lunchtime behaviors. For example, does the client eat alone, or with peers? Which peers? What types of food, and in what amounts does the client eat? How is free time spent after the meal is finished? The lunch period affords me the opportunity to be with my clients in a relaxed, informal manner. Then there are days when I choose to be away from my clients during lunch.

Following lunch, the clients attend two more groups before their day is over. Medicare and other third-party payors stipulate that PHP clients receive at least four separate groups per day. The afternoon time is geared toward exposing the clients to other hospital or outside therapists. Art, recreation, music, dance/movement, and psychodrama are examples of modalities used.

After clients are dismissed for the day (the hospital provides transportation for clients who need it), my time is spent on charting, reviewing the day with my staff, meetings, phone calls, and other activities. Clinical documentation is crucial. The client's medical record presents a picture of who the client is, why he is in treatment, what his goals are, and how he is progressing toward those goals. PHP documentation is done on a group by group basis, using a focus-outcome approach. I strive to document the specific clinical focus of the group the client attended, and what the outcome was for the client, including how that client responded verbally or behaviorally to the intervention presented in the group. Documentation should also reflect why the client needed to be in the particular group, and how the group dovetailed with the client's treatment plan goals. An example group note: "Client attended psychoeducational, which focused on learning a set of assertive communication skills. Client verbally indicated that she understood the material presented. Client agreed to practice the skill with a certain family member, and will report back to peers as to whether she reached this goal. Client clearly needs to learn these skills, as she is currently experiencing conflict with family members, which is causing anxiety."

This typical day involves my spending at least ten hours per week with PHP clients. Family therapy theorists have spoken of the therapist's need to join the client's system while doing therapy. Certainly, if nothing else, the amount of time I have with my PHP clients each week allows me to join them directly and become an integral part of their lives. I don't mind saying I enjoy playing this role with my clients for the time they are in the program. Hopefully, each client can benefit in some manner from their time with me. I know I certainly learn much from them!

My typical PHP client is an adult with a psychiatric and/or chemical dependent history, who is referred because of acute and/or severe impairment of daily functioning. Their psychiatric or addictive symptoms are such that PHP is needed as an alternative to, and prevention of, inpatient treatment. PHP clients are under the order and care of a staff psychiatrist who has made a formal assessment and diagnosis of their condition. PHP clients carry a diagnosis found in the Diagnostic and Statistical Manual of Mental Disorders (DSM). Major depression (sad moods, crying spells, sleep or eating dysfunction, lack of energy, and so on), anxiety, and substance use disorders are among the most common classes of symptoms presented by PHP clients.

Many of my clients are transferring into PHP from an inpatient hospitalization stay. Thus, they can continue to receive daily treatment, yet are able to return home for the evening. Others enter PHP as a less-restrictive alternative to being hospitalized. According to the accepted national standards, PHP clients attend the program five days per week, for a total of 20 hours of treatment per week. PHP is generally intended to be a one- to three-week program, depending on the severity of the client's need. As clients progress in their treatment and become more stabilized, they can step down to an even less restrictive model of outpatient care, commonly known as Intensive Outpatient Treatment (IOP). In this level of programming, clients attend treatment at least two or three days per week for a minimum of three to four hours per day.

Besides addressing the client's core symptoms, the PHP takes into consideration the personality factors of each client. I am seasoned enough as a therapist to realize that the goal is not to alter or change a person's personality (as personality is usually well-ingrained in childhood), but to respond to a client's character in such a manner as to accentuate the client's strength. For example, let's say I'm working with a client who exhibits dependent personality traits. According to Gorski in a workshop I attended, this type of client's life stance is "I'm here to serve others, because others are more important than me." I want this client not to give up helping others in appropriate ways, but instead to learn to help him/herself, as well as others. Thus, in PHP groups, this client can set goals involving realistic and practical skills for self-care. The client's peers can support the client's progress, or can explore with the client resistance to meeting goals. Attempts by the client to inappropriately rescue a peer, which inevitably occurs in the PHP milieu, can also be directly dealt with in the group process, or in an individual session, if needed.

I provide individual, marital, and family therapy, if necessary. Client mental health issues affect family members and vice-versa. A few PHP clients also engage in outside therapy and/or support groups simultaneously with their PHP treatment. I welcome this, and clients usually have no objection to my consulting with their outside therapist.

Another clinical issue that I must contend with is the client's attitude toward being in PHP. Some clients, particularly those with dependent traits, cling to PHP tightly, and resist being weaned off the program. These clients are often isolated, or are in chaotic environments, and they view PHP as a safe haven. Other clients seem to begin treatment with fairly high motivation, but quickly lose interest and drop out. Still others attend out of some level of duress, having to satisfy an outside force such as the court system or an employer. Regardless of the client's motivation level, I keep my therapeutic focus on the purpose of PHP.

In the end, a successful PHP client will have achieved a level of little or no impairment of daily life, will have demonstrated the ability to form and maintain relationships outside of treatment, and will have committed to a specific discharge plan of continuing care. We hold a graduation group for clients on their final day of PHP. During this group, peers affirm the client's work done in treatment and offer best wishes for the future.

Not all PHP clients graduate. Some drop out prematurely, clients with addictions relapse, and others may decompensate and end up re-hospitalized. While client resistance and sabotage clearly exists, I find immeasurable value in learning how I (and my staff) could have intervened with a client differently in such a way as to prevent an unsuccessful outcome.

The stressors I face on my job generally fall into three broad categories: (a) clinical stressors, which all therapists face, such as burnout, responding to client transferences, dealing with my own countertransferences, and frustrations with clients who choose to sabotage their or others' treatment; (b) programmatic stressors, involving staff relations and management of staff, satisfying psychiatrists' expectations, satisfying third-party payors' expectations, monitoring program quality and effectiveness, and proper compliance with state mental health laws and requirements; and (c) industry stressors, mainly keeping current with the trends and changes in mental health care and nationally accepted standards of PHP care.

To assist me with industry stressors, I have joined my state association for Ambulatory Behavioral Healthcare. My state group is patterned closely after a national organization, the Association for Ambulatory Behavioral Healthcare (AABH), which was founded in 1985. The phrase ambulatory behavioral healthcare is the accepted jargon for a continuum of outpatient mental health services ranging from PHP to less structured aftercare programs. In 1996, AABH changed its name from the American Association of Partial Hospitalization—the name change reflects the fact that a wide variety of outpatient programs, in addition to PHP, are now available nationally.

What is the future of partial hospitalization? I believe the coming years will find a continual need for quality PHPs to assist clients who are experiencing acute crisis. However, I foresee an increasing emphasis on IOPs and other intermediate-type outpatient programs that are less intensive than PHP. The broadening of outpatient ambulatory behavioral mental health will be necessitated by such factors as increasingly rigid reimbursements for inpatient and PHP care insisted upon by managed care companies, groundbreaking medications through which clients can achieve a higher level of psychiatric stability with fewer side effects, and the explosive growth of community support groups, whereby clients can receive free and structured support on a daily basis.

I do not know what the future holds for me as a clinical social worker, but for right now, I have found my niche in PHP. I look forward to continuing to serve my clients in this exciting model of mental health care. As one of my clients recently remarked to me, "Ken, you were made for this job!"

Think About It

1. How does PHP differ from inpatient therapy? Outpatient therapy?

2. What is meant by the term "milieu"?

Chapter 24
Life as a Group Home Manager

||||||||||||||||||||||||||||||||||||||||||||||||||||||||||||||||||||||||||||||||||||||||||||||||||||||||||||||||||

by Angela Marie Brinton, BSW

P atience, tolerance, and a sense of humor—the three virtues for working with the mentally ill population. I say this because in the past year, I have been called every name in the book, spit on, hit and, on occasion, threatened by clients who were decompensating, mad, or just having a bad day. It's all part of the territory, but I love my job as the Manager/Director of a group home for young adults, ages 17-25. The first time I assisted in moving a high-risk client out into his own apartment, and three months later he was baking me cookies, I was hooked. I have forgiven (not forgotten) a lot of actions. This is not to say that clients should get by with murder, but clients can change their behaviors. They just have to be taught how to act appropriately in the community, and they have to feel secure. In our program, we preach natural consequences as often as possible. I've been told that our staff work miracles, but it's really our clients.

I received my BSW in May 1992 and started my first "real" post-graduation job in the big city (Kansas City) that same year, as an outpatient case manager for the State of Missouri. I later transferred to my current position within the same organization. I had worked many fill-in shifts, and was therefore familiar with the clients and the program.

The Young Adult Program is very successful, and I am part of a wonderful team of group home staff, case managers, community members, and family members. Our program is located in the inner city, but we serve people from all over Missouri. We are completely community-based. Our clients live in the group home, their own apartments, community residential settings, or with their families. The clients living in the group home have curfews but are able to go out in the community by themselves.

As a part of my job, I am on call to my staff 24 hours a day, 7 days a week. I am responsible for ongoing tasks such as staff training, budgeting, charting, and scheduling. There are two things about my job that I could do without. Those are politicking so that our clients can receive the services they should be automatically receiving and dealing with lazy employees who hate their jobs.

It's 5:30 a.m., well before my usual start time of 9:00, as I trudge into work. I was paged at 1:30 a.m. to talk with Tiffany, who had just trashed her room. We talked about her behavior and why she broke some of her own personal items until about 2:30 a.m., when she finally retired to bed. Her family had promised to visit for about the thirtieth time and didn't show up. One of the staff called me at 5:00 a.m. to inform me that Tiffany wouldn't get out of bed for school and that he needed reinforcements. One of the requirements is that clients go to work or to school every day unless they are dying. Since we adhere to natural consequences, it also means that sometimes we have to have extra staff on very short notice, which explains why Tiffany's case manager and I are here at 5:30 this morning. Tiffany is in her senior year of high school. She will be the only child of 16 in her family to graduate from high school, and she is the only one diagnosed with a mental illness.

When Tiffany came to our program, she wouldn't talk to anyone for about the first three weeks, and refused to get out of bed most days. She had spent most of the last six years living in an inpatient facility. Her solution to every stressor was to cut on herself. She had poor hygiene and low self-esteem. Today she is a clothes hound, hasn't missed a full day of school for two months, and hasn't cut on herself in over a year. She also has not spent one day in the hospital since she came to our program. At 6:30, she is finally ready, and since she missed the school bus, she has to take the city bus, which another client taught her to ride. (We refuse to drive any of our clients to their programs.)

My next task of the day is to work with J.T., who is diagnosed with schizophrenia and frequently cannot tell you what day it is. He has been ousted from every outpatient program in the city, so we have tried to create our own program for him within our group home. He has been at the group home for four years, but for two separate stays. We have taught J.T. how to ride the bus to the mall approximately 75 times. He would frequently forget how to get home once he got there, lose his bus tokens, and show up a couple of hours late. Once the police brought him home, because he couldn't remember his telephone number. After driving about 25 minutes each way to pick him up from the mall one day, with him yelling at me because he thought he had missed dinner, I told myself that it just wasn't going to happen. I was so frustrated that he couldn't figure this one simple task out, but I gave him a bus token again a few days later. After an eternity, J.T. can take the bus about four places. It really can happen, but it has to happen within the client's time frame.

Today, we are making pancakes. J.T. likes to eat, so he's motivated. I have to explain each task thoroughly, from what kind of pan to use to how to turn the stove off when he's finished. We have been trying to teach J.T. how to cook one meal a week, rotating three or four different items. When he first started, he wouldn't stay in the kitchen, but now he'll stay until it comes time to clean up. He's no fool. Before J.T. had his first hospitalization, he was at the top of his class making straight A's and excelled in several sports. He has a near genius IQ.

It's now about ten o'clock, and I have to partake in the scheduling nightmare. We are two staff short and I have a lot of empty shifts to cover, but a budget ceiling that will only allow full coverage for certain shifts. One major downside to the mental health field is that entry level positions pay very little, which makes it difficult to retain really good staff. I have worked very hard to find other ways to compensate employees who go above and beyond the basic expectations.

Unfortunately, completing paperwork is easier said than done, because I always have an array of visitors in my office. Our program is very community-based, so we have a lot of clients who visit. Today, my first visitor is Howard. He has come to tell me about his latest life mishap. He "left his $10,000 paycheck lying on the back porch and someone stole it." Considering that he has no job, one can quickly conclude that there is no paycheck. I ask him if he would like to report it to the police, but he tells me that it's not necessary, because he'll get paid again next week. I ask him what employment he has these days. He relates that he has been working as an undercover agent for the FBI. I tell him that if he ever gets sick of the undercover work, I have a really good program that he can sign up for that pays minimum wage. He thanks me and leaves, only to come back in about a half hour to sign up for the program. I am really excited about this, because I have asked him about 100 times, and this is the first time that he would make the necessary phone calls. I like working with Howard, because he is very challenging. Since I have known him, he's been shot about 50 times, robbed 100 times, and "beat up" more times than I can count, although there is never a scratch on his body. He used to visit the Emergency Room via ambulance about two or three times per week. The staff worked intensively with him, and now he uses the ambulance about once a month.

I am finally back to my scheduling for about 20 minutes before my next interruption from one of our more humorous clients. She meets me at my car every morning to tell me that I look beautiful and that she missed me. It's a great ego boost to hear that every day. Today, Marie is upset because she cannot carry her own spending money. She receives $15 per week. The first time we let her have all of it, she went to the beauty salon and had her head shaved, but then begged me for about a month to buy her a wig. Her reasoning for shaving her head was that she wanted to look like her favorite staff person, Charles. Charles is African-American and wears his hair very short. Marie is Caucasian and female. Marie and I reach an agreement that she can keep five dollars of her spending money per week and that she can buy things with the rest of the money if she will let one of the staff help her with her shopping.

Today is my favorite day of my work week, Wednesday, because we have social night. Any of our clients, old and new, can come. The only requirements are that they have to wear clean clothes, bathe before arriving, and follow the rules. We had to make the prerequisites very specific, because some of the clients would bathe, but then wear dirty clothes they hadn't washed for three weeks. It is a great time. We usually have about 20-25 clients show up, from very high functioning to very low functioning. Today we are going out for dinner to a nice restaurant, a treat for most of the clients. They have to pay for their own meals. I have been asked at least 50 times today when we are leaving. It's about 4:30, and we are trying to get everyone gathered up. Tiffany has just arrived home from school in a really good mood and cleaned up her room without being asked. That's what it's really all about, and programs like this can work.

Most of our clients have been in and out of hospitals most of their lives. Our goals have changed a lot since the program first started. Originally, our goal was for everyone to have their own apartments when they left our program, but through trial and error, we realized that wasn't going to happen. We currently place about 90% of our clients in their own apartments when they leave the program. Approximately 80% of them are still in their apartments after six months. It is difficult to predict how a client will do in an apartment. It is frequently the lower functioning, persistent mentally ill clients who do better in apartments. They will usually take our advice. If we tell them not to go out past 11:00 because they can get killed or robbed, they usually will stay home.

You have to measure success in small increments in working with the mentally ill. What you see as successful may not be to your client. You can't put your values and goals on their treatment plan and have any success.

Think About It

1. Role-play teaching J.T. to ride the bus. What emotions do you experience when doing this?

2. Think about the statement, "You have to measure success in small increments in working with the mentally ill." How would you define success in this job?

Chapter 25
Disaster Mental Health Services

lllllllllllllllllllllllllllllllllllllllllllllllllllllllllllllllllllllllllllllllllllllllllllllllllllllllllllll

by John D. Weaver, ACSW, LSW

People are almost always changed
by the traumatic events they face during their lives,
but they need not be damaged *by those events.*

As I wrote the original version of my chapter for the first edition of this book, I was in the Everglades, near Miami, Florida, on an American Red Cross disaster assignment. Our Disaster Mental Health (DMH) team was working at the site of an airline crash, to help the recovery crews (and the other relief workers) cope with the slow and difficult process of gathering the human remains and the pieces of the plane. I don't get paid for this work (in fact, I often use my vacation time and I lose private practice income to make these trips), but it is very much a part of my professional life as a social worker.

Following that ValuJet crash and, later the same year, the crash of TWA Flight 800, Congress held hearings on the problems surviving family members face in the aftermath of these tragic events. In response to the testimony they received, the members of Congress quickly enacted the Aviation Disaster Family Assistance Act of 1996. Subsequently, and in recognition of the fine work Red Cross volunteers had done following several airline accidents, the National Transportation Safety Board designated American Red Cross the "independent nonprofit organization with experience in disasters and post-trauma communications with families." To meet the needs, Red Cross formed a special Aviation Incident Response (AIR) Team, a rapid-response group that quickly provided assistance to families

185

and to other personnel involved in the relief operations following aviation accidents and other major transportation accidents. The AIR Team has now evolved into a Critical Response Team that can assist with both transportation accidents and other mass casualty incidents, and I have served on both teams.

My full-time job is Casework Supervisor for a county mental health program in Pennsylvania. I am generally in my office by 6:00 a.m. The day there officially begins at 8:30, so while I'm not yet on the clock, I make the coffee, do paperwork, and set things up for the day to come. I also will frequently use this quiet time to write, update my own DMH Internet page, or work on some of my private consulting projects.

On Monday mornings, the early time is often used to finish writing emergency sheets and to phone in reports from weekend on-call shifts. I've always enjoyed providing crisis intervention services, so as one of my part-time jobs, I frequently take 8-10 emergency shifts per month. Depending upon the types of shifts I take, the work involves phone counseling, information and referral, site counseling (with our mobile crisis team), arranging voluntary hospitalizations, and delegating involuntary commitments.

Once my regular day begins, one might find me supervising one of six case managers, overseeing treatment plan writing and reviews, handling complaints, doing utilization reviews, backing up my workers when they are out of the office, writing discharge summaries, answering correspondence (especially requests for records), and attending meetings. I am also involved with annual license reviews, planning, and public speaking on behalf of our program.

Monday through Friday, when my day ends at that job, I head across town to my part-time job at Concern. There I see individuals, families, and some foster children for therapy, and I supervise graduate student field placements. The students and I usually see two to four clients each night. We tend to use cognitive-behavioral approaches and generally see people for a brief course of treatment (five to seven sessions). Concern uses several part-time therapists and offers no benefits; most of us have day jobs to cover our health insurance. I also like to teach one or two night classes each year at a local university, and I do some additional work as a private consultant, specializing in crisis intervention topics.

Far more personally and professionally rewarding to me than the jobs already mentioned is my volunteer career. After graduate school, I served on the board of directors of the local and state chapters of the Mental Health Association. I eventually served for two years as the president of each of those organizations. This kept me at the forefront of consumer advocacy, offered me many opportunities for public speaking, and provided me with a lot of administrative experiences, all at a time when I was working in an entry level position.

More recently, my volunteer interest has swung to the DMH component of the American Red Cross. The Red Cross offers free training to anyone who qualifies and is interested in helping out with DMH, or any of its other relief services (e.g., mass care, damage assessment, family services, health services, logistics, liaison functions, staffing, and computers). I took my first class in 1993 and went out on my first two disasters that year (one on administrative leave time and the other on vacation time). I was hooked.

I have served as a DMH volunteer on numerous major, national disasters and many local events, including work in Iowa during the summer-long Midwest flooding of 1993 and services as coordinator of DMH services for the morgue workers in the wake of a 1994 Pittsburgh air crash that killed 132 passengers and crew. My most memorable assignments were service as Coordinator of the AIR Team's Family Assistance Center following the 9/11/01 terrorist incident that led to the crash of United Flight 93 in Shanksville, PA, and, soon after, my service as an Assistant Officer helping manage the larger World Trade Center relief operation in New York City.

September 11th began as just another day for most Americans. Things changed quickly, though, as the hideous terrorist plot began to unfold. I was in my office at Northampton County Mental Health that morning, helping several other staff members complete a physical office move that had begun the day before. We were positioning desks, file cabinets, and other pieces of office furniture. Someone got word that there had been a plane crash into the World Trade Center in New York City and my co-workers scrambled to get our TV set working to see the news. I simply kept moving furniture.

Before too long, the office was buzzing as a second plane crashed into the second Tower, a third one hit the Pentagon, and another had crashed in western Pennsylvania. Most work came to a standstill as more and more co-workers were watching the news or trying to contact family members and friends. I kept doing what I could to complete the office move. My office mates kept passing by and telling me headlines that seemed more and more surreal as events unfolded and the towers began to collapse. Some may have thought it odd that I kept working on my tasks for the day. Others knew I'd already taken a phone call from the Red Cross, placing me on alert to travel wherever I was needed, as soon as my destination could be determined. Until I was dispatched, continuing the physical activity of the office move was something concrete I could do to help my own office staff as much as I could, before I left the area.

By noon, our County offices were closed. I went home and packed, finally watching some TV coverage. Folks in the disaster relief community plan for "worst case" scenarios, and yet no one imagined this could happen. By the time my kids got home from school, I'd gotten my assignment. I was to drive to the Johnstown area to support the relief operation for the families of those lost on United Flight 93—the "heroes" flight on which the passengers managed to stop the terrorists before they reached their intended target.

For the next 12 days, I served as the Coordinator of the Family Assistance Center (FAC). The FAC is a "safe haven" spot where family members can come together and share their thoughts, feelings, and memories with one another. There they can also talk to mental health workers and members of the clergy, doing so in a secured place designed to protect their privacy. Many prefer to avoid the media, lawyers, and any others who might further victimize them at a time when they are quite vulnerable. Part of our role is to organize family member visits to the crash site, and these are usually followed by a multi-faith memorial service. Most surviving family members need to visit the site—it helps them accept their loss and begin to move forward with their suddenly altered lives.

About 500 family members and close friends of those lost on Flight 93 were served by our team. Helping us serve them were the warm wishes and prayers of people all over the world. We received a marvelous array of flowers, cards, banners, gift baskets, comfort kits, and letters of support. Especially helpful were the touching messages from innocent children, some of whom attended a school near the crash site. These things all gave great comfort to the families and, when we closed the FAC, the items became part of the permanent memorial to those brave souls who lost their lives while protecting the lives of others.

On October 5, I traveled to New York City and began 15 days' work as the Deputy Officer (second-in-charge) for the DMH function for the World Trade Center operation. There, I supervised several other Assistant Officers, as we continued to manage the efforts of some 1,875 DMH workers (1,500 spontaneous local volunteers and 375 National Red Cross volunteers) who were involved to that point in time. From 9/11 to 10/19, there were more than 73,000 DMH contacts made by these workers with family survivors, friends, rescue/ recovery team members, construction/cleanup workers, and fellow members of the various disaster relief teams. I was struck by the size and scope of the relief effort; despite having so many people to help, we needed more. Standing at ground zero and viewing the horror, I found myself thinking that the TV coverage did not properly depict the magnitude of the devastation, nor the great needs of the victims' families, co-workers, and friends.

Located on Pier 94, the FAC was as large as several jumbo jet hangars. In addition to the sizeable number of Red Cross workers, there were people from many government agencies, social service organizations, and support groups. There were therapy dogs and their handlers working the room, in addition to all the other supports. Three or four site visits for families were run from there daily. People were taken by ferry boat/water taxi to a dock near ground zero and then walked in to the viewing location. New York also had many other work sites, including our headquarters office, eight Service Centers (at peak), kitchens, warehouses, lots of mass care emergency response vehicles, a Casualty Contact Unit (a.k.a. Integrated Care Team), and two Respite Centers (RC). These RCs were for recovery workers, police, fire, National Guard personnel, and others who were working on the cleanup effort. They could eat, nap, get a massage, watch TV, surf the net, get first aid, and talk to clergy and DMH. Everyone involved was doing superb work.

In DMH work, we begin with this fundamental premise: less is more (keep it simple). There is nothing we can say or do that will quickly end the shock, ease the pain, or make survivors feel better…but there are lots of things we can say or do that can make them feel (or act) worse! Comments like "I know what you're going through" or "Everything is going to be fine" may seem innocent enough, yet they might easily result in an angry response. We avoid asking, "How do you feel?" Giving eye contact is often enough to get someone talking, and, if not, we avoid being too aggressive in our approaches. Upset people tend to seek us at times when we are most needed. When that happens, it is important for us to simply be supportive listeners and let them share their stories.

Disaster victims are generally normal people who are experiencing very typical reactions to the abnormally stressful situations they face in the aftermath of the event. DMH workers use techniques like psychoeducation, crisis intervention, and defusing/debriefing, to help the victims become survivors and help the helpers (the other relief workers) manage their stress. In most mass casualty assignments, we work to keep the rescue workers from becoming secondary victims. We provide stress inoculation to incoming workers, preparing them for the sights, sounds, smells, thoughts, and memories they will face, and we offer emotional support throughout their assignment. Like disaster and trauma victims, relief workers are forever changed by their involvement in disaster relief activities.

The Red Cross continues to seek help from persons interested in volunteering for future relief efforts. Especially needed are more licensed mental health professionals. Many social workers, psychologists, nurses, counselors, and psychiatrists find their caseloads (patient loads) are too high. As they tire of the same old blend of bureaucracy, politics, paperwork, and pathology, many seek a challenge and some have become DMH volunteers. Once they've qualified and completed free training (which also offers no-cost continuing education units), they too are able to "travel to exotic and not-so-exotic places, meet people whose lives have been struck by disasters—and help them," with the Red Cross covering all disaster-related expenses.

No other moments in my career have come close to providing me the personal and professional rewards that I have experienced as a Red Cross volunteer. I urge you to contact your local chapter and see what it is all about.

Think About It

1. John Weaver finds disaster work personally and professionally rewarding. What rewards do you think you might find in this type of work?

2. How can John use skills from his paid work in his volunteer work, and vice versa?

Chapter 26
Developmental Disabilities in Families

||||||||||||||||||||||||||||||||||||||||||||||||||||||||||||||||||||||||||||||||||||||||||||||||||||||||||||||||||||||||||||||||||||||||||||||

by Toni Murphy, MSSW, CCSW

I was not particularly interested in developmental disabilities before I took the position of Director of Social Services for a nonprofit agency that provided services for children and adults with disabilities. At the time, I was working as a case manager with older adults, and seized the opportunity to work with children and families. Little did I know how limited my knowledge was about disability-related issues. My true "education" was yet to begin.

During the first six to eight months, as I learned about our clients' unique issues, and as I slowly became familiar with and knowledgeable about resources available, I wondered why on earth I was ever hired for the job! My supervisor told me that very few qualified applicants had even applied. I was shocked! The requirements were not especially strict or unusual: MSW, experience working with young children and families, basic case management skills and experience, and a couple of years' post-graduate experience. It seemed the social workers who fit this broad description must number in the zillions. The salary was somewhat competitive, certainly average, and it was a supervisory/department head position—something that looks great on a résumé. The agency also had a long successful history and was well positioned within the community. Why the dearth in applicants? I surmised that the area of developmental disabilities was not widely publicized or acknowledged among social workers.

Now to describe a "typical" day in the life of a social worker in the rehabilitation setting. Upon arrival to our 50+ year-old building, which is cold in the winter and hot in the summer, and leaks year-round, I am greeted by a stack of phone messages, which I take to my little office in the basement to sort through and prioritize. Typical requests are for diapers to be sent home with "Johnny" on the bus following his therapy session, information about our program or community resources, referrals for services, and not uncommonly, requests for help in advocating for a child with special needs to obtain necessary services from other public or private agencies. And there is one woman who calls several times a week for various reasons. She has physical and cognitive disabilities and demonstrates extraordinary insight about these limitations and a tenacious determination to overcome them. She is an inspiration to me, and one of the strongest women I've ever known. Our receptionist doesn't write down her name and number for me on a formal phone message pad. She just lets me know T has called, and smiles.

After my triage treatment of returning calls, it is time to use the city map app on my phone to look up the address for an intake and assessment scheduled for 9:30. Upon locating the address on the map, I realize it is an area with which I am familiar. No problemo. I know my way well. Of course, actually bundling up all of my paperwork, signing out on the board upstairs, asking the receptionist to please take a message (I'm going to be late!), and being detained in the hall by a perturbed occupational therapist who demands to know why one of my clients has missed her last two therapy sessions, are all hurdles I must clear before I escape to my car and make for a clean getaway!

As I attempt a safe merge onto the freeway, I muse about the unique position in which I find myself as a social worker on an interdisciplinary team with physical therapists, occupational therapists, speech therapists, and special education teachers. These professionals are not social workers, and they have different sets of priorities influencing and guiding their work. Specifically with regard to the therapists, a medical model perspective primarily directs their intervention choices and treatment planning. Some conflict between us is inevitable. Later, when I meet with the occupational therapist, I will explain to her that the client in question was recently evicted, and that although their daughter clearly needs therapy, the family is struggling to meet the very basic needs of all their children.

I arrive just in time, and the interpreter with whom we contract is already there. This client moved to the States from Mexico, and Spanish is her primary language. The little house is very dark inside as she tries to keep it cool during the hot summer months. An electric box fan blows across the tiny living room to facilitate air circulation. The mother, A, greets us warmly and somewhat cautiously. The television is tuned to a channel that offers programming in Spanish. The interpreter and I sit down on a small sofa covered with blankets. A sits in a chair near a child's crib. As we begin introductions, A motions for us to approach the crib and meet her 13-month-old son, B. He is beautiful with smooth light brown skin and big dark eyes. He looks exceptionally small for his age and seems to have some spasticity in his muscles. Little B is the reason for our visit.

As we begin gathering information about the child's and family's needs, I find myself feeling increasingly frustrated with my inability to communicate directly with A. (Why didn't I stick with those "Community School" Spanish classes?) The intake takes twice the time it normally takes, because of the time involved in interpreting information back and forth. Halfway through the intake, A breaks down in tears. She explains that all of her family is still in Mexico and she has no friends here. Furthermore, her husband takes the only family vehicle to work, which leaves her more isolated. Since the family lives outside of town, public transportation is not an option.

She continues to describe her frustrations and challenges, particularly with regard to locating and accessing services for her son. Her most immediate concern is that he has been congested for several days, but she has been unsuccessful in securing him an appointment with the doctor. I feel overwhelmed by the end of our visit, and cannot imagine how this young mother must feel. I wonder where I can get a good deal on a magic wand.

Before we leave, we assist A in making an appointment for B with the doctor, and in contacting some other agencies to address various needs. I make a mental note to place this family on my list of high priorities, which will inevitably juggle another family to a lower spot. Some of these decisions are not easy!

It is well into the lunch hour by the time I arrive back at the office. I decide to eat in my office and try to complete my paperwork for this case. At our agency, the social work staff schedule the interdisciplinary team assessments for new clients. I look at the "Evaluation Calendar" and add B in the first available slot. I scurry up the stairs from the basement to check my messages—a manageable stack. I run back downstairs and return a call from a former client labeled "important."

C's child transitioned out of our program about six months ago. While enrolled in our program, D received physical therapy to address his gross motor needs. D is currently in the preschool program at a local public school. C is a single mother with two young sons. She is unemployed, receives public assistance and financial support from the children's father, and utilizes the bus system for transportation. During the two years her son was in our program, I got to know C as a strong, loving, determined advocate for both of her children.

C answers the phone, in tears. It is difficult to understand what she is trying to say, because she is crying so hard. Apparently, D has been ill with an ear infection, and C has taken him to the clinic on two separate occasions this week. Today, when she walked to his school to pick him up, her son's teacher accused C of being a "bad mother" because she let her son go to school when he really needed to see a doctor. C adds that she has felt for weeks that his teacher did not adequately address his needs in the classroom. I feel angry at the teacher's insensitivity to this parent, who struggles to meet the needs of her children, in spite of her limited resources. I also feel frustrated that because of funding and "rules," this is not something I should be spending time on, since the family is no longer a client of our agency.

Fortunately, our city school system has a support program, specifically for parents of young children with special needs. Since I have met with representatives from this program on a number of occasions, I call one of my contacts and explain the situation. Ultimately, a representative from this support program arranges a meeting for herself, C, D's teacher, and the school principal. Much to C's relief, D is placed in another classroom with another teacher. Advocacy is a big part of this job.

As an MSW with this agency, part of my job is to supervise the BSWs on staff. This afternoon, I am scheduled to meet with one of them to discuss a new case involving a diagnosis he has not encountered previously. My supervisee wants to learn more about the diagnosis before his initial meeting with the family. We review the medical information together to identify symptoms and assess what impact this diagnosis may have on the child and family. We consult with a therapist on staff who is able to provide us with more information and resource material for my supervisee to read prior to his intake. One of the many positive aspects of working within an interdisciplinary team is the opportunity to learn from other staff, who collectively and individually possess a wealth of knowledge and experience.

OOPS! I glance at my calendar and realize I almost forgot my Community Task Force meeting! It is a task force comprised of representatives from various agencies in the community who work with parents of young children with disabilities. A local resource was not funded this year, which has caused a gap in services for our clients. Members of the task force combined efforts and successfully accessed grant money to provide these needed services. We now face the challenge of hiring a coordinator for the program and assisting that person with developing a program that effectively meets the needs of families. How will we determine eligibility? How many families can we realistically serve? How much money should be allocated for each family? How will we recruit and train staff? How will we ensure quality services? This is cutting edge social work! The opportunity to create a program that will effectively meet the real needs of clients is exciting! It is also a significant time commitment, and I am fortunate that my agency has allowed me to shift some of my responsibilities in order to participate on the task force.

After I return to my office, I check my messages, gather up my things, and head out to another home visit on my way home. ("On the road again.") The family I am visiting was recently informed that their 18-month-old girl will need extensive heart surgery. Little E was born with a serious heart condition and receives therapy at our agency for mild developmental delays. Mr. and Mrs. F also have two older daughters, six years and eight years old, who truly look like princesses. They greet me at the door with drawings in hand. Mrs. F invites me in, thanks me for coming, and begins to cry. I listen and offer support. She tells me what the doctors explained to her about E's condition, and what to expect following surgery. It sounds quite risky and very scary. Mr. and Mrs. F are involved with their church, which has been their main support since E was born. Mrs. F hasn't needed to cook or clean for the past week! And someone from the church will be with the family at the hospital during surgery.

We say good-bye and I head home. As I pull out of their driveway, I am struck by the difference between this family's access to support and the lack of support A has available to her. Support is a key issue for families who have children with special needs. Some of the most effective programs for this client population are "Parent to Parent" programs that "match" trained support parents with parents in crisis. These programs are available across the country and represent one of many resources available. There are also many organizations that offer information and support for persons with a specific disability. Our agency offers a parent support group and provides transportation as needed, so that everyone has access and can take advantage of the opportunity to share with other parents. I find this aspect of our program particularly rewarding, because clients often establish relationships that continue long after the group has ended.

There are several characteristics that are essential for any social worker considering practice in the area of developmental disabilities. A social worker must be comfortable with people who have abilities different from their own, and understand that everyone has the right to be an individual. Someone who cannot handle seeing children with significant medical involvement may need to seriously consider another area of practice. Families of children with special needs encounter so many people who are uncomfortable with their children. They should not have to deal with professionals who have similar attitudes and behaviors.

Additionally, social workers working with this population must allow parents to make their own decisions regarding their children and families. Parents observe and interact daily with their child in the child's own environment—we don't. It is equally important to allow parents to be where they are in the grieving process. Parents with children who have special needs face incredible challenges every day, yet find a way to make their lives work. Social workers need to demonstrate empathy, offer support, advocate, and provide information. These special moms, dads, and caregivers deserve special praise!

Finally, it will be necessary to communicate effectively with professionals from other disciplines within your own agency, professionals from other agencies, and a wide variety of people in general. Anyone can have a child with special needs, regardless of race, ethnicity, age, lifestyle, or socioeconomic status.

Working in the area of developmental disabilities provides a rare opportunity to share the joys, personal triumphs, and some-times sorrows of everyday heroes. As professionals, we may touch their lives in some way, but the truly most meaningful connection is their lives touching ours.

Think About It

1. Like many other social workers, this social worker juggles many different responsibilities. Does this surprise you? What is your reaction to this aspect of social work?

2. What are your attitudes toward people with physical and mental disabilities?

PART 5:
SUBSTANCE USE
DISORDERS

Chapter 27

Hope Dealer: Social Work and the Opioid Crisis

IIIIIIIIIIIIIIIIIIIIIIIIIIIIIIIIIIIIIIIIIIIIIIIIIIIIIIIIIIIIIIIIIIIIIIIIIIIIIIIIIIIIIIIIIIIIIIIIIIIIIIIIIIIIIIIIIIIIIIIIIIIIIIIIIIIIIIIIIIIIIIII

by Sara Staver, LMSW, CADC

I work with individuals who are stigmatized, criminalized, judged, shamed, jailed, ostracized, viewed as undeserving, and even denied basic human rights. I am an opioid treatment social worker in an outpatient office in the Midwest. I understand the important connection between the strengths perspective and hope. I focus on the resources, capabilities, and resiliency of my clients. I help my clients view the circumstances that brought them through my doors as a turning point—an opportunity to make positive change in their lives. I am a hope dealer.

It's a warm July morning. I sit down at my kitchen table with the newspaper and my coffee, just as I do every morning at 6:00 a.m., before heading to the substance abuse treatment clinic where I work. I open the paper and immediately read that a client I have been working with for the last five years has died of an opioid-related overdose. The article reads, "Melanie is one of the 20 overdoses reported this month...." *They described her as a statistic,* I think to myself. Melanie is a person. Unfortunately, this is not the first time I've experienced the death of a client. *It's the nature of the disease,* I say to myself. I close the newspaper, finish my coffee, and continue with my morning routine.

On my drive to the clinic, I cannot stop thinking about Melanie. I cannot stop thinking about the nature of addiction and its devastating effects. *I despise the disease of addiction,* I say out loud, as if someone were in the car with me, listening to my thoughts. I spend the rest of the drive thinking about all the human suffering, societal cost, and communities devastated by this disease. I think about Melanie, the loss of opportunities, the loss of life, and those who loved her and are left behind, including her 10-year-old daughter and 14-year-old son who will have to learn to live without their mother. I hope they, too, do not succumb to the same fate as the two generations before them. I am angered that there were not more readily available treatment options for Melanie, and for many of my other clients locked in the chains of addiction. Melanie had been on the waiting list for inpatient treatment for more than 30 days. Before exiting my car, I think to myself, *sometimes it is hard to focus on hope, but today, I must.*

I walk gently into my office, recognizing that I must shake the anger, frustration, and sadness I feel. I breathe in deeply and release. *For Melanie,* I whisper. I take one more deep breath and exhale. Upon entering my office, I take a moment for myself, to bring my role as social worker back into focus and bring forth hope. I feel grounded, centered, and present. I check the day's schedule and see that it is packed full with assessments, intakes, individual counseling sessions, and group therapy appointments. I inhale and exhale. I am ready for the day.

My very first appointment of the day is an assessment with Bobby. Bobby called two weeks ago asking if the clinic provided medication to help "a pill and heroin addiction." I remember the call distinctly. Bobby was distraught. The receptionist who answered the phone was concerned about Bobby and asked that I speak with him. When I picked up the phone, he immediately began explaining why he was calling. Bobby had been using prescription pain medications (opioids) and heroin (opiates) for a few years and recently had had a "scare." Bobby explained that to keep from "getting sick" (avoid withdrawal symptoms), he would voluntarily break parts of his body, go to the emergency room, and hope to score opioid pain medication. He described the great lengths that he would go to in order to "stay normal." However, Bobby had recently been flagged by the ERs in his area by the Prescription Monitoring Program (PMP).

"A few days ago," Bobby said, "I wasn't able to score any heroin. I couldn't go to the ER anymore, and I was getting sick. I felt like I was going to die." In a desperate attempt to get back to "normal and feel better again," he asked his wife to break her finger, go to the doctor, and ask for pain medication. She did.

While on the phone, Bobby began to cry. "I can't stand myself any more. I feel so ashamed. I hate myself." The "scare," he said, was an overdose. Later that evening, his dealer had ended up coming through. With the opioids obtained earlier by his wife already coursing through his bloodstream, Bobby had introduced heroin.

"I overdosed, and she had to call 911," he said quietly. "She thinks it's her fault." Bobby said he had been using for the last two days since discharging from the hospital and was running low. He said that he didn't want to score anymore "pills or dope." Bobby would be experiencing intense withdrawals soon, and he was anxious to get started with services.

"Bobby, it sounds like both you and your wife have been through a lot. I will try to get you in as soon as I am able. In the meantime, have you heard of naloxone? It's a rescue drug." Bobby answered, "Yes, the ER gave my wife a dose before I was discharged." While I searched for an opening in my schedule, I explained that we offer a combination of medication and counseling to assist in the recovery process.

In a Midwest city of approximately 100,000 individuals, there are fewer than 10 physicians authorized to prescribe medications to assist in opioid dependency and even fewer options for opioid-specific counseling. The clinic where I work is the only one within a 60-mile radius that offers both a physician on staff authorized to prescribe medication to reduce cravings and withdrawal symptoms from opioid addiction and me, a social worker with specific training and expertise in opioid-specific counseling, otherwise known as Medication Assisted Treatment (MAT). The scarcity of MAT services creates long wait periods for people to get into services and begin the road to recovery.

"I can schedule you to have an assessment in two weeks," I told Bobby. He asked about how long it would take to get started with medication. "Most likely, it will be another two weeks after the assessment before I can get you in to see the physician. But we can get you started on counseling right away." *I must give Bobby hope.* I hung up the phone wishing I could have done more to reduce the 2-week wait time. The best I could do was call Bobby if someone canceled, a rarity in my line of work. Generally, it's during the "no shows" that I can find time to eat my lunch, return phone calls, and catch up on paperwork.

Before I get to the waiting area to meet Bobby, the receptionist catches me in the hall. "Manny is on Line 2." My friend Manny is the county jailer. Manny has been in recovery for more than five years. He has a tender place in his heart for people suffering from addictions, especially those who find themselves under his supervision. Manny embodies hope. "I know you can't say anything for confidential reasons, but Kimberly wanted me to tell you that she is in jail. She was picked up on a possession of narcotics charge and would like you to see her, if possible," Manny says.

Manny has pulled many departmental strings to allow my services into the jail. He has obtained approval for me to provide counseling services, but only to my clients. Manny and I continue to advocate and work together to obtain approval for more expansive services to those in jail, such as group therapy. For now, I take what I can get.

A few years back, Manny and I were enjoying a cup of coffee together, discussing the revolving door of people arrested for low-level drug-related offenses such as possession of paraphernalia (usually spoons or needles used to smoke and inject heroin and pills). They are sent to jail, and those requiring medical intervention are rerouted (usually by ambulance at further economic burden) to the local hospital. The hospital sends them back out the door in less than 24 hours, and the cycle continues. The relationship between the jail and hospitals has become severed. Those arrested are exhausted by this process, and economically, no one wins. From that conversation, I realized that not providing substance abuse treatment to individuals while they are in jail is a missed opportunity. "Another opportunity to deliver hope!" I told Manny. Treatment, regardless of the setting and circumstances, is preferable to no treatment at all.

Before hanging up the phone, I tell Manny I will come by the jail around 4:30 p.m. I should have just enough time between my last counseling session of the day and group therapy at 5:30, I think.

I greet Bobby in the waiting area. "Hi, Bobby. I am Sara. We spoke on the phone. I am glad you are here." I smile and ask, "Would you like to chat with me in my office?" I like to offer a variety of sitting arrangements for my clients—a couple of chairs closer to where I sit and one farther away in each of the two remaining corners of the room. Bobby sits in one of the corner chairs. He is visibly sweating and seemingly stiff.

"I snorted a half of oxy about four hours ago," he says quietly. I ask if "snorting" is his preferred method of use. "No, I usually shoot up." I ask Bobby if he minds that I write down some of what we talk about, and he nods his head in agreement. I lean toward

Bobby gently, lower my voice to match his, and let him know that he is in the right place and that we will go at his pace.

"I don't know if I am ready to stop using," Bobby says. "That's okay. Tell me, what are you ready to do?" I ask softly. Bobby is quiet. I allow the quiet to remain between us. After a bit, Bobby says, "I think I am ready to keep coming here." "Excellent! I think that is a very good place to start, Bobby." I have hope.

On my drive to the jail, my cell phone rings. "Hello, is Sara available?" The only inpatient substance abuse treatment center within 120 miles calls to inform me that a bed has just become available for one of my clients, Jeremy. Jeremy has 24 hours to check in or his bed will be given to the next person on their list. Although this is Jeremy's fourth inpatient treatment, he wants nothing more than to rid himself of the compulsion to use fentanyl. In the last few months, he has begun using "street" fentanyl, an illegally made substance that is generally mixed with heroin and/or cocaine. Jeremy has been close to dying at least twice that I know of. He and his wife have three children.

Four months ago, Jeremy was asked to leave their family home. On the night he was asked to leave, he was found unconscious in an alley. He was taken by ambulance to the nearest ER, treated with naloxone, and given a referral to my clinic. Jeremy and I have been working together ever since. He has been on the inpatient substance abuse treatment waiting list for more than 50 days. Unfortunately, Jeremy did not show for his last appointment with me and does not have a phone that I can contact him on. I quickly make a U-turn and head to the community soup kitchen where I'm fairly certain Jeremy will be for dinner. My quick stop at the soup kitchen will set me back about 15 minutes, but Jeremy needs this opportunity. I find Jeremy and immediately tell him the news. He is thankful and says he will check in at 10:00 a.m. tomorrow. I tell Jeremy I am proud of him, something he rarely hears.

I jump back into my car and head to the jail. By the time I get there, I will have 30 minutes with Kimberly before I have to head back to the clinic to facilitate group tonight.

Perfect, I say to myself with a smile on my face, *just enough time to deal more hope.*

Think About It

1. Imagine losing a client. How would you take care of yourself to ensure you are able to work effectively with others?

2. If you were providing opioid treatment services in an agency or community with limited resources, who would be your allies? Which relationships are most important?

3. How do you feel about criminalizing people who use opioids and other drugs?

4. Think about the relationship between Bobby and his wife. How would you work with the family to address the collateral consequences of addiction?

5. Social workers are crucial to public health infrastructure. How would you support community-based addiction programs and public health?

Chapter 28

Dual Diagnosis: Substance Use Disorders and Mental Health in an Inpatient Setting

llllllllllllllllllllllllllllllllllllllllllllllllllllllllllllllllllllllllllllllllllllllllllllllllllllllllllllllllllllll

by Catherine Lau Crisp, MSW

I am a clinical social worker on an inpatient psychiatry unit at a large teaching hospital in the southeast. I work with the "dual diagnosis service," a part of the inpatient psychiatry department whose job it is to treat people with both a substance use disorder and a mental health issue.

Seventy percent of the people I treat have a substance induced mood disorder; that is, their depression is due to their addiction. Eighty-five percent of my clients have no insurance and little resources to pay for treatment. Many have reached rock bottom in their lives. They have reached the point where they feel a desire to end their lives because they have tried, and usually failed, to triumph over their drug problems. Many of them have been through several treatment programs in the past and are trapped in the web of addiction. With its commitment to the indigent, the hospital where I work is the only option for some people in this area.

My day starts at 7:30 in the morning when I arrive on the unit. Immediately upon arrival, I look over the list of patients assigned to my team. This list tells me who has been admitted since I left the unit and who has left. At any given time, I work with a maximum of nine clients. Additional clients presenting with a mental health and substance use issue are placed on one of the five other psychiatry services.

The majority of my morning is spent meeting with my team and the clients that we serve. My team consists of a part-time attending psychiatrist, a first-year or second-year psychiatry resident (who has completed medical school, is now training for four years before becoming a full fledged psychiatrist, and spends thirty days on the dual diagnosis service), a third-year medical student (who spends six weeks on my team), and a nurse. We generally meet as a team and then make "rounds" to see each of the clients. In working with each of our clients, our goals are two-fold: 1) assess and diagnose the mental health issue and 2) address the addiction. Neither of these is easy. The average length of stay on our service is nine days. Many clients come in with exceptionally high alcohol levels (a blood alcohol level of 0.35 is not uncommon) and/or are in acute withdrawal from the effects of heroin. In a very short time, we are faced with the tasks of decreasing their suicidality and/or hallucinations, detoxifying them from their substances, motivating them for treatment of their substance abuse and mental health issues, meeting with their families, and arranging follow-up treatment for them upon discharge from the hospital. As a social worker, I am involved in each of these aspects, although the psychiatrist and resident will ultimately decide on the diagnosis. I hold primary responsibility for meeting with the families, conducting individual and group therapy, and arranging the discharge plan.

In addition to my work with clients, one of the most enjoyable aspects of my job is the education I do with both the resident and the medical student about the interplay between substance use disorders and mental illness. On several occasions, our team has had lengthy debates about the diagnosis of a particular client. Is he/she depressed because he/she can't get off drugs? Did the depression precede the drug use? If the depression preceded the drug use, at what point did they start to use drugs and how did that affect their depression? What is their diagnosis? Is it substance-induced mood disorder or is it a major depression with a coexisting substance dependence problem? When clients are irritable, is it due to: 1) a component of their mental illness, 2) the effects of withdrawing from their drug of choice (irritability is particularly common among people who are addicted to crack cocaine), 3) a component of a personality disorder, or 4) just a part of their personality style? Many times, each of the team members has a very different opinion about the diagnosis and the recommended course of treatment. It seems like a miracle when we can all agree. At other times, it is clear that we will not reach a consensus. When this happens, the attending psychiatrist ultimately makes the final call about the diagnosis and treatment that we will provide. Although I am surrounded by people with a clear medical model bias, I feel that my opinions and the bio-psycho-social-spiritual perspective I bring to the team are respected and valued by those I work with.

My afternoon consists of individual and group therapy and begins with the group I do each day at 1 o'clock. The group is "required" for all clients on the dual diagnosis unit, but I consider it to be a good day when I have a 75% turn-out. The group focuses on substance use issues and is a combination of psychoeducation and therapy; the content and focus of the group depends largely on the group of clients. There are some weeks when the client population appears insightful, motivated, verbal, and bond together as a group. When this happens, I have fantastic groups. I come in with a topic for discussion and the clients have so many questions and comments that I, as facilitator, play a very minimal role.

In one recent group, we discussed "Consequences of My Addiction." The group members felt close to one another, comfortable with the group setting, and were able to open up and share the pain and losses they had experienced in their own lives and created for other people as a result of their addictions. People cried and shared and comforted one another. I felt I could have left the room and they would have continued with the topic without me. My role was to clarify confusion people had, not to direct them in the discussion. It was a powerful group and one that the clients felt was among the more meaningful groups they attended during their hospitalization.

Unfortunately, groups like the one mentioned above are very rare. Clients are often unwilling to attend groups and need much more individual treatment. Addressing clients' refusal to attend groups frequently presents philosophical dilemmas for the team. Much of the substance abuse theory would advocate a hard-lined approach: attend the group or leave treatment. Mental illness theory would advocate a softer approach: nurture the client and treat the underlying mental illness and the client will be able and willing to attend groups. My team does not have any set rules about how we approach each client; instead we treat each client as an individual and try to understand the client's objections to attending group.

Much of the work I do with clients individually is based on a strengths perspective and motivational therapy techniques. As noted before, many clients have tried and failed many times in their sobriety and have little hope in their ability to recover from their addiction. I attempt to educate them about the process of relapse, help them identify individual strengths and resources that may be helpful in their recovery, confront them on their denial, and assist them in understanding elements of their substance abuse and their mental illness or depression. The most valuable thing I think I offer clients is a belief that if they are willing to do the work, they can recover. I let them know that they have the abilities to recover but, ultimately, must complete the tasks themselves.

When not meeting with the team or clients, my attention turns to discharge planning. I remember quite well the message I received as a student. "Discharge planning begins the day you start treatment with a client." I have never seen this more true than in my work with the dually diagnosed. In considering discharge planning for clients, most of my focus entails connecting the clients with mental health and substance use disorders treatment agencies. For clients without insurance, this entails a referral to the mental health center that serves the area where they live. Many agencies here require that clients contact the agency themselves; my work in this area consists primarily of giving the clients the telephone number of the appropriate agency for them to contact. After the client has made contact with the agency, I send information regarding diagnosis, medications, and course of treatment to the agency.

If the client has been referred by a mental health center, I maintain contact with the referring clinician from the date of admission to the date of discharge. Frequently, clinicians have specific goals that they want their clients to accomplish with the hospitalization, such as decreasing suicidality, decreasing hallucinations, reevaluating medications, detoxifying from drugs and/or alcohol, and providing a more conclusive diagnosis. In addition, the clinician frequently has a plan for the client upon discharge, such as entering residential treatment or beginning intensive outpatient treatment. My role in working with the outpatient clinician is to coordinate services among the mental health center, the client, and the treatment team at the hospital to provide the highest level of care for the client.

In addition to making referrals for mental health and substance abuse treatment, I also assist approximately ten percent of clients with addressing their homelessness. As noted earlier, many of the people I treat are depressed and have hit bottom. Much of this is due to the losses they have experienced as a result of their addiction. It is not uncommon for my team to see people who have lost their jobs, homes, transportation, and families to their addiction. Many clients report living "with friends, on the street, by the river, wherever I can find a place." Despite such seeming desperation, referrals to homeless shelters are often rejected. Clients are frequently familiar with the shelter system and prefer the streets to the shelters. Others report that the shelter system is filled with drugs and not conducive to sobriety. These reports are very frustrating to hear, as the shelters are often the only public resource for homeless individuals. One of the hardest things to accept is that clients may leave the hospital and decide not to change any of the circumstances that led to their hospitalization.

In the course of discharge planning, I also attempt to meet with clients' families. While there is much disagreement about specific approaches to treatment with dually diagnosed individuals, there is consensus that the family is a valuable source of information. Many clients are cut off from their families. They may have stolen from and lied to their families to the point that their families no longer want any contact with them. When I am able to meet with family members, I have two basic goals: 1) obtain information about events in the client's life that precipitated the hospitalization and 2) educate the family about addiction and mental illness. Families are generally relieved when they realize that my goal is not to convince them to assist the client with money or housing, although I freely acknowledge that were the family to do so, my job with discharge planning would be much easier.

I reinforce to families that it is important to set consequences for the negative behaviors of their family member and in doing so, to validate the limits that they have or want to set for the addicted member. After meeting with the family members, I invite the client in to join the meeting. This is a useful time for both the family member and the client, because they have a safe space with a mediator to express certain issues. The intensity of the emotions can get quite high, but by and large, these meetings are productive for the client (who hears previously unspoken feelings and thoughts from the family member), for the family member (who has been given a chance to be a part of the client's treatment and has obtained information about the treatment), and for myself and the treatment team (who now have a more complete picture of the client's life and history, thus enabling us to provide better treatment to the client).

As you can see, theoretical dilemmas are common in working with dually diagnosed individuals. Anyone who wishes to work with this population must have a good understanding of theory regarding both substance use disorders and mental illness. In addition, one must be able to handle both the theoretical and the direct practice conflicts. These conflicts fascinate me. The potential for a variety of approaches in work with this population is enormous.

I never know what to expect from moment to moment. The client population is as diverse as any group of clients; I have treated angry alcoholic men who lost $100,000 jobs and depressed women who were addicted to prescription pain killers. The range of psychiatric diagnoses varies from the more common substance-induced mood disorder to the less common somatoform disorder. The common denominator is the substance use issue and the common ground that our clients share.

Think About It

1. As in other chapters in this book, a team approach is used. Why do you think this is a useful approach in social work? What might be some difficulties with it?

2. Why are there theoretical dilemmas in working with dually diagnosed clients?

Chapter 29
Adventure-Based Practice

IIIIIIIIIIIIIIIIIIIIIIIIIIIIIIIIIIIIIIIIIIIIIIIIIIIIIIIIIIIIIIIIIIIIIIIIIIIIIIIIIIIIIIIIIIIIIIIIIIIIIIIIIIIII

by Christian Itin, BSW, MSW, Ph.D.

I awaken, it's bitterly cold outside, the sun has barely risen. It's about 6 a.m. I roll over to light the stove and start the water for some hot tea. Now comes the hardest part of the day—getting out of my warm sleeping bag and starting the day. You see, I'm a social worker whose area of practice is adventure therapy. "Adventure therapy," you say. "What is that? Is that a form of practice that social workers engage in?" We certainly do, and for the last 14 years or so, this has been my primary area of practice. I'd like to tell you about a day in the life of a social worker engaged in adventure-based practice. This particular program is a four-day course run by the Colorado Outward Bound School as an adjunct to inpatient treatment for substance use disorders.

As I greet the morning, the only thing I know for certain is that the day will be uncertain. Regardless of the population I'm working with, or the length of the course, the beauty of adventure-based practice, and particularly wilderness-based practice, is that each day is a new adventure for me and the clients. The day brings with it all the unpredictability of life, with its moments of joy and elation, and despair and frustration. Though I might have a sense of what the activity of the day will be, I cannot know how the participants (I prefer this to clients, because it clearly reflects the participatory nature of the experience) will respond, what the weather will provide in terms of challenge, or what other unforeseen forces will be at play. Flexibility on my part is a critical skill in effectively using the lessons that the day will present.

The day starts with making sure the participants are up and beginning breakfast. You see, we have become a community, dependent upon each other for our survival. If each member of the community does not contribute to the tasks that need to be accomplished, the entire group suffers. Since much of my work is with individuals and families in recovery from some form of addiction, understanding the mutuality of support is critical. It is one thing to talk about relying on the support of others, and being responsible to (as opposed to responsible for) others; it's quite another to get up in the cold morning air to start the stoves, fetch water, and begin breakfast as a critical contribution to the community. The nature of living together, participant and social worker, facing the same obstacles, opens up new frontiers for exploration.

After breakfast, the group cleans up, packs up, and prepares for the day's activity. Today it is rock climbing. Yesterday we engaged in some problem-solving activities, some trust building activities, and a high ropes course. Tomorrow we have a peak climb planned. On a longer course, there may be many days of backpacking, including climbing high passes, fording rivers, and traveling off trail. However, on a four-day course, we often engage the participants in rock climbing on the second day, because of the dramatic nature of the activity.

There are two major components to rock climbing—the technical skills and the process. Therapeutically, I am interested in both. The technical skills enable participants to become fully involved in the activity. They must learn how to "belay," a term that means to hold. Each participant will be asked to belay another, to literally hold another person's life in his hands. Participants learn the skills of belaying and practice on the ground before they have to use the skills on the rock. This is a perfect metaphor for the course and therapy in general. The participant is provided an opportunity to practice new behaviors and new ways of approaching old problems in the relative safety of our program. By learning belaying, participants are also able to feel a sense of mastery and accomplishment in learning a new skill that will be directly relevant to their lives. Though this relevance is short-term (most will not continue to rock climb), it provides an excellent example of mastering a task, just like tasks in recovery must be mastered.

Once the skills of belaying are mastered, we head to the rock face. But before we climb, we set the stage, or frame the event, and help establish an isomorphic link for the participants between the climbing and their recovery. This is the process of the activity. I share with the participants that climbing is not so much about getting to the top, but is more about how you get to the top. The rock is waiting to provide you with lessons about how you approach obstacles in your life. Do you hug the rock, limiting your vision, your options, your choices; or do you attempt to lean back and increase your vision? Do you engage in the activity in isolation, by yourself, seeking to get it done as quickly as possible; or do you ask for support from others, enjoying the experience? The rock, like life, does not care what you do, and how you do it; but your experience of the rock will be different depending on how you approach it and work with it. The participants' experiences of the rock usually have implications for their recovery, in reflecting how they are approaching their recovery.

As the participants climb, each has lessons to learn, struggles to encounter. Some participants rely on others, others battle the rock; some are hesitant to try, others are more eager. My job is to help them process the experience and explore the opportunities fully. For those reluctant to try, I work with them, attempting to help them make choices that are actual choices, rather than ones based on default. For example, one person is refusing to climb because he is afraid. In exploring the fear, we discover it is not a fear of height or a fear of falling, but rather a fear of not succeeding. For this person, it is better not to try than to try and not succeed. We talk about the implications for recovery, about the implication of this choice, and about what the worst thing that could happen would be. After some discussion, soul searching, and consultation with fellow participants, the participant decides to attempt a climb. It's not really important if they summit or not, but it is important that they discover something new about approaching fear.

The day is long, and what started out as a cold day has turned into a blistering hot afternoon. I run around the cliff checking the safety systems, watching the participants belay, consulting with other staff, and not least of all paying attention to participants' therapeutic goals. Every part of the day holds potential lessons for the participants. As the belayers, what do they experience holding another person's life in their hands? As the climbers, what can they learn about dealing with challenge, with obstacles, with unforeseen circumstances? As some are not "actively" involved, what do they do to support others, what do they do when they are not the center of attention? My job is to provide the opportunity for each participant to be conscious of the lessons presented throughout the day and to relate their personal treatment goals to the day's activity, or to help them stay alert to the opportunities to work on a treatment goal.

Often, participants come with treatment goals related to asking for help, focusing on their own goals and not others, dealing with anger appropriately, or any number of other goals. The true power of adventure-based practice is helping participants work on these goals through the activities, not through simply talking about them. In recovery work and Outward Bound, we are fond of the expression "walking your talk," which is really about doing what you say you want to or are doing. The experiential nature of adventure-based practice challenges participants to walk their talk, to follow through with what they have said they want to or need to do. Treatment goals become concrete experiences that they can take with them in their recovery.

We head to camp, but the day is far from over. There is dinner to prepare. It takes effort to accomplish those things necessary for the community when everyone is tired and would simply like to sleep. The effort required is not like the effort required for recovery; making dinner is a necessity. The challenge for participants becomes how to use this experience as a beneficial part of recovery. Some of the most profound conversations between participants happen while cooking dinner or doing the dishes afterwards. As some participants prepare dinner, the staff members gather to plan the evening group. Group will be a formal time to integrate the lessons from the day, to give participants a chance to share and work through concerns from the day, and for the group to plan for tomorrow's adventure.

After dinner and clean-up, we gather for group. The participants share their experiences, their frustrations, the lessons they are taking away from the day, and what they hope for tomorrow. Some of the participants express satisfaction with the day; others wish they had done something different. Some make clear connections to their recovery; others see no relevance. The group is challenged to work with the material that comes up in the group and to help each other make connections with recovery. I also work to help the participants make connections and engage with each other. Often, I challenge participants with an observation from the day or a comment they made earlier, or invite a fellow participant to challenge a peer. Group is an opportunity to take care of the business of the community as well. Who will cook breakfast? Who will get water?

As the group winds down, it is nearing 10 p.m. I still have progress notes to write and sleep to catch before the sun rises again tomorrow. It's not like other work where you get to go home in the evening, to family and friends. You are with the clients 24 hours a day. It's been a full day; one with unexpected surprises in the lessons learned by both participants and staff. I've seen participants challenge themselves and their perceptions of themselves. I've seen acts of courage and compassion as members have worked to help each other. I've also seen participants shirk away from responsibility, choose not to be honest, fall into old negative patterns of behavior. Part of the beauty of this work is that there is always tomorrow.

I was first attracted to this type of work by an article by Janice Kaplan, which suggested that Outward Bound was a treatment modality unexplored by the social work profession. I later came to the Colorado Outward Bound School in part because of another article written by a social worker, Nelson Chase, who had founded the Health Services Program at the Colorado Outward Bound School. In the 14 years I've worked in adventure-based programs, I've met numerous social workers doing this type of work. One of the professional associations I'm active in, the Association for Experiential Education, has a professional group called Therapeutic Adventure, to which social workers belong. Social workers have considered adventure-based practice, though it probably remains relatively unknown as a specific area of practice.

Outward Bound is the most well-known adventure-based program, but not all adventure-based programs are Outward Bound. In fact, most adventure-based programs now are less wilderness-based and actually often occur in an urban environment. The most common form of adventure-based practice usually involves what is termed a ropes course (a series of obstacles suspended by cables in the air), problem solving initiatives, and trust activities on the ground. This form of adventure-based practice can be conducted at a treatment center, a school, or local community center. The advantage of this type of adventure-based practice is that the social worker can return home after work, and usually is paid a salary commensurate with other standard treatment personnel in the agency. In wilderness programs, staff are often paid a much lower salary than others with similar responsibilities in a treatment context.

The social worker looking to get involved in adventure-based practice can often work in conjunction with someone who has the technical skills to conduct the activities (though I strongly encourage social workers to develop the skills necessary to conduct the activities, as it makes the practice more integrated). There are numerous avenues for gaining the training necessary to facilitate the process of adventure-based practice. Unfortunately, most are not formally recognized within social work education.

I invite social workers to consider adventure-based practice. It is a form of practice I've found invaluable in working with adults and adolescents, men and women, those dealing with addictions, and those who are survivors of violence, as a means of bringing communities together and as a means of organizational change. I have found my professional education in social work to be invaluable in conceptualizing adventure-based practice. Adventure-based practice requires a blending of individual and group practice skills, an understanding of community and organizations, and an ability to act as a manager and administrator. My education focused on an advanced generalist perspective with an emphasis on integrated practice. This base has served me well as I have developed professional competency in adventure-based practice.

Think About It

1. What is meant by a "community" approach, and how does it help clients?

2. What privacy/boundary issues might come up in a setting, such as this one, where the social worker spends 24 hours a day with clients?

Chapter 30
A Very Special Nursing Home in the South Bronx

‖‖

by Kim R. Lorber, CSW, MSW

Each morning, I travel to a nursing home in the South Bronx. This is a unique setting for people with AIDS who are in recovery from substance addiction. Treatment is offered by an interdisciplinary team comprised of a permanent staff of social workers, doctors, nurses, a dietitian, substance abuse counselors, case managers, recreational therapists, an education department, and a bevy of consultants. Interdepartmental relationships are strong, reinforcing effective team treatment for residents while also modeling cooperativeness and mutual affection. Improvements in medical treatment have changed the direction of practice from sobriety for limited survival of residents to a skills-building program for the vast majority, who will graduate to live in society.

I am buzzed into the facility and receive the smiles and greetings of those residents whose responsibility it is to monitor the "front point" and document the goings and comings of their peers. Some I know better than others from our work together in groups or individual therapy; most I know fairly well from our initial psychosocial assessment interview. I marvel at the growth they have accomplished in only a few months.

Residents range in age from their early 20s to late 60s. Many grew up in the foster care system and are survivors of physical, emotional, and sexual abuse. The majority are African American or Hispanic. Most have not finished high school. Some have never worked. All have little self-esteem and belief in their own abilities to change. Most are mandated to the home by a legal agency as an

219

alternative to incarceration. Often, the date of arrival is their first time substance free. Over time, the symptoms from withdrawal will wane, but it is not a fast or easy process.

Our program requires abstinence and promotes recovery, a change of behaviors, attitudes, and perceptions. It has a three-phase structure. Orientation lasts for approximately three months, during which residents participate in in-house activities and develop cohesiveness as a supportive group. Primary Care is a 4- to 6-month phase during which residents begin to attend appointments and recreational outings unescorted. Re-Entry is the third and final phase, requiring completion of an 8-week discharge planning group, which I co-facilitate. Upon completion, mandating agencies will be notified that residents have completed the program and are ready to return to the community.

They will now begin to look for housing, a process that can take two or more months through the Division of AIDS Services (DAS). Their support systems, including family, support groups, Narcotics Anonymous or Alcoholics Anonymous meetings, medical care, individual therapy, and a food pantry, must be in place. Registration with a local agency offering case management and many of these services is essential. These networks will replace the support inherent in our structured program and are coordinated through the social work department.

I check the marker board in the clinic to see who is on bed rest. A review of the "House Changes" clipboard notes Debbie's hospital admission. I call the hospital to find out Debbie's room and telephone numbers. I fax a request to hook up her television and then call her. This is her fifth stay in as many months. She is in pain, lonely, and feeling isolated. Debbie tells me about toiletries and clothing she needs and asks me to contact her brother in New Jersey. She earlier signed a consent form permitting me to speak with her family as needed. Her brother is not at work, and the home number Debbie gave me is incorrect. With her permission, I contact her mother, who knows very little about AIDS. She is concerned about her daughter's treatment and cannot understand why Debbie continues to be plagued by various serious illnesses. I remind her that Debbie's vulnerability is due to her compromised immune system, and that Debbie has returned "home" to our facility feeling better following each hospitalization. Debbie's mother tells me she will kill herself if Debbie dies. I listen, appreciating her worry. There is little more I can say. I offer Debbie's telephone number, but she hesitates. "I live on a fixed Social Security income. I can't afford to call," she says. I suggest taking it for Debbie's brother or daughter. She accepts and thanks me for calling. I call Debbie to let her know I reached her mother, but I do not tell her it is unlikely she will hear from her. I am relieved to learn later that she has called, after all. Debbie hopes for a reunion with her family but, after 25 years of heroin addiction and abandoning her six children, their support has been minimal. I contact our substance abuse department and relate Debbie's supply request.

Rachel arrives eager to know if I have heard anything from her lawyer, who has left me angry voicemail messages. Rachel is also a mother of six, all boys, who have been raised by others for most of their lives. She is eager to appeal the termination of her parental rights (TPR) and to gain custody of her 2-year-old son. I have written to the judge and her lawyer and left several messages on the latter's voicemail asking about the status of the appeal process. We are waiting to receive papers for Rachel's signature to be submitted to court. A new attorney will be assigned for this phase. Rachel is eager to "have my baby back." She has seen Richard once in almost two years; he has lived since birth with a foster care family eager to adopt him, as they have his three older brothers. I feel conflicted between my professional responsibilities to help Rachel in her self-determination efforts and my personal preference to leave the child with his brothers and the only family he has ever known. I remind Rachel she should be patient and that she is doing everything she can, having begun a Parenting Skills Class run by the Administration for Children's Services (ACS) and my in-house Parenting Support Group. She has been drug-free for nine months. I forewarn her that ACS is concerned with Richard's well-being. Rachel leaves and I jot a note, which I will transcribe later into her chart, regarding the progress of her case and our latest efforts on her behalf.

Mitchell needs a letter to help his 18-year-old daughter and her baby find housing. They live in a shelter and lived with him prior to his readmission to our facility. I document his current status, date of admission, and the dates of his admission and discharge during his previous stay.

Lawrence wants to vote in today's primary elections. He has been in the program for a week. I advise him to speak with his counselor to arrange for an escort. Residents are not permitted to leave the facility within the first 30 days of admission, with the exception of legal and medical appointments. Later, Lawrence tells me he has decided not to vote. Meanwhile, I have called the Voter Registration hotline to order forms for other residents.

At 10 a.m., I co-facilitate the Re-Entry discharge group with my office mate. We begin with a review of the importance of keeping a schedule. We solicit updates about the clients' developing outside support networks and distribute calendars for the coming week. I remind them that half of our discharged graduates have relapsed when they lacked outside support. We review the changes they will find from living within an institutional environment to independent apartment life. I remind them of their complicated medication regimens, which most still have dispensed to them throughout the day. Some residents take 40 or more pills daily. They are encouraged to seek self-medication status so they can become familiar with this responsibility before they are also required to shop for groceries, cook, and have meals ready.

Residents typically are excited to be phase-advanced to Re-Entry and see that as the time to find an apartment and "get out." They are eager to be independent, feel good about having been clean for approximately seven or more months, and are tired of living in a structured environment offering little privacy. While their frustrations are understandable, it is the purpose of this group to help them prepare for independent living. Some will have their own apartments. Others will wait for a city-furnished scattered site apartment. They are encouraged to begin going independently on recreational outings. Sometimes we are forceful in our comparison of what they are doing versus what they say they will do once they have moved. Those who think they will join groups and go to movies later when they haven't during their time with us, probably won't. We conclude with a discussion of reestablishing family ties, and residents candidly discuss their family histories, shame of having lied and stolen from their relatives, repeated attempts to be forgiven, and what often feels like final rejection. They are encouraged to be patient with others with whom they need to renegotiate relationships. They are reminded of the importance of focusing on their own recovery and goals, to avoid bad feelings that might trigger a relapse.

I next meet with Michael, a poetic, sensitive man who enjoys writing, reading, and classical music. He is a member of my Creative Writing Group. We periodically meet to discuss literature or something Michael has written. Today he is tired from an unrelenting bout of pneumonia, and he offers me a poem he has written. I accept it gladly and assure him I will read it soon. I do not make any effort to edit or critique his work; I will share with him the parts I understood and enjoyed best and compare it to other things he has written or we have both read. This is a lovely break before lunch.

During lunch in our cafeteria, Elsa approaches me. I make an afternoon appointment around therapy and group commitments. After lunch, I check my voicemail messages. Elsa arrives eager to know if I have communicated with the foster care agency about her scheduled child visits and next court date. Elsa's son Johnnie is five years old; she left him with his father three years ago. Johnnie entered the foster care system one year later, after his father abandoned him, and has been living with the woman he knows as "Mommy." Elsa is mandated to our program and arrived newly "clean." She located Johnnie with the help of our family social worker. I began to work with her and arranged a visitation schedule with the monitoring agency, one hour every two weeks. The agency had been ordered by the judge to begin the process of terminating Elsa's parental rights, which they postponed with her reappearance. At her request, I arranged for her to attend an ACS Parenting Skills Class and my in-house Parenting Support Group. She completed and received certificates for both. Elsa is currently in the frustrating situation of waiting for the next court hearing, in two weeks. The last one, two weeks ago, brought some surprising results. The supervising agency and the foster mother are eager for the eventual reunification of Elsa and Johnnie. The caseworker, eager to present to the judge this rehabilitating mother and documentation supporting her success, was instead held in contempt of court for not having begun the previously requested TPR process. She is to return with her own attorney. The judge has also ordered that Johnnie be moved to a preadoptive home, in order to become eligible for adoption sooner. Elsa is understandably distressed. I assure her we will find her an attorney to arrange adequate representation. I give her a referral slip to the Bronx Family Court, where she can request to see the court record and find out her attorney's name. Elsa is most concerned about Johnnie being uprooted while she pursues custody. She is waiting for news from the supervising agency but knows little will happen before the next court date.

Jennifer arrives for individual therapy. Her boyfriend has been discharged and did not leave any contact information. She is very sad, certain he will live with his son's mother and that their relationship is over. While relationships are discouraged within our environment in order to prevent distractions and other "addictions" during the recovery process, they happen regularly. She is the House Coordinator, the highest level within the residential structure, overseeing all resident responsibilities. Jennifer wants to be alone now and discusses how to negotiate some privacy while she deals with her feelings. We discuss how she will be able to do this now and later when she is working and having her daughter, temporarily in kinship foster care, living with her again. She is overwhelmed by the thought of these responsibilities. We focus on developing her outside support system and discuss her frustrations in securing an apartment. She is articulate and insightful and we reflect on her ongoing growth. I encourage her to continue attending her codependency and stress management groups, and we hug at the end of her session.

I return to my office and check my voicemail. There is a message about a lease for a resident to sign and take to her DAS worker. I call the front desk and, learning she is out of the facility, leave a note for her with the pertinent information and a referral slip so she can get a pass for tomorrow. I have checked the DAS worker's availability and the resident's schedule for any conflicting legal or medical appointments.

It is 3:00 p.m. and time to prepare for my Parenting Support Group. This 8-week certificate group allows residents the unique opportunity of being validated as parents by discussing their experiences. Most have not raised their own children or have done so while using substances. The process of recovery includes reconciliation with family whenever possible. Painful memories and current confrontations can make this especially difficult with children. We focus on familial patterns and how the clients as parents are watching their grandchildren being raised as they were raised themselves, and as they raised their children prior to separation. They have genuine concerns about understanding the cycle and how they can create change in their own lives and those of their loved ones. Rachel does not come. Gloria cries as she shares her amazement at the evolution in her relationship with her two daughters. She came to the facility angry that her 14-year-old daughter had told her school social worker 10 years earlier about Gloria's drug use, which resulted in her children's removal from her home into the foster care system. Gloria was unable to look at her own responsibility until a recent relapse, during treatment, which helped her to focus on her need to grow and become a role model for her daughters. Their relationships have improved significantly.

Group is over at 4:15 p.m. I go to the clinic to complete my chart notes. I am ready for my last meeting, an interdepartmental daily review at 4:30 p.m. with the substance abuse team. There are no significant resident problems to discuss, and I head back to Manhattan at 5:00 p.m.

Think About It

1. How does Kim's work with HIV patients differ from Michael's work in Chapter 8?

2. In the case of Rachel, what ethical dilemma exists?

PART 6:
PRIVATE PRACTICE

Chapter 31
Private Practice and the Eclectic Social Worker

IIIIIIIIIIIIIIIIIIIIIIIIIIIIIIIIIIIIIIIIIIIIIIIIIIIIIIIIIIIIIIIIIIIIIIIIIIIIIIIIIIIIIIIIIIIIIIIIIIIIIIIIIIIIIIIIIII

by Diane Rullo-Cooney, MA, MSW, LCSW, CADC

Private practice in social work creates an array of emotion from excitement to fear. An understanding of the week of a private practitioner takes you from seeing individual patients in a private office to standing in front of sixty students teaching the ideals of social work practice. This story is a journey through thirty years of accomplishing the dream to be a SOCIAL WORKER.

In identifying my role as a social worker today, I must start more than twenty-five years ago. Somehow, in my early adolescence, I knew the phrase "social worker" but had no concept of the meaning of that role. When I was thirteen and someone asked what my future goals were in life, I would respond, "I want to be a social worker," not understanding exactly what that meant. I held onto my dream many years before it came to fruition.

Life, as tumultuous as it is, did not take me directly onto an educational track. Like so many others in my family and social circle, I went to work full time after my high school graduation. At nineteen, I was promoted to a manager's position, but I wasn't fulfilled. I might have had a strong future in business, but I knew this was not a perfect fit. I enrolled in evening classes at a local college. Surprising myself, I did well. I became even less satisfied in my employment and changed jobs to become a sales representative, thinking this was the answer to my happiness.

It wasn't. I envied my colleagues at sales meetings who appeared more sophisticated and confident. I decided that one major difference between myself and the rest of the sales force was a college degree. I made one of the biggest decisions of my life, quit work, and returned to school full time.

I was naïve about the educational system, and unaware there were specific programs for social workers, so I entered a psychology program. Perseverance paid off. I received my undergraduate degree in psychology in two and a half years. During this time, I was required to do field work, which led me into the working world of being a clinician. I volunteered as a peer counselor and later in a grass roots community counseling center that had recently opened. My supervisor at the community counseling center was attending school for her master's degree in social work, which awakened me to the specialization of social work.

Still, I returned to school and obtained my Master of Arts in counseling. I was employed as a mental health clinician, substance abuse counselor, and a clinical supervisor in addiction services. I worked for years in the mental health field, not fulfilling my original goal of becoming a "social worker."

Twelve years after I originally returned to college, I entered an MSW program. Working full time, I entered a full-time Saturday program and completed my second master's degree. I had finally achieved my goal. I was now officially a SOCIAL WORKER.

Over the years, I worked in hospitals, community agencies, family agencies, and free-standing programs. Looking for autonomy, I decided to venture out into private practice. I am a clinical social worker. Conducting individual, group, and family therapy is my love, my destiny. I consider my work fun, not torturous. When I wake up in the morning, I do not dread the work day. The excitement persists because I have managed to make my job eclectic. I assume many different functions in one week. The following is a composite of the roles I undertake during a week's time.

My major role is that of a private practitioner. Having a private practice is a double-edged sword. I have autonomy. I do not have a supervisor or administrator monitoring me. My evaluations are based upon the return of my patients to my practice, and the ongoing referrals. (NOTE: The field of social work identifies individuals as "clients." I use the word "patient" to emphasize the importance of the situation [as one is viewed when seeking treatment from a physician] and to establish the validity of mental health treatment.

I believe patient eliminates a moralistic and value laden focus on the individual.) It is exciting to be able to, as I put it, "run my own show." All decisions are mine alone. I schedule appointments when I choose. I decide when I want to work or relax. Flexibility is my nature. I keep my work week open seven days. This gives me the advantage to block off time any day of the week and still be available for patients.

Looking at the other side, private practice is frightening. The economy and health care benefits play a role in the income I receive. If the economy is experiencing a recession, mental health treatment is not a priority. Individuals will not spend money on a "luxury" such as therapy unless they are completely decompensated. Managed care companies and insurance companies determine fees. As a private practitioner who accepts insurance, I am at the mercy of the health care system to determine my income. There are no employer-paid benefits in private practice. I do not get paid vacations, sick days, health insurance, or a retirement plan. When I choose to go on vacation, I need to make sure I have covered myself financially for the month.

My day starts by checking to see if I received any messages. I return emergency calls from home. I have an additional telephone line in my home, on which I keep the ringer off. This line is solely to return calls, protecting myself from caller IDs and anyone getting my personal number. As I drive to the office, I think about my schedule and the patients I am to see today. This includes reviewing last week's session for each patient and assessing the therapeutic treatment plan. I try to make an effort to identify any transference and countertransference issues that may have arisen.

Private practice is a business as well as a community service. While my goal as a social worker is to help patients change unwanted behavior, I must be aware of the need to keep the business financially stable. There is always a concern about patients canceling appointments, which reduces my weekly income. Some private practitioners choose to charge for missed appointments. I have a theory about cancellations and patients not showing up for their scheduled appointments. When individuals have a mental illness, it affects all parts of their lives. I do not believe in penalizing a patient for his or her pathology. Missed or canceled appointments are a result of the person's pathology, and as a clinician I need to resolve this with the patient. Balancing the fear of reduced income and understanding the patient's pathology is a process I have successfully undertaken.

The element of worry about cancellations subsides quickly as I pull into my office complex. Upon entering my office, I once again check to see if I have messages. Private practitioners must continuously review calls for patient emergencies and new referrals. The core of our business is new referrals. When a call comes in, the successful clinician returns the call as soon as possible. This is how to build a business. Additionally, as a sole proprietor, I don't have someone else covering emergencies, so the telephone system becomes an important tool. Some added expenses to being in private practice are having a pager and a cell phone. When my patients have emergencies, I am available. Luckily, emergencies do not happen very often.

I wait for my first appointment. My appointments are scheduled for fifty minutes. This leaves ten minutes to regroup for the next patient. My fees are on a sliding scale basis, and I accept insurance. Establishing fees and collecting money are two of the hardest things for me to do. Social workers have been indoctrinated to think of their work as a community service requiring little to no payment for the work accomplished. Social workers often feel guilty about accepting payment for treatment. Society, including social workers, believes social work is a job requiring little compensation. This is detrimental to our profession. We are highly trained and highly skilled. By charging an appropriate fee per session, we are able to accommodate the patient's needs in a private office setting, while validating our accomplishments. As entrepreneurs, our business is one of helping others.

Private practitioners are unable to receive immediate gratification in discussing a case with colleagues. When a session is difficult, there is no other clinician around. The responsibility of this person's treatment is solely in my hands, combining a sense of power and fear. It is helpful for private practitioners to build support networks, connecting with colleagues for case discussion. This reduces the isolation.

A priority for the private practitioner is to establish a billing system. I have set up my computer with a small business software package to monitor patient billing and outstanding fees. I put time aside weekly to input data about sessions for the past week. I send invoices out two times per month to insurance companies, to keep a regular flow of income.

After seeing patients in the morning, I go to the university to perform my role as an adjunct professor. I enjoy academia, both learning and teaching. One of the most productive ways I have found to become proficient in an area of social work is to teach in that area. Students are challenging. I must be at least one step ahead of the students and have a solid understanding of my ideas to be able to relay the information.

I derive satisfaction from watching students integrate the information into their training. The role of adjunct professor is time-consuming. Preparation for a class takes between two and five hours per week. I read the material, take notes, and decide what information to put forth to the students. Highlighting the important aspects of a topic and giving examples are part of the preparation. Bringing in other citations and philosophies will encourage students to expand their research. This is a continual process of new learning for me.

Deciding on how to grade the course and what type of system to use, then making up tests or reading papers, takes several hours. Balancing a private practice with hours for preparation and review is difficult. During a semester, I do not consider my time to be my own. Every minute of the day is taken for some task to be done. Students also want time to talk to the professor. I receive calls in my office about papers and tests. The role of adjunct professor is not just the three hours I am in the classroom. I teach three classes a semester, which totals about seventy students per semester. I had to learn to manage my time appropriately to complete all tasks efficiently.

An additional role I have is one of instructor. I teach one-day to five-day workshops. Preparation for this includes making an outline and copies of all handouts to be sent to the facility. The time to prepare for workshops is done months in advance of the presentation. When the actual event comes close, only review is needed.

Moving on further in my week, I do administrative work for the continuing education department at the university. I develop workshops for clinicians who are Family Preservation Service (FPS) workers. FPS is a short-term, intensive in-home program that teaches families skills to prevent the unnecessary placement of children outside of the home. My role here is to conceptualize the training needs of the workers, locate instructors who are experts in that area, and arrange for a training site for each workshop. I then develop the brochure and prepare it for print.

This work really is seasonal. The main functions are done during the summer for the Fall semester and in January for the Spring semester. The remaining months consist of gathering statistics, writing up the quarterly reports, and monitoring workshops. This job balances out with being an adjunct professor. The time-consuming part is during the summer when classes are not in session, unless I take a summer teaching position.

The last role that I take on is the role of student. I am currently attending school full time for my Ph.D. I would like a future in academia, and that is not possible without a doctorate. My classes fit into one full day, and when I return home, I go back to my office to see patients. Time needs to be put aside at some point within the week to do readings, research articles, or write papers. I find myself with a book, paper, or laptop computer at meals. I have found my laptop to be one of the most functional pieces of equipment to have with my lifestyle.

My various roles all have a function. Private practice never guarantees an income. I am more secure with a safety net. Private practice is my first desire, but I gain more security by having positions with a regular income. My goal is to obtain a full-time position as a professor and to maintain my private practice. Obtaining my doctorate and teaching at a university are steps toward that goal. I also have the personality of one who likes diversity. Keeping my professional lifestyle active contributes to my enjoying every minute of my work.

Think About It

1. Rullo-Cooney uses the term "patients." Other social workers use "clients," "participants," "consumers," and other terms. What does each term connote to you? How will you decide what you will call the people you work with?

2. Rullo-Cooney has several different jobs. How would you like an eclectic career such as this?

Chapter 32

An Office to Call My Own: Private Practice in the Lesbian Community

|||||||||||||||||||||||||||||||||||||||||||||||||||||||||||||||||||||||||||||||||||||||||||||||||||||||||||||||||

by Amy Blake, MSW, CSW, ACSW

On the day I walked away from the "real world" of my profession, I felt as if I had just launched myself into outer space with no way back. Leaving a hospital-based program for survivors of sexual trauma was not easy for me. I had an illusion of security there in a regular paycheck and benefits. My disagreements with the administration; the fact that my program was dissolved; and a growing awareness that that environment was killing me emotionally, physically, and spiritually brought me to a crossroad. I took a leap of faith to become self-employed in work I care about, which is helping people heal. In my dreams of private practice, I longed for the freedom but never counted on the depth to which I would have to draw on my inner strength and resources. I battle the incessant voice of doom and despair that tells me I cannot do what I am doing, that I should get a "real job" and put to rest this silly notion that I can make it on my own. Never mind that I have been able to support myself.

Being diagnosed with Chronic Fatigue Syndrome has given me pause to reflect and act on my ideals of health and well-being. Private practice has helped to hold me accountable to my ideals. The more I take care of myself, the more able I am to be present for my clients. I have had to adjust to the need for mid-day naps, no super late hours (which, unfortunately, is when most clients need appointments), time for cooking good food, and time for my meditation practice along with yoga and Tai Chi. Some days, taking care of myself is my full-time job. I have thankfully beaten back the fear of not being able to take care of myself, and I have recovered a great deal of my energy.

I chose the world of private practice after seven years of psychiatric hospital work and a stint, which felt like a lifetime, in the geriatric division of a university medical school residency program. I also had the good fortune to experience teaching at the university level in Women's Studies. I currently work with individuals, couples, and groups for lesbian and bisexual women survivors of childhood sexual abuse. The focus of my counseling work has been healing from abuse and trauma.

As it turns out, my work is the polar opposite of my major area of study in social work school. I studied Social Policy and Planning and received a Certificate in Gerontology. One of the things I love about being a social worker is how fluid the movement can be from one aspect of social work to another. All roads can lead us to exactly where we need to be in our work and in our lives. I have found it so unfortunate and aggravating in interviews when my background was viewed as a limitation rather than a source of information and a different perspective.

My social work education prepared me to be in the trenches with people's pain. Social work school taught me about opportunities in life and about being an active participant and change agent in my own life. Being in the trenches has to be a choice. I have to want to be there and I have to be able to be present with my client's process. To do this, I have to know that I do not have to, that I have a choice to do something different.

Education aside, it was my personal healing journey that led me to clinical work and eventually private practice. Once I began experiencing the healing power of therapy, I knew I could help others. I draw deeply on the success of my own healing process when I am struggling in the face of a client's hopelessness and pain. I am not convinced that that kind of experiential knowing can be taught. The advanced training that I have found most beneficial has been that which challenges me to grow as a person and as a therapist. So far, I have been fortunate to find such an environment for personal and professional growth in a Grove Metaphor Therapy Training and consultation and currently in an IMAGO Relationship Therapy Training.

The private practice teeter-totter plays independence and isolation against one another. Having my own office and setting my own schedule is appealing—I get to work any twelve hours of the day that I choose! Hearing about people's pain and trauma can skew my view of humanity, especially if I am not careful to find a balance in my life. There is no more walking down the hall for collegial companionship. Lunches, peer supervision, and networking all need to be arranged more formally. It is very easy to become unbalanced when the last thing I want at the end of the day is to talk to people, but it is exactly what I need to challenge the day's experience of senseless violence. To battle the isolation, I talk with other therapists, and I helped to start a gay and lesbian therapists' networking group in my area.

I happen to like the slower pace and the quiet of my office. I have been able to create a space for healing, and clients and others who visit my office comment that they feel safe and they can really talk there. I am sure it is not because of my rag-tag and borrowed furnishings I've picked up along the way, although they do add a certain atmosphere.

"Hi, I got your name from the Gay and Lesbian Hotline. Do you charge for counseling?" the voice on the phone asks.

The financial instability of private practice is a struggle. Putting a dollar amount on my worth as a therapist and asking people to pay it is an evolving process. I generally do not work with insurance. I believe that there will always be room for high quality, confidential therapy. I have managed to keep myself out of the managed care crisis and I hope to keep it that way. Seeing clients who pay out-of-pocket creates other issues.

I work most directly with the lesbian community, and the community seems to have a love/hate relationship with therapists and therapy. At times, fees can be a major issue, and I am confronted with an expectation that my service to the community should not come with a price tag or it should be greatly reduced. My gay male colleagues do not face this same issue. To me, it is an ingrained piece of sexism where it is hard to pay a woman for emotional support, because of an expectation that it be given freely. It is a challenge to negotiate the financial rules of therapy. I have to remind myself that my sick days, vacation days, and insurance benefits come directly from the work I do and not from some company. On the other hand, I have also had the experience of having a client, who pays a low fee, decide to give me a raise because she appreciated the work she was able to do.

"Oh, you own the women's bookstore? I tried dating the other woman there and she said, 'No,' " a woman tells me.

The "other woman" at the bookstore is my life partner and business partner. We decided our town needed a feminist, lesbian and gay bookstore, so we set about creating A Woman's Prerogative Bookstore. I saw it as a great way to focus my social work on the positive aspects of community building. It is another way for me to balance the pain and trauma side of my work. People come into the store and find themselves in ways they never expected, whether that is a growing feminist consciousness or coming to accept their gay or lesbian identity. I also get to see how there are many paths to growth and healing.

I am actively involved socially and politically in the community I serve, which poses some interesting boundary challenges. On a busy Saturday, I may see a client in group, ring up her purchase at the bookstore, and end up being seated very near her at the women's coffee house that evening. My house, my office, and my bookstore are all located within a quarter mile. I thank my lucky stars that I have a love relationship that precedes my arrival in the metro-Detroit women's community. I cannot fathom dating in such a fishbowl. Boundaries tend to be a rather frequent topic in my sessions, as well as with my peers. The tough part for me is the battle I feel around the need to assert my right to have my life and the feelings of constriction I experience when I run into a client socially. I think this setup, although not ideal, can be powerful and growth-producing when handled with extreme care and when the power dynamics are acknowledged and kept in check.

The best part about the life I've created as a social worker is that I like the foundation I have established. I get to live my life according to my values, and when I go to work and hate my boss, I have a major say so in how things change and get resolved.

Think About It

1. Amy Blake specialized in one area in school but works in a different area. Think about the possibilities of this happening. Why/how is this possible?

2. What do you see as the pros and cons of being in private practice?

3. What boundary challenges does Amy face?

PART 7:
CRIMINAL JUSTICE

Chapter 33
Social Work in a Police Department

||||||||||||||||||||||||||||||||||||||||||||||||||||||||||||||||||||||||||||||||||||||||||||||||||||||||||||||||||||||||||||||

by Claire McCullough Godfrey, LCSW

I place my badge against the lockbox, and the gates of the parking garage begin to slowly squeak open. I have arrived for my overnight shift at the Police Department Main Headquarters, and after squeezing into a spot between two huge F250s that could eat my Subaru for breakfast, I dash inside the station to grab my gear. Police radio, cell phone, and car keys in hand, I head out to find my work car for the night.

By the time I get to the car, I am sweating. It is August in Texas, and the black pavement of the garage has been soaking up blistering rays for months now. Even though the sun is setting, the heat index is 105 degrees, and I know I will be sweating for most of my shift. I begin the process of logging on to the computer that is docked on the car's dashboard, when flashing lights of blue and red momentarily blind me. I look up to see that a patrol officer next to me is also starting his shift. I watch and listen as he tests his lights, his siren, and the PA system. He slowly circles his vehicle, checking that all is in order. His Taser buzzes as he tests the charge, and his shotgun snaps back as he checks its functionality. These are the sounds of the start of my day.

I proceed to do my own vehicle inspection. This car is my office, and I will spend most of my shift driving from crime scene to crime scene providing crisis counseling and support to victims of crime, their family members, and other people who have experienced tragedy. The Victim Services Division of the police department employs 37 counselors, most of whom are clinical social workers, and all of whom have their master's degrees in mental health oriented fields. Some of the counselors work in the investigative units, carry caseloads, and support victims throughout the investigative process. Others, like me, respond directly to crime scenes and provide one-time clinical interventions.

I check my supplies, verifying that everything is present—five car seats of varying sizes, water bottles and snacks, toys and coloring books, bug spray, diapers from preemies to pull-ups, blankets, two soccer balls, a bright yellow vest, 911 cell phones, and a variety of pamphlets on area resources. These are my work tools for the night.

On the computer, I quickly scan all of the scenes that officers are currently working. Another counselor (there are three of us logged on at the moment) tells me there is a call holding in the north sector of the city. I cue up on the radio and take the call. Dispatch chirps up "10-4, Crisis22, I have you 76 to 134 Lions Drive for a Check Welfare Urgent." "10-76," I say. I'm on my way. Check Welfare does not tell me much. It means the 911 caller is concerned about something—usually a person they have not heard from in a while. I check the computer, and sure enough, the caller has not heard from his brother in two days. The missing brother's car is outside, but he is not answering the door, and the deadbolt is engaged.

I start driving and continue to listen to the radio traffic while en route. The officer on scene asks dispatch to have the homicide detective call him, and I can hear screaming in the background of the radio traffic. The missing brother is dead. I know already, and I prepare mentally for the call and all the stages of grief accompanied by frustration, shock, devastation, and heat—it is still hot, and we will be outside for hours. After the sun sets, the heat radiates from the ground instead of the sky. Sticky and enveloping.

I pull up in front of the house to an array of flashing lights and emergency personnel. Two EMS ambulances, an EMS commander truck, a fire engine, and four squad cars. The sun has now set, and I can see the outlines of others, non-uniformed and hunched over on the ground. That must be the family. "Crisis22, I'm 10-23."

An officer approaches and gives me the rundown. The missing brother (Dominic) is dead. He is lying in his bed with no apparent trauma and no visible cause of death. The officer continues, "He just got out of rehab last week. We haven't searched the house, but this may be an overdose. Oh, and his girlfriend is here, too. She's also dead in the bed."

I am surprised to hear this, and my brain is churning. Homicide/suicide? Suicide pact? The officer knows what I am thinking. He says he is confused, too, and the homicide detective is on her way. The officer introduces me to the family. The surviving brother, his parents, and assorted other family and friends talk to me about Dominic—his life, their love for him, and their confusion about who the girlfriend is and why she is also dead. The mom is struggling to take it all in and asks me repeatedly if he is really dead. "He is dead," I say, clearly and compassionately. It hits her like she is hearing it for the first time, and her family huddles around her.

I make my rounds and meet with as many of the family and friends as I can. They all want to see him, to get into the house, to hold his body and look for the cause. They are desperate. I explain why they cannot enter, why it is being treated as a crime scene even if it turns out not to be a crime. We talk about evidence collection and the importance of preserving everything for the eyes of the trained detective. When she arrives, I introduce her to them. "This is Detective Wilson. She is here to help investigate what happened to Dominic." Some detectives like to talk to the family after they have processed the scene, but this detective always says hello first. She understands the family is on edge and wants answers, and she knows the power in giving them a few minutes of her time from the beginning.

We wait. The family cycles through quick rounds of grief—they are angry at the girlfriend, certain this is her fault. They are in denial and beg for his life to be returned. They are heartbroken and melt to the ground in waves of anguish. They comfort each other and hold each other up. I am counselor and manager, attendant and organizer. I bring water and tissues and blankets for people to sit on.

I enter the house to ask for updates, only allowing myself to do so every 45 minutes, so as not to create more delay. I honor the bouts of frustration with how long the investigation is taking, and offer physical aid as people collapse and regain composure. Twice, we call for an ambulance for the mother. The DSM calls this "ataque de nervios," although I call it being a parent who loses a child. When I am able to step away, I research the girlfriend, aware that her family does not know she is dead. We have her name now—Elizabeth—and with the help of the officers and the police database, I find her father's information and his address. She has no

Days in the Lives of Social Workers

known husband or kids, and her mother appears to be deceased. I make a mental note to notify her father as soon as the scene clears.

Hours later, the detective emerges along with the medical examiner, who arrived long ago and quietly slipped into the house. They explain what they have found, qualifying their findings as preliminary. Dominic has no trauma to his body and neither does the girlfriend. They found drug paraphernalia in the trash can that is consistent with opioids. There is no suicide note or indication that the deaths were purposeful (although again, the qualifier, we do not know everything yet). It may have been an accidental overdose. Dominic's body will be taken to the medical examiner's office for an autopsy, and from there he will go to a funeral home.

The family asks questions and weeps. I prepare them for the bodies (covered, bagged, on a gurney) to be removed from the home. Some family members leave, others stay, wanting to see the bodies, needing the final proof that their loved one is truly gone. When the transport team wheels out the bodies, they collapse again, the final guttural, primal, anguished sobs. And like that, the bodies are gone and the family begins to depart. I provide a final round of information, re-explaining the next steps, the order of legal next of kin, and the process of choosing a funeral home, the investigation, and the issue of the girlfriend. I tell them I will find her family tonight and tell them she is dead. I will do it in person if I can. They thank me for helping them, the mother hugs me tightly and weeps, and they leave.

Once they have gone, I dash over to the detective and medical examiner, eager to catch them before they leave. I share the information I found for the girlfriend's father. They were able to identify her body from an ID that was in the house, so I am given approval to make notification. The approval process is always odd—asking permission to ruin a person's life by telling them their loved one is dead—but it is a check and balance system, and I am grateful for it. Best to make sure everyone agrees on someone's identity before telling their family they are dead.

I get back in my car and plug in the address of Elizabeth's father. He lives on the south side, and I start to drive. On my way, I switch radio channels to the correct sector and say I need an officer to meet me down the block from this address. When I arrive, I see the patrol car sitting patiently in a church parking lot with its parking lights on. I drive up next to him, so that our driver's windows are nearly touching, a favorite way of communicating amongst law enforcement in the summer—stay in the A/C as long as possible! I know this officer. I have worked a few calls with him, and he is patient—that will be helpful. I explain the circumstances to him and tell him I will be making a death notification. "I'll handle the talking if you can just make sure no one shoots me"—my favorite line for these types of calls. A little levity for us before we dive into the depths of despair. Self-preservation is another word for it.

He chuckles and nods, and we drive together to the house. We get out quickly and walk to the door. We have both done this before and know that you have to get to the door fast, or people will meet you halfway down the driveway, anxious to know why an officer and a lady with "victim services" written on her shirt are parked outside.

We get to the door, and he knocks—the loud police knock that I can never do correctly. A woman answers the door, but I know we are looking for a man, the dad—Larry. She says he is home, and just then, he walks up behind her. "Hi, Larry, I'm Claire with Victim Services, and this is Officer Birmingham. We have some information to share with you. May we come in?" Concerned looks usher us inside, and I immediately see children's toys. I know this will be heavy, and I want to tell the father first, before any children, if I can. This will give us a chance to strategize how to tell the kids about the death, a luxury we rarely have, but worthy of effort.

I ask about kids, and he says his 7-year-old twins are home. Just then, they come bounding into the room, two girls with big smiles on their faces. I explain that I would like to meet with their father privately, and the woman quickly takes the children by the hand and leads them upstairs. When I hear a door shut, I turn back to the father. He says, "Is this about Elizabeth? She's always getting in trouble." I say yes, it is. We sit down in the living room, and I confirm Larry's identity and his relationship to Elizabeth, and then I tell him.

"I'm sorry, Larry. Elizabeth is dead." A deep yell comes from his body, but I do not think he hears it. "WHAT?" he says. "WHAT! WHAT! WHAT!" He pauses, and I say it again, "She is dead. She was found today." I have more to tell him, but I know he is not ready to hear it. He stands and yells, "NO NO NO NO"—and I know what is going to happen. He is going to break things.

We stand, and I gently place my hand on the officer's arm and push backwards. Together, we take three steps back. Now we are close to the door and out of immediate reach. The father is screaming and crying. He is punching walls and flipping tables. He opens cabinets and flings out the contents. Glass is shattering and breaking, and the sounds are all so loud. I consciously arrange my face to look compassionate and calm and understanding. A side-glance to the officer shows me he has done the same, and I am grateful for his presence, his restraint, and his demeanor.

We wait. The father breaks all the things, and we let him. When he is done, he is heavy with breath and tears. He sobs loudly and sits back down on the couch, and we join him. The father asks why, how, when, who, all the normal questions. I answer, and I tell him that another body was found with hers, a boyfriend. This is unusual and rolls off my tongue with hesitation, because I do not know how he will respond. He looks shocked with a flash of anger and asks if his daughter was murdered. I explain the process of the investigation and the initial findings.

The moment I say that they were in rehab together, he softens and through tears explains that he always knew his daughter would die of an overdose. He tells me the story of her life, the ups and downs, the death of her mother and the aftermath, of the first time he realized she had stolen his pain pills, of the jail trips and rehab trips, the havoc it caused their family, and the love he always felt for her, despite it all. It is more than I need to know, but it is my favorite part of the job—to share in this person's history, feelings, and grief, and to provide enough support to get him through this hour, the first hour, of the rest of his life without his daughter.

When he is done with her story, I reflect on how much he tried to help her, how much he loved her. He cries and nods silently, then asks about next steps. Now he is ready. I explain all the steps, write them down, give all the numbers and the contacts, and then approach the subject of telling his other children. By now, I know the twins are Elizabeth's half-sisters and they hardly knew her. He says he wants to do it himself, but he asks for guidance. I explain the concept of death in the eyes of 7-year-olds, and we talk about their past experiences of death (a dog), the family's religious beliefs about the afterlife, the words to use, and the reactions to expect.

When we finally stand to leave, he thanks us for our time. We show ourselves out and breathe in the night (still hot) air. When we get to our cars, I pause and look at the officer. We can now let down our masks, and he says, "That was terrible!" Years later, I will see this officer again, and he will tell me it was the worst experience of his entire professional career in law enforcement—watching the father physically and emotionally grieve his child's death. I join him in his feelings, let myself acknowledge for a moment how terrible it is—the things we must do in this job. We take a deep breath and he smiles. His emotional shield is back up, and he says he is off to find a taco. I smile and realize I have not eaten, used the bathroom, or had a drink of water in six hours. "Me, too," I say. And we part ways.

Before I can get to the taco (but after I find a bathroom), I am paged to respond to a scene in the east sector. The call text says the narcotics unit has served a high-risk arrest and search warrant, and there are children present. When I arrive at the house, I see that a hole has been blown through the patio wall. I can see the kitchen sink from my car. On this scene, there are no flashing lights or patrol cars. I see unmarked police cars and an armored vehicle, a battering ram, and other tools used to breach a residence quickly and before anyone inside can react and grab a weapon.

An officer in tactical gear comes up to my window and taps on it with a gloved fist. He is holding his long gun, wearing all black gear, an exterior bullet-proof vest, goggles, and a helmet. My natural response is hesitant, because his outfit is intimidating, but he chirps a friendly, "Hey, lady, how ya been?" and I realize he is an officer I work with often—a reminder that their uniforms often mask gentle souls.

We have a quick chat, and he tells me updates on his children, including his youngest who has Down syndrome and needs special care. Then he explains the scene. They arrested a woman who is a high-level narcotics smuggler in a major cartel. She accepted shipments for thousands of pounds of drugs and sent them off to New York, Chicago, and Philadelphia. He is proud of his unit for catching her—she is a major player in the drug trade and may face life in prison, he says. They also successfully arrested her without anyone getting hurt. It is a win for the police department and for the war against drugs. And yet, she has two young children, and they were in the home at the time of the breach. His tone and affect drop as he describes finding them huddled in a closet crying, how they only speak Spanish so none of the officers have been able to communicate with them, and how they are still crying on the couch.

My mind starts churning with tasks and concerns about the impact of this traumatic experience on the children. I grab a few stuffed animals and coloring books, remembering that play is a route to emotional safety for children. I hurry inside, past officers counting boxes of money and categorizing drugs. When I step in the door, I am shocked at the destruction. The impact from the wall exploding has left wreckage everywhere. There is sheetrock dust in the air, and the search of the house resulted in the cabinet doors hanging open and ajar, furniture turned upside down, and thousands of dollar bills strewn across the floor like a carpet. I look at the officer with confusion, and he explains that the money on the floor exploded from the wall and the ceiling during the breach. That they found money and drugs hidden everywhere. That the money they are leaving behind is counterfeit.

I find the children sobbing on the couch. The girl is four and the boy is six. They are still crying loudly when I crouch down in front of them and smile. In Spanish, I explain who I am and why I am there. I offer them teddy bears, which they take and cling to tightly. I acknowledge what they have just experienced and how scary it was, and I ask if they have questions. "Where is mommy? Why was it so loud? Why did they make a hole in the wall?" I answer them in the ways I can, which are brief and basic, emphasizing that mommy is safe and they are safe. I ask them to show me their favorite place in the house, and they guide me to their shared room, which is filled with toys and games. I ask about their favorite things, and they slowly, and then quickly, begin to run around and point out toys, games, books, pictures. The pieces of their lives. An officer joins me, and I ask him to stay with the children for a moment so I can talk to the mom. He agrees, and before I can get to the door, he is on the ground building something with Legos with the kids.

I find the mom in the back of a patrol car with an officer standing guard. I ask permission to speak with her, so I can discuss placement options for the children. Again, asking permission, a reminder that I, a social worker, am a guest in the world of law enforcement. And even though they are happy (and relieved, and grateful) to have me here, they are also in charge and I must be careful to work within the confines of their process. He agrees, and I talk to the mom. I explain that I will be finding somewhere for her children to go. I ask about family, friends, neighbors—anyone she knows and trusts to care for her children. She is crying as I talk and shakes her head. There is no one. They are all in El Salvador, and they have probably already been killed by the cartel. Everyone will die, she says. She begs me to take her children home with me, to care for them, to hide them. The cartel will find them and kill them. She says this over and over. She is crying the tears of a mother who may never see her children again and is no longer able to protect them.

In this moment, even though she is a high level drug smuggler working for an international cartel, I feel sadness for her. I explain that I cannot care for her children, but that I will call an agency named Child Protective Services, and they will take her children to a safe place. She has never heard of CPS and looks afraid. I do my best to reassure her, but the reality is that I myself have doubts about the long-term safety of these children. How dangerous is this cartel? Will they find the children? I acknowledge her fears and tell her I will make sure they go somewhere safe tonight. It is all I can do.

I arrange a quick good-bye between the children and their mother. It is heart wrenching, and they sob when she leaves. I call CPS, and while they are en route, they ask that I pack up a bag for each child. I go into the closet and see that there are thousands of pieces of clothing, all designer, most with tags still on them—the products of drug money that will now be left behind and never seen by this family again. I find two small suitcases and begin to pack them. I pick clothes that have been worn before. Maybe they hold memories; I hope so. I pack a few small toys, the ones I saw each child select as a favorite. I walk around and look for pictures of the children with their mother. I take the pictures off of the wall and fridge and tuck them safely into the bags. The officers watch silently and begin to hand me things they find that might be useful or special—a few passports, finger paint artwork, a picture of their mother as a young girl. I wonder if these are the only items they will ever have from their mother, their birth family. I wonder if they will remember this day.

CPS arrives. The children are playing in their room, and I take the momentary reprieve from their attention to tell the worker everything. I emphasize the danger the children may be in and the gravity of what they have experienced tonight. She says she understands. She gets her car ready, and we pack the suitcases in the trunk. Together, we go back, and I introduce her to the children. I explain that she is a good and safe person who is going to take them to a safe place where they can sleep. By now, it is 5 a.m., and they are visibly exhausted. They protest in unison, as they want to stay in their room, or with the officer who has been playing with them, or with their mother in the jail, or with the neighbor upstairs with the little dog. We give them time, explain it in different ways, and then there is no more time. We must leave.

We make it to the front door before they start to fight the forward movement. They scream and kick and cry, and in the end, the officer and I have to carry them to the car and strap them into the seats. I try to reassure them, but they cannot hear me over their screams. This is the outpouring of trauma, the real and true grief of everything they have experienced tonight. Their fear of the unknown has come to fruition. I look at the CPS worker, and she appears shockingly calm. She smiles and says this happens all the time. She will go through the McDonald's drive-thru for Happy Meals, and that will help. I nod and thank her and shut the car door, and off they go.

I turn to the officer, and he has tears in his eyes. It is momentary, but I see them through my own blurry vision. He quickly regains his composure, clasps me on the shoulder, and says, "PHEW! That was tough. Thanks for coming. I couldn't do your job." I respond "I couldn't do yours!" and I thank him for helping me with the children—our mutual acknowledgment that the work is hard and exhausting, and that to do it in the best way possible, we must help each other.

The end of my shift has come and gone, and I am now in the familiar territory of being held over. I am going on hour 13. I head back to the station and plant myself in front of the computer to write up my reports. I am tired and emotionally exhausted, so it takes longer than it should, but finally all is complete and I can log off.

The sun has risen, and the heat that never left begins to thicken again. I squeeze myself back into my Subaru, which is now lodged between two different trucks, and take a few deep breaths. Each night is a journey, a rollercoaster, a marathon of crisis and calm, despair and hope, loss and gain. I honor, for the briefest of moments, the lives that were changed in this 13-hour period and my role in their experiences—lessening trauma, supporting through grief, shining light into darkness and confusion, connecting with help, extending kindness, holding sorrow, ushering to safety.

A few more deep breaths, and the details will begin to shift from my awareness to my memory, a final survival technique in the long game of doing this type of work. Then I turn on the car, blast the A/C, and head home.

Think About It

1. What are your initial reactions to reading about the scenes that this social worker responded to? How do you think you would feel working crime scenes such as these?

2. Crisis intervention requires the social worker to build rapport quickly. What rapport building techniques would work in this setting?

3. What biases do you have, whether positive or negative, toward law enforcement? How would you be able to navigate these biases to effectively collaborate in a law enforcement setting?

4. This role requires self-management and extensive time separated from co-workers. In what ways might you care for yourself and find support in a role such as this?

Chapter 34

Social Work as a First Responder in an Anti-Trafficking Program

||||||||||||||||||||||||||||||||||||||||||||||||||||||||||||||||||||||||||||||||||||||||||||||||||||||||||||

by Stephanie Taylor, MSW

I am driving toward Disneyland just a mile or so from the police department, where I will be meeting a victim of human trafficking. As I watch the Disneyland fireworks start to light up the sky from the freeway, reality settles in just miles from the happiest place on earth. Human trafficking is real, and it is a big business.

It's not unusual for my days to begin much earlier than anticipated. Tomorrow's work day starts tonight at 9:30 p.m.

Working in the field of human trafficking, there are often multiple roles a clinician plays. Tonight starts the direction that tomorrow will take when I pick up a phone call from our task force law enforcement partners.

They state that they have a victim who is in need of an advocate, resulting from a traffic stop that was conducted earlier in the evening.

I pull into the police department where our task force law enforcement officers are stationed. My role is victim advocate tonight. I advocate for what makes the victim feel heard, safe, and understood. This often looks like getting her food, something warm to wear, and letting her talk about her boyfriend. This boyfriend is the same man who was just arrested for human trafficking because he would pimp her out and made a profit off of this exploitation.

This particular case is different from many. This victim is familiar. I first met Lisa when I was called out on a similar call six months ago, in the middle of one night last fall.

Tonight is different for Lisa.

Six months ago, when I made contact with Lisa, she had just been picked up on a sting operation. She had made a date with one of our undercover investigators. When the date was confirmed, our undercover investigator showed up at a motel room as a sex purchaser. Money was exchanged, solidifying the transaction, at which point she was apprehended and brought into the police department. She was not being arrested for prostitution, but rather she was being brought into the station to start an investigation against her trafficker, who was also her boyfriend and her pimp. During that first call out, she was detained for questioning, and I was her victim advocate. She refused services at that time, because she did not see herself as a victim of human trafficking.

In accordance with the NASW *Code of Ethics,* we honor self-determination, despite how obvious the abuse and exploitation appears in her relationship with her pimp. In honoring self-determination, it is important to assess for immediate safety concerns, assessing whether there is a plan to harm herself or someone else. Through an assessment, Lisa did not appear to be a harm to herself or anyone else, so my role as her victim advocate was to honor her decision. I provided her a safe place to stay for the evening, assuring her that if she ever needed anything, she could reach out to me directly and we would assist her with services. I did not expect to see her again.

Here we are six months later. She was picked up by police while in the car with her pimp. An investigation began on the night of that sting operation. Although Lisa refused to cooperate with law enforcement previously, she fit the definition of a victim of sex trafficking. Since that night, law enforcement has been determined to find and arrest her trafficker. This six-month investigation caught a break tonight when police stopped her pimp on a traffic stop because they suspected he was in the company of a minor, along with Lisa. Over the months, this investigation revealed to law enforcement that Lisa's pimp has trafficked many girls up and down the state of California. He is a high-level trafficker. Law enforcement has been determined to identify, arrest, and prosecute this trafficker with or without the help of the victims involved, including Lisa.

Lisa remembers me. I can feel a sense of relief from her when she sees me. She isn't the hard and uncooperative young woman that she was six months ago. She is scared and unsure; the circumstances are different now. Her boyfriend, the declared love of her life, is now in custody. She doesn't have a place to go, and she has no money and no one to call. The relationship between her and her boyfriend no longer exists; it's over. She is alone.

Tonight, her whole life has changed.

She is not completely aware of just how much her life has changed yet. I know this because I have knowledge of this investigation. I know our law enforcement team has been looking for this pimp for months. Tonight, her only concern is to see her boyfriend and make sure he is okay, and to understand what is going to happen to him. She doesn't understand that he is going to be charged with human trafficking.

I am relieved that she has a familiar face to come in contact with at this moment. Although she appears hesitant, she is cooperative with the investigation and communicates that she is glad that I showed up again.

My clinical role tonight, as a victim advocate, is one of addressing basic needs and starting to build the rapport necessary to continue providing services to Lisa. My clinical role looks a bit different this evening. It is approaching midnight before I am able to sit down with her. I am tired and can only imagine how tired she must feel. I learn that she has not slept in 22 hours. She was working all day and into the night for her trafficker. She had a quota that needed to be met each day, and she worked until she met her quota. An average night ends for Lisa only when she has $2,000. Each service breaks down roughly to $75-$150 per sex purchaser, depending on the service the purchaser requests. This provides an idea of the number of men she comes in contact with each night. However, despite her life changing tonight, the victim sitting in front of me doesn't exhibit behaviors most would assume of a sex trafficking victim.

She is a victim who claims she chose "the life"—even though she has never been able to use any of the money for herself, she needs permission to buy anything, and she sits here with no options for a place to go. This young woman believes she makes her choices and she chose this life. It is always challenging to listen to this logic. Choice should always have freedom as a component, but her boyfriend controls her freedom. Human trafficking victims are often more reminiscent of domestic violence victims in the type of trauma they endure. However, the trauma that victims of human trafficking experience can be much more extensive.

Tonight, I work to show her that there are people—outside of her trafficker—who will meet her needs. There are people who will meet her basic needs without requiring her to meet a quota. I learn that she hasn't eaten since this morning. (Her pimp wouldn't feed her beyond breakfast until she met her quota.) I feed her. I provide her with a pair of sweats and an emergency backpack full of toiletries that I carry in my car, for this exact occasion. Familiarity benefits me in this situation, because she saw I wanted to help her six months ago, and she sees that I am here now.

After law enforcement finishes their questioning, I take her to our emergency shelter to get some sleep. I assure her that I will be by in the morning. She asks to confirm that I will be the one to see her in the morning. I assure her that I will. She has no idea that I am plagued with the knowledge of what will happen to her trafficker. In this case, I know that my clinical role will be to help her understand the gravity of his charges of human trafficking and provide support when she realizes that she will not see him again. But tonight is not the time for that. She needed food, and now she needs sleep.

My schedule has now changed a bit for tomorrow. Lisa is the priority, because she is in acute crisis. I need to assess for safety and suicidality, and begin a case plan for her. I will meet her in the morning at the time we agreed to meet. It is important to help her feel heard and understood.

My work can look different each day, because we are working with such a volatile social issue. I am the program director for a nonprofit that provides services to meet immediate crisis needs and continues to provide holistic, victim-centered, trauma-informed comprehensive case management to victims of human trafficking until they reach a point of self sufficiency in their own lives. As a director, I spend most of my time working to fight the issue of human trafficking on a macro level. Most of my days are spent advocating for funding and educating law enforcement and services agencies that are seeking training specific to working with human trafficking victims/survivors. I work with policy makers to inform policy from the perspective of those who are working in direct service with victims/survivors.

I also have the privilege of training and supervising graduate level MSW interns. I teach a class, as an adjunct professor, specifically equipping students to work with victims of human trafficking after they have been identified and are receiving services. Most importantly, I keep a small caseload of my own, because it is important for me, as a clinician, to remain in close proximity to the population, so I can advocate for them appropriately.

It is now morning. Today, my morning will start with Lisa. I will keep her as part of my caseload. I have cleared my schedule so I can provide her with the appropriate time and care to help her process the events of last night and start looking ahead at a potentially new life.

I ask her how she slept. She responds, "I couldn't sleep at all. I just dreamt about him."

After all the abuse she has endured from this man, her only concern is that he is okay. She spends the morning asking me about his case: *Is he being charged? Will he be released? Can I go and see him?*

I have learned over the years working with this population that appropriately timed honesty, no matter how painful the truth, is key to the healing process. This allows a precedent to be established, and results in a sincere and honest working relationship. Explaining the extent of the case to her last night would not have served her or our working relationship well. The crisis was acute, and she was hungry and exhausted. She needed to feel safe and taken care of, to some degree, last night. Even though she is still in crisis today, I know that, ethically, it is time to answer her questions. By doing so, I treat her with dignity. I am not withholding information, and she can trust me. The chances of Lisa receiving this information and allowing me to be a support in this are better today than they would have been last night.

So, I share with Lisa the extent of the charges that the District Attorney is pursuing against her boyfriend. I am careful not to speak against her boyfriend. I am relaying information to her, and my concern is providing support to her during this loss. It is important to understand that she is grieving a person, a future, and a life she believed that she envisioned for herself. In this moment, I choose to remain neutral about the case, despite my inner bias, because she needs someone to sit in her pain with her, without having an opinion.

To be effective social workers, we must constantly be aware of our bias and our countertransference. I listen to this young woman talk about her relationship with this man, and I have plenty of thoughts and opinions. Although I understand the victimology of an abusive relationship, I can't help wondering what deficit this relationship filled for her. What did she receive from this man that she was lacking in her life and her heart? I am aware of the monster that he is, but she felt loved and understood by him, in some capacity. This is her reality, and I have to take that into account. Until I try to comprehend her reality, without judgment, I won't be able to address and provide the services that are necessary to fill the needs that her trafficker met. As I work with her through a victim-centered and trauma-informed approach, I address the countertransference that I begin to experience in working with her, because I am fighting to understand things from her reality. This support is unfamiliar to her.

In the time that I work with her, I am determined to provide this young woman with a corrective experience. My hope is that she encounters people who are concerned about her, with no strings attached, no quota to meet, and no expectation of getting something in return. Only then will she be capable of truly choosing—with freedom—the life she wants for herself.

Think About It

1. What bias of your own did you notice about Lisa's story while reading this chapter?

2. What interventions would be most effective in working with someone in this situation who does not self-identify as a victim of sex trafficking?

3. What clinical framework(s) would be most effective in working with this population?

4. Describe next steps in developing a comprehensive case plan for a victim of sex trafficking.

5. How would you prepare for this work with victims of trafficking? The challenging clients? The nature of the hours required? How would you take care of yourself in this work?

Chapter 35
A Hard Day's Night: Working with Assaultive Men in Prison

by *Michael Crawford, MSW, RSW*

It's only a short drive from my home to work. That's long enough for me to start focusing on the tasks ahead and just long enough at the end of the day for me to clear out the stress and strain of my work and get ready to enjoy time with family.

I used to think that prison was an odd place for me to practice my craft. Having been trained in both mental health and family therapy, I was comfortable with fifty-five minute hours spent in the privacy of a quiet, clean consulting room. In sharp contrast, the damp and dark quarters of an aging portable trailer, which, when not used for therapy groups, doubled as a school house, seemed decidedly unprofessional. Over the years, I have developed considerable comfort in places like this. Prisons are places where social workers should feel quite comfortable. We have been working in prisons since well before social work was considered a profession.

I don't work in a prison full time, but rather on a contract basis, conducting group therapy. My other job is teaching in a school of social work. I need to work hard to put the jobs I have waiting on my desk at the university out of my mind, so I can focus on the tasks at hand.

Today the sun is shining and the temperature is climbing quickly, as the sun burns the fog off the mountainside. I know that the trailer will be hot today. The breeze I always hope for never materializes and probably wouldn't help anyway. The windows in the trailer are just too small to do much good.

I walk into the minimum security farm camp with its low wire fence, through gates that are wide open during the day. The trimmed grass and ornamental bushes are beautiful, and I catch a scent from a fragrant flower bed. The men enjoy the task of caring for the grounds, as it gives them an opportunity to be outside and work at a job that is more relaxing than most.

Frank is pulling weeds today and greets me with a warm smile. His smile makes me think that people can make their own happiness, even in places where one might think there is little joy. I mumble to myself, wishing that more of the guards would show a lighter side.

I sign in and Mr. Richardson, a senior correctional officer, tells me, with what I think is a cheeky grin, that I should have a full group today. I smile and give myself permission to think that the system is working, all the while remembering that last week two of the group members were inadvertently sent out on a work party and missed the group session. Mr. Richardson and I seem to be developing an understanding about the place of social work in corrections. He was the officer who told me that licorice was contraband and that I couldn't bring it to the group, even if it was Easter. "Rules are rules," he said in response to my attempt to make sense of the declaration: "These guys aren't here because they missed Sunday School." There are so many rules in prison, and breaking them takes little effort. What's harder, though, is dealing with the punitive attitudes held by many of the staff.

With pass key in hand and name tag firmly pinned to my shirt, I head over to the portable. Several men shuffle about outside waiting for the door to be opened. I see black running shoes and dark green work clothes for everyone. What an ugly color to have to wear day in and out. The men understand this for what it is. They freely describe this stripping away of their personhood as part of a systematic method that robs them of their uniqueness and individuality. There is no misunderstanding possible about who is in charge and has control here. My mind wanders back to the psychiatric hospital, where I worked many years ago and the time I was stopped at the door when trying to leave a locked ward. My protestations that I was indeed staff were not enough to free me from the steel grip of an enthusiastic and newly-hired orderly. The nursing unit manager came to my rescue and soon freed me, but not before I had a small taste of what it's like "inside." Being scared and powerless are common themes in my work with abusive men.

The therapy group consists of men who have been convicted and are now serving sentences of two years or less for assaulting their partners. Each of them has been court ordered to attend a twelve-session family violence program. I usually have about ten men in the group and work with a female colleague. Working with Sandra is great; I would hate to do this work alone. She brings some balance to the group and really challenges the men, and sometimes me, on our sexist beliefs and attitudes.

The men are restless today, and we spend the better part of the first hour dealing with a conflict that has come up between two members. It's loud and pointed. I don't want the group to get out of hand, and work as skillfully as I can toward a peaceful resolution. I wonder who in the group would get involved to break up a fight if one started, all the while knowing that there has never been any assaultive behavior in the many years that I have facilitated group sessions with abusive men. One man last week couldn't handle the conflict in any other way than to excuse himself from the group. Walking out was a giant step in the right direction for that man. This was one of the few times in his life that he had had to deal with conflict so positively. His earlier response, and one that he is struggling to change, was to start throwing punches. The other men recognized his progress and shouted some praise in his direction, as he slammed the door behind him. I make a mental note to call on him later that day. I can tell from the look on Sandra's face that she is exhausted. I am, too. We have worked hard to help the men work through this problem, and we know we have made some gains.

Today, Bob tells us that his wife has decided to leave town and head back east to be closer to her parents. His eyes are filled with tears as he tells the group that he knows this is the end of his marriage and that he probably won't see his children anymore. Some men make empathic responses and others, maybe because the issue hits too close to home, just hang their heads. Lou, whose mother has just passed away, talks about his own loss and encourages Bob to ask others for the support he'll need to deal with this in prison. Prison is so isolating. The men sit back and watch life go by on the "outside," unable to influence or control it in any way. "Letting go" is harder for some men than for others. It's particularly hard for those like Phil who are serving their first sentence.

The men struggle a bit with our presentation today. Our aim is to introduce the men to a gendered analysis of woman assault, and we use an exercise that asks them to discuss male dominance and their need for power in the relationship. This is hard for most men to do, and these men are no exception. Some struggle with the exercise and others reject our ideas entirely. One man talks about how his girlfriend must have felt living with him. However, he comes to understand her and have empathy with her victimhood, he says, by living under a correctional system that to him seems to set and enforce arbitrary and senseless rules. Great insight! I hope he is able to carry through with this and translate that thought into some behavioral changes. Other men just want to talk about how messed up the "old lady" is. Our feminism offends the sensibilities of some of the men, but we seem to have come to an arrangement in the group. Sandra and I gently invite them to consider our ideas about violence and accepting responsibility as they review their lives and plan for the future.

At lunch, I am reminded again of the divisiveness that is everywhere in prisons. We eat at separate tables. The men sit on benches, while the staff are afforded more comfortable chairs near the windows. The food's good. In fact, most days the food is great! I suppose that it's used as something of a pacifier, keeping the men content. Regardless, the men like to complain about the food, but privately most agree they don't eat that well when not in prison.

I finish my day after a few interviews in which men and I plan for their continued therapy once released, some telephone calls, and of course, the requisite hour for recording. I feel good about my work today. When I first started working as a social worker, I had a boss who told me that if I really wanted to feel good about my work, I should work with clients about whom others feel most hopeless. He gave me my first opportunity to work with violent men, and I have thanked him for this many times. This is great work. Some of the men simply fight their way through therapy and gain nothing, but I don't choose to focus on those at the end of the day. The men who have had the courage to face their situations honestly and make decisions about living nonviolent lives are the ones that bring the greatest satisfaction to this job.

As I drive home, I allow myself the luxury of thinking about how torn I am between the clinical social work I practice daily and the political social work I know needs to be done. For me, it's a happy discomfort. I would hate to feel the complacency that I see in some social workers who have accepted that things don't change. Every time I walk into that prison, I see the poor and the disadvantaged, the physically and the mentally ill, the alcohol and drug addicted, the uneducated, the abused, and the Indian men who are disproportionately represented. I don't just see criminals, and I don't just think about how they need to change. I wonder about our social, economic, and political system, and how we in Canada imprison more people than most industrial countries in the world. I wonder about a country that has so much wealth but so little interest in distributing it fairly. My work with social justice groups is important to me and provides me with the hope of systemic change, but today my clinical work brings me satisfaction.

Heading home, I wish that others could experience the happiness that I experience in my life.

Think About It

1. What might be some difficulties in practicing social work in a "punitive" environment, such as a prison?

2. What do you think about the statement, "...if I really wanted to feel good about my work, I should work with clients about whom others feel most hopeless"?

Chapter 36
Residential Treatment for Adolescent Sexual Offenders

IIIIIIIIIIIIIIIIIIIIIIIIIIIIIIIIIIIIIIIIIIIIIIIIIIIIIIIIIIIIIIIIIIIIIIIIIIIIIIIIIIIIIIIIIIIIIIIIIIIIIIII

by Ronald M. Arundell, Ed.D., ACSW, LISW

I will describe an average day in the life of a social worker practicing social work in a residential treatment facility in the Midwest. This facility specializes in the treatment of adolescent males who have committed sexual crimes.

There is evidence that sexual offending behavior begins in adolescence. In 1989, Becker and Kaplan found that approximately 58% of adult sexual offenders first began their perpetration activity in their teens. What these data indicate is that juvenile sexual offending behavior is a serious social problem and needs attention.

Treatment for adolescent sexual offenders is provided in both community-based outpatient and residential modalities. Many of these programs employ both BSW and MSW social workers.

The residential treatment center consists of 24 male adolescents ranging in age from 13 to 18. The Juvenile Court refers most of the residents who have had convictions ranging from rape to gross sexual imposition. More than 80% of the residents have convictions for other antisocial acts, such as breaking and entering, theft, possession of drugs, running away, and assault. The average length of stay is four to six months. The facility utilizes a behavioral level system common to most juvenile facilities.

The day begins at 8:30 a.m. I grab a cup of coffee and check in with the director. We briefly review issues that have arisen from yesterday and discuss incidents that need addressing in group session this afternoon. The unit leaders are also present to report on the behavior of the residents last evening. A couple of residents had their levels dropped because of abusive language and failure to follow the rules. The team agrees that these issues need more attention in group.

At 9:00 a.m., I conduct an intake interview. In the waiting room, I introduce myself to the new resident, his probation officer, and his mother. I usher them into my office and try to join quickly with the young client, John, by asking him if he is nervous. John responds by looking at his shoes and saying, "A little." I then begin the interview by disclosing information about my experience and the overall philosophy of the treatment program. I briefly review the intake forms, rules of confidentiality, level system, and the treatment program rules and regulations. I then ask John to go with a staff person to unpack his clothes and see the facility. I inform him that his mother will be over shortly to say good-bye.

I review the court documents, probation reports, and victim impact statements supplied by the probation officer. I explain to the probation officer and Mom that the first couple of weeks will involve a thorough assessment that will include psychological tests, a psychiatric consult, and a complete social and sexual history. After obtaining this data, the treatment team will develop a specific behavioral plan. The social worker will consult with Mom and the probation officer for their input and suggestions.

After answering questions that Mom has about family therapy, phone calls, and visitation, I escort her and the probation officer on a tour of the facility. We end the tour at John's unit. I say good-bye and inform John that I will see him in group.

As I walk back to my office, I have strong feelings of sadness, anger, and powerlessness. I feel for both John and his mother, who are struggling with behavior that neither understands. John sexually molested his 6-year-old sister and his 8-year-old cousin. John has his own history of sexual abuse and experienced severe physical beatings until the age of eight. His mother struggles with her own feelings of shame, guilt, and powerlessness as she attempts to do "the right thing" to help John and her daughter.

I check my messages before getting into my car to go to Juvenile Court. There is to be a hearing to review a resident's progress in treatment. As I am driving, I begin to reflect on how I became involved in the treatment of juvenile sexual offenders.

A few years back, when I was a social worker at a psychiatric hospital for children, I became aware of the extensive sexual and physical abuse that 80% to 90% of our residents experienced in their lives. At the time, there was a significant level of denial about this phenomenon. Today there is more awareness, but still not enough. My own clinical social work experiences led me to a recognition that young people were acting out sexually, but mental health professionals did not seem to be addressing this behavior.

I joined the Association for the Treatment of Sexual Abusers (ATSA). I involved myself with researchers, social workers, and other mental health providers who shared a similar concern about these issues. Through conferences and personal contacts, I learned about the dynamics and treatment approaches from pioneers in the field such as Gene Abel, Judith Becker, Meg Kaplan, Bill Marshall, and Fay Honey Knopp.

My generalist social work training, coupled with the specific knowledge of the dynamics of child sexual abuse and sexual offending behavior, provides me with a solid foundation for professional practice in this special area. Although the work is stressful and discouraging at times, there is also a sense of fulfillment that comes when I witness significant behavioral change in my clients. There is also the knowledge that as a social worker, I am contributing to the prevention of sexual offending behavior in the future.

I find a place to park, grab my notes, and walk quickly to the Juvenile Court building. Outside the courtroom, I greet the resident, Bill, and the residential staff person. We review the details of the hearing. Bill and I have discussed this hearing in individual and group sessions the week before.

The bailiff calls the case and we enter a small hearing room. The referee reviews the treatment reports, asks me to comment on Bill's progress, and asks Bill how he is doing in treatment. There is also a discussion of future discharge plans. The referee congratulates Bill on his progress and schedules a final hearing in six months.

As I leave court to go to my car, I have a feeling of accomplishment. Bill has done well in treatment. He learned the cognitive behavioral techniques of Relapse Prevention and how to apply these techniques to his own life. He also has a good aftercare plan. His prognosis is good. The hard work by Bill, his family, and the treatment team resulted in a positive outcome. I stop at a streetside vendor, get a hot dog and a soda, and enjoy the moment.

After court, I return to the facility and attend clinical staffing. Our treatment team conducts clinical staffing weekly for about an hour. The social workers, psychiatrist, psychologist, art therapist, recreation therapists, and mental health technicians from the units discuss the progress of the residents in treatment. We review, discuss, and modify treatment plans. The social workers report on the residents' progress in individual, group, and family therapy.

Clinical staffing is lively with a free exchange of ideas. There is a climate of mutual respect and support as we debate various treatment approaches. I briefly report on Court and the outcome. The team members congratulate me on the fine work I did with Bill and his family. The positive feedback feels very rewarding, and I thank the team for their support and cooperation.

After clinical staffing, I have two individual therapy sessions scheduled. The first is with Randy, where I will be completing his sexual history. The second is with Andrew, who is preparing for discharge. We will discuss his safety plans and his thoughts and feelings about returning home in the next two weeks.

When I complete the individual sessions, I prepare for group with my co-therapist Melody. Melody is a graduate social work student in her final year. Melody will be leading the group on the sexual assault cycle. She will review the cycle using charts and handouts and will have each group member report on his own sexual assault cycle that was part of his homework assignment from the day before. Melody and I discuss various approaches and strategies that we might use as co-facilitators.

Group consists of twelve adolescent males who have committed various sexual crimes. Group takes place four times a week for an hour and a half. The group uses a cognitive-behavioral model that incorporates the sexual assault cycle, thinking errors, and Relapse Prevention Model. There is a defined structure to the group, and the social workers play an active role in the group process.

Melody reviews the components of the sexual assault cycle. We both assist each resident in describing his own cycle and how it applies to his sexual offenses. The group goes well.

After group, I briefly visit with some of the residents. We discuss their progress in treatment, visits, problems at school, and discharge issues. I remind certain residents of upcoming assignments. Bantering and joking takes place between the residents and myself. I return to my office feeling very positive.

One of the interesting outcomes for me in doing this work is to experience the wide range of positive and negative emotions.

In struggling to teach these young men how to get in touch with their own feelings, I learn how to do this myself in a deeper and more effective manner.

I check my messages, do some paperwork, confirm family therapy appointments, and prepare to call it a day. I feel tired but fulfilled.

This work is challenging and requires the social worker to apply social work knowledge in multiple modalities. It offers many opportunities for social workers to be innovative and creative. This field also provides a social worker the chance to make important contributions to clients and to society.

In the years I have worked with adolescent sexual offenders, I have found this work to be exciting and growth enhancing. In the process of serving others, I have learned much about the world in which I live and myself.

Think About It

1. Role-play going to court to testify about a client.

2. What do you think might cause an adolescent to become a sexual offender?

Chapter 37
Forensic Social Work: Mitigating Death Penalty Cases in a Capital Defense Unit

||||||||||||||||||||||||||||||||||||||||||||||||||||||||||||||||||||||||||||||||||||||||||||||||||||||||||||||||||||||

by Lisa Orloff, ACSW

(Note: The death penalty has been abolished in New York since this chapter was written. Thirty states still have the death penalty as of February 2019.)

In September 1995, New York state reinstated the death penalty for certain crimes defined as first degree murder. The return of the death penalty after a 21-year absence brought with it challenges not only for the legal community, but for social workers as well.

The death penalty is the ultimate statement about the worthlessness of a human life. When a jury imposes the death penalty, it has concluded that this person's life no longer has value, sense, or purpose—a concept completely antithetical to social work. We know that a person is more than the worst thing he or she has ever done, and thus, capital cases demand a social work perspective.

I am the social worker for the Legal Aid Society's Capital Defense Unit. I work in Brooklyn, NY. The unit also includes five attorneys, two investigators, two paralegals, an administrator, several law students, and several social work volunteers. The inclusion of an in-house social worker as part of the defense team is an acknowledgment that social workers bring a special body of knowledge, skills, and abilities necessary in the representation of people charged with capital crimes. In my work, I perform traditional social work functions, and some that are not so traditional.

The most obvious role I play is that of advocate. In no uncertain terms, the state is trying to kill my client, and I advocate for my client's life: I tell the client's "story." This is called mitigation. In order for the judges, juries, and district attorneys to understand my client's actions, the actions must be placed in an extensive social history of the client's life. A social history is constructed through client interviews, collateral interviews with multigenerational family members and others, and the collection and evaluation of life history records (school, hospital, child welfare agencies). The presentation of mitigating factors can be used at different stages of a case, but it is predominantly used in the beginning. For example, the District Attorney has 120 days from a client's arraignment to decide whether or not to seek the death penalty. Along with a multitude of legal issues that can be raised during this time, the defense team can produce evidence of mitigation to persuade the District Attorney that *this* is not a death penalty case.

The range of mitigation evidence is as diverse as our clients, and the presentation of mitigating factors is written into the criminal procedure law. I explore and explain the forces acting on the client—I discuss the people, places, and things that shape a client's life. The person-in-environment perspective is crucial to this work.

At the foundation is my relationship with the clients. What I need from them is information. I need to understand them, and this is most definitely a process. Much of what will be our mitigating evidence is our client's own victimization. Getting a client to reveal horrific stories of abuse and neglect is a skill requiring good interviewing techniques, empathy, patience, and frequent contact over a long period of time. I've heard this referred to by the lawyers as "hand-holding," and I wish it were that easy. The more time I spend with my clients, the more they will trust me and the more they will tell me, and this is one of my goals. Another reason I spend so much time with them is because of what they are telling me. For example, when a client relayed the details of his father's suicide, I did not scribble in my legal pad, thank him, and wrap things up. It took some time to "debrief" with him. I'm not my clients' therapist, but I do counsel them. To do less would be exploitive. Sometimes, however, I go visit a client without an agenda. Sometimes, I go just to talk, break up their monotony, show I care.

Unique clinical issues are raised with a client who may be facing the death penalty. For example, depression is common for a client who feels as if he is waiting to die, and a challenge arises in trying to keep him engaged in the complex processes of a capital case. Often, our clients express suicidal thoughts or even attempt suicide. Consequently, sometimes my own anger is peaked. I feel, "Here I am trying to save your life, and there you are trying to end it!" I absolutely understand where it's coming from: their vision of their future is bleak, and in reality it is. In most cases, if the client does not receive the death penalty, he will spend the rest of his life in prison without the possibility of parole. The challenge is to get the client to take baby steps with you: let's get through the first 120 days, then the trial, and so on.

Collateral interviews are vital in this work. It is a huge mistake not to question what my clients tell me. Some clients will make things up because of the desperation of their situations or because of their mental illness. Some clients will not remember their own childhoods—a function of trying to repress traumatic memories.

Gathering a social history from a family most often involves convincing them to reveal painful secrets: mental illness, addiction, physical abuse within a family. Sometimes the collusion is incredibly strong. Protecting the family secret appears more important than saving the client's life. This can be ameliorated by social workers, as we are trained and educated to do not only thorough diagnostic interviews, but sensitive collateral interviews.

It is also vital to go into the homes and communities where my clients come from—to experience firsthand (albeit for a short time) the chaos and poverty. If I expect to tell my clients' stories, then I need to immerse myself in their worlds.

Reviewing client records is one of my favorite parts of the job. I learn most about my clients by reading their records, and I get independent verification of our mitigation. Records are paper trails. For example, a school record may refer to a psychiatric hospitalization a year earlier, which the client has not told me about. Or, a certain caseworker is mentioned over and over and will be contacted and interviewed. The records must be closely read and read with a creative mind and with an eye toward the future. I ask myself, *Where does this record lead? What agency record will we request next? What person from the record should we contact?* Reading records also allows me to take the information back to the client, whose memory might have faded about a significant life event.

I educate the rest of the staff with regard to the mental health or disabling conditions our clients face. For example, we discuss how to effectively communicate with a client who is mentally ill, or we discuss what schizophrenia looks like. I don't think I've cringed harder than when one of our lawyers referred to a client as "weird." It was a perfectly accurate description of a very disturbed client, but after a discussion, the lawyer understood the importance of not referring to a client in this way.

I network with mental health experts. Clients frequently need psychological testing, psychiatric examinations, and neuropsychological testing. I serve as the unit's liaison with these mental health professionals. Together, we discuss what testing is appropriate.

The biggest frustration I feel revolves around our time limitation. Most often, we have 120 days to build our case—that is, to uncover and substantiate from all angles, for example, sexual abuse. This is a tall order. Most social workers know that it can take months or years for clients to even begin to discuss sexual abuse.

There are several lessons I learned very quickly in this field. The first thing I had to learn was to redefine success. I used to think success was measured in terms of how well a treatment plan worked, or how much a person's functioning improved. Success in a capital defense unit is when the state decides not to kill your client.

I also learned that the social worker in this field needs to be able to seek out support and ask for help. This was the first job I had in which I started to dream about my clients. My most personal moments were being invaded by work, and I realized some need was not being met during my waking hours. I went into therapy for the first time and bought clinical social work supervision.

I came to this work through a logical evolution. Most of my volunteer experience as an undergraduate was working with victims. I worked as a rape crisis counselor and in battered women's shelters. While living in London, I had my first experience working with "perpetrators"—male prostitutes. What I came to realize in my first week was that most of these kids (all under 21) were victims of some type of familial or stranger sexual and/or physical abuse. My first paying job out of graduate school was in the Legal Aid Society's Criminal Defense Division. Again, I was working with people accused of committing crimes instead of working with the victims of crimes. And again, I found that a huge percentage of my clients (mostly felony offenders) had been victims of trauma or were survivors, and many were re-enacting their trauma.

Legal Aid's Capital Defense Unit was assigned to the first murder one indictment in New York City. Manhattan District Attorney Robert Morgenthau appointed a committee of senior Assistant

District Attorneys to help him weigh the factors in the case. Several members of the Capital Defense Unit, including me, met with this committee after I submitted an extensive psychosocial report outlining mitigating factors. In his first decision in a capital case, District Attorney Morgenthau announced that he would not seek the death penalty.

It has been shown that the death penalty is not a deterrent to violent crime. It has also been shown that it is applied capriciously and disproportionately to racial minorities. And obviously, it is irrevocable. This is the most challenging position I have held as a social worker, and by far it is the most rewarding. The pay-off is huge. It's indescribable. The feeling I had when I went to tell my client the District Attorney was not going to seek the death penalty against him cannot be duplicated.

I am proud to be involved in this difficult fight by bringing a social work perspective to death penalty work.

Think About It

1. How do you feel about the death penalty?
2. How do you feel about working with people who have committed violent crimes?

Chapter 38
Victim Services

IIIIIIIIIIIIIIIIIIIIIIIIIIIIIIIIIIIIIIIIIIIIIIIIIIIIIIII

by Staci A. Beers, MSW, LSW

It is 7:15 a.m. and I start the day with an hour and fifteen minute commute to work. On my morning commute, I ponder the question I get asked the most when I tell people what I do—"How did you get involved in this line of work?" I didn't exactly grow up and say, "I want to work in victim services."

It all began when I attended West Chester University. I majored in criminal justice and minored in women's studies. One day, a counselor from the local victim resource center came to speak to my women's studies class. She spoke about the services of the center and volunteer opportunities. It sounded interesting. I was planning on attending law school the following year, with a focus on women's issues in law. I contacted the center and signed up for the next training class. The classes were quite educational. I learned a lot about myself as well as the victim experience. I began volunteering three nights per month. My role as a volunteer was to provide support for victims on the hotline or at hospitals when a victim would come into the Emergency Room for the rape exam. Every night I was on call, I waited patiently, eager to put my newly-acquired skills to work. I graduated from West Chester University five months after I became a volunteer.

I decided to attend graduate school and was accepted at Marywood College School of Social Work in Scranton, PA. During my interview, it was clear that I would be able to gain experience with victims of crime during my internship. I interned at a comprehensive victims' center in a nearby county. The first year, I worked

274   *Days in the Lives of Social Workers*

with sexual assault survivors in group and individual counseling, as well as on the hotline and in the emergency room. I will never forget my first "run" to the ER with a female adolescent. She was sexually assaulted in a group home and was not sure she wanted to press criminal charges. Her caseworker took her to the ER for the exam with the intent that criminal charges would be pursued. I explained the exam and told the young woman that the choice to prosecute the perpetrator was hers. The caseworker disagreed. I quickly learned that we, as social workers, may have the same basic training, but the agencies that we work for have many different philosophies that will mold our work ethic. I was able to diffuse the situation by separating the young woman and her caseworker and explaining the importance of choice and regaining the control that was lost from the assault. They both agreed that the choice lies within the victim.

The more I worked with sexual assault victims in the emergency room, the more I came into contact with law enforcement. I decided that my second-year internship would be within the criminal justice system. I worked in the victim witness department at the same comprehensive victims' center. I provided accompaniment to all court proceedings, assisted victims in filling out victim compensation claims, and provided training to the local law enforcement community. It was at this point in my career that I was exposed to different types of crime victims.

It was also at this point in my career that I worked with survivors of homicide. I was fortunate to co-facilitate the Adult Homicide Survivors Group. The members of this group allowed me to walk with them through their grief process. I am forever grateful that they allowed me to be with them through some of their most difficult and personal times. They taught me more than any textbook or class could teach. In the final semester of graduate school, I put together a handbook for these survivors. We received a grant, the book was professionally printed, and we used it when we met with families for the first time. The handbook covers different types of grief, the criminal justice system, and a simple glossary of terms. This handbook is available at no charge for all homicide survivors.

As a victim witness coordinator, I learned to deal with different professionals who did not necessarily share my philosophy and ethics. I worked with many police officers and detectives who were good at their jobs but lacked empathy needed to work with victims. I was able to provide the bridge that was needed to communicate between the victim and law enforcement. I also worked with many prosecuting attorneys. Again, they were good at their jobs, but some lacked the compassion it takes to work with victims of crime. Sometimes plea agreements were taken without the consent of the victim. Other times, the victim was not believed. I was fortunate that the core group of district attorneys I worked with were extremely compassionate and understanding. They worked with the victim month after month, and week after week, before going to trial or taking a plea.

After working at the county level for four years, I was given the opportunity to work on behalf of victims of crime at the state level. It was a difficult decision to leave clients I had worked with over an extended period of time, as well as the many professional relationships that I had made. However, I made the move to work in a newly-created office designated for victims of crime in the post-sentencing phase. Most of my work with victims is through telephone contacts. It consists of notifying victims when the inmate is eligible for parole.

It is 8:30 a.m. and I venture into the office. I begin the morning by scanning my in-box, which is overflowing from work that I never got to yesterday. I try to prioritize the many things that are awaiting me. By 9:00 a.m. my two co-workers and I are scanning the piles of files that are flowing into the office. We try to prioritize the piles; however, all are equally important. The piles consist of (1) files that we need to notify victims of the parole decision, (2) files that need to be checked to make sure all of the victim information is complete, so the parole decision can be made (if the information is not there, we must notify the victim), and (3) files that have come to our office because a parolee has violated his parole, come back into the system, and either brought more victims with him or we need to notify the others.

As we scan the piles, the phone rings. Soon all of us have an issue that needs immediate attention. The in-box can wait. I receive a phone call from a woman who is a domestic violence survivor and is receiving death threats from the inmate, who will soon be paroled. I try to track down the file in our file room. I find an "out card" that is unclear and must go on the first of many "file hunts" today to find out who has the file. I locate the file and immediately type up a memo to the decision makers to notify them of the new threats. I tell the domestic violence survivor that we may be able to keep him in prison a bit longer; however, he will complete his sentence in nine months, and he will walk out of prison a free man with no supervision. I refer her to her local domestic violence center, so she can start to work on a safety plan in the event that he attempts to carry out his threat on her and their children. As I hang up the phone, I feel like a Band-Aid. I am only able to stop the bleeding for a short amount of time. One day, the inmate will get out, and the vicious cycle will start over again. I pray that if he enters the system again, it is not for murder.

It is lunchtime and very quiet in the office. I try to dig through my in-box, separating memos from victim input. I sign letters that will notify victims of their offenders' status. Some victims will be happy that the inmate has been refused; some will be terrified that the system can no longer house their offender, who is paroled.

In the afternoon, I weed through the victim statements received in today's mail. Some speak of the abuse suffered at the hands of the inmate. Some speak of the loss of their loved ones who will never come home, because the offender decided to drive drunk. Others speak of the betrayal they feel because the offender is someone they loved and trusted. The statements are placed in a confidential file for the decision makers.

As the afternoon steamrolls ahead, I take several phone calls from anxious victims who are awaiting the parole decision. I tell them there has not yet been a decision, but we will notify them when it comes back. I encourage them to call again if they want to check on it from time to time.

I receive a phone call from a past client of mine whose brother was murdered several years ago. The murder is still unsolved. A few weeks ago, she called me and asked me to advocate for her on the state level. She gave me permission to speak to whoever I could that would help her. I contacted the District Attorney's office handling the case. The DA would not talk to me, instead relaying an answer through his staff. I was referred to the investigators. They were surprised that I was calling and inquiring about the status of the investigation. They assured me that the puzzle was beginning to fit together. Now, several weeks later, my past client is calling to tell me that my phone calls have helped a great deal. The case has not been solved, but it looks as if it will be soon. I am happy for her. I hope she soon gets the answer she deserves.

The end of the day is nearing. I have acquired some new things in my in-box that will have to wait for tomorrow. The piles have dwindled. However, I know that more files will come flowing in. It is never-ending. I never would have imagined that working at this level would be so stressful. We cope with the stress through humor. Sometimes, all I can do is laugh!

As I commute home, I am again reminded of what it takes to work in this field. First, it takes dedication and determination. I did not enter victim services for financial gain. Second, it takes the desire to learn. Every day is a learning experience for me. I work with so many different individuals. They are from various ethnic, socioeconomic, and educational backgrounds. They teach me what they have learned. Third, it is imperative that anyone working in this field deal with their own personal biases and issues. It is difficult to be effective as an advocate when you have not done this. Finally, it takes the perseverance to want to make a difference in the lives of others. Victim services is about helping people in need at their time of trauma and thereafter. It is about walking with them on their journey of healing—if they allow you. It is about getting their voice heard by the decision makers, including elected officials.

As I pull into my driveway, my family and my Black Labrador, Chelsea, greet me. I leash Chelsea up and we go for a very long walk, unwinding from another "typical" day.

Think About It

1. Discuss the statement, "I feel like a Band-Aid."

2. How would you cope with the volume of work that Staci describes? How can humor help?

PART 8: OLDER ADULTS

Chapter 39
Social Work With Survivors of the Holocaust

IIIIIIIIIIIIIIIIIIIIIIIIIIIIIIIIIIIIIIIIIIIIIIIIIIIIIIIIIIIIIIIIIIIIIIIIIIIIIIIIIIIIIIIIIIIIIIIIIIIIIIIIIIIIIIIIIIIIIIIIIIII

by Paula David, MSW

I never considered social work as a career. In fact, I wasn't sure what they did. I wanted to be an artist, a teacher. or a writer; somehow finding a palatable platform that would recognize my interests and inclinations to creativity and communication. So I studied drawing and painting, did an undergraduate degree in art history, critiqued other artists' work helping the public see behind and beyond the obvious, and spent many hours teaching people of all ages to use color, design, and mixed media to help them give visual expression to their feelings. I didn't know then that I was acquiring the ideal training for social work.

After completing art school, followed by a B.A. in Art History, I applied to the Community Development and Planning program at the Faculty of Social Work. I had always been interested in town planning and assumed that's what the Faculty of Social Work was advertising. They offered me a spot, and as the two-year master's degree matched the timelines of my husband's academic obligations, I happily accepted, looking forward to forging a new career in town planning. It was quite a shock on the first day of classes, when I saw the course descriptions and discovered what community planning involved, and that social work did not entail planning town and social environments for developing communities. It turned out that my course selection was likely the most fortuitous error of my life and the beginning of a long and rewarding journey into the world of social work.

I have spent 15+ years as a social worker at the Baycrest Centre for Geriatric Care in Toronto. I also never considered working with older adults, but within a month of starting at Baycrest, I knew I had found my place. Up to that point in my life, my only experience with older adults was within my own family, but four loving grandparents had given me an open acceptance to this new adventure. Even then, I associated aging with illness, loss, and death. I had no idea that within those landmarks and major events were so many life stories, each one richly interfaced with the fabric of my own identity, family, culture, city, country, and history. Not a day passes when an older adult does not, either directly or indirectly, teach me something new or help me look at my life and my world with a different perspective.

Today, I arrive at work knowing that the day will focus on the needs of older adults, some with cognitive impairments, some with physical impairments, and all who are struggling, coping, and enduring the gamut of challenges of aging. Their chronological age ranges from 70 to 103, their health status ranges from pretty good to pretty bad, and their stories and life experiences range beyond the scope of the normal imagination. I can't imagine any other area in which every client has lived longer, experienced more, and acquired more wisdom than all the professionals involved. I also can't imagine a richer or more exciting client base with which to work. The nature of this work brings the social worker into intimate contact with family members and friends, and we often become close allies in easing an older adult's journey through the complexities of aging.

The Baycrest campus includes a hospital; the Jewish Home for the Aged; supportive housing; day care services; and a range of specialty services, community medical clinics, and outreach programs. A significant percentage of patients and clients are Jewish, and of those, almost half are Survivors of the Nazi Holocaust. They are the remnants of Europe's pre-war thriving communities and are now facing the challenges of the aging process.

I enter the complex and head toward my office, located on the administrative floor of the hospital. My desk is in its usual array of organized chaos—a pile of papers waiting to be filed, a stack of phone messages waiting for follow-up, another heap of newspaper clippings needing to be mailed to the appropriate people. My computer beckons with a screen saver that conjures images of dozens of new emails containing questions, assignments, meeting requests, and reminders of tasks waiting to be done. Finally, there is the permanently ensconced "to do" list, whittled down on a daily basis while simultaneously and exponentially growing in size. I usually try to get in well before my 9:00 a.m. starting time, as I know that the quiet hours before my colleagues arrive provide rare uninterrupted time and the opportunity to organize myself.

As a social worker in this setting, my ongoing and continuous clinical work is to positively motivate, support, and encourage the process that the frail elderly in general encounter with the aging process. With the Holocaust Survivor in particular, the work must focus on the same process, with the legacy of the Holocaust inflicting and intruding itself upon every aspect of daily living. The Holocaust and the impact it had on the Survivors, their families, and humanity in general is a complex and never-ending area of study. Every day, my mandate is to coordinate that study, investigate the unique needs of this special client group, and work with a multidisciplinary team to ensure that we respond to those needs in a context of optimum care, research, and education. Every day is a new adventure in responding to this mandate.

There are some fixed programs, such as the groups. As a longstanding group worker, I find that group work's tradition of emphasizing mutual aid and the best potential of individuals in an empowerment context is ideal for my practice. The Terrace Holocaust Survivor's Group, the two Second Generation Groups, and the two Child Survivor and Hidden Child Groups are all well attended and have taught all the social workers involved a great deal. These groups force me to deal with my own emotional involvement both with the overall impact of the Holocaust and the havoc it wrought on so many lives. Today, I am meeting with the Terrace Survivors Group, an open-ended group that I've been running for eight years.

I am looking forward to this group, but it wasn't always so. At the beginning, the Survivors claimed that I wouldn't be able to bear the burden of their grief should they share it, and initially I shared their fears. I had to find a comfort level for myself that coincided with theirs, and then develop a trust with a group of individuals who have every reason in the world to be leery of trusting. Years ago, our first meeting was unique. Mrs. L. crossed her arms over chest and said, "Thank you dear for asking me, but I will never talk." Four women followed suit. Three more didn't have the strength, and just sat weeping. It was a long, tearful, and painful process. We came up with operating guidelines and limits, with the members continually dealing with and clarifying their own needs for support, company, or solitude. This took place over time, and the physical and emotional toll the meetings took on the members was sometimes overwhelming. As a group worker, I don't remember a series of opening meetings of any other new group where almost all the potential members arrived already in tears, and the group leader was almost as frightened as they. Patience and persistence paid off, and time allowed everyone to develop faith and trust in the group process. Eventually, we all learned how to talk and listen and learned to support the pain and honor the strength. I came to realize that no matter how difficult or draining the process might be for me, I always walk away from meetings with a sense of privilege and satisfaction.

As this and the other Holocaust-related groups evolved, so did our knowledge base, and the need to disseminate it. I spend a good part of every day writing, talking, and pulling together the bits and pieces of information that we are accumulating on a regular basis. Following the Survivors Group, I prepare for an orientation of new staff. I am allocated a 30-minute segment of their first day at Baycrest and I must introduce a mixed group of social workers, nurses, dietary, housekeeping, research, and support staff to the issues surrounding aging Holocaust Survivors. This is an opportunity to convey both the difficulties and the rewards of individualized care and the unique needs of Survivors. This particular task forces me to focus my thoughts and condense a great deal of material into something meaningful and hopefully something that will make the new employees want to learn more. As important as our learning is, the sharing of that knowledge is even more important.

To achieve this, the computer and related technology have become an integral part of my work. Technology has expanded the scope of both the Holocaust Resource Project and the concept of social work in this setting. Emails arrive from around the world, from Survivors, from their families, and from their healthcare providers. Some require straightforward practical advice about resources, others ask for some clinical input, and many are tinged with heartbreaking stories of loss and trauma. I moderate a range of discussion lists, one for child Survivors and hidden children, one for adult children of Survivors, and one for healthcare providers.

Following a quick lunch, I return to my computer to read and respond to the various discussion groups. Throughout these exchanges, concrete advice, riveting stories, and therapeutic venting all take place. Some of these groups require almost daily contact, while others connect when a specific clinical question arises. Most importantly, a community of people who work with, for, or are related to Survivors has formed and joined hands with Survivors to work on enhancing all aspects of their lives. Developing and sustaining these connections in cyberspace is an aspect of community development that continues to evolve in my practice. The ability to sit at my desk in Toronto and "talk" to and consult with individuals around the world has enriched both the practice and the outcomes.

It is a broad job description, which in turn gives great variety and scope for innovation within the day-to-day activities. This afternoon a new intern has requested a meeting. She is a young German woman and has some concerns as to how Survivors might receive her. We spend some time discussing her fears, her family, and her knowledge of the Holocaust. She leaves my office with some literature and increased confidence about meeting her new clients. I have explained how quality care, honesty, and sensitivity to individual need can overcome most obstacles. I am also feeling very good about the caliber and commitment of new staff that is coming to the facility. Staff must learn about the historical aspects of the Holocaust and have an idea of what our clients endured. In the context of patient/client experience, they must also focus on quality care.

A large part of my job carries an educational component, and it is one that is extremely satisfying. In the process of training staff, students, family, and community members, all of my communication skills, my creativity, and my empathy is required. I am presenting difficult material, sometimes raise traumatic memories, and can offer no foolproof solutions. It is a wonderful opportunity to complement the traditional clinical aspect of social work.

Working with older adults can be compared to working in uncharted territory. When I began this work, "old" was perceived as around 75-80 years. Today we have many clients who have reached their 100th birthday. There are times when I feel overwhelmed by the depth of the pain and the extent of the trauma that I hear when Survivors share their stories. There are days when I feel I cannot listen to one more gut wrenching heart-breaking narrative. At those times, I know that I need to pull back, and rethink my role. Bearing witness is perhaps the most challenging part of the job, but it is also the most rewarding. It is both a humbling and an energizing environment that demands ongoing learning and commitment to a flexible approach to practice.

Since each day involves some teaching, my exposure and excitement about this component led to expanding that role to teaching gerontology at a local university. So today, and once a week each academic term, I leave work a little early and drive down to the campus. (This time will be made up later in the week, when I stay late to facilitate the evening Child Survivor Group.) Since I started teaching, I have found that in each session, there are only one or two students who are really interested in a social work career with older adults. The others are there to obtain the credit. One of my goals has become to share some of my enthusiasm for this work and present the material in such a way that the students will catch a glimpse of the scope of challenges and rewards found in gerontology, realizing the rich learning that is ongoing in supporting and working with older adults. My satisfaction comes from, by the end of the term, discovering a few "converts."

After class and some informal discussion with students, I arrive home by 10:00 p.m., tired but satisfied. It has been a long but productive day. My position with the Holocaust Resource Project is an adventure in clinical evidence-based practice, knowledge transfer, and opportunity. I am blessed to be actively participating in the lives and events of a group of people that most others are studying in history classes. In working with Survivors of the Holocaust and their families, I am allowed to share in their sorrow and pain, celebrate their resilience and achievements, and witness their capacity for life.

I have found that the social work profession's commitment to social justice and systemic empowerment is an important presence in the range of services necessary for older adults in general, and Holocaust Survivors in particular. Sadly, our society continues to marginalize its elders, not recognizing them for the resource they are. Add illness, cultural diversity, and early life trauma, and they have the potential to become further isolated. In the case of the Holocaust Survivors, part of my job is helping to create an environment that will not tolerate any further indignities. Since this is a systemic challenge, it takes a social worker's perspective and the support of a committed multidisciplinary team to work toward optimum care. I have long recognized that working with Survivors of the Holocaust and their families is both a joy and a privilege. Each day is a new adventure in social work practice and I know that I am fortunate to be at Baycrest at a time when so many Survivors from all over the world are turning to us for care, support, and understanding.

Think About It

1. What do you know about the Holocaust?
2. Why is it important to hear and preserve Survivors' stories?
3. What are the effects of historical trauma on future generations?

Chapter 40
Nursing Home Social Work

IIIIIIIIIIIIIIIIIIIIIIIIIIIIIIIIIIIIIIIIIIIIIIIIIIIIIIIIIIIIIIIIIIIIIIIIIIIIIIIIIIIIIIIIIIIIIIIIIII

by Patricia Gleason-Wynn, Ph.D., LMSW-ACP

All nursing homes or facilities are required to provide for the medically-related social service needs of each resident. Medically-related social services assist the residents in maintaining or improving their ability to manage their everyday physical, mental, and social needs. Federal regulations state that nursing facilities with more than 120 beds are required to employ a qualified social worker on a full-time basis. Facilities with 120 beds or less must provide services based upon the needs of the residents. In these homes, the social worker may be employed on a part-time or contractual basis. A qualified social worker has (1) at least a bachelor's degree in social work or a bachelor's degree in a human services field, including but not limited to sociology, special education, rehabilitation counseling, gerontology, and psychology, and (2) one year of supervised social work experience in a health care setting working directly with individuals. In many states, the individual must also be certified or licensed as a social worker to practice social work in that state.

I started out as a nursing home volunteer while in college studying to be a social worker. Initially, I was offended by the unpleasant odors and frightened by the advanced age and cognitive decline of many of the residents. However, I came to realize that my caring and attention meant a great deal to the residents, and I learned much about life and also about United States history from them. I was hooked! After graduating with my BSW, I was offered a job as the only social worker in a 180-bed nursing facility. Though

I had little practical experience and training as a nursing home social worker, I took it. The job turned out to be a great learning experience, as well as very challenging. Even after obtaining my MSSW and Ph.D., I have continued to work with older adults in and out of nursing homes.

There are many things I like about my job. First, I like working with older adults. Most of the residents have a wealth of insight and wisdom about everyday living, and are willing to share if asked. The residents seem to appreciate the caring attitude and attention. As an advocate for the residents, I look for ways to help them achieve their own personal goals and wishes. I seek to empower the residents by helping the staff understand the residents' needs for autonomy and control over what remains of their lives. I believe social workers play an important role in enhancing the residents' quality of life.

The second thing I like about the job is the autonomy. Even though my administrator is not too clear about what my job as a nursing home social worker involves, she knows that I know what has to be done to meet the psychosocial needs of the residents, and provides me the freedom and flexibility to do it. A nursing home social worker needs to be self-directed and able to work independently. I have been the only social worker in all the facilities where I have worked. There are no other social workers telling me what to do next or how to get it done.

Third, I like the diversity of the job. Though the tasks may be similar day to day, I work with different residents, family members, and volunteers daily. Diversity requires one to be flexible, as well as a wise time manager. Throughout one day, I may practice a variety of social work roles—a coordinator of services, liaison between the resident or family and staff, counselor, advocate, and educator. The days are usually quite busy, and may include meeting and assessing the needs of newly-admitted residents; documenting social histories, assessments, periodic reassessments, and progress notes; consoling a resident over a recent loss, perhaps a roommate's death; attending meetings such as weekly resident care planning meetings, monthly quality assurance and periodic department head meetings; visiting with individual residents; providing weekly reminiscent group therapy; and working with the resident, family members, and community services to arrange a successful discharge to home.

Finally, I enjoy the opportunity to work as a member of an interdisciplinary team. I have to communicate and work with other nursing home personnel: nursing, dietary, activities, and ancillary services, including rehabilitative therapies. Communication is necessary in order to avoid conflict and fragmentation or duplication of services. With the other team members, I assist in directing care toward meeting a resident's physical, mental, spiritual, and social needs. It is challenging at times working with different disciplines, assuring the resident's right to choice, and meeting various expectations set forth by the administrator and corporate office.

A typical day in my life as a nursing home social worker is as follows. The facility is licensed for 90 beds, and I work part-time. I like to arrive at work by 8:00 in the morning. There tend to be fewer interruptions in the early hours. Thus, I have some time to get my paperwork done. In my mailbox, there is a note from the night shift nurse informing me that Mrs. Smith needs a new pair of house shoes, and Mr. Brown's wife died at the hospital late last night. I add Mr. Brown to my mental checklist of residents to see this morning, and make a mental note to call Mrs. Smith's niece about the shoes. A look at the resident care plan conference list indicates there are twelve residents who will be reviewed this week. I need to see these twelve residents prior to the care conference to reassess their condition, evaluate their current psychosocial needs, and document their progress made toward achieving the goals set at the last quarterly meeting.

As I leave my office, I pick up my notebook. In it, I document the various social service requests I receive from residents, staff, and family members, in addition to my own observations and interactions as I am walking through the facility. I can refer to my notes later at my office, make the necessary phone contacts, and then check off the request after it has been met and documented in the resident's medical record. It keeps me organized.

I visit the three nurses' stations, review the 24-hour notebook and talk with the charge nurse about any changes in the residents' conditions, as well as any need for social work intervention. There are no referrals this morning. I breathe a sigh of relief, because I need to see the twelve residents for care planning and get their paperwork finished.

I stop to talk to Mr. Brown about his wife's death. His son and daughter are with him, and he's picking at his breakfast. I offer my condolences to Mr. Brown and his family. The son and daughter take the opportunity to go get a cup of coffee while I visit with their dad. I sit and listen while he talks about his marriage, how much he loved his wife, and how much he will miss her. He is also worried about who his next roommate will be, now that his wife won't be returning to the room. I assure Mr. Brown that I will inform him as soon as I know about a potential roommate. This seems to give him some relief. I give him a hug and tell him I'll see him tomorrow morning before the chapel service for Mrs. Brown.

As I walk toward Mary Jones' room to begin her reassessment for care planning, Bertha McDougal hollers out, "Honey, honey... come here, honey!" Mrs. McDougal has advanced dementia, probably of the Alzheimer's type. Though she does not seem to recognize who walks by her room, she calls out, because she is alone and likes to have her hand held. Significant conversation is difficult with Bertha, because she cannot follow the train of thought. She enjoys having her hand held and patting the hand of the visitor. After a couple of minutes of pleasantries, I offer to take her to the Activity Room where other people are gathering. She goes willingly.

Before lunch, I am able to see nine of the twelve residents who are going to be reviewed at the care conference. As I complete the required paperwork, I am interrupted by three family members asking questions about their relatives, by a call from Mrs. Smith's niece saying she will bring the house shoes tomorrow, by a resident who is going home soon wanting to know if I have contacted the home health people yet, and by a few residents who are disoriented and want to know where to go. I plan to finish the other three residents' reassessments tomorrow morning.

There is a Quality Assurance meeting during the lunch hour. I am the secretary for the QA meeting, so I have to go. The meeting ends about 1:15 p.m. After checking my mailbox for messages, I head out to the floors to complete individual visits with residents who are room bound because of physical or medical conditions, residents who are having difficulty adjusting to placement, and residents who have been assessed as requiring social work intervention such as remotivation, supportive counseling, and social interaction. The visits are completed amid interruptions for phone calls, questions from the Admission Coordinator and Director of Nursing about potential admissions, stopping to offer reassurance to residents who are confused, and saying good-bye to Bert Black, who is going home with his wife.

I stop to see Matilda Church, who was admitted yesterday. Miss Church has no immediate family. A neighbor provided minimal care for Miss Church until Miss Church fell last week and fractured her hip. Matilda is in the nursing facility receiving physical therapy, and hopes to return home within the month. I review the Resident Bill of Rights with Matilda, provide her with a copy, and document the interaction in the social service progress notes. I make a copy of her Living Will and Durable Power of Attorney for Health Care and place them in her medical record. I obtain the information I need to complete Miss Church's social history and initial psychosocial assessment. She wants to return home as soon as her hip is healed. We discuss various options for discharge planning. I assure her that I will work with her, the staff, and her neighbor to make the discharge a successful one. It's after five o'clock; it's time for me to go home.

There are a number of challenges facing social workers who choose to work in nursing homes. One of the challenges is the lack of training or preparation for the job. In their formal education, social workers rarely receive any training in the field of aging, much less in how to provide services to the nursing home population. When confronted with the reality of the work place and what one can realistically achieve, the social worker may experience tremendous dissatisfaction. The social worker is typically confronted with time constraints and high caseload ratios.

Lack of understanding by other staff, including administrators, about the social worker's role and functions is another challenge. Social work services are not always tangible, e.g., emotional support services vs. obtaining house slippers; thus, others outside the profession do not always see or understand the importance of the social worker's job. The staff needs to be educated about the functions of the social worker and come to view the social worker as a valuable team member and trusted advocate.

As nursing home social workers, we experience death and dying daily. We are constantly saying good-bye to residents and family members or friends who have touched us significantly. We have to handle our own grief while consoling others who are grieving.

The days are busy and at times long. I believe it takes a person with strong willpower, desire, and determination to make it as a nursing home social worker. The job holds personal rewards and benefits. These rewards include the hugs and smiles from residents and thank yous from the family and staff.

Think About It

1. Have you ever visited a nursing home? What do you think of? Think of the smells, the sounds, the sights. What is your reaction?

2. Do you work better in an autonomous role, such as that of the social worker in this chapter, or in one where you are given more direction by a supervisor? Explain.

Chapter 41
Senior Adult Coordinator

IIIIIIIIIIIIIIIIIIIIIIIIIIIIIIIIIIIIIIIIIIIIIIIIIIIIIIIIIIIIIIIIIIIIIIIIIIIIIIIIIIIIIIIIIIIIIIIII

by Madeline B. Cohen, MSW, CISW

My days as the Senior Adult Coordinator at the Tucson Jewish Community Center are never "typical." Each day presents new faces, new challenges, and new ideas. Join me on my daily journey into the wonderful world of seniors.

Coordinating activities for senior adults at a Jewish Community Center incorporates the basic tenets of social work practice, as well as the creativity of program planning and implementation. My scheduled activities range from "Lunch Bunch," a daily kosher lunch/socialization program for frail seniors, to "Young at Heart," a weekly lecture program for active seniors. "Lunch Bunch" includes chair exercises for seniors with limited mobility, as well as conversational Yiddish, current events, movies, and Bingo; a special luncheon complete with Hebrew ceremonial blessings is held every Friday to welcome the Sabbath. It is indeed incredible that fifteen regular members of "Lunch Bunch" are over 85 years of age. In fact, I was inspired to create the Nifty Nineties Birthday Club for any senior who reaches this special milestone.

The "Young at Heart" lecture series provides an opportunity for cultural and educational stimulation. The enthusiasm of this well-informed, politically astute group never ceases to amaze me. The members have a program committee that votes on their speakers, makes the calls to the prospective lecturers, and even writes the thank you notes. Topics range from famous artists to medical technology. Other senior activities are Bridge Club, Stamp

Club, Chess Club, and Friendship Club, a senior support group. A comprehensive sports and fitness facility is also available at the Jewish Community Center to meet the seniors' recreational needs.

My daily responsibilities include developing and implementing activities, making social service referrals to appropriate community agencies, and providing emotional support. Because seniors have very special needs revolving around their physical, emotional, financial, and social problems, a seasoned social worker is needed to assure appropriate referrals to community resources. I interface with the State Department of Family and Children's Services, mental health partial hospitalization programs, community physicians, and nursing homes on a regular basis. Family members often call me for guidance in dealing with their aging parents.

Providing growth-oriented supervision to paraprofessional staff, student interns, and volunteers is the key to a smooth operation. In addition, excellent organizational skills are a necessity in managing this fast-paced job, where each day brings new demands. I have learned that being tactful in difficult situations is imperative in establishing good rapport with older adults. I encourage monthly council meetings to allow the seniors an opportunity to verbalize and ventilate about their likes and dislikes. Since many of our participants were professionals before retirement, they need to feel a sense of empowerment in this new phase of their lives.

My interviewing skills are always put to the test when prospective members call to learn about activities. Many have just lost a spouse or recently moved to Tucson to retire. I must quickly assess each individual's needs and issue a personal invitation to at least one specific group activity. Patience is a virtue in this role. Since many seniors have no other contacts in their lives, they often want to share their thoughts, opinions, and grief with me. Empathic listening is required at all times, even if I have heard the same story one hundred times.

One of the positive aspects of this job is the opportunity for one-to-one relationships with a population that imparts wisdom, wit, and often a little "chutzpah" (nerve). Moreover, program development allows one's creativity to soar to new heights. It is always crucial to develop new activities for this population. I have found that anything is possible, from a drama club to bagel brunches. Day trips to local attractions and special holiday programs are quite popular. My position also requires planning one overnight trip each year. A scenic bus trip to a Nevada hotel/casino proved to be memorable for all of us.

Working with nearly one thousand seniors means that I will invariably run into one of "my" seniors in the community. It is indeed a treat to see a familiar face in the supermarket, mall, or library and to be greeted enthusiastically.

Unfortunately, the senior social worker must also cope with the physical deterioration of the aging and the inevitability of their deaths. My experience in bereavement counseling comes into play, as I must support the grieving family as well as the seniors who have lost a friend.

How do I cope with the emotional and physical demands of the job? The staff organizational design provides the answer. The Senior Department at the Jewish Community Center falls under the auspices of the Adult Services Department. This team concept allows for shared ideas, as well as peer support. The Center incorporates a yearly staff retreat for team building and enhanced customer service skills. I have had the privilege of serving on the planning committee, which has led to heightened camaraderie with my colleagues.

In addition to my agency, there are several organizations that provide ongoing support to the senior worker. The Pima (County) Council on Aging, a joint funding source for our kosher lunch/socialization program, sponsors periodic training on the nutritional aspects of aging, as well as governmental regulations. The National Association of Social Workers and the Institute of Continuing Education, a branch of Jewish Family and Children's Services, offer various conferences and group discussions with networking opportunities, as well as continuing education units to keep my social work certificate current.

I chose this specialty because of my commitment to community service and my desire to utilize my creative talents. My experience for this position includes years of group work in a mental health setting and enjoyable summers as a unit leader at a coeducational camp for Jewish children. Working with a vital senior population has allowed me the opportunity to grow both personally and professionally.

Think About It

1. Which part of this social worker's job do you think you would like best? Why?

2. Which parts of this job might be difficult for you? Why?

3. What surprises you about the senior adult coordinator's role?

Chapter 42
Home Health Social Work

IIIIIIIIIIIIIIIIIIIIIIIIIIIIIIIIIIIIIIIIIIIIIIIIIIIIIIIIIIIIIIIIIIIIIIIIIIIIIIIIIIIIIIIIIIIIIIIIIIIII

by Judith J. Lacerte, MSW, LISW, G.S. (Geriatric Specialist)

Home health social work requires flexibility, patience, and a genuine concern for the older adult population, the chronically ill, and their caregivers. Professionally, I came to home health social work from within a public health setting, as a result of my prior position. It introduced me to direct practice with the frail adult and the successful collaboration between a department of social services and department of health in serving the needs of the community. I discovered during this time that I relate well to senior citizens. I especially enjoy working with the very old.

The majority of my time is spent visiting patients in their homes, as opposed to seeing people in an office. My car acts as my office, with my beeper and cell phone facilitating communication among the office, patients, and other agencies. I work as part of a multidisciplinary medical team that includes nurses, physical therapists, speech therapists, occupational therapists, nutritionists, and personal care assistants.

I have a lot of autonomy and freedom, two things I like best about my job. For the most part, I choose how to use my time, and the days go according to the schedule I set. However, flexibility is still a key to enjoying this work. The best planned visit schedule may change one or more times during the day, depending on patients' availability (doctor appointments or unplanned hospital trips) and patients' needs. Although there are few social work emergencies, the work is fast-paced. Counseling for depression, anxiety, or pain management requires a more intense visit regimen than resource coordination.

I am on a beeper between 8:30 a.m. and 5:00 p.m. I choose to start my day early, at my home desk away from the commotion of a busy office, charting visits made the day before. I go to the office to hand in paperwork and make myself available to other staff. Nurses ask about resources and the psychosocial impact of a particular illness or social condition on patient care. As team leader, I assist other social work staff with questions about community resources and documentation around unusual visits.

Home health work is done in a prompt and timely manner. New assessments are ideally made within three working days of the referral and not more than seven days. Charting is turned in weekly, and statistics are collected monthly. In some ways, I am always "under the gun," so I can never get very far behind. My weekly schedule of visits is in place on Monday morning, indicating slots available for new referrals. I see patients 1-2 times per week for 4-15 weeks. Visits, in combination with the follow-up paperwork, meetings, supervision times, and being available for phone calls and questions, create a full schedule. I visit many agencies to coordinate resources. It is often easier to drop by an agency than to go back to the office and call. I work full time and have benefits, but the trend is toward pay per visit.

I rarely take lunch, as I am usually on a "roll" by noon. I stop to pick up coffee and eat my apple, carrots, and nuts while I drive. If there is time, I return to the office to check the mail, check the referral book, and follow up on phone calls. I use my "lunch time" to run a personal errand as needed.

I evaluate all patients for community resources and long-range health care planning. I counsel patients and their family members on issues relating to behaviors that may impede optimal health or adherence to a medical regimen, or that may require changes in activities of daily living. All follow-up visits involve aspects of one or more of these areas. I pride myself that I can move easily during one day from completing a psychosocial assessment to doing a relaxation therapy session with a patient in pain to arranging for another to be connected to community resources. I continue by counseling a patient for depression, assisting a family with nursing home placement, and educating a family on techniques for managing a family member with Alzheimer's Disease.

Medicare is the primary payment source and determines how charting is done. I format goals that are behavior specific, time specific, and outcome measurable. I devise treatment plans for each goal and address them in each charting. I do progress notes every 30 days and after a hospital discharge. The entries are brief, but specific. The prompt charting regime keeps me focused on patients' needs and treatment outcomes. I don't visit to visit. My role is clear as a professional helper. I am there to do a job, and the patient and/or family member sees the result, or knows what the barriers to care have been.

A typical day could easily include the following cases and interventions:

Mrs. Smith, 88, has a diagnosis of emphysema and middle stage Alzheimer's Disease. She lives with her husband of 55 years in a well-appointed trailer. Her husband is exhausted after seven years of caregiving and refusing all offers of help. Recently, his wife has become verbally and physically abusive. Afraid he was on the verge of hurting her and himself, he accepted his physician's recommendation for home health services. *Presenting problem:* Counsel spouse to cope with current situation. *Intervention:* This was considered an urgent referral and I cleared my calendar preparing for a 2-hour visit. After completing a psychosocial history and allowing time for the spouse to tell "their story," and share his feelings of guilt and grief, I identified with him the problems, needs, and possible solutions. The patient needed a way to control her outbursts, and the spouse needed respite and coping skills and requested nursing home placement for his wife. From the patient's home, I called the doctor to ask for a prescription to calm the patient without sedating her. I called several nursing homes, and forms were faxed to the physician's office for prompt attention. I gave Mr. Smith a mini-course on Alzheimer's Disease and the phone number of a 24-hour Alzheimer's hotline and support group. Our agency assured him a daily personal care assistant for his wife for two weeks. Before I left, Mr. Smith said he felt for the first time that there was hope, and he believed he could cope without taking drastic action.

Mr. Thomas, 81, has a history of cancer and rheumatoid arthritis with prior histories of drinking, depression, and chronic pain. He lives with his caregiver wife. He makes frequent doctor visits, but obtains little satisfaction. *Presenting problem:* Chronic pain and inability to sit still. *Intervention:* I had made several prior visits to this home. During this visit, I again led the patient in a 30-minute relaxation and visualization exercise. He remained perfectly still. He stated he expected to be pain-free for several hours. During the visit, the patient agreed to purchase a cassette player and relaxation tapes for pain control.

Mrs. Williams, 90, has a diagnosis of chronic heart failure and middle stage Alzheimer's Disease. She lives with her developmentally disabled but very solicitous son, age 62, in a small town. There is a long history of community involvement from churches to government services. *Presenting problem:* Mrs. Williams is increasingly hostile and has periods of refusal to speak, eat, or participate in self-care activities with the personal care assistant or her son. *Intervention:* I had made two visits to this home before. During this visit, I used Naomi Feil's techniques of Validation Therapy, to assist the patient in interacting with her environment. She was becoming responsive to me. Today, Mrs. Williams started actively cooperating with caregiving activities.

Mr. Jones, 65, has recently recovered from a stroke that left him paralyzed on one side. He lives with his elderly and frail brother in a relatively new, but "broken down" mobile home. Because of his successful recovery, the nurse and personal care assistant were preparing for a required discharge. *Presenting problem:* The patient's lack of safety without a personal care assistant and need for equipment in the home for patient self-care. *Intervention:* My first visit was a psychosocial assessment. I learned the toilet needed repair and that a shower bench, a shower rail, and hand shower would permit the patient to safely enter the shower stall and bathe safely without a personal assistant. Mr. Jones also needed glasses to read the labels on his medicine bottles. On this second visit, I brought with me a donated shower bench. I also brought a shower rail and a hand-held shower, which the patient agreed to purchase. In between visits, I called a local church, and one of its members, a retired plumber, agreed to repair the toilet and install the shower equipment. They further arranged for another member, an ophthalmologist, to obtain the glasses. The patient was discharged and able to perform his personal care needs without risk of injury.

On a day such as this, there is no time to return to the office. I go home, feeling productive and tired.

I love my job, because it is challenging and daily calls for innovative practice skills. It is undergirded with outcome-oriented charting that provides stability to fast-paced practice.

Think About It

1. Some social workers work in an office, some in the community, some out of their cars. Which do you prefer, and why?

2. Compare home health social work to hospice social work.

Chapter 43
Geriatric Care Management: A Growing Profession

|||||||||||||||||||||||||||||||||||||||||||||||||||||||||||||||||||||||||||||||||||||||||||||||||||

by Peggy McFarland, Ph.D., LCSW

Over the years, I can't tell you the number of people who have asked me, "Why would you want to work with all those old people?" I think back to my undergraduate days when I was obtaining my bachelor's degree in social work. I knew I wanted to work with older people, but all of the social work majors in my classes wanted to work with children. I was fortunate to find a professor and advisor who encouraged me to research and complete my field work in geriatrics. I went on to complete my MSW and Ph.D. in social work, all with a special emphasis on geriatrics.

What many new social workers don't realize is that the issues of aging and older adults are linked with many fields of practice—addictions, child welfare, health, and family counseling. Therefore, it is important and necessary for all social workers to have knowledge about working with older people. If you are not comfortable working with older people, I would suggest taking advantage of some volunteer opportunities working with older folks. I predict that you might find a new passion, because the need is so great and their appreciation is so genuine.

Why not go where the jobs will be? If you look at the demographic changes predicted in the world, by the year 2050, one out of every seven people in the world will be 65 years old or older. I call that guaranteed job security!

My passion for working with older people began at the age of 13, when I started working as a candy striper at the county home.

Even though it had another name, people still referred to it as the "county poor house." The needs of these residents found a place in my heart that has never died. I was one of those lucky people who found a passion early in life and stayed with it my entire career.

Starting my own geriatric care management business was something I felt called to do after working for other agencies for 10 years. I worked in home health for seven years and then started and ran a hospital-based adult day care for another three years. In both of these jobs, I found myself as the person who always thought outside of the box with an entrepreneurial spirit. I may not be the typical social worker, because although I want to help others, I also like the idea of developing a business and making money. I was scared when I first started the geriatric care management business, because even though I was confident in my knowledge of working with older folks and their families, I was not sure if people would pay privately for this service. I still remember being nervous quoting my price to one of my first clients, and yet the client did not bat an eye. Actually, I find that many of the adult caregivers pay for my services rather than having me bill their parents. Check out the Aging Life Care Association website at *http://www.aginglifecare.org* to learn more about these types of services.

My geriatric care management business includes work with geriatric clients and their families, corporate contracts with companies to provide eldercare information and referral for their employees, and contracts with employee assistance programs (EAPs) as a subcontractor for the clients who have eldercare concerns.

On this particular day, I start my morning at 9:00 by heading out to see a family that I have been helping for the past three months. The husband is a caregiver for his wife of 40 years, who has mid-stage Alzheimer's disease. They have two sons who live long distance but are very involved and concerned about their parents. I have been meeting with this couple to help them explore community options such as assisted living, home health aides, and respite care. The husband is becoming overwhelmed with the situation and needs to accept some help from others. The sons are pushing for them to move to a retirement community, but the husband doesn't want to move. I spend time today educating the husband about some of the behavioral techniques he can use to calm his wife down and to keep her safe. I also gently review retirement home and care options, in case we need to move in that direction. I think he trusts me, because I can be supportive and objective. He has given me written permission to discuss details with his two sons, so I will email them this afternoon when I get home.

At noon, I am scheduled to provide a "lunch and learn" seminar at one of the companies where I have an eldercare contract. As part of the contract, I agree to conduct a number of seminars on topics of interest for employees who have eldercare concerns. In the past, I have conducted seminars on selecting nursing homes, caregiver stress, Alzheimer's disease, and community resources. Today, I am presenting a seminar on "Family Decision Making and Planning for Long Term Care." I selected this topic because I have found that adult children are often concerned about their older relatives but don't know how to begin the conversation or what plans they need to discuss. Today, my group consists of 14 women and three men who are all involved in some aspect of caring for older relatives.

I am always surprised by the questions that arise during the seminars because of how much misinformation is out there. At this particular seminar, I discuss the need to have key documents in order, such as living wills, power of attorney, health care power of attorney, and wills. One participant tells me that she thinks her parents have a will and asks, "Isn't that enough to take care of everything?" I try to explain the difference between a will and a living will and what could happen if her parents don't have a living will in place and are placed on life support. I offer a list of elder law attorneys in the area to those who may need this contact information.

Another participant states that she is afraid to have these conversations, because she doesn't want her parents to think she is trying to take over their lives. She is having trouble making the transition from a child to caregiver. Although I don't see this as a therapy group, I ask if anyone else has experienced these types of feelings. Several folks share their thoughts about how they talked to their parents and tried to get involved in the decision making. I encourage participants to always include their loved ones in the process and to allow them to remain as independent as possible.

Another participant talks about how guilty she feels because she has to go to work every day and leave her mother home alone. We discuss how difficult it is to be a working caregiver, especially when your mother needs you to take her to doctor appointments when you are supposed to be working. She is a single woman who needs to work full time to support herself. At this point, I am able to share information about the free transportation available for older people in the community and to mention the family leave policy that employees can discuss with their human resources department.

Although I always feel as if these sessions could go on for hours, all of these employees need to get back to work, so I ask for one more question. My last question of the day is a difficult one: *What do you do when your parents refuse to allow help to come into their home even though they could benefit from it?* I try to have this particular caregiver think about why her parents may be refusing care. Are they concerned about the cost, don't want a stranger in their house, or afraid to give up their independence? Sometimes if we understand the cause, then we can help people move ahead with the process.

I end the session by reminding them all that part of their elder-care benefit allows them to call a toll-free number at any time to discuss their concerns or to request information about community resources. They can use this service no matter where their older relatives live in the country.

When I arrive back at the office, I return several calls to corporate clients who called the information and referral toll-free line. One of them needs the names of hospice programs in another state, which I research online. Another client wants to know about the Medicaid regulations related to paying for nursing homes. I often get this question, so I send her several pages of materials that I have developed on the subject. I find that in my line of work, I have to stay current on all the community resources and health care regulations. Sometimes I feel like a detective trying to track down information on services in other parts of the country.

I finish my day by emailing the sons of my morning client to keep them posted on my meeting with their parents. Since they live so far away, I know they are relieved that I am monitoring the situation with their parents.

Why would you want to work in geriatrics? So you can feel a sense of accomplishment at the end of every day!

Think About It

1. What traits would you want to see in a social worker who is helping your aging parents or grandparents?

2. Why don't many bachelor's level social work students want to work in geriatrics?

3. What aspects of working with the older population might be rewarding to you?

PART 9:
END OF LIFE
AND LOSS

Chapter 44
Hospice Social Work

IIIIIIIIIIIIIIIIIIIIIIIIIIIIIIIIIIIIIIIIIIIIIIIIIIIIIIIIIIIIIIIIIIIIIIIIIIII

by Daniel Liechty, Ph.D., D.Min., LSW

Hospice medical care is a growing field for master's-level, licensed social workers. In other areas of medicine, social workers too often find that in the economic pinch, social work services are considered secondary in importance. Nursing professionals have been very ambitious to extend their field of activities, and RNs now perform many of those social work duties that are considered vital. This has not been the case within hospice medicine. Medicare guidelines are very explicit about the need to preserve the interdisciplinary nature of care.

There are five core hospice disciplines, each making its own unique contribution to the care of the patient. Medical nursing services assume responsibility for the overall medical treatment. Typically, this includes aggressive pain and comfort control, bowel and bladder regimen, wound care, and monitoring nutrition and fluid intake. Home health care services focus on the personal care of the patient. Volunteer services focus on social visitation for patients and also clerical or public relations functions within the hospice program. Because Medicare regulations stipulate that at least 5% of the work hours for the hospice must be done by volunteers, hospices take very seriously the task of training and coordinating volunteer services. The Volunteer Coordinator position is often filled by a master's-level social worker. Pastoral counseling services are another of the core disciplines, a recognition by those formulating Medicare guidelines of the importance of spiritual issues in the face of mortality. It is with these professionals that the hospice social worker forms a patient care team, a team that closely consults, plans, and carries out the care for each individual patient.

Social work services focus on the psychosocial needs of the patient and family. This may begin with connecting the patient or family to available public and private services. The more a social worker knows about available services and the qualifications for each service (means, age, specific disease, geographic location), the more that worker can be of service in connecting the patient or family to relevant services. Individual and family counseling skills are extremely important in hospice social work. Assisting the family in organizing its available resources for caregiving is usually necessary. Family members may be available and ready to provide the care. Yet it is not uncommon for even very competent people to be stumbling all over each other. As a less emotionally involved outsider, the social worker can play a valuable catalytic role in such very concrete tasks as assisting the family in working out a schedule and assigning care tasks to specific family members.

Care for a dying loved one always stirs up death anxiety and related emotional stresses within a family. The hospice social worker remains available to the patient and to each family member for supportive counseling and for psychotherapy related to death anxiety and anticipatory grief. Such issues vary widely from family to family and are strongly influenced by such factors as age, ethnic and religious background, the patient's place in the family system, and past experiences of resolved or unresolved grief. The worker also needs to know his or her limitations, both in terms of personal expertise and limitations imposed by the function of the agency.

Most hospice cases are paid at a capitated rate. This means that the social worker does not increase agency income by making more visits. Therefore, hospice social workers should be generally less tied to productivity rates than in other agency-based work, and also have greater freedom to concentrate services on those clients most in need at any given time.

There are cases of complicated grief that are either beyond the expertise of the worker or would require an investment of time that is beyond the function of the agency. Recognizing when to refer to specialists is one of the hospice social worker's most important tasks. Hospice social work perpetually moves between practical experience and theory. The hospice social worker will be engaged in expanding his or her theoretical knowledge through studied reading and further education. It is clear that the psychosocial care of hospice patients and families demands the attentive concentration of a trained and highly professional social worker. In addition to membership in the National Association of Social Workers, affiliation with either the National Council of Hospice and Palliative Professionals (Social Work Section) or the Association for Death Education and Counseling (ADEC) is important for keeping you up to date.

Let us now look at an actual day, a Tuesday in February, typical in my practice. I arrive at the office by 8:00 a.m. The first thing I do each time I enter the office is to check the RIP notices. This tells me which patients, if any, have died. That information is very important, because it affects all other scheduling. If a patient has died, I prepare a discharge summary and the paperwork for bereavement follow-up. In larger hospices, bereavement follow-up is handled by a bereavement specialist, often a master's-level social worker. But in my agency, I handle that task as well. I spend about an hour looking over paperwork, answering mail, and calling patients to schedule the appointments for that day. I see some patients on a regular schedule each week, but most patients are scheduled on the day of the visit. This allows more scheduling flexibility for me and allows the patient to easily decline a visit if he or she does not feel up to it on a given day.

I usually begin visits by 10:00. Social work visits are not generally appreciated before the morning routine is over. This particular morning, however, will be a bit different. My hospice is hospital-based and I have been asked to lead an in-service on death, dying, and grief for the dialysis group in the hospital. Health care professionals are placed in emotionally paradoxical positions. They possess a body of knowledge and skills that makes them adequate transference objects for suffering patients seeking assurance. Yet this same body of knowledge and skills also forces them to acknowledge less-than-optimistic prognoses in many cases. Coping mechanisms for shouldering this paradox, as well as the personal death anxiety stirred up by working day in and day out with extremely vulnerable patients, is the theme of this in-service. Such in-service leadership adds a dimension to my job that would not be possible except in a hospital-based program. Another example of this added dimension is my participation as a standing member of the hospital's medical ethics committee.

The in-service runs until 10:30, so I schedule my first patient visit for 10:45. My first visit is with a 96-year-old man. Although a cancer patient, he is still active and mobile. It is the first warm day in months and, as I expected, he wants to get out for a walk. We walk out to his barn and he explains each piece of equipment to me. He has done this many times before, but each time, I encourage him to remember different stories that go with the use of each piece. This allows him to keep his mental faculties stretched and active, and also allows him to make narrative closure on his life as a whole. I finish this visit at 12 noon. My next client is scheduled for 1:00 p.m. Driving time will be about 20 minutes. I could go back to the office to write up my notes, but in this case, it makes more sense to go to the public library.

There are a few tricks of the trade a hospice social worker needs to know. One of these relates to equipment. You need a good, comfortable and reliable car, but not one so nice that it bothers you when it gets to be a total mess inside. You need a detailed map of the catchment area, one that shows every single street. You may prefer Google Maps or another app. When I was in the field, I used a book-type map with a comprehensive index, marking landmarks on that map. These included diners and fast food places, where I could grab coffee and a bite in a hurry; libraries, where I could do paperwork in peace and always find a public rest room; and any other public rest rooms I could find. Your toolbox will also include an accordion file with at least five copies each of every form of your paperwork and documentation; a good set of black pens; a pocket dictionary of medical terms; a professional book or journal you are studying, which can be read in 5-minute slots; and back at the office, a copy of the "bible," Therese A. Rando's book, *Treatment of Complicated Mourning.*

I leave the library at 12:45 p.m. and eat my lunch in the car on the way to my next appointment. My one o'clock appointment is not actually a hospice patient, but rather a home care patient. Like my agency, many hospices find it most cost-effective to be teamed up with a home care service agency. In smaller agencies, this allows for better utilization of nursing personnel and more advantageous quantity pricing for pharmaceuticals and medical equipment. My agency employs a home care social worker—I only see home care patients if the longer term plan is to discharge them to hospice.

In this case, however, I have been asked to visit the woman to find out why she has been absolutely resistant to the presence of home health aides in her home, a form of assistance she desperately needs by all objective standards. She is 89 years old and lives with her 94-year-old husband. She suffers from advanced vaginal cancer, which has spread to the liver, and was discharged from a recent emergency hospital visit into home care. She could easily qualify for hospice services, but she is unwilling to accept hospice. I met with her a few months ago after another hospitalization to speak with her about this. She equates accepting hospice services with "just giving up." We in hospice don't see it that way at all. We see ourselves as continuing an aggressive fight against the illness. But it is a fight on another level. That is, after diagnostic medicine has done all it can to fight the illness directly, palliative medicine continues that fight on the level of combating the ability of that illness to rob the person of the maximum quality of life, however that person defines it, for the time that person has left.

The equation of accepting hospice with giving up is a common social prejudice. The price people pay for that prejudice is continuation of torturous, agonizing, and invasive treatments months after such procedures can do any good for the person and may actually be doing harm. It is sad, but as respect for patient autonomy is a cardinal hospice and social work value, it is a situation we must live with until a shift occurs in the values of the larger society.

The woman rants and raves about the inept housekeeping skills of the home health aides she had during the first two days. She angrily told them not to come back! I am lost for a way to turn. She is ethnic Italian, so I ask about her own special recipe for pasta gravy, just to make friends. Her face lights up as she explains the delicate nature of stewing red sauce and adding the right spices (at least one of which, of course, will go with her a secret to her grave). At last she sighs and says she no longer has the strength to cook like that. I sense an opening and ask her to talk about her earlier days, before she and her husband moved to this small apartment. She goes on and on about what a great housekeeper she had been. Her house, her garden were the envy of the neighborhood!

"I was strong! Not like now, worthless, useless..." I form a hunch.

"Did you help any of the older ladies in the neighborhood to cook and clean?"

"Of course, all the time! They needed me!"

"Did you view those ladies as worthless and useless because they needed your help? I can assure you, nobody views you as worthless and useless now that you really need help with your cooking and cleaning."

Once that connection was made, her attitude changed rapidly. By the end of the visit, she and I together called the home health services supervisor to request an aide for the following morning. She only asked that the aides ask her what needs to be done before just jumping in and doing it, and that they tell her where they put things when they do the cleaning. Easily respected requests.

It is a short drive to my next visit, and I arrive at 2:15 p.m. The patient is a 67-year-old man with end stage lung cancer. In many ways, this is the diagnosis I dread the most. The patient is hooked up to oxygen, has no energy, and gasps for breath with even the slightest exertion. At this late stage, there is also often a tradeoff between pain control and mental alertness. He has chosen pain control and is sound asleep when I arrive. I spend the session with his wife, who spends the time reminiscing about their happiest times and tearily seeking my reassurance that they are doing the right thing.

These kinds of visits wrench my guts. It is easy to see that professional burnout could be a problem in this line of work. My style is to meditate purposefully and regularly on my own mortality—not on a sweet by and by, a reincarnation or some other emotional escape, but on my own death, finality, ultimate personal limitation. I find this allows me to truly stay with people emotionally who are hurting because of their mortality, yet also relieves me of any messianic complex, of assuming responsibility to carry their pain with me constantly and to fix everything.

I'm back at the office by 3:30 p.m. If this were Monday, I would be leading a bereavement group at 7:00 p.m. As it is, however, I have just enough time to write up the paperwork on these last two visits before leaving for home at 4:30. Maybe I'll have time tonight to watch that tape of my favorite episode of *ER*....

Think About It

1. What is the underlying concept of hospice?

2. Why might some clients/patients be resistant to accepting hospice services?

Chapter 45
Pet Loss Support Group

IIIIIIIIIIIIIIIIIIIIIIIIIIIIIIIIIIIIIIIIIIIIIIIIIIIIIIIIIIIIIIIIIIIIIIIIIIIIIIIIIIIIIIIIIIII

by Juliet Sternberg, LMSW

Thursday is my Monday, the start of a busy four days of work. As the practice director of Hope Veterinary Clinic, which I run in collaboration with my veterinarian partner, I walk to work on Thursday mornings anticipating all the tasks that need to be accomplished. These include meeting with staff members, responding to client emails and voicemails, managing the finances, and ensuring that the environment is in good shape.

We do not charge for my counseling services—they are instead part of the comprehensive services that Hope Vet provides. Rather, I am paid to manage the practice. This works well unless there is a billing dispute involving someone I have been counseling. In this event, I delegate the issue to one of my assistants—the office manager or head receptionist—rather than enter into an awkward and ethically conflicted exchange with a client.

It is not until early evening, when I take a walk to collect my dog from daycare, and stop at home to feed him and my cats, that my thoughts turn to the evening's Palliative Care and Grief Support Group. I wonder who will come. Because it's a drop-in group open to anyone (Hope client or not), and to people nursing their pets through end-stage diseases, as well as people experiencing loss, participants vary each week. However, similar issues recur no matter the number or demographics of the attendees. Most people come once or twice, and occasionally someone will come for many months. Sometimes, people will return after a break or

315

seek individual therapy from pet-sensitive social workers to whom I refer them.

I still have a little performance anxiety and worry that I won't be of adequate help, but after 10 years of running this group, I reassure myself that the magic of the group will prevail.

Although animals have lived around the human fireplace and grain store for thousands of years, it is only in recent decades that pets have been recognized as integral members of the family. Sadly, the social work profession seems to be lagging behind our clients in this regard. Numerous bereaved clients have reported that their therapist has stated something to the effect of, "You should replace your lost pet and realize that it was just an animal." Needless to say, this does more harm than good, and clients end up feeling even more isolated and unbalanced when, in fact, they are experiencing a very normal response to a profound loss. I apologize too often for my profession and hope that the next generation of social workers, recognizing pets as family members, will be more empathic.

This evening, three people attend the group. Josie is in her 70s. She walks using a shopping cart for stability, the result of a stroke a decade ago, which robbed her of her dancing career. In the interim, she and her husband divorced, and she has recently lost her 12-year-old dog, Mikey, to cancer. As she speaks, it becomes clear that the impact of the cumulative losses is wearing on her. Josie has been coming almost weekly for five months and says that the group is helping her find community and support. For the first four months, she was focused entirely on her stated inability to get over this loss. "I miss him so much," she repeats. "I should be over this by now." Encouraged by the other participants, Josie is gradually acknowledging the multiple losses and that "getting over this" would mean not needing the group anymore and giving up the last identity of being a loving pet owner. Finally, she acknowledges that she doesn't really want to work on "getting over it" at all, and that this is okay. She is convinced that she didn't love Mikey enough, and is berating herself for this, in spite of doing things like wrapping gifts for him and putting them under the Christmas tree. We know her well enough to tease her gently about her perceived lack of love, and she laughs.

People commonly express feeling guilty that they didn't do enough—and the group finds itself discussing what is "enough." The participants conclude that it is indefinable, and animals thankfully have remarkably low expectations about "enough" where love, care, and quality of life are concerned. For a moment, Josie can acknowledge that she wouldn't be feeling this much pain if she hadn't loved Mikey, and the others reassure her that Mikey certainly experienced that love. I expect Josie to attend the group for a long time.

Amanda is a new attendee tonight. She reports that she lives alone and has recently lost her cat, Sammy, the admitted love of her life. "I had to wait all my life for the right man, and when he came, he was a cat!" she says. The group laughs, easing any tension she has about being here for the first time. Amanda expresses her spiritual beliefs about Sammy being in heaven and worrying that he might not know how much she loved him and that she wanted only the best for him. This leads to a more general discussion about the spirit world and animals' place in it. This is a common theme, and I am often reminded of my social work training to "meet the client where the client is." This means never imposing my own spiritual beliefs, but always trying to support clients in exploring their beliefs and thoughts. Ritual is often meaningful for clients, and Amanda talks about doing something to honor Sammy's memory. The group helps her with suggestions about making a scrapbook of photos and memories, writing letters to Sammy telling him how important he was to her, and inviting friends to a memorial gathering. All have been used in the past to good effect depending on circumstances and appropriateness

Monica is the third attendee tonight. Her border collie, Jackson, is in the end stages of intestinal cancer, and she is here for support during this intense nursing and caretaking experience. We used to separate people whose pets are in the throes of palliative care from people who have lost pets, but we have found that combining the groups can be cathartic. And so it was tonight—Josie and Amanda helping Monica to make quality of life decisions, and Monica reassuring Amanda and Josie that they were indeed great "pet parents." We talk with Monica about the paradox of this experience—becoming intensely closer to her beloved Jackson, all the while knowing that she will soon lose him. Amanda says that this has been a life-changing experience, and Monica is agreeing with this. She is using the time of reflection and intensity of emotion to consider a career change to work with animals, or volunteering at an animal shelter after she loses Jackson.

The participants all say how helpful the group experience is to validating their feelings and being able to share similar experiences with one another. I find this to be the essential power of the group over an individual counseling session—the sharing of common experiences helps normalize feelings that they may have believed to be abnormal, and it decreases the isolation so prevalent after a profound loss. And no matter how dissimilar participants might appear at the outset, ultimately the common bond of love and loss makes for a potent and moving group experience.

Typically, four consistent themes emerge in pet loss groups:

1. Clients need reassurance that they aren't crazy for feeling so devastated about the loss of their close companion, and the loss of their caregiver role.

2. People need reassurance that they made good decisions and need not feel guilty about treatments they decided to pursue or the decision to euthanize their pet.

3. Clients are sometimes angry after a pet has died. If they are angry with the doctors at our clinic, I have to try hard to not take it personally, but rather to recognize that it is a normal part of the process of trying to rationalize their pet's death.

4. The emotional pain of the loss will eventually not be so intense but will never completely fade. New pets may be adopted and may become equally as loved, but can never ever replace the lost pet.

I am often tired and have low energy when I come to group. It has almost always been an exhausting day. But when the group ended tonight, as in most weeks, I am left feeling what brings us all to this profession—the satisfaction of using my skills and experience, of helping people to feel a little better, and giving them some supportive tools to use to help them during the coming months. And I am warmed by the participants' gratitude of finding a supportive social worker and a group of pet owners who understand the importance of their relationship with their pets and the deep pain of their loss.

Social work students often contact me enquiring about working with animals. While I believe that there is a tremendous need for social workers to work with animals and people, and that animals are a largely underutilized social work intervention, the most challenging aspect of obtaining work in a private veterinary clinic is the difficulty of getting paid for doing clinical work. I am paid at Hope to be the administrator. Other social workers have obtained veterinary nursing degrees or sought training in animal-assisted therapy. Provided that new social workers demonstrate self-reliance and creativity, there is no reason why they shouldn't seek to make a career in this emerging social work field.

Think About It

1. Think of someone you know (perhaps yourself) who has lost a pet. How did you respond to that loss? Being perfectly honest, did you consider that the pet was a family member? If so, why? If not, why not? And how did this feeling influence your response to the loss?

2. How do you feel about death, loss, and grief? It is something we will all experience in our lives, but is something with which few people are comfortable. What can you do to feel better prepared to help yourself and other people cope with the experience of loss?

3. How might pets be of benefit to people with various needs? How could pets be used at your internship placement or in your social work practice?

(Note: This chapter was originally published in Riding the Mutual Aid Bus and Other Adventures in Group Work.*)*

PART 10: MANAGEMENT

Chapter 46
The Daily Life of a National Association Executive

IIIIIIIIIIIIIIIIIIIIIIIIIIIIIIIIIIIIIIIIIIIIIIIIIIIIIIIIIIIIIIIIIIIIIIIIIIIIIIIIIIIIIIIIIIIIIIIIIIIIIII

by Elizabeth J. Clark, Ph.D., ACSW, MPH

E ver since childhood, I have liked being busy and having a variety of experiences. I don't do well with repetition, with maintenance, or with wasting time. In graduate school, my favorite book was Howard Parad's *Crisis Intervention*. I realized early on in my social work training that I loved crisis intervention and would not be happy doing long-term therapy or any job that required similar activities day after day. As I look back on my career, I realize that I have chosen venues—mainly hospital social work and administration—that allow me to use all of my skills and that present different challenges each day.

When asked to write a brief chapter about my position as executive director of the National Association of Social Workers (NASW), I happily agreed. I believe social workers make excellent administrators, and I hope many of you reading this will consider the positive impact you could have by joining a management team.

Under NASW structure, the executive director is the Chief Staff Officer. It is a paid position. Our president (elected for a three-year term) is the Chief Elected Officer. The President is a volunteer and chairs the Board of Directors. The executive director is responsible for the day-to-day operations of all entities of NASW.

The easiest way to showcase the variety in my job is to chronicle one day. It is a fairly typical day from a time and activity perspective, but each day is unique. That's what I like most about my job.

I start my day by scanning several news programs on television. NASW has social justice in its mission, so political issues are important to us. I generally leave the house around 8:00 a.m. and have an hour commute by train. If I don't have an early meeting, I like to arrive between 9:00 a.m. and 9:30 a.m., after people have had their coffee and conversation and settled down for the day.

I have three assistants. Two are executive assistants who divide administrative duties. The third is my special assistant. She holds an MSW and works on most projects with me, attends meetings, speaks on my behalf, and manages the Social Work Reinvestment Initiative.

One of my executive assistants arrives at 8:00 a.m., and she scans emails that have arrived during the night and early morning, forwarding important ones to me via my smartphone. I can often address them while I am on the train. I am an ardent fan of my phone. I am exceptionally good on one and hardly ever use a computer anymore. I use my smartphone for correspondence, but also for any writing projects, including reports, grants, and this book chapter.

When I arrive at the office, my second executive assistant hands me my calendar for the day. One of the things I learned early on in my position is that only one person can keep my calendar. Requests always go to my assistant, and he schedules appointments and travel. That, and meeting preparation, is close to a full-time job.

First on my agenda is a staff meeting to review our flexible health benefits package. Our program administrator is present to give guidance and discuss why the program is a good choice for staff. I only stay for the introduction.

I have approximately 100 staff in the national office. NASW is what is called a 501(c)(6) under the federal tax code. That designation is a membership association or guild, and we have 56 chapters as administrative units. We also have a separately incorporated foundation (a 501(c)(3) organization), a Political Action Committee (PACE), a Legal Defense Fund, and a separately incorporated for-profit insurance company—NASW Assurance Services—that provides liability insurance and group life benefits for our members.

The NASW Foundation houses many programs, including the Center for Workforce Studies, the newly formed think tank, the Social Work Policy Institute (SWPI), and the Social Workers Across Nations (SWAN) Initiative. Each of these programs has a social worker as a director. These programs represent research, policy, and international practice.

We also have a Social Work Practice Division, where social work staff develop practice standards and updates, represent NASW at relevant meetings, and work in coalitions. We hold the profession's *Code of Ethics* and manage the peer review process for ethical violations. We offer professional credentials and continuing education programs. We also have a press that publishes a dozen or more social work books and five professional journals each year. In addition, we have a communications department that manages our public relations activities, including our website and social media functions, and a marketing department for the association. Our legal department is composed of three attorneys who handle both chapter and national legal issues, write and file amicus briefs, and develop our *Social Work Law Notes* publication series.

To meet our social justice mission, we have a Government Relations Department that includes our lobbyists, our PACE (Political Action for Candidate Election) activities, and our field organizing program. We also have the Social Work Reinvestment Initiative, which includes the Dorothy I. Height and Whitney M. Young, Jr. Social Work Reinvestment Act in Congress.

On any given day, I can spend time in meetings with staff from any of the areas just mentioned. On the day I am describing in this chapter, several of these areas require attention.

After the staff meeting regarding benefits, I am scheduled to attend a meeting with a Congressman's staff. It is scheduled for 11:00 a.m. That means I need to leave the office by 10:30 to allow enough time for travel and to get through the security at the Rayburn House Office Building. It can be exciting to be on Capitol Hill. It can also be time consuming. Two staff accompany me to the meeting. We discuss the plan for reintroducing the Social Work Reinvestment Act in the 112th Congress, and how our Social Work Policy Institute could assist our social work colleagues on the Hill.

I am 20 minutes late for an informal luncheon planned for noon in my office. The chair of our National Committee on Nominations and Leadership Identification is in town to conduct a virtual meeting to develop the slate for the next election of our national Board.

I have a few minutes to see what is pending in the office. I review all correspondence, blogs, and marketing materials. There are several reasons for my review. First, anything put on the web is there forever. I also want to see anything that is going out under my signature. The main reason I like to review materials is to stay informed on activities within the Association.

At 1:30 p.m., I join the virtual meeting on nominations. I welcome the committee members and thank them for their service. Fifteen minutes later, I am back in my office. I have a few more minutes of free time to check emails. My emails are screened by my staff and are identified by a color code to help me determine which ones I need to act on first. It is not unusual to get 300 emails per day. These do not include listservs or junk emails.

At 2:00 p.m., I attend our monthly leverage committee meeting. There are about 20 staff in attendance. They represent our various departments. I established the leverage committee several years ago to deal with the numerous requests we receive each week, such as inquiries asking NASW to be part of a coalition, support a program, provide funding for an event, attend a meeting, or join an initiative. Each request is carefully considered using a set of guidelines. Relevant staff are prepared to present the request, to discuss the pros and cons, and to show how our agreeing to the request will leverage the association and the profession.

At 3:00 p.m., I have a meeting with my financial team to review the monthly financial report. The team includes our COO (Chief Operating Officer), who is a talented social worker; our controller; and our assistant controller. My special assistant (another talented social worker) also attends most of my meetings. She keeps track of issues, follows up on pressing items, and she manages my project list.

We had a solid month financially, so the meeting goes quickly. We identify a red flag area or two, and agree on which budget line items will be more closely watched for the next month. At the conclusion of that meeting, the COO stays to discuss a personnel item.

At 4:00 p.m., I have a meeting with the executive director of the North American Association of Christians in Social Work, one of more than 40 sister social work associations. We have met previously, and we have a nice collegial relationship. My special assistant also sits in all meetings with outside organizations. In the 45 minutes we spend together, we come up with several ideas for enhancing our partnership.

It is now past 5:00 p.m. Three staff are waiting to see me. Staff can set up formal meeting time, or they can check my schedule and try and catch me between meetings or before I leave in the evening. The assistant director of development wants sign-off on the end-of-year fundraising campaign for the Foundation. Next, I meet with the governance relations associate who manages the board nomination process for an update on the virtual meeting. Finally, I meet with the director of our Social Work Policy Institute, who is leading a social work research delegation to Cuba early next year. We review the letter of invitation that will be sent in the coming week.

My last meeting is with my executive assistant, who needs to confirm calendar entries and conflicts. We also review some travel arrangements. I travel approximately twice per month for meetings and speaking engagements. Many of these meetings are during the weekend. Although I don't mind the travel, and I love speaking and meeting social workers around the country, I never get to recoup the weekend days. That means that some work weeks are extra long.

My executive assistant also asks me to review a final copy of the report we are submitting to the People to People Ambassador Program. The report is an overview of the activities of the social work delegation that NASW led to Russia a few weeks ago. It looks terrific. We have a wonderful in-house graphic designer, and she works magic on our printed materials. The report is 40 pages and needs to be read before it is submitted. I take it with me to read when I have time.

Tonight, there is a dinner meeting in Virginia. A group of social work leaders will be meeting the following day, and a pre-meeting dinner has been planned. Dinner is scheduled for 7:30 p.m. My special assistant travels to Virginia with me. Because it is rush hour, it takes us about an hour by train. The dinner goes well. It's almost 9:45 p.m. when we leave.

When I came to Washington ten years ago, I thought I would enjoy the Washington social and cultural scene—galas and dinners and evening events. I now try to avoid many of them. They are surprisingly similar and predictable. They often end quite late, and I still have an hour commute to get home. I prefer to leave the office at seven. My COO and I travel on the same train. Frequently, we leave the office together and spend another 45 minutes addressing issues we couldn't get to during the day. If we don't ride together, I use my smartphone to finish correspondence or make staff assignments.

Tonight I go home about 11:00 p.m. I usually get home about 8:00 p.m. If my husband is in town, I cook dinner. My phone is off. I seldom do any work after dinner, and I seldom watch television. I am, however, an avid reader and I always have a novel on my Kindle.

Reviewing my day, it is easy to see why I love my job. I am never bored. On any given day, I have the opportunity to use many social work skills and to be involved in a wide variety of activities that serve thousands of NASW members and advance the profession. I deal with social work practice, research, education, policy, and administration. My schedule today covered insurance, human resources, operations, finance, policy, governance, collaboration, international affairs, marketing, development, public relations, and social networking. I made one trip to Capitol Hill and one to Virginia. I had both lunch and dinner with social work colleagues. The day was full, busy, and productive. Best of all, I know tomorrow will be different.

Think About It

1. What social work skills do you currently possess that would be useful in an administrative position?

2. What micro skills do you use on a regular basis that would transition to macro practice?

3. How would you feel about working the extended hours and weekends required to fulfill the responsibilities of leading an organization?

(Note: Elizabeth J. Clark was the NASW executive director/CEO from 2001 to 2013.)

Chapter 47

Life as an Agency CEO

||||||||||||||||||||||||||||||||||||||||||||||||||||||||||||||||||||||||||||||||

by Judith C. Czarnecki, MSW, LISW

I awake with a start at 4:45 a.m., the remnants of my Board Chairman's words in my head and the answer to the question he had posed forming in my mind. I reach for the notepad I keep by my bed for just such occasions and jot down a few things "to do" in order to get the information needed. Most of my CEO friends report having the same type of experience. I'm one of the lucky ones, though. My inspirations usually come close to dawn instead of the middle of the night. It's 5:00—only a half hour before my usual rising time. I read the parts of the newspaper I didn't get to last night and, by then, it's time to arise. Every morning, five days each week by 6 a.m., I'm at the gym. I believe it's important to be in good physical shape to be a CEO. My days as CEO of a social service agency are long, and hundreds of decisions can be made within them, so I need endurance, energy, and stamina. The morning is really the only consistent time I have, because of various meetings and other events that need attention. Some days, like today, I have to cut my exercise routine short to go to early morning meetings. This week, I have only two early meetings—some weeks I have five.

My first meeting begins at 7:30 a.m. It's with two Board members at an area restaurant to discuss plans for new programs. It goes well, and I leave with minutes to record and four different program ideas to research within the next three months. I arrive at the office in time for my 9:30 meeting—a brief session with the Vice President of Finance and Administration. She has an update on the audit, which will be completed soon, and needs some financial reports signed for some of the mental health boards. We also briefly discuss the requirements for the new MIS manager we will be hiring soon. It's critically important for the CEO to keep very close tabs on the finances. This is an area most social workers learn little about in school, so it requires additional training and constant work to be sure everything is in order. A large part of it is assuring the agency has a knowledgeable, well-qualified accountant in charge of the fiscal area. The agency now has about a $3 million budget, and this is my fifth controller in six years. I think I finally have someone who really understands accounting. She has never worked in the not-for-profit sector, so both she and I spend some extra time to be sure she learns the intricacies of the requirements of our various funding sources.

At 10:30, my next appointment is waiting. The new Chairman of the United Way is making a courtesy call with the President of the United Way. They are making the rounds of the funded agencies to learn about them and get input from the executives regarding the United Way's new three-year investment plan. I proudly review the agency's services (we are the United Way's second largest investment, as we receive more UW money than any other program except the Red Cross) and share with them my concerns about the new plan. The UW has decided to withdraw its support of programs for domestic violence perpetrators, as it believes this is a criminal justice issue. Although it is too late to change the UW's plan, I present my case to help my visitors understand the impact this decision will have on our agency and services to families where domestic violence is present. I haven't decided yet how we will handle this internally and, so far, have informed only the administrative team. We're still investigating the possibility of reclassifying the program in order to get it funded. After all, we have the equivalent of two people doing that work and serving about 200 batterers per year. It would be difficult to terminate this service.

It's 11:40 when they leave—just enough time to check my messages before leaving for my noon Rotary meeting. I note that I missed a call from the VP of one of the local hospitals, whom I've been trying to contact for the last month. I also need to call the Council on Accreditation. We're up for our re-accreditation this year, and I'm a Peer Reviewer and a member of the Central Accreditation Commission—it's hard to tell which of these items needs attention today. I pull out the notes I made when I awoke this morning and put them on top of the "to do" pile.

The Rotary meeting is important for making business contacts necessary to the agency. It is a little difficult, as I am one of about 20 female members in a group that numbers more than 500. Most of the other women are also from social service agencies, so we have somewhat of a bond. All of us, however, are in Rotary for the same essential reason, so competition is common. Especially as resources (financial and personnel) become scarcer, competition increases. So far, all I have gotten for the agency from my membership is one computer set-up (about $2,400). I've tried getting funding to help with a couple of other programs, but haven't yet been successful. I really need to spend more time getting to know the right decision makers.

It's 1:20 when I return from the luncheon. It was good—I was able to connect with the President of a local bank. He will put me in touch with a trust officer to determine if there is a fit between some of our programs and some of the bank's trusts. I just have time to review my notes before my 1:30 appointment with two representatives from a local foundation, who want to discuss our application. We've requested $30,000 to fund a program working with fathers of children born to teenage, unwed mothers. The representatives are here with questions from their review committee, and they want to take a look around our facility. It's really good news, because this meeting means we made the second cut in the review process and, if all goes well today, we'll probably get the grant. We won't know for another two months, but it's looking good for now.

It's 2:25. I have 35 minutes before the meeting with the United Way to review the part of the investment plan into which our Home Care program falls. I check phone messages again and return the call to the hospital VP from this morning, but he isn't available, so it's another round of phone tag. The call to the Council is more successful—they ask me to review an agency in Florida. I accept, although I'll be the "Team Leader," which means more work. The reviews are a lot of work (about 40 hours before we get on site and another 24 or so once we're on site), but they are excellent learning experiences. Every time I do one I learn something—either a new program idea or, just as important, I learn how NOT to do something. The on-site visit won't be for three months, although the work will start when the materials arrive, in about a month. I return three more calls, leaving voicemail notes on all. It's now 2:50 and time to head downstairs for the United Way meeting.

4:45—I'm back from the UW meeting. I check my messages and find one from my Board Chairman. I forgot to make the calls I thought of this morning, so I hurriedly call another CEO friend of mine to get some background information before calling the Board Chairman. I reach him at 5:10—a good time to get him. We discuss the information I have that he needs for a meeting day after tomorrow, check a few other items, and set another time to talk.

5:45—Time to review the mail, check the rest of the messages, attend to things that need to be done, and be sure I have everything in order, as I'll be out of the office the rest of the week. I leave the office at 7:00 and head home to eat, then pack for a three-day conference in Milwaukee. Before retiring, I mentally review the day, realize there was something I forgot to tell my secretary, make a note to call her from Milwaukee, pack, read the mail and most of the paper, and retire around 10:30.

Most days are similar to the above. As the President/CEO of an agency, the only way to get time for planning and research is to block out time from the schedule. If it's not blocked out, the secretary will book it! Being a CEO is demanding, exciting, stressful, fun, frustrating, sometimes lonely, and fulfilling. It is hard to get used to the impact your words and actions carry and harder still to understand that no matter what decision you make, someone will be upset. Especially in today's ever-changing environment, there is never a dull moment. Salaries range from about $40,000 for a small organization to over $120,000 for very large (over $15 million) agencies (a few not-for-profit CEOs who head national organizations can make even higher salaries).

I am one of the "old time" CEOs who received a master's degree in clinical social work, and started out as the director of a branch office of a larger organization where I did a lot of clinical work, as well as provided administrative oversight of the office. That's back when agencies hired "executive directors" and wanted them to be "practice experts," not necessarily "expert managers and leaders." With the changes in the corporate world, Board members now have much less time to devote to agency activities, and they delegate more responsibility to the CEO. This has occurred at a time when the social services world is in the throes of major restructuring and long-range planning has been reduced to about three months. This requires more business acumen on the part of the CEO—things often not acquired in graduate schools of social work.

A recent trend in social service agencies is to indicate a preference for hiring someone with an MSW and an MBA. The second preference is to hire someone with an MBA, and the third is to hire a person with an MSW or other related degree (MPH, MPA, Ph.D). Although this preference pertains mostly to larger (over $2 million) agencies, there is a similar trend among smaller agencies in larger communities. Agencies in smaller rural areas still look for MSWs and, preferably, one who can provide a combination of administration and direct clinical work.

Being a CEO is a demanding job. However, it can be quite fulfilling. There is nothing quite as rewarding as developing a program, getting it funded, and knowing that you have been responsible for helping people change their lives in ways that may not have been possible without your agency's help. It's the spirit of social work, and it's what makes all the long hours and frustrating moments worth it.

Think About It

1. Brainstorm ideas for keeping the program for domestic violence perpetrators going.

2. Which is more important—for the CEO of a clinical agency to have clinical expertise or business expertise?

Chapter 48

Transferring Micro Experience to Macro Practice: Working at the Child Welfare League of America

IIIIIIIIIIIIIIIIIIIIIIIIIIIIIIIIIIIIIIIIIIIIIIIIIIIIIIIIIIIIIIIIIIIIIIIIIIIIIIIIIIIIIIIIIIIIIIIIIIIIIIIIIIIIIIIIIIIIIIIIIIIIIIIIIIIIIIIIIIIIIIIIII

by Roxana Torrico, MSW

It is a 30-minute metro ride into the city. It is usually a race to get on the train, only to be squeezed in between tons of people in business suits reading their papers, eager to begin their day. I get off at Union Station and slowly walk down North Capitol. As I look up, I am struck by the beauty of the Capitol. I am also stunned by the sight of several homeless men and women sleeping on the streets, begging for food or money. I look around and wonder: *Does anyone notice or are we so used to seeing this type of poverty that we are not affected by the sight of homelessness even on the streets of our nation's Capital?* I am always shocked at how one of the richest countries in the world does not have enough money to provide people with enough supports and affordable housing. And then I am reminded of why I have chosen this line of work.

As I walk into my office building, I remember how as a graduate student, I was certain that I wanted to work with families in a direct service capacity, not realizing how intense and challenging this work would be. After graduation, I went on to work full time with a local child welfare agency as a foster care social worker. At the time, I was also employed part time as a case manager for homeless families in a transitional housing program. In my work with homeless families, I was faced with many former foster youth who became homeless as adults. I remember wondering if there was a link between the two systems. It did not make sense to me how three out of seven of my homeless clients used to be in foster care.

After about 18 months, I recognized that direct service in a child welfare agency was not a good fit for me, and I accepted a position as a Program Manager for the Child Welfare League of America (CWLA). CWLA is the nation's oldest and largest membership-based child welfare organization. It is an association of almost 1,100 public and private nonprofit agencies that assist more than 3 million abused and neglected children and their families each year. At last, I would be able to combine my professional experiences with the child welfare and homeless systems to act as a change agent. Although I knew when I accepted this position my work would be different, little did I know how different it would be!

Today is Monday. List of Things To Do: *(1) review draft for housing poster, (2) finish PowerPoint presentation, (3) schedule interviews (Utah, California, Washington, Oregon), (4) attend NPEYH.* I begin EVERY morning by checking my email. I scroll through several internal and external emails—confirming meetings, providing policy updates, and requesting information regarding housing options for youth.

I click on the most important email, a request for information. A worker from Colorado is interested in knowing what kind of housing options are available for young people in her state. I pull out my Colorado folder—I have one for almost every state. Fortunately, Colorado has a very promising housing program. I provide the worker with a contact name and send her several attachments with details about Colorado's Family Unification Program. The Family Unification Program (FUP) is the use of time-limited (18 months) Section 8 vouchers for youth aging out of the foster care system. Young people ages 18-21 who have left foster care at age 16 or older are eligible for housing assistance and aftercare services. I explain that in October 2000, Congress passed legislation that made youth aging out of the system eligible for these time-limited Section 8 vouchers. I also send her some information about other program models that are assisting youth with housing upon discharge from public systems. I make myself available for further assistance and update her on current CWLA projects relevant to housing options for young people. I click "send" and take a minute to process. I get these emails from workers all over the country. Usually they are surfing the Web or receive information regarding a recent presentation. I am always hopeful that they find the information useful.

After responding to the information request, I move on to the first item on my "List of Things to Do": *(1) review draft of housing poster.* One of the deliverables from my grant is to create marketing materials for youth and adults regarding housing options. In an effort to do this, I have collaborated with a national network for foster youth to create a poster to educate young people, member agencies, independent living coordinators, community-based workers, policymakers, and advocates on the importance of safe, stable, and affordable housing for youth aging out of the foster care system. I have been working closely with the designers to make sure that the pictures are culturally diverse and the wording targets both young people and adults. I call the designer again to discuss some more changes in the poster—I would like one of the pictures changed. After a long conversation and yet another brainstorming session, the designer and I decide since this poster will be distributed all over the country, that we should take advantage of the space on the back. We decide to add national statistics on the cost of housing and resources on the back panels. Off to work to gather more information. Who knew how much time went into creating a poster? I have been working on this for months!

Next item on my list: *(2) finish PowerPoint presentation.* I am scheduled to attend a conference in Austin, Texas, to discuss housing for youth. I have done this presentation in the past, but I always like to add some local information when I present. I spend some time doing some research on the Internet, so I am able to incorporate housing costs for Texas in my presentation. "Found it!" According to the National Low Income Housing Coalition, the cost of a one-bedroom at the Fair Market Rate is $543 a month. The hourly wage to afford this one-bedroom is $10.44. I didn't make that much when I was 18. But here is the kicker—the number of weekly hours (at state's minimum wage) that a young person must work to afford this apartment—81! This is both powerful and shocking information that I must add. Professionals need this type of information to make change. I always incorporate a policy and practice perspective to my presentations. The people who do the work need this information to inform policymakers on the need for change. "How can we expect young people with no outside supports to afford housing on their own? How can we be surprised by the intersection of foster care with homelessness, incarceration, unemployment, and high pregnancy rates when we don't provide these young people with the tools and supports for a successful future?" I could go on and on.

I save my changes to my desktop—ready to make copies to pack up for the upcoming presentation.

On to the next item on my list: *(3) schedule interviews (Utah, California, Washington, Oregon)*. I spend the afternoon making phone calls to the Independent Living (IL) Coordinators on the west coast. I am currently leading the efforts of a collaborative project with other national partner organizations aimed to improve the housing outcomes for youth aging out of the foster care system. A major component of this effort involves identifying and describing promising efforts designed to address their housing needs. As a first step, I am conducting interviews with state Independent Living Coordinators across the country. The purpose of these interviews is to gain insight into each state's discharge policy, use of funding, and housing options offered to the numerous young people as they age out of the foster care system. Unfortunately, I have to leave messages for all but one of the state Independent Living Coordinators. The IL Coordinator from Utah answers the phone! I introduce myself and give background information on CWLA and our recent initiative on youth housing. He is very interested and is willing to set up a time to do the interview. I explain that it should only take 20-40 minutes. He asks "Do I need to do any research before the interview?"

My response: "There are only two questions you need to be prepared to answer: (1) How many young people age out of your state's system every year? and (2) How much of your Chafee funding is being used for room and board services?" In an effort to assist youth in their transitions to adulthood, the Foster Care Independence Act (FCIA) of 1999 established the John Chafee Foster Care Independence Program, allowing states more funding and flexibility to assist young people in their transitions to adulthood. States received increased funding and were permitted to extend Medicaid eligibility to former foster children up to age 21. Additionally, the Chafee program allowed states to use up to 30% of their federal funds to provide room and board services to youth 18 to 21 years of age. This includes young people who move into independent living programs, age out, and/or lose touch with the child welfare agency and then return for assistance before reaching the age of 21. He is thankful for the opportunity to share this information. We schedule a time for the following week.

I am scheduled to spend the rest of the afternoon at a National Partnership to End Youth Homelessness (NPEYH) meeting. I take a short metro ride to the meeting. I always enjoy having meetings somewhere else—change of scenery. I arrive to the meeting just in time. The National Partnership to End Youth Homelessness, a national coalition that represents the fields of child welfare, juvenile justice, mental health, homelessness, and housing is committed to ending youth homelessness. We have a meeting about every six weeks. Today, we are having a guest speaker to discuss the issue of reentry—juveniles being discharged out of public systems without an effective discharge plan. This is an issue that the group has been interested in for some time. Our speaker is very interesting but unfortunately reinforces what NPEYH already knows—"There isn't enough research to support that juveniles coming out of detention centers are becoming homeless." We spend the last few minutes of the meeting brainstorming next steps relevant to the issue. We look up at the clock. Time to wrap up. We schedule our next meeting. On the agenda: The Issue of Reentry.

Done for the day. Off to the metro. I spend the next half hour working on my "List of Things to Do" for tomorrow.

I usually find that unless a person has worked with or knows someone who has been in public systems, it is not something that they think about. However, approximately 20,000 to 25,000 young people age out of the foster care system each year, many without familial or economic support. Not only has it been frequently reported, but I have also witnessed foster youth leaving the care of the child welfare system without the skills or support networks necessary to enable them to become self-reliant adults. My professional experiences as a trained social worker have allowed me to witness the economic losses and the emotional, physical, and psychological impact of abuse and neglect on children and families. As a result, I recognize the importance of sound practice and policies, cross-training among disciplines, and comprehensive, culturally competent wraparound services to ensure the well-being of children, youth, and families. I am thankful that I am able to combine practice and policy to make change!

Personal characteristics that are helpful in this type of position include the ability to be organized and work independently. I cannot survive without my "List of Things to Do." I am often invited to meetings and events, so it is also important that an individual in this type of position be comfortable with networking and public speaking.

This position requires that an individual have a master's degree in social work or a related field with at least two years of experience in housing, homelessness, and the child welfare system. Salaries are commensurate with professional skills and experience.

Macro level social work (policy, research, program planning) is very different from micro or mezzo level practice. The most important thing to note is that there is no face-to-face delivery of services. If you enter this level of social work practice, you will serve as a change agent. Therefore, I strongly recommend that you either work part time in direct practice or volunteer, so you do not lose touch with reality. It is often easy to forget how we arrived to the social work field when we are spending so much time in meetings and writing reports.

Think About It

1. Which organizations are analyzing and influencing policies, conducting research, or providing consulting or training at a national or state level in your areas of interest?

2. Which organizations are stakeholders in housing, homelessness, family preservation, or child welfare issues?

3. Do you feel that it is important for a social worker to work "in the trenches" before working in an organization on a macro level? If so, why?

(Note: This chapter was originally published in More Days in the Lives of Social Workers.*)*

PART 11: VETERANS AND THE MILITARY

Chapter 49
Family Advocacy in the Military

||||||||||||||||||||||||||||||||||||||||||||||||||||||||||||||||||||||||||||||||||||||||||||||||||||||||||||

by Carol Hendler, MSW, LCSW-C, LICSW, LCSW

It's 5:30 a.m. I stick my arm out of the covers to turn off the strident beeping of the alarm clock. Oh, how I would love to turn over and sleep for another couple of hours! Wouldn't it be nice to have a "normal" job with people who don't think the day begins before the birds waken? What in the world is a former flower child type like me doing working for the Army, anyhow?

I force myself out of bed, turning on the bedroom light to help begin the transition to Ms. Hendler, Clinical Social Worker. A quick shower, tending to the cat's needs for fresh water and food, my own breakfast, and I'm in the car, thankful to be going to the military hospital where I work in the Family Advocacy Program of the Department of Social Work.

It took something of a circuitous route for me to enter civil service. I worked for two years in the Family Advocacy Program at a nearby Army installation under a contract with a private firm, which filled social work positions at the various military bases around the country. It was in this position that I learned about the unique military culture. Confidentiality in the military regarding a soldier's personal affairs is applicable for soldiers who seek assistance. Even then, if commanders wish information about their soldiers, they have the right to ask, but the clinician is only required to surrender the information when directed by a military lawyer. This release of information to a commander is on a "need to know" basis, which allows the clinician to stick to the minimum and "nothing but the essential facts."

The Family Advocacy Program was designed to assist commanders in dealing with the distractions their soldiers experience when there is a child or spouse abuse situation. In fact, F.A.P. (in the military, if anything can be reduced to an acronym, it will be) is called a commander's program. The function of the Armed Services is to defend our country. When a person enters the service, it is made quite clear that he or she is now a military asset. Being victims of familial abuse not only deters the soldiers from their mission; it also might harm government property, the soldier's body. Being perpetrators interferes with soldiers' ability to do their job and brings their judgment into question. I've been told by many soldiers that they have been told they are expected to control their families. Therefore, it seems the violence is sometimes the result of a soldier's felt impotence in that endeavor, because, as those outside the military community recognize, it is not within the scope of healthy human relationships to control others. As soon as a report of family abuse is received at F.A.P., the commander of the sponsor is notified. The sponsor is the military member of the family who is responsible for his or her family members, also known as dependents.

Despite doing the same work as Federal employees, while working for the contractor, I was paid 10 percent less and had much poorer benefits than my equivalent civil service colleagues. I entered the civil service system by taking a job at the commuting distance Department of Veterans Affairs in a long-term drug and alcohol treatment program. I stayed a year and missed being in Washington, so I applied for a civil service social work position in the Family Advocacy Program at the hospital where I am now employed. The experience with the drug and alcohol program was invaluable, as a high percentage of F.A.P. cases involve addictions.

By 0700 (7:00 a.m.), the main parking lot is already filling up fast, despite the fact that work, even for most military personnel, doesn't begin until 0730. There is a frantic scramble, like ants at their hole, as civilian employees and soldiers try to secure the quickly evaporating spaces before they are all gone. The process is generally completed in another 2-3 minutes. The smaller lots closer to the main hospital and main buildings on the installation have filled up at least a half hour before. No sense in looking for a place there, wasting precious time while the big lot fills up. My car joins the row, front bumpers all lined up at attention.

I walk the equivalent of a couple of city blocks to the mental health building, our new quarters as of this past September. It's a nice feeling, walking into the clean, modern edifice. Our old quarters were next door in an ancient, patch painted building with inadequate ventilation and a broken water fountain. When we moved into our new building, we all received individual offices with new computers and maroon and tan color-coordinated furniture. Within the sanctuary of my office, there's enough room to accommodate four adults and one child. Because the furniture was part of the contract for the construction of the building, we were faced with another of the strange thought processes that occur in the military. Despite the fact that the mental health building houses the Department of Psychiatry, the Department of Psychology, and the Department of Social Work, chairs in the offices look ideal for people applying for bank loans. Comfortable, relaxing therapy chairs they are not. *I must find some second-hand cushy seats to replace these as soon as I can,* I think to myself as I enter my office.

After locking my purse in the cabinet over my desk and disengaging the call forwarding from the front reception desk, I check the email for any important bits of information. Today there is a reminder about the in-service presentation to be held after the Case Review Committee (C.R.C.) meeting. I pull out yesterday's statistics form, which itemizes my time in 15-minute increments, and add up the figures. My door is open, and colleagues are filtering down the corridor to their offices, stopping to wish me and each other a good morning, filling coffee pots with water, and exchanging a few pleasantries.

My phone rings. "Good morning, Carol Hendler here." "Good morning, Ms. Hendler. This is Alice. Do you have a few minutes?" she asks, hesitatingly, soft spoken, sounding timid, frightened. Alice is typical of several civilian wives in my spouse abuse case load. They tend to be polite, passive, and unhappy, and hope their husbands will someday have a sudden awakening to how their inconsiderate behavior is hurting their wives. At the time of this realization, the husbands will change their behavior and become loving, involved spouses. Many of these wives say they endure continuing abuse, in addition to the documented dynamics of abuse, because they were told during their indoctrination as military wives that their husbands' careers depend on maintaining a "good" family. Family problems could lead to demotions with their attendant reduction in pay, bars to reenlistment, discharge, or in extreme cases, Courts Martial. They are often fearful their husbands will take out their rage about being disciplined on their wives. A reduction in pay also affects the entire family, so most of the women keep silent. To counteract this situation, the Congress passed legislation called the Transitional Assistance Program. This law provides the families of soldiers discharged because of abusive behavior with twelve to thirty-six months' salary.

When a commander is called and informed that his or her soldier is involved in an act of family violence, the case manager can make the recommendation that the commander place the soldier in the barracks for a few days, providing a cool-down period. Commanders have no authority over civilian family members. In the case where a female soldier, living in military housing, is being abused by her civilian husband, it is the wife who can be ordered out of the home. When there are children in the home, these judgments seem to require the return of King Solomon.

Alice's situation came to the attention of the Family Advocacy staff when the unit's administrative coordinator received a call from the on-call social worker. All the civilian social workers take a week's worth of turns providing after-hours and weekend coverage. The turns occur two to three times per year. On the previous evening, the on-call social worker received a call from the emergency room reporting a possible Family Advocacy case of a wife who had a scratch on her neck and a bruise on her upper right arm, which the wife stated had occurred during a fight with her husband. Her husband had come home at 0100. They argued. It became physical when he grabbed her by the arm and pushed her against the wall. She can't remember how she got the scratch on her neck, but she didn't have it before the fight. At this point, the wife was able to reach the front door and run to her neighbor's. The couple lives in Army supplied quarters a couple of miles from the Army hospital installation in a community setting.

The on-call social worker checked to be sure there were no children in need of supervision, then called the soldier's commander, who went out to the home and ordered the soldier into the barracks for a few days for a cool-down period. The social worker spoke with the wife, who said her neighbor was with her and could drive her home. The wife was informed that someone from the F.A.P. would be calling her to set up an appointment. The F.A.P. supervisor referred the case to my co-worker who, as part of her standard operating procedure, called the Provost Marshall's (P.M.) Office and the Criminal Investigation Division (C.I.D.) to report the cases. I provide individual therapy to the wife. The case manager has enrolled the husband in the anger management group, which F.A.P. pays an independent contract clinical social worker to lead. As the couple shows they are ready for conjoint sessions, they will be given that opportunity. Had this been a child abuse or neglect case, the Child Protection Service in the appropriate county would be notified immediately.

The case manager has written a synopsis of the case for presentation to the C.R.C. As 0800 approaches, the F.A.P. staff and a multidisciplinary team from various hospital agencies assembles. New cases and cases up for review are presented with only a number to identify them. Reviews are generally on a three-month basis, but can be scheduled sooner depending on individual circumstances. The commanders related to each case have been invited to attend and are generally present. Following the case presentation and any questions asked and answered, a vote whether to substantiate or unsubstantiate abuse or neglect is taken on new cases. Most votes follow the recommendation of the case manager, but not always. The C.R.C. determination carries. This is not a court of law. The goal is to provide treatment for the family to prevent violence from occurring again. Therefore, only a preponderance of information that an incident occurred is required to substantiate a case. On rare occasions, a C.R.C. has recommended that a Commander initiate administrative action against a soldier. In such cases, it is usually when the soldier is noncompliant with the treatment plan or is declared a treatment failure or has had other incidents of abuse.

Following the C.R.C. is the 1½-hour in-service presentation, at the main hospital building, about a city block away. One of my social work colleagues is presenting a case study of a client with bulimia. Following this is lunch at the hospital cafeteria and a return to my office to spend the afternoon in two individual sessions and one conjoint couple session. It's now 1600 (4:00 p.m.) and time to return to what feels like a very different world.

Think About It

1. What are some unique issues in working in a military setting?

2. Would you like this job?

Chapter 50
Employment Outreach With America's Heroes

IIIIIIIIIIIIIIIIIIIIIIIIIIIIIIIIIIIIIIIIIIIIIIIIIIIIIIIIIIIIIIIIIIIIIIIIIIIIIIIIIIIIIIIIIIIIIIIIII

by Doris Nelson, LMSW

It is a busy Tuesday morning. I press the control key on the computer keyboard to find that there is another client on the log. "I just finished with one person and now there is another one. It has been steady since we opened at 8:00 a.m.," I think. It seems that each client I have seen for the past two hours is "desperately" looking for work, realizing, after six months of hit and miss job hunting, that they are at their last week of receiving unemployment benefits. I think, "Don't these veterans remember those days of being in the military, of getting things done and done on time, never to procrastinate? What are they thinking about?" Anyway, I hit the F1 key to see if the veteran has looked up three jobs on the job site intranet, so I can give him more details about where the position is located, the salary, and job description of the position of interest. There are no jobs selected. No other notes have been keyed in to reference what the veteran needs. "Well, what does this person need?" I wonder.

The Department of Labor is not just a place to file for unemployment benefits and look for a job from the job site intranet the agency lists every day. The agency is now known as the one-stop career center, where people can file for unemployment, look for jobs, and get assistance in going to school if they qualify. Partner agencies are at the labor department on assigned days to receive referrals for clients needing public assistance, such as food stamps, housing, vocational rehabilitation, training for those over 55 years old, and more. There is a resource center that offers computer classes, résumé and cover letter classes, interviewing classes, and classes for those who are transitioning from incarceration. We see hundreds of people every day seeking assistance in job placement, academic/technical training, or social service assistance. Because our time is limited with each client, an average of 15-20 minutes, we work fast and, in turn, a few clients become revolving clients, fall through the cracks, or leave with a bad taste in their mouths that they did not get the help they needed. I am the only licensed master's level social worker in the agency. Many of my colleagues do not possess any degree, but newcomers to the agency are expected to have at least a bachelor's degree or four years of experience in a human service agency and familiarity with unemployment insurance. Being fresh out of graduate school and passionate about working with America's heroes are the factors that drove me to accept the position, even though the pay is lower than that of a secretary.

Many of my clients have recently gotten out of the military through retirement, finished their enlistment term, or have been out for many years. Many have stated to me that they still think back on their military days and the "can do" attitude they had in getting tasks accomplished when told to, but now it seems since they have hung up the BDUs (Battle Dress Uniforms), the drive they once had has dwindled away. Many of my clients are used to a structured environment—when their supervisor or NCO (Non-Commissioned Officer) told them to do something, it was done without question. I remember my own experience in the military. I liked the structure, the traveling all over the world, the "yes, sergeant" or "no, sergeant" or "can do, sir" remarks. There wasn't a dull moment in the military! I had many dreams and goals to accomplish, but they ended very quickly because of a disability that I incurred. I couldn't see a light at the end of the tunnel. I asked, "What am I going to do? Where am I going to live? What can I do to obtain suitable employment that I would enjoy and be capable of doing with a lifelong challenge that I have to accept?" Many of my veteran clients have similar challenges that have them wondering, "What, when, where, how, and why?"

My next client is a retired Army Vietnam/Persian Gulf veteran. As I call his name, he gets up and follows me to my cubicle office. I greet him and he speaks softly. At my cubicle, I introduce myself, saying, "My name is Doris and I will be working with you today." He says, "Thanks," and holds his head down slightly. I ask about his military career and what job he is seeking. He talks briefly, but his sad facial expression speaks louder than his words. I listen and watch. He states, "I got to be honest with you, ma'am. I lost my job, my marriage is over, and my spouse took all my money. My bills are overdue and I am getting ready to be put in the street."

"What a mouthful to swallow," I think. I look at him—silence. He covers his face. My brain is rolling with questions. I know my counseling will be limited to finding a career and landing a job. All the other issues this veteran has going on are things I am not to address very much. It isn't part of my job. I know I can only work with him no longer than twenty minutes, but he has many concerns and issues that cannot be brushed away. How can he effectively get back in the job market and obtain a stable job and deal with his other worries at the same time? What does he have as far as other family support, community, and other personal resources? What is his mental capacity? Any suicidal thoughts or harmful intentions to others or himself? I begin to talk softly, showing concern and asking questions. Thankfully, he does not have any intentions to hurt himself or anyone else. His eyes fill with tears.

He reports that half of his military retirement check is allotted to his minor child. He has a few friends he did some landscaping and carpentry work for, and they have offered him extra money to help him stay above water. "I do with what I got, but it is getting harder and harder. I feel like I am sinking and I can't get up," he tells me. We begin to work on what strengths he has right now and how to utilize them in the areas that are causing concerns or hindrances.

The client opens his briefcase and pulls out his credentials—a résumé that needs to be updated, a DD 214, a Social Security card, certificates, awards. I look at his résumé and the other articles. "This is good," I tell him. The résumé is well written and states all his skills from his military career. I see many skills that could help him in two positions we currently have listed on the job intranet. He has supervision and leadership skills. I tell him about the positions and we begin to review them.

After three meetings and six telephone counselings, the veteran revises his résumé to target the positions that we have reviewed— one for a local charter school as a superintendent of housekeeping and a federal position on the military base. I feel that he would want something paying a lot more than $30,000 a year that is being offered for the position—Custodial Superintendent. He doesn't. He states, "I had to wax floors, clean rooms and toilets in my military career, so I don't mind the work."

The tasks seem hard and tedious. In the military, everything was done when it was supposed to be done, he says. He is used to everything being structured and done on time. I tell him it has to get harder before it can get better, but hold on and continue to do what is necessary to meet your goal. After the veteran has sent and re-sent the needed paperwork for the positions, I advocate and negotiate with the employers, playing phone tag to set up interviews. The light at the end of the tunnel begins to appear. My client is able to work out housing accommodations with his friends. He has been offered both positions, and has to make a choice. Success! He calls me from time to time to say hello and to thank me for helping him. I tell him, "It was the determination in you to get the task accomplished."

It's not all in the money you want to make, prestige you want to hold up in lights, or the recognition in everything you do. It is the gratification in helping human beings who felt that their whole world would crumble, and we as social workers let them know that the power is within them. We are just the vessel used to give guidance and allow them self-determination in setting their own goals that are suitable for them and not us. Everything that may be right for us is not always right for them.

Working with veterans is a challenge within itself, because many have so many skills from their military experience and want to utilize them in the workforce. Many employers do not realize that the skills veterans have learned while serving in the military in just a few years is as much experience as someone working a whole lifetime. The challenges they face, especially those who served in wartime, make them able to see beyond the surface of what we see. They feel that they are not appreciated. The benefit that they have given us is the freedom to come, go, and sleep at night while they, the veterans, have stayed up all night in the cold, the heat, or sleeping on the ground, giving their lives to ensure that those not serving will be safe.

These are the heroes that I give honor to and ensure that they are able to give back to us the experience that keeps us free.

Think About It

1. What are your feelings about working with veterans? Do you feel employers should treat them differently from those who did not serve in the military? Explain.

2. In what way would you work with this veteran, knowing you
    had only 20 minutes to come up with a plan? Would you have
    done any more or less than the worker did? Why or why not?

(Note: This chapter was originally published in More Days in the
Lives of Social Workers.*)*

PART 12:
HIGHER AND
CONTINUING
EDUCATION

Chapter 51
A Social Work Educator's Day

||||||||||||||||||||||||||||||||||||||||||||||||||||||||||||||||||||||||||||||||||||||||||||||||||||||

by Stephen P. Cummings, MSW, ACSW, LISW

My path to becoming a social work professor was not direct. When I earned my MSW in 2002 and became a medical social worker in a large, trauma-focused hospital, I thought I'd reached my professional goal. However, even during the early years in that role, the opportunity to become an educator was evident. I started instructing students in the field. I became an adjunct instructor, teaching an evening course on family violence. I chaired our hospital social service department's education committee, planning continuing education events for our department members.

During this time, another opportunity was emerging. We started accessing patient records digitally and charting in web-based applications. Professional technology became more prevalent in our hospital's daily work. Technology has always been an interest of mine, so I actively sought ways to develop technology-based supports wherever I could, as a form of service to our department. Then, a major professional shift happened—I applied for the position of Clinical Assistant Professor at the University of Iowa School of Social Work, where I'd take on the role of Distance Education Administrator. This post seemed to blend all the key components of my work at the hospital into a full-fledged faculty role: technology use, program development, and social work education.

A "typical" day involves a few factors: what my teaching deployment looks like in a given semester, what productivity and service I'm engaged in at the moment, and what administrative duties I need to address. As the distance education administrator,

I'm often traveling to one of our program's education centers off-campus or teaching online, as well as meeting with committees, giving presentations, or writing.

An outline of my week could look like this:

- **Monday:** I have a face-to-face class in a center a couple of hours away in Des Moines. I pick up a university vehicle around 8:30, stop by the campus office to get any deliveries for the center, and I'm on the road.

- **Tuesday:** I have committee work to review and emails to answer. Fortunately, few people leave voicemails in this setting (a major contrast from my hospital days). If homework has been submitted, now is a good time to start grading.

- **Wednesday:** This is usually a day set aside for faculty administration. Our monthly faculty meeting starts at 9:00 a.m. and faculty connect from all sites in person or via Zoom videoconferencing. The faculty scholarship meeting follows, where research or other productivity is shared and feedback is provided.

- **Thursday:** I meet formally with our Des Moines faculty to review any concerns and plan for upcoming events. Then I prepare for my evening online course.

- **Friday:** This is my productivity day. I plan the weekly podcast as part of my partnership with the #MacroSW Collaboration; I work on proposals for national conference presentations; and, I confess, I do catch-up work from earlier in the week.

A typical day may look something like this:

6:00 a.m.: Still at home, I've set aside this time to review my calendar for the day, responding to any emergent emails from students or colleagues. (A few students send messages in the middle of the night but I'm not awake; or, if I see the message, I'm not responding until 6:00 the next morning.) This slot of 30 minutes helps me focus, especially if I'm commuting a long distance in the morning. Today, I'm just traveling to campus, but I still value the early morning time, as it's still quiet and any problems that may come up likely won't happen until I'm heading to work. My wife usually joins me to visit and work on her own goals and projects.

8:30 a.m.: I've dropped off my son at his school, and I've navigated to my office. I allow for campus travel, which includes avoiding throngs of students crossing the street.

8:45 a.m.: I'm in the office, saying "hello" as a way of an informal morning check-in with our program director and program staff. I'm a member of our department's administrative team, so this time allows me to get updated on any higher administrative issues or concerns that may have just come up. For example, my director may have learned of a policy proposal that could affect our distance education students.

9:00 a.m.: I go over my class material. In my role, it's common to be deployed to teach both online and face-to-face courses. Regardless of the class environment, for any homework I assign, I handle it through our course management system online. The University of Iowa uses the Canvas platform, so I have one online dashboard to review. I grade submitted work and provide feedback using the online rubric. I confess, it's easy to pretend the next semester is still far away, but if I'm honest with myself, I'm probably behind in my course planning. During this time, I can work on preparing for the inevitable next semester.

10:30 a.m.: Administrative work. I'm still in my office, but now I need to shift gears and look over any issues involving our distance centers. Last year we had to move our program centers to a new location, and a lot of details came up during the transition that needed to be addressed. If I didn't catch emergent issues at 6:00 a.m., I'm following up on them now.

11:30 a.m.: If I have time between now and 1:00 p.m., I will work on projects. This could be preparing for this week's online macro social work (@MacroSW) Twitter chat, an article for *The New Social Worker* magazine, or abstract proposals for an upcoming conference. I note that for some projects, I use Slack, an application that allows team members to communicate and share files. I'm often chatting with team members asynchronously using this application throughout the day.

1:00 p.m.: Administrative Team Meeting. This is the formal meeting among administrative members of the faculty and staff, where we present and review pressing issues or concerns. For example, if I'm working on a project that involves support from administrative team members, now is the time to make this idea known.

2:30 p.m.: I'm heading over to the geographic center of campus, where the campus faculty assembly is held. I attend as a representative of our unit, and it's here I can ask questions and take note of campus-wide concerns and issues I may need to report back to my department. This is something I volunteered to do last year, and represents a form of university service.

3:30 p.m. to 5:00 p.m.: Office hours. While I can only be in one space physically, students at any of our centers (including our online MSW program) know they can reach me during this time. My door is open, my email is front-and-center on the desktop, and my campus-based Skype phone number is live. If students would like to drop in via Zoom videoconference, they are encouraged to let me know ahead of time. (That said, I have a set address students can click on if they wish.) This all takes a little harnessing; if a student connects via Zoom, I shut the door with a note that I'm meeting with a student, and also update my status on Skype to reflect this.

6:00 p.m. to 9 p.m.: I'm home, teaching my evening Human Behavior in the Social Environment class online. The class is offered through Zoom, which makes it easy to facilitate breakout groups. I spent a few months prior to this semester preparing this course, including recording short presentations, building online quizzes, and essentially completing the entire course design before the first session was held.

My rank is clinical, rather than tenured, a distinction in which I take pride. The rank of clinical is something ported over from the medical campus—the "clinical" speaks to how social work practitioners provide insight from practice in the higher education setting. Although I left my clinical role behind when I became a professor, I'm able to keep at least a little contact with clinical practice. I continue to provide clinical supervision to hospital social workers seeking advanced licensure. This is also another way I'm able to "give back" to the profession.

Typically, a clinical professor requires a terminal degree in social work (the MSW) and background in direct practice. This position is sometimes classified as a Lecturer; however (in my case, at least), the Clinical Assistant Professor title carries the expectation of consistent productivity. For me, this includes publishing and presenting on topics related to social work practice. I'm not expected to engage in extensive research work. This is the key difference between my role and my tenure-track colleagues.

The most significant change for me is long-range planning. For all my skills working at the hospital, each day began and ended at a set time with a few exceptions (sometimes it's not possible to leave during a patient crisis mid-stream). On some days, my work as a professor can feel like a life where I'm perpetually but passively on-call; my email inbox is constantly filling up with student questions, committee updates, and invitations to partner on a project. So, yes, I no longer carry a pager, but the volume of contact just shifted to a different path. This isn't a complaint, just an observation on how the volume and intensity of the work has merely shifted. To hit goals and complete long-range tasks, I have come to rely on a "Work In Progress" (WiP) board in my office, helping me visualize what I'm working on and how close these projects are to being finished (and when it's a good time to say "no" to new work).

Working with colleagues has changed, too. At the hospital, I worked with social work colleagues relatively closely, often handing off patients or receiving hand-offs. I was accustomed to constant interaction with team members, patients, and families. Work was charted daily, and each month I submitted a census count of patients with whom I engaged. In my educator role, the level of autonomy I experience has increased dramatically. This is most clearly reflected in my annual review process. At the hospital, my reviews were short and to the point. The refrain "keep doing what you are doing" was something of an unofficial motto. Now, I provide an annual written statement summarizing all areas of my work, including my short and long-term goals, along with my updated Curricula Vitae. At the hospital, I summarized high points. Now, I include and annotate everything I do. This seemed foreign to me at first, but without this detailed information, my senior colleagues would have little idea of the work I'm doing over time.

This also speaks to the culture of social work practice to which I grew accustomed. I developed my practice in an environment where "tooting one's horn" was seen as a negative. This fits with my view that social workers, engaged in the empowerment of others, aren't as accustomed to alerting the world to our successes. I appreciated being recognized for good work, but I wasn't inclined to ask for praise too often. In higher education, professional promotion absolutely requires it. I continue to adapt to this.

After several years in this position, I believe my favorite part of my role as a social work educator is the constant engagement with students, coupled with the ability to develop programs and interventions so closely connected to my interest in technology. It's really an amazing experience to be able to teach both theory and practice courses based on my experience working in the health care field. The increased presence of online programs like the one I've helped develop and execute continues to be controversial, but I believe the ability to connect to students this way, obviating the need for students who are committed to their communities to relocate to our physical campus, speaks to a component of social justice that reflects my commitment to social work as a profession.

Think About It

1. How does this description align with your perception of clinical social work faculty?

2. If you are a clinical social worker, are there features of social work education in which you currently engage? What interests you about social work education?

3. In your experience as a social worker or social work student, does the field of social work practice represent what was taught in your program? How is it different?

Chapter 52
A University Counseling Center

‖‖‖

by Laura Crawford Hofer, MSSW, LCSW, ACSW, BCD

I anticipated an easy day today in my role as a counselor at the university's Counseling Center. I had checked the black notebook on the secretary's desk for my appointments and found that, because it was early in the semester, just three students had appointments scheduled with me today. I also had time blocked off to meet with the director of the Counseling Center about the Crisis Response Team, to prepare for a group interpretation of the Myers-Briggs Type Indicator, and to attend an Academic Leave Committee meeting.

Suddenly, a hurricane appeared in the doorway. My first student was here. I invited Donna into my office. The tall, gangly, raven-haired woman in front of me described again what it had been like growing up with Attention Deficit Hyperactivity Disorder (ADHD) and not having been understood. Still hyperactive at thirty and unwilling to take medication regularly, she could barely sit still in my office on the red plaid couch. Her thoughts darted around as actively as her long, brown limbs did. Sometimes she didn't even complete sentences. It was, nevertheless, easy to hear the pain as she talked about playing basketball, her skill and love for the sport, and how often she would be prevented from going to practice by detention. Blurting something out in class or not being able to find her homework earned her detentions, even though they were due to her impulsivity and disorganization, both hallmarks of ADHD. Today she was grieving again, as I listened, for the many years that she had been misunderstood.

361

Her thoughts switched to the waiver that she was hoping to secure for the math requirement at the university. An English major, she felt hopeless at math. Each math problem looked new to her. She could not remember the processes she had used before to solve a similar problem. If she didn't receive the waiver, she threatened, she would drop out of college. I knew that Donna was not willing right now to be tested for a learning disability. She was already grieving her ADHD and felt that she could not handle being diagnosed with another problem. But I also knew that without testing, Donna would be unlikely to be granted the waiver. She and I had already discussed this and she knew, too.

Suddenly she brought up her "twin" brother, Richard. Exactly one year older than she was, the two had been very close as they had grown up. Richard had died eight years ago in a car accident. The anniversary of his death would be Thursday. Donna wept as she remembered him. She longed for him to be here now so he might understand her anew, as she was coming to understand herself and her experiences. As the session ended, Donna commented again on how tired she was after every session. Not used to experiencing feelings for anything but the briefest time, the sessions with me focused her on what was going on inside.

After Donna left and I had written a few notes on the session, I knew that I had to meet with the Director of the Counseling Center, Dr. Joanne Wells. Joanne and I had been instrumental in the development of the Crisis Response Team (CRT) at the university. It included representatives of many of the organizational units in the university: campus police, housing, faculty, students, campus ministry, health services, athletics, counseling center, the Dean of Students, the Vice President for Public Relations, and the Vice President for Student Affairs. Joanne and I had already led this group in a process that had established the purpose and basic functioning of the team and had produced a written protocol. Now she and I were responsible for the once-a-semester training.

Before we started, I told Joanne how deeply Donna's pain had moved me, how I wondered if it could really be possible to resolve the profound losses that she had to bear, and how concerned I was that she might act impulsively again and drop out of the university. Joanne heard my pain, my doubts, and my questions. Then I was ready to move on.

For the CRT training, we wanted to provide a hypothetical situation. We brain-stormed. What crises had we heard on the news lately that had occurred on a college campus? We considered a sexual assault, a suicide, and an apparent love triangle in which a jealous husband had assaulted a professor and left him in critical condition. This time, because we knew that there were gang members attending our university, we settled on a gang-related incident. We fleshed out the hypothetical incident. A gang member and a fraternity brother would have words in White Hall. Someone would bump into the rattled gang member. The gang member would draw a gun and shoot wildly. A nursing professor and a nursing student would get hit. We gave the student a fictitious name and laughed as we thought about the professors that we'd like to shoot and the ones that we knew that the students would like to shoot. Our good judgment won out, though, as we settled on someone who was genuinely liked and respected in all parts of the university community. We would let the team decide what happened after the shooting and how each organizational unit could best respond to this scenario. The secretary, Sally, knocked on the door. Both Joanne and I had students waiting to see us.

A tall man in his mid-twenties, Bruce almost always wore a black leather jacket, black jeans, small round sunglasses, and multiple silver earrings in his left ear. On warmer days he wore a ripped shirt exposing a pierced nipple. The bottom third of his head was shaved and his long hair gathered into a ponytail at the nape of his neck. Flamboyant and unconventional in his appearance, I knew Bruce also to be a gentle and thoughtful person disturbed by his relationship with his girlfriend, Danielle. A recovered alcoholic, Bruce had just begun to experience the relationship as destructive. Danielle toyed with him, he felt, and yet he couldn't give her up. Today he continued. He compared Danielle to alcohol. Bad for him but feeling so good. He knew the relationship hurt him. She hurt him when she told him that she had seen her old boyfriend and when she had hinted that they had had sex. And, she hurt him because he was not focused on studying. But he knew he would call her again. He knew that when she called him, he would respond. *What was it that made him want to call her and want to respond?* I asked in numerous ways. Bruce could see Danielle only negatively and couldn't identify right now what was magnetic about her to him.

When the session ended, Sally asked if I could see a resident assistant, or RA, who had walked in without an appointment. RAs are upperclass students who receive free housing at the university in exchange for their support to a section of ten to twelve students in the residence hall. RAs generally only come to the Counseling Center if they have students about whom they have serious concerns. So I agreed to see Shelley.

An RA in our one residence hall with apartments, Shelly explained that all three of the apartment mates of another student, Rose, believed her to be bulimic. They had come together to see Shelley the previous evening and had reported that Rose often excused herself from a meal and that they could hear her vomiting in their shared bathroom. When they had confronted her, Rose had passed it off as a virus, but she had gone into the bathroom to vomit so many times now that they no longer believed her. Two of the apartment mates were nursing students and were aware of how damaging repetitive vomiting was to one's body. The woman who shared a room with Rose also had seen laxatives in Rose's purse.

That Rose was possibly using both laxatives and vomiting to control her weight made this an emergency situation. Losing so much fluid from the body could cause not only dehydration but an electrolyte imbalance, a heart arrhythmia, and death. I asked if Shelley had told her boss, the resident director (RD), what was going on. She had. I asked Shelly to set up a meeting in the Counseling Center later today or tomorrow with Rose, her roommates, and herself present. The meeting would be an opportunity for Rose's roommates to describe exactly what they had seen and heard, to express just how worried they were, to learn whether or not action was warranted, and what action would be taken.

Shelley and I then talked about how she would approach Rose about the meeting. Shelley thought she could tell Rose that her roommates were very worried about her and needed to talk with her at the Counseling Center. But she feared that Rose would deny all of what her roommates had observed and would refuse to come to the meeting or would come but refuse to follow through on any plan. If Rose refused at either level, I pointed out, we could use the university's judicial process to force Rose to act, since she appeared to be exhibiting behavior that endangered herself. But hopefully, I continued, Rose would be moved by her roommates' worries to worry herself and to want to act.

I knew that, depending upon what came out in this meeting, it was likely that I would be recommending to the student that she have a full evaluation for an eating disorder. She would need a physical as well as a psychosocial evaluation that included specific questions about weight and dieting history, body image concerns, and family history of eating disorders, sexual abuse, drug or alcohol use, and mood disorders in order to fully address what appeared to be a very serious problem. Shelley was relieved when she left my office. It felt good, she said, to have a plan.

Many things were crowding my mind right now. I was quite concerned about Rose and about her physical condition. I knew that I had to tell Joanne about this situation. I was concerned about Donna, since she seemed in the midst of a crisis, and about Bruce who was stuck. Then there were my kids. I had applied for this job, in part, because it offered a 10-month contract. Like school social work, I could have two months during the summer to be with my family. Except for occasional evening events, such as a workshop, class, or speaker that I was responsible for, most of my hours at work were hours that my children were in school. The university also offered an exciting, intellectual environment. But today I had to work late. I had an Academic Leave Committee meeting. Tuesday meant that my 13-year-old had swim team practice after school and that my 10-year-old would be home alone for awhile. Even though she knew that I would be late and would call Sally to check in, I knew that she was likely to be apprehensive.

I had a few minutes now to begin preparing for the group interpretation of the Myers-Briggs Type Indicator for the class on interpersonal communication. I thought back to my training in the indicator and how often I had used it since then. Professors in certain classes, RAs, and sorority presidents had all requested that I do an interpretation for their groups. A useful tool to help people sort out some innate differences in behavior, the indicator also teaches respect for those differences. I enjoyed watching groups learn, for example, that some people think and talk almost simultaneously while others process their thoughts internally for a while before they are ready to speak.

Sally broke into my thoughts, asking if I would take a call from a professor who was concerned about a student. A professor in the business school, Dr. Foster, had a student who had become increasingly withdrawn. Friends of the student had told Dr. Foster that the student's father had died two years ago and his mother had died just last month. The friends were worried that he was drinking excessively and might be suicidal. Dr. Foster had observed that he was participating less in class and had stopped handing in homework. Dr. Foster himself had had a friend die by suicide and was worried that this student might be at risk. He wondered what he should do.

We talked first about setting up a meeting with the student. Dr. Foster needed to talk with the student about the change in his behavior in class and about what might have precipitated it. With the permission of the other students, or if the student said

anything to indicate that he might be suicidal, Dr. Foster could address that question directly. Dr. Foster wondered if he could make
the student think about something that might not yet have crossed
the student's mind. I explained that if the student was not thinking
about suicide, he would simply dismiss the idea. If he was thinking
about it, he would probably be relieved that someone had asked.
If suicide *was* on the student's mind, I continued, the professor
should escort him to the Counseling Center. Someone would see
him immediately. *And today was supposed to be easy!* I mused to
myself, as I hung up.

My next student was waiting. Denise entered my office almost
soundlessly. She sat on the couch without moving, but I knew that
beneath her surface calm she struggled with profound and disturbing feelings. Today she talked again about her decision to file sexual
harassment charges against a staff member at the university. He
had touched her and tried to kiss her. She had been frightened
and tried to avoid him at first. A year ago, she said, she would not
have been able even to consider confronting him. Now she was
angry. She described her anger as being like a volcano within her.
She never knew quite when it was going to erupt. Sometimes, she
said, she was afraid of her anger, but it was better, she said, than
the feelings of helplessness that she had endured for so long. I was
reminded of Denise's history of being raped twice, of not being able
to tell anyone because of her shame and fear, and of not having
had words for many years for these parts of her experience. She
had certainly come a long way.

As I wrote up notes on my session with Denise, a very relieved
Dr. Foster called me again. He reported that the student was sad
but had said he was not thinking about suicide. He had also been
referred by his boss to a therapist and had started therapy during
the past week.

Sally reminded me that I was now due at the Academic Leave
Committee meeting. I sighed. I felt like I hadn't had a moment's
breathing space all day. As I walked to Berkshire Hall, I thought
back over the applications that I had reviewed: the English professor who had requested time to finish the final chapters of a book
on the medieval Norman author, Marie de France; the librarian who
had requested two summers' leaves to investigate and write about
the life of Deems Taylor, an American composer, critic, and author
from the '30s; the art professor who wanted time to explore the

Basque region in Spain, his ancestral home, and hoped to produce a visual record of what his trip meant to him. While these were written in a layperson's English, one application about rainfall patterns and el Niño from the meteorological department was so technical, I knew that I would be relying on the expertise of other committee members to help determine how significant a study it was and whether or not it was worthy of a sabbatical.

I thought back to starting on the committee. I had felt uncertain of my place at first, but I had learned quickly that my comments were heard and respected. The group had a norm that encouraged everyone's active participation and disagreement. I looked forward to lively discussion.

After the meeting, I walked quickly through the light rain and stopped by the office briefly to check my schedule for tomorrow: five students on the calendar. It looked like Shelley had been able to put together a meeting for Rose and her roommates, and Donna wanted to see me again.

I looked forward to tomorrow.

Think About It

1. The counselors joke about a hypothetical scenario in which people on campus get shot. How can they joke about this? What purpose do you think this joking serves?

2. What might be some typical issues that surface in counseling college students?

Chapter 53
Providing Continuing Education to Social Workers

IIIIIIIIIIIIIIIIIIIIIIIIIIIIIIIIIIIIIIIIIIIIIIIIIIIIIIIIIIIIIIIIIIIIIIIIIIIIIIIIIIIIIIIIIIIIIIIIIIIIIIIIIIIIIIIIIIIIIIIIII

by Barbara Alexander, LCSW, BCD

Today began early, at 3 a.m., when I awoke in an adrenaline fueled panic, remembering that I had not sent interview questions to my next speaker. Her interview is in two days.

This is one of many situations in my life as a continuing education provider and small business owner that lends itself to anxious moments. I'm my own boss, and if I want things to go well—or "go" at all—I'm the only one who can make that happen.

Let me begin with what I *don't* do as a continuing education provider. I don't plan conferences. I don't arrange travel or book hotel rooms. I don't sell tickets or organize "Meet and Greets." And especially, I don't walk away from my own business at the end of the day. It is always on my mind, because this is a business, and in a way, it's like most other businesses. You develop a product, you market the product, you take orders, and you fulfill them. Then you provide whatever customer service is indicated. You pay your bills and keep whatever is left—after you pay your taxes. But most businesses don't provide a product that is vital to the life of the customer. If anything goes wrong with On Good Authority's continuing education products, it could put the customer's career in jeopardy—the customer could lose his or her license. I can't afford to make mistakes. That's enough to keep me in a perpetual cold sweat, or hot flash, as the case may be.

Here's what I do as owner of my business, On Good Authority. I produce continuing education programs consisting of recorded interviews with psychotherapy experts. These are then compiled by topic, say, a series of interviews about grief and loss, for example (see *http://www.ongoodauthority.com*). These programs are available online for download any time of day or night. Mental health professionals purchase and listen to (or read) these interviews, take a short quiz online, and print out their own CE certificates upon successful completion of the quiz. Because the programs are all approved for continuing education credit, the listeners may use them to fulfill license renewal requirements.

The best part of my business is developing and producing the programs. First, I decide on what program to produce next. There is no shortage of ideas, but it's crucial to know what topics would be most important and necessary for the professional. Getting that right is what drives sales. It's a very interesting and creative process. Sometimes I survey my listeners, and other times I hit on something topical on my own, inspired by a scientific, scurrilous, or intriguing item in the news. Several years back, I did a number of interviews related to Woody Allen and his step-daughter. Very juicy. Is this relationship incest? Had his gazillion years of psychoanalysis made any impact on him? If so, what was he like before? Good grief!

Once I decide on the topic, the research begins. The Internet has made this much easier, but it still takes weeks to review what is already known about the subject, and then to find speakers who would not only be knowledgeable but interesting. I take pride in my "faculty" of more than 200 speakers, all of whom have written, presented, and are active, expert clinicians. First I have to locate them, which isn't always easy. Next, somehow I have to find a way to listen to their voices, usually on their phone machines, to be sure they aren't real "soft talkers" and are easy to understand. I also try to see comments or reviews of their books and their presentations. If I like what I find, I invite them to participate.

When I have the speakers lined up, I read everything they have written on the subject, so I can develop questions. This involves putting myself in the place of the clinician, thinking about what a clinician would want to know. I've found that post-graduate mental health professionals don't want a lot of theory—they want practical help, as in "How do I find out if my patient is suicidal? How do I get my patient to open up to me about it?" But without some operating theory, one's work is just a shot in the dark, so I try to find a balance.

So, at 3 a.m., I write my questions for the speaker. I try not to script the interview, as I want it to be spontaneous, sort of like a consultation or conversation with a colleague who happens to be an expert in his or her field. But this is going to be a challenging interview. The subject of the program is "Suicide," and this speaker has a very deep and unusual understanding of the problems of returning combat soldiers. I have interviewed her before, and she is so knowledgeable that she is hard to slow down. She is so exciting, it is hard for me to slow myself down! If I can keep my focus, I will be pleased with her ideas and my listeners will enjoy the interview and learn from it.

In two days, my sound engineer will come to my house, bringing his computer, his microphone, and headphones. Sometimes I use a sound studio, but not this time. I will sit on my sofa, having turned off all the phones in the house. I will have my notes all around me and some water nearby. I will have a cushion in front of the little refrigerator behind me, because it hums and I worry about the noise. I will be a bit nervous. Will the sound be okay? Will the phone line be okay? Will I ask the right questions to get the best out of the speaker? Will I sound intelligent? How much will I have to prompt the speaker? Or cut off the speaker? Most important: will the speaker deliver, as I hope she will? Sounds like it shouldn't be all that difficult, right? After all, I'm a seasoned psychotherapist myself, with decades of clinical experience to draw on. I keep reminding myself!

When the interview is done, the first round of the editing process will begin. I will listen to the recording, outline it, and tell the sound guy what I want cut. After he does that, the interview gets shot over to one of my transcribers. I worry about how much I will have to nag her for the transcript. Once I have it, the final editing of sound and transcript is done. Then I will combine this interview with the others I have recorded on suicide and write my introductions and editorial comments.

Writing the multiple choice test questions is fun. I used to have some psychologists write the tests, but they made the questions too complicated and too tough. After all, I'm competing with the relative ease of conference attendance, where a mental health professional can sign in to a seminar, collect his or her CE certificate, and never have to take a test. I have to make the multiple choice questions user-friendly and yet significant enough to satisfy the approving bodies.

Fortunately, I know some very witty people, my husband in particular. I write the one correct answer and the so-so answers, and he writes the "always wrong" answer. The conversation can get pretty silly. For instance, one question had to do with assessing ADHD: "What are the most significant indicators of ADHD?" His answer: "The sound of the mother hitting her head against a wall."

Back to today. I've sent off the questions to my speaker, and the sun has risen. No point in going back to bed, so now I turn to managing the business, which is the most time-consuming part of my day. On any given day, I could be developing marketing plans to let people know about my products, contacting my ordering people about sales, updating customer files, providing tech support to customers, streamlining my website (under the strict orders of my webmaster), nagging my transcribers, and keeping current on the continuing education rules of 50 states and six professions (social work, psychology, licensed professional counselors, marriage and family therapists, addictions counselors, and professional guardians). That's 300 state boards to monitor. And, of course, I could be paying bills. The variety of things to do is endless and relentless. But at least I'm no longer packing boxes and shipping tapes, since On Good Authority's programs are now all online as MP3 files and transcripts.

So I check my email and take care of any customer service issues. I had not anticipated how much hand holding would be involved. For instance, one customer has multiple email addresses, has changed them often, and thus could not log in to access her tests. She and I have gone over this several times. I wonder why I can access her tests on my computer and she can't. Finally, I have her fax her test to me and, logging in as her, I enter all her answers online. As the *Saturday Night Live* character, Roseanne Roseannadanna, used to say, "It's always something!"

When I began On Good Authority, I never thought it would survive this long, and I never realized how hard I would work. Plus, I ran into surprising resistance! In the beginning, I received some very snooty responses from my colleagues: "Oh, yes, you're doing that entrepreneurial thing!" Social workers tend not to have positive thoughts about business. We tend to have a "service over self" mentality—we're not supposed to personally benefit from the work we do. But of course, that mentality doesn't pay the bills.

This brings me to the subject of how my social work education prepared me for undertaking this business venture. Well, it did and it didn't. Obviously, it prepared me for interviewing speakers, for researching possible topics, assessing needs, and for handling customer service issues. But it in no way prepared me with business skills, nor would I have expected it to. That is a different area of knowledge, which I had to acquire on my own.

When I was elected president of the Illinois Society for Clinical Social Work, I was quite intimidated by the thought of running this organization. So I hired a business consultant, who taught me how to structure board meetings (although I had served on many nonprofit boards by that time) and how to read a profit/loss statement and a balance sheet. But the rest of it—marketing, pricing, developing ads, website management, database administration—all these skills were developed "on the job," and I am still learning.

This "still learning" is also a valuable part of being a social worker—recognizing the value of keeping an inquiring mind about our patients, ourselves, and the world around us. Any therapists who think they know all they need to know are heading for trouble.

It's 11 a.m. I'm still in my pajamas, and I haven't eaten or worked out or done any of the healthy things I need to do to live my life. So that happens next.

Then I pay those bills. For the first time in 18 years, this is a somewhat pleasurable experience. Up until a year ago or so, I made no money whatsoever. Everything I made went back into the business, to expenses, such as paying secretaries, sales tax, telephone bills, licensing fees to all the state licensing boards, webmasters, web servers, sound engineers, CD duplicators, professional newsletters for advertising space, and so forth. But now in addition to my retail sales, I have agreements with a number of larger companies and receive royalties. "Royalties!" What a wonderful word! "Royalties!" Finally there is some reward for all these years of providing continuing education to thousands of therapists.

Jumping two days ahead:

The interview went very well, but I'm a bit drained, so I'll listen to it tomorrow when I'm fresh. I try to remember that a perfect job done in an infinite amount of time is worth absolutely nothing.

I fiddle around with my iPod and work on some transcriptions. Now it's dark out—the work day is over except for the thinking part, which never ends.

You know, I do love all this. I learn so much and use so much of myself. All my clinical experience comes into play, and I draw on it extensively. Doing the research and doing the actual interviews makes me very happy. I get a chance to speak to people I would never otherwise have access to. It's more than the money, or I certainly would have closed up shop years ago. This business keeps me alive, vital, current. When you're in a clinical practice, you can't really talk about your work. But as a continuing education provider, I can and I do. I'll keep at it as long as the continuing education beast needs to be fed (which will be as long as continuing education remains a requirement for license renewal) and as long as I have energy and a functioning brain.

Now I think I'll watch the new episode of *In Treatment!* And hope I sleep through the night.

Think About It

1. Is being an entrepreneur consistent with being a social worker?

2. What ideas do you have that could be turned into a social work business?

3. What social work skills does the writer use most in her day-to-day work?

PART 13:
INTERNATIONAL
SOCIAL WORK

Chapter 54
Consulting in Armenia

||||||||||||||||||||||||||||||||||||||||||||||||||||||||||||||||||||||||||||||||||

by Jerry L. Johnson, Ph.D.

Suddenly, it seemed, I was standing in front of the city council building on a sunny March morning trying to shake off the fogginess of jet lag. I needed to pay close attention in my first meeting. After a 36-hour trip, I had arrived in Yerevan Armenia at 4:00 a.m., just five hours earlier. As a consultant for the United Nations Development Programme (UNDP), I thought that my job was to develop and implement a region-wide media campaign against substance abuse. Yet, I have discovered that nothing is certain in international practice.

In five minutes, I had a meeting with my hosts from the city council and UNDP—assuming, of course, I had found the correct building. I was supposed to have a driver, but he failed to appear at the hotel that morning. So I walked the three miles to what I hoped was the city council. Simply walking around a busy city, hearing the noise, nearly choking on the overwhelming smell of car exhaust, and listening to the melody of an unrecognizable language is a learning experience. I'm glad the driver didn't show up.

I walked past the guard at the door and up three flights of marble stairs to the office of International Affairs. I knocked on the closed door. A woman answered, and in halting English said she was in another meeting, but I was welcome to sit in while she finished. The room was a busy place. People were talking, others were knocking and entering, and one woman was grinding coffee beans by hand. How can these people hear each other?

Ninety minutes later, after sitting in a smoke-filled room unable to understand even one spoken word, my meeting still had not begun. In Armenia, as well as many countries around the world, time means very little. The telephones and public transportation did not work well, so people simply showed up hoping to squeeze in at least one minute at some time during the day. If I wanted to telephone someone, I had several people try to call all day, hoping that at least one person would be lucky enough to get a message through. I was lucky to get one meeting completed during any given workday. It was normal for 9:00 a.m. meetings to begin after lunch. Waiting is a fact of life. Everybody waits up to several hours for meetings, food, and transportation. This is a difficult lesson for time-obsessed Americans to learn. For me, it is easier on my mental health to leave my wristwatch and planner at home.

When I accepted the assignment in Armenia, I had been a social worker for 15 years. I worked as a therapist, community organizer, administrator, and consultant during that time. Yet, I did not really learn to be a social worker until I began international practice. It is stimulating, challenging, and exciting, while at the same time quite humbling. You see, many years of practice experience in the United States are not always helpful outside the United States. I believe that theory and practice are, for the most part, contextual. In other words, my expertise in substance abuse prevention and treatment ended as soon as my airplane crossed out of United States airspace.

To be successful, social workers in international settings must carefully study the culture, politics, and lifestyle of the locals. They must be willing to make plans and develop strategies "on the fly," relying heavily on local needs, wants, and volunteers. Pre-planning is normally a useless exercise, often leading to a dangerous single-mindedness that when implemented results in an ugly version of practice colonialism. It certainly results in little or no success.

A social worker should take nothing for granted in international practice—even the assignment. In fact, I am more surprised when things go as planned than when they don't. Thus, on this assignment, I was not surprised by what transpired next. After two hours and two cups of very strong Turkish coffee, my meeting finally began. My hosts began by telling me what I was partially expecting: my assignment was not what it appeared. I was not in Armenia to work on substance abuse prevention after all. This was a ruse to get a social worker with community-based experience into the country. Substance abuse prevention was the only pocket of untapped money locals had left to pay for a consultant, so they developed the substance abuse prevention project. It worked.

I was actually in Armenia to help UNDP and local leaders with "democracy building" efforts. They wanted me to develop a project to stimulate local interest and participation in community service through volunteerism. They wanted my ideas the next day.

Finally, some of my training and experience was helpful. As an advanced generalist practitioner, I was prepared to work closely with different systems at different levels of society to develop a project that best fit local needs. If it were not for the jet lag and personal intercultural adjustment dilemma faced by all social workers in international settings, this would be easy. However, in international practice, social workers not only have to learn to work differently, but their efforts are confounded by the sometimes overwhelming task of learning to live in the foreign setting. That can be a daunting task, indeed.

Just as we were beginning to discuss different project ideas, we were interrupted by a harried-looking woman who, after one loud knock at the door, rushed in and grabbed me by the arm. She wanted me to go somewhere, but she was speaking in hurried Armenian and I had no idea what she wanted, or why she was grab-bing me. Through a translator, I discovered that I was now very late for another meeting my hosts had scheduled that day with 20 police officers from the surrounding area. They wanted to know my ideas, and had many of their own to share. Great! I am off to meet with a group of people about a project I have just learned is not the project I had planned.

For me, the most important thing for a social worker to accom-plish before intervention planning is to learn about the country and its people. Armenia was no exception. My first trip to Armenia came during one of the most difficult times in its long and interesting history. In the seven years prior to this trip, Armenia had survived one of the most deadly earthquakes in world history, the breakup of the Soviet Union, war with Azerbaijan, and complete blockade as a result of the war by Azerbaijan and Turkey leading to a complete collapse of its economy and way of life.

When I arrived, the Armenian people had lived four years with less than two hours of electricity per day, and they had survived harshly cold winters with no heat source. Food and water were scarce. Basic services were nonexistent, meaning that schools were closed, garbage was left to pile and rot, and transportation was a nightmare. People were living day-to-day simply trying to feed their children and survive. They didn't have the time, money, or inclination to abuse drugs, or volunteer for community service, for that matter.

After a harrowing car ride through the city, dodging huge potholes and oncoming traffic on streets without functioning traffic signals, we arrived at an older-looking stone building for the meeting. My translator, Sona, the harried woman from the city council, informed me as the meeting began that I was her first subject as a translator, but I had no reason to worry. She would do her best.

We sat around a large wooden table, all in overcoats, as there was no heat and winter's chill still made it uncomfortable, even indoors. As is typical in meetings all across the former Soviet Union, I opened the meeting by telling about my project, explaining my credentials, and describing my experience. Then, I listened as each person made his or her statement. Since I had no idea what this project was at that point, my opening remarks were brief.

Sona did a nice job translating as people stated their ideas about community service. A good job, that is, until one woman in military uniform seized the floor. She stood at her seat and proceeded to give a twenty-minute speech, punctuated by yelling and fist pounding. After about five minutes, Sona stopped translating. Now, this usually means that the translator does not want me to hear what the person is saying. Therefore, I assumed the woman was telling me to leave Armenia on the same plane I flew in on earlier that day. I kept tugging gently at Sona's arm saying, "What is she saying?" I was reading her body language and, in America, she was unmistakably angry.

Fortunately, I was wrong. She was vigorously saying that the work I was intending to do—as yet undefined—was needed in these difficult times and that they (the police) should do whatever they can to help. However, she warned me that any efforts to organize people might be mistaken as Communist policy, so I should expect difficulty getting people to trust the sincerity of the effort. This was, in fact, prophetic.

This experience demonstrates how unfamiliarity with the local language is a significant barrier in any international setting. I misread words and body. I had a translator, but as I found out in this instance, translation is unreliable and difficult. It takes time and experience together to build the relationship of trust needed to make third-person translation work well. I did develop this type of relationship with Sona later; however, the trust was not present at this meeting. When I spoke, did she translate my words accurately? What if she did not like my ideas—would she change them? Would she make me sound foolish, and would she let me in on any nuances of speech and communication that might be unfamiliar? These were only a few of the questions racing through my mind as the meeting progressed.

At meeting's end, each person shook my hand and offered his or her assistance before leaving. It turned out to be a successful meeting, despite my limitations and lack of ideas. Yet, participants in this meeting agreed that I should develop projects to address the growing problem of idle youth. The blockade and power shortage had forced the closing of schools during late fall, winter, and early spring. In addition, the end of the Soviet regime also ended the existence of a large network of youth clubs and activities. As such, youths had nothing to do but idly "hang out" on the streets. The police (and most others I interviewed in the coming weeks) believed this was a dangerous precursor to crime and delinquency. This ultimately became the organizing theme of my work over the next two years in Armenia.

By this time, it was well past noon. After a short lunch break, we went to meet the director of the Department of Social Work at Yerevan State University. After waiting for nearly an hour to no avail, we learned that she had been unable to get to the office that day because of transportation and electrical problems. This was typical. When the power went down, the subway did not run. Often, public buses simply ran out of gasoline, leaving people to walk from wherever they stopped. So, we rescheduled for another time.

Without power, days end early in Armenia. By 4:00 p.m., it was time to go home before it became dark and impossible to travel. Therefore, I walked the two miles back to my hotel, hoping to write notes about the day's events. That night, like every night for six weeks, I made handwritten notes by flashlight instead of typing them on my portable computer. Nights were long and dark; so dark that I could not detect the city outside my hotel window. It is a strange experience to sense the presence of a city, but be unable to see it. For more than five years, over three million Armenians lived without light.

After six weeks, I (with much help from my hosts) recruited 25 local people to serve as volunteer organizers. We developed a grassroots youth center, run by adults, that provided youths with cultural and community service opportunities. While changes in local politics ended the youth center after one year, the initiative demonstrated by the local people did not die. Out of the core group of volunteers, two other non-governmental organizations (NGOs) were born. One group of women completed the first qualitative study of women's lives in Armenia, while the other publishes and distributes literature to help educate and motivate the citizenry to vote in democratic elections.

Yet, in the beginning, the task was difficult and the barriers plentiful. Culture, politics, economics, and history conspired to make democracy-building in Armenia hard. It is a challenge to motivate people to care about the community when it is questionable whether they will have food or heat on any given day. However, the spirit of the local volunteers was remarkable and admirable.

I have worked in other countries (Albania, Belarus, and Russia), but few have had the difficulties of the Armenians. With all the barriers present in daily life, it is difficult to accomplish much in one day. By international practice standards, this day—my first in a new land—was successful indeed.

Think About It

1. What are some cultural boundaries that one must overcome in international social work?

2. Are there differences in the concept of time even within our own culture with respect to various social work settings?

Chapter 55

Working with Unaccompanied Minors in Britain

IIIIIIIIIIIIIIIIIIIIIIIIIIIIIIIIIIIIIIIIIIIIIIIIIIIIIIIIIIIIIIIIIIIIIIIIIIIIIIIIIIIIIIIIIIIIIIIIIIIIIIIIIIIIIIIIIIIIIIIIIIIIIIIIIIIIII

by Holly Anderson, BSW, BA

I am standing in the rain at a tube station, and it's 7:30 in the morning. I am dutifully sipping a Starbucks Latte. There are some things that I just can't let go of from North America. I am surrounded by suits and overcoats staring blankly ahead, completing their morning commute almost mechanically. For me, I am travelling across London, to a foster carer's where I will find my first client of the day, Mahammed.

I am a Canadian social worker and have been working in London for six months. I am working with "Unaccompanied Minors," a client group who come to the UK without family or supports, who arrive illegally to seek asylum, often escaping war, poverty, or political persecution. Their families are missing, dead, or have desperately sent them here to have a better life. These children are taken into care and cared for under the *Children Act, 1989*. They are placed in foster care and given access to education, health, and social services.

My role as their social worker is to ensure that all of the statutory requirements for their care are met under the Children Act, such as housing, education, health, and religion. I believe that it is also my role to empower them, to befriend them, and to support them through an incredible cultural transition. I am working with a diverse caseload of approximately 15 young people ranging in age from 12-18, who come from a variety of countries across the globe.

The "Looked After Children" system in the UK is a robust system with many levels of procedures and protocols. As a result of the *Children Act 1989,* social work for children who have come into the care system is prescriptive and rigid. The system is logical and fail proof in many regards. There is a rigid structure of meetings, forms, and reports that must take place when a child comes into care, and continues to take place while the child is in care. As a social worker for Looked After Children, the role can be very administrative, and focuses more on case management and coordinating services rather than direct client work. In Canada, I was used to more in-depth work with my clients and having the freedom to spend time with them, irrespective of structural expectations. In the UK, it seems that the focus is on structural outcomes and the Looked After Children Framework. Certainly, it is robust in its approach with a long list of statutory requirements. Young people are entitled to have a place in education, to have yearly medicals, and to have regular visits from social workers. This is then all followed up at a Looked After Review, which is a three- or six-month review of the young person's circumstances. These reviews have been set up to assure that the health, education, and placement needs are being met for the young people and that their voices are heard.

The young boy I am about to see is a 12-year-old unaccompanied minor from Afghanistan, and I am worried about him. He is new to this country, having been here for just over three weeks, and is desperately unhappy. Mahammed left war torn Afghanistan after rebels killed his father, and his mother feared for his safety. He was told he would reside with his "cousin" in London. My gut feeling was that Mahammed didn't want to be in this country, but wasn't given the choice in Afghanistan. We have talked about his returning home, but he has stated it is not what his family wants.

One of the reasons for Mahammed's unhappiness is that he was not placed with the "cousin." I have met Abdullah before, a 20-year-old asylum seeker, who has presented at our office with two other "cousins." It appears that he arranges for them to come over with Agents (people who are paid to bring children to the UK), collects them at the airport, then cites that he cannot take care of them and drops them on Social Services' doorstep. I was almost confident that Abdullah was at the bottom of a long chain of child smuggling, but had no proof. At any rate, Mahammed cannot live with Abdullah. I know this (having visited the flat, which is more of a rooming house packed with other Afghan asylum seekers, and certainly no place to raise a child), and Abdullah knows this, but Mahammed doesn't understand this. He has cried on the four visits I have had with him, stating over and over again (through an interpreter) that he wishes to live with his cousin. I am confident that today will be the same.

I am progressing through the Looked After Children Framework for Mahammed and have completed all the relevant papers, forms, and meetings. I am heading nicely to the first review, to be held in a week, and know that the file is prepared for this scrutiny. He is on a wait list for education, has had a statutory medical check, attended a local mosque, and has been placed in foster care. However, as thorough as this system is, it isn't meeting his needs. I am not sure that a British structure of social work is capable of meeting his needs.

After traveling on two tubes, an overground train, and a bus, I arrive wet and cold at the foster carer's. The foster carer is a good carer who seems genuinely concerned about Mahammed, and is trying very hard to make him feel settled. The language is a constant barrier, as Mahammed doesn't speak a word of English. She is feeling hopeless as her attempts aren't working. It is going to be a difficult path for Mahammed in this country. At the age of 12, his life circumstances are incredibly overwhelming and will force him to grow up quickly. In some ways, these children come to this country to have a safe childhood/adolescence, but in other ways they almost miss those years, having to cope with adult worries at a young age.

When the interpreter arrives, we begin discussing his current circumstances. Mahammed again expresses his unhappiness and begins to cry. I explain to him that I have requested Pashtu-speaking foster carers for him, but this will be a long search, as there aren't many. He says he wants to live with his cousin, and that I am going against what his family wants for him. This is a difficult situation, complicated by the use of an interpreter and cultural barriers that I am not sure we can cross. I do my best to listen to his concerns and validate his feelings, but I cannot give him what he wants—a placement with his cousin. I leave feeling hopeless and misunderstood.

Now I am on a series of tubes and buses to get to my next client, Alban. I spend a lot of time in a day traveling. Foster carers and semi-independent placements can be anywhere in London, and getting from one to another can take hours. After grabbing a sandwich at a tube stop, I arrive at Alban's placement. Alban is about to turn 18, which should be an exciting time in a young person's life. In

Britain, for children who have been looked after, there is a Leaving Care Act that supports young people through this transition and ensures that their education, housing, and financial needs are met. Nonetheless, in the case of unaccompanied minors, this transition is tumultuous and confusing. The majority of unaccompanied minors are granted Exceptional Leave to Remain in the UK until their 18th birthday when they come into the country. This means that they are entitled to remain in the UK until their 18th birthday, but no longer. Alban came from Kosovo at 14, when his father arranged for him to come as he feared for his safety because his father belonged to a democratic party. The family received death threats and thought it was best to send Alban to the UK. After traveling for ten days in the back of a truck, he came and started a life here. The British Red Cross offers a family tracing service for asylum seekers, and Alban has tried to find his family. However, there has been no word, and Alban believes them to be dead. Now, he is facing potential deportation, and is fearful. He has nothing to return to, and has begun a life here. He remains close to his foster family, is enrolled in college, and has a girlfriend. For Alban, deportation means returning to a blank slate and leaving behind four years of a life that he has worked hard to achieve.

Alban is doing well in semi-independence and I meet with him and his support worker first. The support worker sees Alban once a week, gives him his allowance, and helps him with budgeting, shopping, and general independent living skills. After the support worker leaves, I spend some time checking in with him. I have been Alban's social worker for six months and we have begun to form a relationship. He isn't attending college as often as he should be and we discuss the implications of this. Alban has the right to apply for an extension of leave to remain in the UK, which he has done. It is hoped that this extension will at least be granted for him to finish his education. The outcome is still pending, and he isn't feeling confident. Again, through the robust system of Looked After Children, Alban's basic needs have been met. He has had access to education, medical and dental treatment, and has been well taken care of since arriving in this country. The system offers opportunities and stability to British care leavers, yet because of the immigration laws, can't offer the same to unaccompanied minors. *The Children Act* and the immigration system don't compliment each other, and often as a social worker I feel trapped in the void between the two.

Finally I am about to return to the office. I work in northwest London, in a very diverse, poverty stricken borough. Social services are divided into boroughs, with each borough responsible for delivering services under the *Children Act*. I work in a team of eight social workers, only two of whom are British. I enjoy the diversity of the office as much as the diversity of my caseload. We have a manager and a deputy manager who are responsible for supervision. Supervision is very perfunctory in the UK and ensures that statutory requirements are met and the cases are progressing according to the Looked After Children framework. It doesn't allow for a larger reflection on practice—for this I have to seek out like-minded colleagues. This has been a shift for me, and at times very challenging.

I arrive at the office to check my emails and glance at my messages before my last client of the day, Hasan. Hasan often pops into the office, and enjoys having a social worker. He is from Somalia, leaving extreme poverty and war to come here. Hasan is now 17 and is probably my most content client. He very much has the outlook of being given a second chance in life and is going to make the best of it. His own resiliency has aided him through adapting to life in the UK, and I know that it is this resiliency that will create opportunities for him as an adult in the UK. We chat for a while, and go through some statutory paperwork. He's a rare person who has been granted Indefinite Leave to Remain in the UK, allowing him to remain in the country indefinitely with no restrictions. He adds some light to my busy day, and I am grateful for that. As long as he is in full-time education, he will continue to have a social worker until he is 24, and he is eligible for housing benefits and income assistance on his 18th birthday. I have very few worries about Hasan, and our relationship is an easy one. I think Hasan sees the social worker role as a positive thing, and enjoys the extra support and security of being in care.

After Hasan leaves, I start the overwhelming paperwork side of my job, ensuring that every visit is well documented and the appropriate forms and paperwork completed. This offers me the opportunity to debrief my day in my head, and make plans for the next visits and the next day.

Being a social worker in the UK working with this client group is an opportunity for which I am grateful. It has added to my practice in unexpected ways and offered me insight into the political and personal experiences of asylum seekers. I am very glad that I have experienced it, and feel richer for it. In the back of my mind, however, there remains the knowledge that I will be returning to Canada. This has always been a humbling thought, and effectively demonstrates the social and political barriers between my client group and me. I have a safe, democratic country to return to, a thought that I often take for granted. For the children on my caseload, this is potentially their only opportunity, and it may be time limited. Even after six months of working with these children, it is difficult to grasp the intensity of their plight. I do my best to walk through their experiences with them; however, I know there will always be barriers, and some that we cannot cross.

Think About It

1. As a social worker, what do you see as the limitations and opportunities of practicing social work with an interpreter?

2. How do you think you would balance administrative and organizational requirements with client-centered practice to ensure best practice for clients?

3. What issues of power and privilege do you need to be aware of when practicing social work with this client group?

Chapter 56

Working with Raskal Gangs in the Highlands of Papua New Guinea

|||||||||||||||||||||||||||||||||||||||||||||||||||||||||||||||||||||||||||||||||||||||||||||||||||||||||||||||||||||

by Gerhard J. Schwab, Ph.D., MSW

I wake up in the house of John Taka, a former "raskal" gang leader. He lives in a typical Highlands "bush-house," which is made of local timber, bamboo, and grass. The entire house is basically one big room with a fireplace in the center. The roof is the highest above the fireplace and rests on a circular wall that is low and does not have windows. As all other houses in the village, John's house does not have electrical power, water supply, or any of the other conveniences that we are used to in the industrialized world. During my village visits, I sleep in my sleeping bag, which I always carry with me. However, after years of living in Papua New Guinea, I am still getting annoyed by fleas that find their way into my sleeping bag, suck my blood, and keep waking me up during the night. So it was this night. I did not sleep well and although I know it is morning, I am still tired. Hence, I try to rest as well as I can for the time left until I hear people starting to prepare fire to boil sweet potatoes and coffee for breakfast.

Through the little door, the only opening in the house, I see that it is dawning outside. I get up, go to the river, and take a bath in refreshingly cold water. After my river bath, I enjoy sitting at the river shore. As the warmth of the sun energizes my body, I reflect on my situation and think about what an interesting and challenging job I have. I am employed by the Austrian Institute for Development Cooperation and am part of an effort to build an association of criminal youth gangs, "raskals" as they are called in Papua New Guinea. The primary goal is to develop income-generating projects with gangs so they cease criminal activities. The salary I get for my work is split into two parts. I am paid about US $450 each month into a savings account in my home country. The purpose of this is that I have enough savings for my reintegration when I return home. In Papua New Guinea, the actual place of my work, I get free housing, food, and a pocket money allowance. In terms of social security and health care, I have the same benefits as any public servant employed by the Austrian state. Funds for this project are provided by the Austrian federal government, the Catholic Bishops Conference, and the local Catholic Church in Papua New Guinea.

When I come back to John's house, I see that he and his family are already sitting around the fire, drinking coffee and eating sweet potatoes. I join them and immediately get a plate of sweet potatoes and a big cup of coffee. Our conversation turns into a review of plans we have worked out over the last few days to develop a business to farm potatoes in John's village and sell them in a town at the northern coast of Papua New Guinea. However, my mind is eager to move the conversation to our plans for today. We are going to meet with two other gang leaders to prepare a conference with gangs of several other tribes in a particular valley. I am very excited about these kinds of conferences we conduct in more or less regular time periods. Over a couple of days, we meet with raskal gangs and analyze economic, political, and social structures and developments in the Highlands. Within this community framework, we then move on to learn about the reasons why they engage in criminal activities. This broadened understanding of Highland communities and criminal gang activities then provides a base to develop economic projects utilizing relational and social recourses of raskals to generate income for gang members and their families.

It takes us nearly two hours to get to the place of our planned meeting. The road is in bad condition and requires 4-wheel-drive cars to get through to the village at the end of the valley. The car we are using is a 4WD Suzuki; it was donated by a Catholic aid organization and belongs to the Catholic Archdiocese of the Highlands province. Along the road, women and children are walking to their gardens, carrying gardening tools in their hands; men we see are carrying axes. Naturally, many of them would like to get a ride, but they have to recognize that our car has only limited seating. We are aware that we would have to walk with them for at least a whole day to get to our meeting place, if no people in Catholic churches around the world would donate money for cars in "mission countries."

As soon as John and I arrive at the village, we are greeted by village elders and church leaders. We briefly talk about the purpose of our coming to their village and are then taken to the house of a village elder. They obviously are pleased about our coming and have already prepared a meeting place. Two village elders and three church leaders sit with us, and we all wait for the arrival of the two raskal-gang leaders we are supposed to meet with. I have learned to view these times as opportunities to learn about people and their communities. However, in this situation these village leaders are more interested in hearing from us than telling us about themselves and their village. They are eager to find out what other projects we have started with raskals from other areas. We are proud to tell them about some of the projects we have started and are very open with failures and frustrations we have experienced. Our most successful projects are farming projects, primarily vegetables and coffee, and work contracts with governments, such as road maintenance. The biggest problems we have are a few members of our raskal association who secretly continue to engage in criminal activities after they have become members of the raskal association. This puts the legitimization of our association at serious risk and endangers our positive working relationship with governmental and business organizations.

When the raskal leaders arrive, the village elders tell us that they now know enough, promise us their full support, and leave. Initially, the two gang leaders are suspicious, but are willing to engage in a discussion about the goals of our work as soon as they find out that several well-known raskals have joined our association and have started viable businesses. We share with them our main reason for wanting to meet with them: to invite them to co-sponsor a conference for raskals of their valley. They very quickly realize that we do not come to "save their souls," but that we want to work with them on a specific project, a conference to analyze the reasons why young men form raskal-gangs. The more they hear about what we want to learn from them and the more they see how we define their possible roles in the proposed conference, they realize that we are willing to engage in a partnership with mutual risks and dependencies. After about two hours of talking, I hope that we have enough of a common denominator to agree on organizing a conference that will take into account new ideas that we have generated during the meeting. I am somehow disappointed that we are not able to set a time and place for the proposed conference, but nevertheless I am glad that we all agree to meet again in two weeks.

In the late afternoon, we drive back to John's house. I drop him there and drive on to the main township in the area to have dinner with the Archbishop and three priests. These four men constitute the community I live with when I am in town. They are a great group of men, and I enjoy being affiliated with them. They are all "movers and shakers" and are deeply dedicated to values of human dignity and social justice. There is no doubt in my mind that our association of raskal gangs only could get started because of the full backing of the Archbishop. Dinner with them is always fun and serious at the same time. We freely talk about our personal issues, laugh with each other, challenge each other, and do business at the dinner table. Tonight, among other things, we talk about arrangements I need to make in order to duplicate the budget of the provincial government with a commentary I wrote about it. Budget analysis of provincial and national government is a key element in our raskal conferences. My friends at the dinner table help me in thinking through some possible budget implications and give me valuable help in improving my commentary. Additionally, one of them edits my commentary and thus helps me to improve my writing skills in Pidgin, one of the three official languages in Papua New Guinea.

After dinner, everybody gets out for their evening engagements. I have scheduled a meeting with an Australian business man who operates a hardware store in town. We meet in his house in a very pleasant living room. He knows I am Austrian and puts on Mozart's *Eine Kleine Nachtmusik* to make me feel comfortable. Our discussion circles around gang activities and the problems they cause for his business. He wants to explore with me ways for him to get involved with our raskal association. After I point out to him some of the difficulties gangs have in managing their businesses, he suggests that he will design an accounting course for project leaders. He personally will attend the next conference to get to know some of the raskals and then design a course, which will be implemented by his staff together with a selected group of raskals.

It is close to midnight when I leave his house and go home to a small two-bedroom house in town that the Catholic Church provides for me. I share the house with two Papua New Guineans who are students at the nearby teachers' college. When I enter the house, they are already asleep. I greatly enjoy my first warm shower after several days and am looking forward to sleeping in a bed without fleas. In bed, I read a few pages in Saul Alinsky's

Rules for Radicals and a few pages in the Bible. I use these readings to help me reflect on the day and to live with the conflicts,
complexities, and paradoxes of doing international social work
in Papua New Guinea.

Think About It

1. How does this approach to working with gangs differ from other
   approaches you know about?
2. Discuss the role of religion in social work.

Chapter 57
Working with Russian Immigrants

IIIIIIIIIIIIIIIIIIIIIIIIIIIIIIIIIIIIIIIIIIIIIIIIIIIIIIIIIIIIIIIIIIIIIIIIIIIIIIIIIIIIIIIIIIIIIIIIIIIIIIIIIIIIIIIIIIIIIIIIIIIII

by Julia Ostropolsky, LCSW

I'd like to work with the Russian-speaking elderly and disabled," I said, an MSW practicum student. "I think they need social supports."

"Nonsense," I was told. "Their adult children support the elderly. But if you wish to, go right ahead."

I began going to people's homes, asking them what problems they had, what issues they were facing, and what needs they could think of. Very early on, it became evident that there were so many gaps in social service delivery to older Russian-speaking New Americans that the agency began writing a grant to support my position, and created it to meet the needs of the clients.

Today I have my own agency, stemming from my years of practice as a social worker and therapist. My work has been challenging, successful, and fulfilling. It has a lot of unforeseen experiences, both good and bad, and gaps, and room for growth.

"Julia, I hope it's not too early." The client's voice wakes me up at 7:00 a.m. Urgency, and apology in the desperate attempt. "My husband is out of his medications, and we can't call anyone to bring them, or for the pharmacy to mail. It's been a very bad night for us. He was crying with pain."

And so another day begins. I call the pharmacy and ask them to deliver the medication. I plan to visit the family later in the day, to put a call in to their doctor, and to request medication management.

It seems the husband has taken a monthly dose of painkillers in 20 days—information easily missed, especially when interpretation is involved. I have located a home-visiting doctor for this family, in an attempt to postpone placement. What's better is that the doctor's assistant speaks Russian fluently and is able to visit with the patient to get the history and examine needs.

Each day is a new day, filled with new visits, new requests, new hopes, and outreach. My first appointment is with Irene, who has recently been hospitalized with major depression. She and her spouse came to the U.S. to join their son, but their joy was short-lived, as the son stopped talking to them three years ago, refusing them a chance to see their grandchildren, and not giving them the benefit to work it out. Irene, a Holocaust Survivor, has been suffering nightmarish memories and anxiety associated with her impending citizenship exam. She doesn't speak English, but if she fails the exam, she will no longer qualify for public benefits. Fear of this has worsened her symptoms of depression. When we meet, I offer to apply for a waiver of the exam, based on her poor health condition and failing memory. She agrees. We spend an hour talking over a cup of tea. She feels supported. She calls it a visit. I call it therapy.

I go to my next appointment. Lucy's spouse has been diagnosed with Dementia of Alzheimer's type. As we talk, he walks about laughing, picking up odd things here and there, and showing them to us, forgetful of the words, no longer able to name things or people. Lucy has decided that she cannot put him in a nursing home. Instead, she suffers through the agony of sleepless nights, angry outbursts, when he doesn't want to be changed, and barriers in not having the luxury of English. She brings a pile of letters to me, the ones she doesn't understand: Social Security, an application for food stamp benefits. "My son's English isn't good enough," she explains. "He can't read these." So, I do. I am a social worker. I fill out the applications, explain the benefits, read the letters. I think she struggles for money, so I offer to help with incontinent supplies. I make a few phone calls, place the family on a waiting list with Missouri Area Agency on Aging, and contact a few local food pantries. There are a few minutes left in this hour, so we discuss how better to react when her spouse refuses to brush his teeth or pours his soup into a bowl of a freshly cut up salad. Simple behavior modification. Everything doesn't have to be perfect. Lucy is a "good student." She is learning to let a few things go and to delegate some to the home aide. We still have to work on medication compliance, though. Lucy will not take medications for herself, and she refuses to give them to her spouse. She doesn't let the doctor know. Instead, she tells me in secrecy, and respecting the confidentiality, realizing that this decision isn't life threatening but instead, life burdening, I try to explain. Tomorrow I'll put a call in for a pharmacist to visit.

As I leave, a local mental health agency representative phones me on my mobile line. They heard that I do diversity training seminars and request my services. They can't pay, though, and I agree to do it for free. Overcoming the cultural barriers is one of the goals I have set early on, so I try not to turn down any requests. I have to make a few other calls myself. I do have an office, but spend very little time there, utilizing my mobile phone to the max. I call the local Russian newspaper and inquire whether the editor received an article I sent for the Social Work page. This is additional pro bono work I do, writing articles for the Russian paper. This one had to do with all the major changes within the Medicare system. Readers need to be informed.

Another phone call is to a homemaking provider agency. There is a concern about one of the clients we serve, so we try to work it out with increased monitoring by an aide. I have yet to call the Division of Senior Services to report this issue. I am concerned about this particular client's ability to make decisions. Money management and other supports provided by our agency aren't enough. She recently walked out of her home, wearing nothing but a gown, in the middle of a cold winter night.

As we deliberate over the phone, I make my way to the door of another client. This woman is battling severe physical illness. She no longer can leave her home and suffers bouts of depression and anxiety. On occasion we can both sit back and indulge ourselves with relaxation therapy, proper breathing exercises, and meditation. She reports that deep breathing at night before falling asleep helps.

My staff calls and informs me that the paperwork is in order and is ready for my signature. We are applying to become a Medicaid provider. Until recently, I worked almost for free and was not aware of such a thing as being a Medicaid/Medicare provider. I just did what needed to be done, and relied on small reimbursements from the Division of Senior Services for the few clients that agency approved for counseling services. All is well. I'll be by the office at 5 p.m., and will sign the papers then. I now need support of staff, because there isn't time to bill and to make phone calls. I work until

7 p.m. most of the time. That is because I don't believe in turning people away or placing them on waiting lists (a policy I know I will have to rethink one day).

Next I have a lunch meeting with an attorney. He is a friend and has agreed to take on a case of my clients who were wrongfully accused of causing damage to their rental property. As we eat, we talk about setting up something formally. He is a smart man, very giving, and kind. He wants to help, himself having Russian roots.

Now I am running late. As I drive to my next appointment, I realize that I forgot to complete my case records, and I need to schedule a visit to the Social Security office for a 65-year-old gentleman who asked me to help him apply for Medicare benefits. I make a note, sitting at a red light.

My phone rings. My mother asks me about my day. My phone rings. A voice asks me to stop by when I am in her building next. My phone rings. A concerned mother states that her teenage daughter has begun skipping school, doesn't sleep at night, and seems to have delusions. She doesn't say "delusions." I advise her to schedule an appointment with a psychiatrist, and/or if things are terribly bad, to take the child to an emergency room. It may help to see a physician, but the mother refuses to see anyone, because she heard that I can help in these matters and wants me to meet the daughter first. I promise to call back to get additional information and schedule a meeting.

My days are unpredictable and full of challenge. Yet, I know that I am able to help. There are a lot of unmet needs among New Americans. Don't let anyone tell you that they "take care of each other." They do, as much as anyone else would and does, and their needs are accelerated by lack of knowledge of English, confusion within a new culture, and many other barriers. So, as a social worker, I decided to help those who can't always help themselves. I do so, hoping to empower them, educating them and the larger community in the process, and knowing that what I do makes a positive difference, if even in one of many lives.

Think About It

1. Why is it important, in working with members of a particular culture, to understand the views that members of that culture typically hold toward help-seeking?

2. What is Julia's role in working with other agencies and other professionals to help her clients?

PART 14:
POLICY PRACTICE

Chapter 58
Policy Practice in a Legislative Office

IIIIIIIIIIIIIIIIIIIIIIIIIIIIIIIIIIIIIIIIIIIIIIIIIIIIIIIIIIIIIIIIIIIIIIIIIIIIIIIIIIIIIIIIIIIIIIIIIIIIIIIIIIIIIIIIIIIIIIIIIIIIIIIIIIIIIIIII

by Brad Forenza, MSW, Ph.D.

It's 9 a.m. and, as I check voicemails from last night, there are already new calls on hold for me. I actively wonder why—in this day and age, when everything is electronic—a landline even exists in my office, let alone a landline ringing off the hook. The answer becomes clear as I scribe notes for follow up: my boss, a liberal state legislator, was asked by the governor to chair a benefits reform committee (whatever that means). Since the committee started meeting in earnest, I've become the unwitting target of lobbying efforts from public employee unions (police, teachers, and others) and individual public servants alike, as well as from homeowners, boards of education, and myriad taxpayer groups. The phone is the quickest way for each interest to communicate—sometimes loudly and often colorfully—its urgency. In politics, issues are often framed as life-or-death.

When I am finally able to answer a call in real time, it's a prosecutor wanting to know if prosecutor pension vestment will change for new hires. I tell him, "No," because yesterday—at the state capitol—I was explicitly told that prosecutor benefits were non-negotiable. This time last year, when I was an MSW student, I wonder *who knew that I would soon be communicating prosecutor pension policy?*

Last summer, sandwiched between two MSW field placements, I had secured an internship in a Congressional office. There, I helped constituents resolve issues related to labor, health, and human services at the federal level. Post-MSW, I wanted to pursue more of this macro work. Since political jobs are not widely advertised, I sent my unsolicited résumé and cold cover letters to state and federal legislators throughout my region. I made uncomfortable follow-up calls, and—two months later—I was finally invited to interview for an anticipated vacancy in my own state legislator's office. Per my social work training and experience, I was hired to manage constituent affairs for her small, local team. My job entails all the hallmarks of social casework: helping residents identify community resources, making referrals.... But since this whole benefits thing erupted, I've become the local policy contact, as well. *I wasn't trained in this,* I think. What do I know about public employee pension and benefits?!

I learn on the fly that public employee pension and benefits are perceived to be driving up property taxes in the state, which is why the governor and legislature want to act. I also learn—through meetings with myriad stakeholders—that these benefits function as social insurance for the people who receive them. *So why are we doing this?,* I ask myself. Why did the governor and my boss decide that this was the month to tackle such an albatross of an issue? Cynically, the answer could be political expediency. Altruistically, it could be a sense of what is right and just for taxpayers. (I learn in my macro practice that there are rarely winners in politics—just trade-offs.) I don't have time to fully answer my question, because the next call is her: my boss. "Did you tell the prosecutors they were exempt from benefits reform?" she asks.

"Not exactly," I respond.

"Well, they think they're exempt, and they've already sent a memo to the governor saying as much," she replies. "His office wants to know who would give them that impression." My impulse is to think, *I was only trying to help!*—but information is power, and information can change at lightening pace. "Don't stress too much about it," she tells me, "but don't fall for that again, either."

I remind my boss about a visit to a school we are making in the afternoon. Coordinating community events is another job func-tion—one that my social work training prepared me well for. My boss has been invited to this school as per her efforts in securing additional state funding for stem cell research. "Great," she says. "Do you have a speech for me?" And just like that, I realize that I'm floundering again. I feel a small palpitation for yet another fresh-man mistake. In this, my first post-MSW job, I'm not yet versed at anticipating my boss' needs, or the needs of the dynamic political arena, where policy itself is only one slice of the pie.

"I'll get you something," I tell her.

I understand why my boss wants talking points. Politicians are generalists. My boss knows public budgeting like the back of her hand, but that's just one area. As a legislator, she is called on to communicate state finance just as expertly as stem cell research, autism treatment, lead-based paint removal, or any other substantive issue. Fun for me is the fact that—at the state level—the vast majority of policies are domestic, social ones. And it's my job to analyze and communicate those policies on her behalf.

My boss hangs up, and there is a constituent waiting for me—a resident from the downtrodden, former manufacturing town where our office is housed. This individual, an unemployed taxi driver, has an appointment with me. In spite of the day's chaos, I want to honor my commitment to him. For the next 40-ish minutes, I ignore all calls and help Mr. G. identify what he needs to accomplish to get his driver's license reinstated, so he can get back to work. In short, the state motor vehicle agency tells me that Mr. G.'s traffic violations are manageable, but his child support arrears are considerably steep. While I wish Mr. G. could have been more diligent in honoring his child support order, I know better than to judge him. I help Mr. G. work out a payment plan with the state, and—although he leaves my office as unemployed and license-less as when he walked in—I silently celebrate his small victory and hope that he can do the same.

After lunch, my phone still rings (my phone is symbolic for the rapid-fire nature of this job). It's apparent that there is misinformation out there—likely a conscious spread of misinformation—about what the benefits reform committee actually purports to do. The committee's emphasis is on modifying benefits for new employees, not current or retired employees. Yet, every other call is from a screaming retiree demanding that the state make good on its promise to him or her. And from a social justice perspective, I hear every caller loud and clear. I promise to convey each and every concern.

As the afternoon inches on, I remember I have to write that speech. Stem cell research, stem cell research...what do I know about stem cell research? I shut the ringer off my phone and start searching the Internet for anything and everything written on the topic. In the next hour, I become a street corner expert on all things stem cell, as well as the ways in which stem cell research is funded in the state. I layer conversations about federalism and social justice into my boss's speech. This is the realm of my job that I excel most in: communicating dense policy via user-friendly terms. And when that policy has implications for health and well-being, which is abundantly true for stem cell research, I feel all the more empowered. I may not be the one making the speech, and I may not be the school's intended guest, but my words are shaping the audience's understanding of an issue related to human welfare. And for me, there is power in that.

The students are intrigued by everything my boss has to say about stem cell research. I wonder if they knew who she was or what she did prior to today's assembly. I wonder if they knew that the funding afforded to each student in the room and the services each is entitled to are informed, in part, by her efforts. And I wonder if they knew that behind every legislator is a team of people—some social workers, some lawyers, some political scientists, some of everything, really—helping to shape an agenda on behalf of a local community.

Being at the school seems like a good way to end this work day. But when I think of all the voicemails I'll have to retrieve tomorrow morning—each of them related to public employee pension and benefits—I wonder if, in fact, I would have been better off staying back at the office. There's a gala for the State Firefighter's Association tonight, I remind myself. I bet they'll be talking benefits there, too.

Think About It

1. What social work skills does the writer utilize in his macro practice? In what ways is social work training useful for working in a legislative office?

2. In what ways does the writer learn on the job? How is on-the-job learning the same as, or different from, classroom learning?

3. What does the writer mean by "there are no winners in politics, just trade-offs"? What does he mean when he says "policy is only one slice of the pie"?

4. In what ways can you identify and celebrate small victories with your clients?

Chapter 59

A Day in the Life of a Policy Practitioner

||||||||||||||||||||||||||||||||||||||||||||||||||||||||||||||||||||||||||||||||||||||||

by Joan M. Abbey, LMSW

Stepping out of the shower, and reaching for a towel, my brain runs down today's schedule while the towel rubs down the body. It is going to be a long day, and I have to be in several places at once. I am not sure how I will do it, but I will try. Working as a child advocate is never easy.

The Governor's Executive Budget recommends eliminating the entire Division of Day Care Licensing. I once worked as a child care provider, so I understand the importance of licensing to assure quality child care for working families in our state. While driving to the State Capitol, I wonder what will be the outcome of today's public hearing on this Executive Budget recommendation. Arriving at the hearing room at 7:45 a.m., I can barely get in the door. In addition to child care providers, advocates, bureaucrats, and concerned parents, there are a number of journalists jammed into the hearing room. It seems the discrete phone calls to the press telling them about the hearing got results. There is no place to sit. Inching up to the front of the room, I lean against the wall.

At 8:00 a.m., the public hearing begins. From his body language, it is clear the director of the department that houses Day Care Licensing is uncomfortable with the presence of so many media and people holding signs protesting the Executive Budget's recommendation. The director explains the rationale for the recommendation in the Executive Budget. In turn, the committee members ask a number of pointed questions. Point and counterpoint, time wears on. My feet begin to hurt, and I wish I had worn flats. The director and committee chair are speaking loudly, neither swaying the other's position on this issue. Catching the attention of one of the committee staff members, I slip her a question. *Who will be responsible for investigating abuse and neglect allegations in child care centers if the Division is eliminated, since this function is the responsibility of Day Care Licensing?* A few years back, responsibility for investigations in day care settings moved from Children's Protective Services to Day Care Licensing. If the state should abolish Day Care Licensing, an entire class of children in our state will not receive equal protection under the law. In essence, the state will violate the Fourteenth Amendment of the U. S. Constitution. The department director is new to the state and may not know about this policy. The staff person slips the question to the committee chair. He glances at it and shoves it under a stack of papers. After a few more heated exchanges between the director and committee members, the committee chair asks the U.S. Constitution question. The director looks stunned, his voice falls several decibels, and he answers, "That function will not be covered." The audience gasps with the realization of the import of this statement. The chair strikes his gavel and announces the hearing is adjourned. The media swarms the director. I head to the door. It is noon and I am already an hour late for a board meeting.

Arriving at the board meeting, I apologize for my tardiness, drop into a chair, and slip off my shoes. I hate being late for anything. As the lone social worker on this board and as a general membership representative, I want to make a good impression with this group of health care providers and administrators. Worrying that my tardiness works against that, I quickly scan the agenda, while listening to the conversation to figure out which item is being discussed. The issue under discussion is lead screening and abatement. A municipality in the state is about to lose federal funds to enable the safe removal of lead from older homes. There are problems with public outreach to identify unsafe homes, and the local health department is experiencing personnel problems. We vote to write letters to the federal government, the Mayor, and the local health department director encouraging cooperation among all parties and expeditious action. Also, we agree to use our networks to distribute fliers to parents educating them about the danger to children from lead poisoning in older homes. The fliers will also tell parents where they can call for lead screening and abatement assistance.

The board moves through the remaining agenda items, and I hope no one notices my stomach growling. It has been a long time since that breakfast bagel and coffee. When the meeting ends, I grab a sandwich from the lunchroom and head back to the office.

I place a call to several children's legal rights organizations and ask their opinion about whether abolishing day care licensing is grounds for a class action suit on behalf of children in child care. They confirm this to be the case and offer their assistance to the local early childhood organization in drafting and filing the suit. I call the director of the local early childhood organization and put him in touch with the legal rights groups.

It is after 4:00 p.m. The security guards will lock the building and set the alarms at 6:00 p.m. I have just enough time to dash off a couple of letters and return some of the calls in my voicemail box. The other calls will have to wait until tomorrow, and I will respond to my email from home tonight.

Driving home, I turn on the radio to catch some late local news and traffic. The reporter is saying that the Governor's office is swamped with phone calls from parents and others concerned that children in child care will not be protected from abuse and neglect. It has been a long day, and it is not over yet. No one told me in graduate school that to be a policy practitioner, I would have to be a press agent, politician, legal expert, and budget analyst rolled into one. It would be nice if the job paid the salaries of all four jobs rolled into one, but the work has other rewards.

Pulling into the driveway, I stop and collect the evening paper and the mail. Glancing at the newspaper headlines, I see that the day care public hearing made the front page. Inside the house, I kick off my shoes and think out loud. "Sometimes you lose, sometimes you win, and we may win this one after all."

P.S. After receiving 10,000 letters and phone calls, the state did not eliminate the Division of Day Care Licensing.

Think About It

1. How does the writer illustrate the connection between policy issues and practice issues?

2. What are some strategies you would use to prevent the closing of the Division of Day Care Licensing?

408   *Days in the Lives of Social Workers*

PART 15: WORKING IN COMMUNITIES

Chapter 60
Social Work in the Public Library

||||||||||||||||||||||||||||||||||||||||||||||||||||||||||||||||||||||||||||||||||||||||||||||||||||||||||||||||

by David Pérez, MSW

I t's winter, and the holidays are a distant memory. It's back to work from holiday vacations and back to school for Monmouth University. It sure is cold at the Jersey Shore in the winter. The wind blows hard inland off the ocean; can't wait for summer. This is Long Branch, New Jersey, "the Friendly City on the Jersey Shore." This is the same city that became famous for having been frequented, as a vacation location, by seven U.S. Presidents: Ulysses S. Grant, Rutherford B. Hayes, James A. Garfield, Chester A. Arthur, Benjamin Harrison, William McKinley, and Woodrow Wilson.

The Long Branch Free Public Library is where I'm headed for work. Yes, that's correct. I am a social worker, doing social work, at a public library. I agree, the library is not your typical venue for a social worker, but nevertheless, it is an effective model for community development. In my library director's office, there hangs a frame with the following quote: "There is not such a cradle of democracy upon the earth as the Free Public Library, this republic of letters, where neither rank, office, nor wealth receives the slightest consideration," by Andrew Carnegie. As a matter of fact, the Long Branch Free Public Library is the last of the 36 Carnegie libraries to be built in New Jersey. It would seem only natural for social work to thrive in such a structure, built by such a philanthropist.

As I drive up to this historic building with the words "Public Library" and the signature Carnegie columns in the front, I see the familiar patrons. They are slowly making their way to the library. I park my car and walk to the entrance, where I'm greeted by a male patron, "Mornin', Dave." I return the greeting, "Mornin', brother. How are you today?" "Cold," the patron replies. I already knew the answer to that question, because this patron sleeps in a tent on the outskirts of our city, and our overnight temperature was in the 20s. Every morning, the patron wakes and hikes right back to the library, where he finds warmth and bathroom access, books to read, and public computers to watch movies or conduct whatever type of research the patron may need to conduct. This is more than a library; it's the patrons' "home base."

The library opens at 10:00 a.m. I come in at noon and will be here until 8:00 p.m. As I approach our front circulation desk, I'm told that there are two patrons waiting for me outside my office, and I'm handed a sticky note with the name and number of someone looking for information on affordable housing. I make my way to the elevator and la Senora Sanchez spots me.

"Hola, David."

"Hola, Senora Sanchez. Como estas hoy?" "Bien David, pero necesito tu ayuda en llenar las formas de almuerzo para mi hijo."

"Okay, Senora Sanchez, te puedo ayudar a las 1:00."

"Okay, gracias, David."

So, I am a bilingual social worker, fluent in English and Spanish. Mrs. Sanchez has requested help in filling out school lunch forms for her son. I ask her to come back in one hour, since I already have two clients waiting for me.

It's a good thing my Monmouth University interns are all due to come in today. I can certainly use the help. I supervise three School of Social Work interns from Monmouth. I am thankful that all three interns are already here and have initiated the intake forms for our new clients. I enter our social work office, put down my personal belongings, introduce myself to our new clients, and pull up a chair next to Robert, one of my interns. This is a great opportunity for me to observe the intern and attend to the client's needs at the same time. The client has come in today stating she has lost her live-in caretaker job, thus becoming unemployed and homeless at the same time. The patient she was taking care of decided to move to a senior retirement community. That one decision now has our client living in her car without any money for food or rent. Since we, as library social workers, serve as resource and referral agents to our community, I suggest an organization that specializes in placing home health aides, as well as the Department of Social Services to help her with basic needs like housing and food.

I then move to the next desk and sit next to my other intern, who is filling out an intake form for a client. I introduce myself and engage with the client. The client has been referred to us by Intense Supervised Parole (ISP). This client is an ex-offender and is seeking re-entry services: employment, housing, healthcare, driver's license restoration, food, and help with other basic needs. I offer to escort the client to the library's Technology and Career Center. We have computers that have direct access to the Department of Labor's database for jobs. Our library was selected by the DOL, and we were awarded a grant, with which we hired two part-time employees who are dedicated to helping our clients/patrons with their job search, as well as building their résumés and cover letters. So, the intern has made an appointment with the client for next week. I give the client my business card, which has all my contact information, and then walk the client to our Technology and Career Center to introduce him to our career coach, who will continue to work closely with him in his job search.

As I am on my way back to our social work office, I am called to the circulation desk. There is a client on hold who just called asking for me. I pick up the phone, and it's Mrs. Johnson, following up on our visit from yesterday. Mrs. Johnson is seeking disability services for her foster child, who has been diagnosed with Attention Deficit Disorder (ADD). I advise Mrs. Johnson that I have not heard back from the agency we called yesterday, assuring her that I will contact her as soon as I hear back. As it turns out, the agency takes three days to call me back, and Mrs. Johnson calls me twice a day until they do. This can become the most frustrating part of my job—waiting for other agencies to call me back regarding help I am soliciting from them for my clients. My dedication to the community is to pledge my partnership with them, in helping them to identify their own strengths and helping them to help themselves, navigating through policies and procedures that at times are discouraging.

It's now 2:00 p.m., and I have a meeting with my Director at 2:30. We are having a stakeholders' meeting with New Jersey State Parole Board, Monmouth County Re-Entry Task Force, GEO Re-Entry Services, New Jersey Office of the State Librarian, and Monmouth University School of Social Work Field and Professional Services. At the meeting, we discuss a new collaboration/pilot program, in which the Long Branch Public Library (LBPL) will become a "Re-Connection Center" for re-entry services in Monmouth County.

The state agencies are working on a federal grant proposal and will refer clients to us at the LBPL. Monmouth University will place social work interns in libraries throughout New Jersey, and these libraries will also become Re-Connection Centers. I will not only supervise the LBPL interns, but will travel to the other libraries to provide social work supervision to meet social work professional and ethical standards. The 2:30 meeting goes well, and we all agree that the process is steadily moving forward.

I go back to our social work office and meet with the interns from 3:30-4:00. We discuss the day's cases and clients. Together, we discuss possible solutions and work through any challenges. The interns all leave at 4:00, and I take my hour break.

At 5:00, I am back at the library, covering the help desk at our public computers. For the next three hours, I will assist our patrons in basic library functions. I don't mind this, even though it is not "social work"—or is it? I think it is important for a social worker in a library to truly identify with where he or she is—you are in a library. At the end of the day, it will always be a library. That being said, it is important for a social worker in a library to identify with librarianship—whole person librarianship. When we accomplish this whole person librarianship, although we are a totally different profession with specific standards and ethics, we can become one with the librarian. We can share a common vision and goals.

In between assisting the patrons, I am preparing and planning for our next community cultural event. We just completed our Black History Month events, where we invited local historians, amateur rap artists, fashionistas, painters, and medical professionals. All of this was to celebrate the diversity of our community and to honor the African American and Afro Latino communities. Now it is time to coordinate the annual Latino Fest, to take place in September.

It is 7:00 p.m., and we are closing the library in one hour. I am going through my emails, and I notice an email from Mr. P at the New Jersey Department of Military and Veterans Affairs. We are collaborating on a Veterans outreach program here at the library. The Department of Labor has identified a trend in veteran unemployment in Long Branch, so we will join forces to reach out to this community. We are planning a summer event. Mr. P wants to meet, so I confirm a meeting for next Monday. This population is very special to me. I am a disabled Army Veteran myself, and I would not be a social worker if the VA had not paid for me to get my MSW degree.

At 7:30 p.m., the closing announcement is dispatched through-out the library. The teens turn in their laptops, and the remaining patrons bring their books to the circulation desk for check out. The children log off of their computer games. The homeless patrons begin to put on their several layers of clothing, hats, and scarves. Back to the cold, back to the tent, back to their reality. I wish I had a magic wand, a genie in a bottle, a winning Powerball ticket.

"Good night, Dave."

"Good night, brother."

Think About It

1. How can a social worker remain politically neutral in a free speech environment such as the public library?

2. How does the social work profession "fuse" with "whole person librarianship"?

3. How can a library gain support from local governing bodies and trustees to justify having a full-time social worker on staff?

4. How does a library provide confidentiality for social work clients in a library space?

Chapter 61
Community Organizing for Social Change

IIIIIIIIIIIIIIIIIIIIIIIIIIIIIIIIIIIIIIIIIIIIIIIIIIIIIIIIIIIIIIIIIIIIIIIIIIIIIIIIIIIIIIIIIIIII

by Asherah Cinnamon, MSW, LCSW

My favorite part of my work is getting to know and have close relationships with a very diverse group of people in my community, and working with them to empower the community toward change. The most satisfying part of the work is being able to do something effective and positive about the problems of racism, sexism, classism, anti-Semitism, and all the other "isms." I am able to do the work that has my heart, and get paid to do it. As a social change agent and community organizer, I get to be involved with a wide variety of people working toward systemic change.

I am Director of the East Tennessee Chapter of the National Coalition Building Institute, and serve as one of its national trainer/consultants. NCBI is a nonprofit organization that builds teams of local community leaders and future leaders and trains them to handle controversial issues and intergroup tensions in their own organizations, among their own identity groups, and in the community as a whole. This training, team building, and outreach to community leaders are all part of my job. I coordinate the activities of the chapter with a completely volunteer team of 20-30 local community leaders and students, whom I have recruited and trained over the past three years. I have no paid staff, which also makes me a Jill-of-all-trades.

Three days in January, though not routine for me, nevertheless represent the culmination of three years of local organizing and relationship-building. At 8 p.m. on a Monday night, I hear that a

Black church in our city has been burned to the ground in the early morning hours. Recovering from shock, outrage, and grief about this, I begin making phone calls to find out more about it and learn that the church is one of more than 20 that have been burned to date in the Southeast USA in the past 16 months. I spend two hours on the phone with a Methodist minister, who is a volunteer on my NCBI chapter team. That same night, we put together a statement of support to present to the congregation of the burned out church as quickly as possible. Calls go back and forth at 10 p.m. with the first draft of the statement, to check in with the NAACP president and several chapter members to make sure that the statement is appropriate and will indeed be seen by the African community as a genuine offer of support.

Early the next morning, I begin sending the statement out to key community leaders, especially white church and synagogue leaders, for their signatures. By sheer luck, it is time for all the Methodist ministers in the district to hand in their year-end reports, so we obtain permission to meet with the district superintendent the same morning, and we have a copy of the support statement ready for signatures. At noon, we have over 50 signatures from district ministers and the bishop. Other signatures come in from the Catholic Bishop, the Director of the Jewish Federation, the Presbytery, the Episcopal Bishop, a rabbi, and several Baptist ministers and lay leaders. I make more phone calls to encourage other local leaders to sign the statement in time for the next church meeting, and pass it along to others.

I talk with the Director of the local Neighborhood Development Center, an active member of my NCBI team, about possible workshop offerings to bring people together around this event and the issue of racism in our community. She and the NAACP president, who has participated in one of our trainings two years earlier, agree to co-sponsor the first workshop. I find free space, get a team member to agree to lead the workshop with me, and we set the date.

The vast majority of people I speak with thank me for giving them the opportunity to show their support. Many say they did not know what to do, and their shock kept them immobile until I called. A few are not eager to sign or join the coalition of workshop sponsors—they are cautious. One of the frustrations of this work and its most important challenge is to overcome the fear and hopelessness that masquerade as caution. Equally challenging is the internalized oppression of members of groups who have been the target of prejudice and find cooperation difficult. This can disable whole organizations from taking effective, cooperative action when it is clearly needed. Others, often with political pressures on them, are unable to take what is for them a bold step, for fear of making a mistake and being criticized for it publicly. Given our cultural propensity to trash leaders as soon as we think they have goofed, I can't entirely blame them, though I would like to indulge in that comforting pastime.

Not all caution leads to refusal or opposition. A key religious leader calls to ask if we should be sending a statement about the racist motives behind the arson before we have proof of them. I point out that our support statement has been worded specifically not to depend on such proof, but to give local leaders the opportunity to make a renewed commitment to fight racism in the community, regardless of the motive for the arson. I inform him that late-breaking news reports say racist graffiti was found on the scene of the arson and has been linked to the time of the arson. He thanks me for my patience and signs the statement immediately, telling me the name of another leader to contact and giving me permission to say that he encourages his colleague to sign. I am elated. Often, people who may seem to be fighting what we are doing turn out only to need more information and some listening time to join in fully.

I make many calls trying to reach the minister of the burned church or his associate pastor, whom I met earlier in the year when he interviewed me on the church-run music and talk radio station. The station had been broadcasting from the building adjacent to the church. It too has been destroyed in the fire, along with a brand new church-sponsored day care center. Finally, I reach the associate pastor, who remembers me and says he is sure the congregation would like to receive our statement of support that same evening at its service. He says he will check with the minister, who has been deluged with calls and is having difficulty returning them all, including mine. I am pleased to hear that he is receiving mostly supportive calls.

That evening, I meet with the Methodist minister who helped me draft the statement, to attend the prayer service in the parking lot of the burned out church. It is a freezing January night, and I am grateful for my New England training in how to dress for cold. Still, it is not enough, and our toes feel frozen soon after we arrive. We are introduced to the presiding minister, who welcomes us and invites us to read our statement of support after the service. I do so and then list some of the community leaders who have signed. I notice the faces of the 50 or so congregants who are gathered in this place of violent destruction. As I read, I see one woman elbow her friend with an excited air as she hears the names of the signers. Others nod their heads solemnly, moved, and also still numb from the shock of the violation of their sacred building and the destruction of their base in the community. One woman's eyes sparkle with unshed tears. She watches intently as I read the list of signatories. It is a small thing, really, to put words together and send around a statement of support. But for these people, it is a sign of hope, and a contradiction to their isolation as victims of violence and their isolation as members of a minority group in the midst of a majority culture which has too often let them down.

The statement of support is only a first step in our response. We quickly begin plans for a series of workshops to teach bridge-building skills to some of the people who signed the statement and members of the burned church. Three months later, 70 people participate in the first Leadership for Diversity Workshop, including members of local law enforcement, who have been criticized by the Black community for not doing enough to apprehend the arsonists, and an FBI administrator, who has just moved into town in the midst of it all and has not yet met anyone. He sits down unknowingly behind the minister of the burned church, and the group gasps in anticipation of tension, as they see the chance placement of the two men. As we go around introducing ourselves, the minister turns and shakes hands with the FBI agent, showing much grace, and breaking the tension for us all. The rest of that workshop day would be a jewel in the life of any social worker. Participants are honest, kind to each other, and unusually open to each other's point of view.

As I have become more experienced in this work, I have also been invited to present workshops for the profession at national conferences and for national groups. This gives me the added perk of meeting people from all over the country in my field, and making lifelong friendships that endure even when I move to a new state. Similarly, the fact that the organization I work for has grown to international scope gives me at least semi-annual contact with people who do the same work I do from all over the U.S., Canada, and Europe. The National Association of Social Workers and the National Association of Human Rights Workers are additional networking resources for me.

As is true for staff in many social change/community organizations, my job includes fundraising and grant writing, activities that are necessary to raise the money to pay myself and the organization's expenses. Most of the time, I work on contract, with no benefits, and I have a lot of independence to set the direction for my chapter in conjunction with my local team. Contract work is not for the timid. It varies widely and there are seasonal and geographic swings, as well. As the mother of a young child, this seasonality has given me time off during holidays and much of July. So it has its advantages.

On the other hand, the hours are irregular. Evening and weekend work are not uncommon, since reaching out to a whole community means going to community events and scheduling meetings when people who volunteer and have paying jobs elsewhere can attend. Sometimes, there is a push for a certain event, a workshop or training, and I am enfolded in my job for days and nights at a time. My family is not always thrilled, even though they are supportive. My husband volunteers with our chapter, and I have recruited my mother-in-law to make phone calls for us once a month. My daughter and my mother have participated in our workshops and other community events. One benefit of community organizing is being able to include my family in some aspects of my work. This feels more natural to me than the rigid division of family from work, though it does not suit everyone, and it requires clear boundaries nevertheless.

In the fall, I will have an MSW student in field placement with me. I have always found it a very mutually rewarding experience for myself, my organization, and the student. As our local volunteer team develops, the growing sense that I am not alone in this work makes all the hard work especially worthwhile. Social change is often best done at the local level, changing attitudes and bringing people together across traditional barriers. Working cooperatively with neighbors, making new friends, overcoming obstacles on the way to goals we choose together from the depths of our hearts— that is the best kind of work I can imagine.

Think About It

1. What are some important skills for community organizers?
2. How would you like the irregular work hours of this type of social work?

Chapter 62
Epilogue: I Am Still a Social Worker

IIIIIIIIIIIIIIIIIIIIIIIIIIIIIIIIIIIIIIIIIIIIIIIIIIIIIIIIIIIIIIIIIIIIIIIIIIIIIIIIIIIIIIIIIIIIIIIIIIIIIIIIIIIIIIIIIIIIIIIII

by Linda May Grobman, MSW, LSW, ACSW

It was about 36 years ago that I began my first post-MSW position as a social worker. I earned $11,998 per year as a full-time employee in the inpatient adult mental health unit of a state hospital. I felt like Mary Richards from *The Mary Tyler Moore Show*. I could hear the familiar line from the theme song, "You're gonna make it after all," playing in my head as I happily practiced my new profession.

I am a social worker. My diploma says so. My state license says so. But mostly, I say so. I am a social worker.

The following is a composite "day" in my life. Some of these activities typically happen over a period of time, rather than in one day.

I wake up and, after the morning's activities at home, go to my office. I begin my work day by reading and answering emails, and responding to telephone calls. I spend a good part of my morning on social media. I post the link to the latest *The New Social Worker* article on our Facebook page, Twitter, Pinterest, and in the LinkedIn group. I post a Social Work Month meme on Instagram.

I am going to the annual conference of the Association of Baccalaureate Social Work Program Directors (BPD) next week, so I pack several boxes of books and materials to ship to the conference for my booth in the exhibit hall.

I will spend about 3½ days at the conference talking to social work educators and students about the books I publish, *The New Social Worker* magazine, and other projects I am currently working on and may want to collaborate on with them, as well as discussing their current activities and projects. I cherish the two times a year (sometimes more) when I meet with colleagues at this and similar conferences. It is a time to renew friendships and professional connections, to make important contacts, to learn what is happening in the field nationally, and to get a refreshed perspective on things. I hope I'll be able to take some time away from my exhibit to attend some of the conference workshops. Conferences have so much to offer, both educationally and through informal networking.

Next, I check the SocialWorkJobBank.com site. SWJB is an online job board I launched in 2001, where social work job seekers and employers go to, hopefully, find a "perfect match." I have always had an interest in social work career development, and I enjoy seeing people find the right job. Two new job postings so far today! And good ones, too—an administrative position in state government and an entry level BSW position.

I am a social worker. My current "job" is publisher and editor at White Hat Communications/The New Social Worker Press, a social work publishing company that I started. I am a social worker. It's what I am, but is it what I *do?*

It's time for lunch. I like to get away from the office at lunch time. It breaks the day into manageable chunks. I guess this is a throwback from my days as a hospital social worker. I always felt that a change in scenery in the middle of the day was a good, healthy idea. It is part of my daily self-care practice.

My husband Gary and I go to the Chinese buffet down the road. A local social worker, someone Gary knows, stops by our table to say "hi." Gary introduces us to each other, saying, "You're both social workers," and pointing to each of us. The woman says, "Well, I used to be." *Hmmm,* I think. Then she says to me, "Are you *still* a social worker?" I think to myself, *I didn't know I could UN-become one once it was part of who I am!* (And I don't want to.)

I am a social worker. Does she mean do I *do* social work? Does she mean is social work my *job title?* What is the meaning of her question, "Are you *still* a social worker?"

When I got my MSW, I chose the mental health concentration. That was my main area of interest, and I figured that regardless of what setting I worked in, I would be working with people on emotional issues, so a mental health background would be good preparation. I also remember writing in my MSW application, as part of my personal statement, that I wanted to accomplish social work goals through my writing.

In my first professional job after graduate school, I worked in a mental health inpatient setting. A "state hospital." Every day started with reading patient charts. Then leading the morning "community" group. Then the morning team meeting, individual sessions, charting, and other paperwork, before lunch. After lunch (away from the hospital, with colleagues), there was therapy group, then more individual sessions, family sessions, charting, and more paperwork. Sometimes a hearing for involuntary commitment, and a couple of times a month, a family education and support group that I co-developed and co-led with another social worker at the hospital. My days were fairly structured, although never quite the same from one day to the next. And it was clear. I was a social worker. My job title said so. And I was doing social work.

My next job was at a children's hospital. Patients ranged in age from infancy to late adolescence. Their presenting problems could be anything from a life threatening illness to injuries suffered in an accident or other medical conditions. Social workers were assigned to patients and their families who needed some help with community resources, emotional coping, and other social issues. My job title was Social Worker, and I was employed in the Social Work Department. Every day, I would find out about any new patients in the hospital who were assigned to my caseload, and I would check to see who on my caseload from the previous day was still there. Then I would head out to "the floor." I would go to their hospital rooms, hoping to find their parents or other support people to talk to. Referrals came from doctors, nurses, and other staff. Social workers were involved if there was a specific reason to be involved. It might be suspected child abuse, emotional adjustment to a new diagnosis of cancer, a need for financial assistance, discharge planning issues, or something else. Most of my day would be spent going to rooms and talking to children and their parents, writing in charts, consulting with doctors and nurses, making phone calls, and sometimes meeting with an interdisciplinary team.

But back to today. I am a social worker who publishes. Social work is part of who I am, not just what I do. I have several manuscripts on my desk that people have sent to me for possible publication in *The New Social Worker*, the national magazine I started and edit and publish. I get excited each time I receive an article. I especially enjoy finding new and interesting social work writers!

The first article looks good. It's about public speaking skills for social workers. This is just the kind of article I want to publish in *The New Social Worker.* I email the writer, letting her know that the article has been accepted and attaching the necessary paperwork.

I read each manuscript carefully, paying attention to the content presented, the writing style, the writer's credentials, sources of information, and especially, the article's relevance to our unique niche of readers—social work students and recent graduates. I also need to be aware of warning signs for such things as plagiarism and inaccurate information.

I am a social worker. So, how did I get to be a publisher? I am often asked this question when I attend social work conferences, and someone will probably ask me again next week. It's sometimes difficult to explain. Even though I sometimes describe myself as a publisher, I know I'm primarily a social worker. Even though I am an entrepreneur, social work is where my core professional values lie. I am a social worker who has a social work publishing business.

To me, social work is not just a job that one learns and does. It is a way of thinking and being, as well. Social work education is a transformative process. It teaches you theories and skills, and gives you a professional title, and helps you understand the "why" and "how" of some things you may have already known instinctively. But it doesn't just teach you *about* social work. If successful, it turns you *into* a social worker.

I became a social work publisher so I could use my skills in editing and writing, along with my social work values and skills, to help other social workers in their career development. This was one of my interests from the beginning of my own career. As I developed my own career path, I became interested in social work career development as a whole. I found it interesting and exciting to be able to help other social workers find their niche.

I once had a part-time job working with a college student organization, and I enjoyed this population. It was a mix of association management, leadership development, and individual and group counseling. I became involved in the National Association of Social Workers, first as a volunteer leader, and then as a staff person. I worked at two state chapter offices of NASW, editing state newsletters, staffing committees, and performing other functions. I liked being able to serve other social workers.

Eventually, I had some ideas that I wanted to put into action. I wanted to publish a magazine for social workers. I wanted to write or edit a book or two, help social workers find jobs, and foster career development in social work colleagues. I created this niche in the form of a social work publishing company.

As the end of my work day nears, I think about the book I am editing, the fifth edition of *Days in the Lives oof Social Workers*. It is a collection of social workers' stories—social workers in different roles, and in different settings. They all have different jobs, but they all have a professional social work education and do their work from a social work perspective. They are all social workers.

Before I leave for the day, I reach into my box of "Ask Me About Self-Care" buttons and pull out a few to take to the conference next week. I will proudly wear the big round, green buttons with these words in large letters, to let everyone at the conference know that, as professional social workers, it is important to take care of ourselves, whether that means taking a lunch break, going to a yoga class, or investing in our own therapy.

I think many social workers have careers that evolve and transform over time, as mine has. Their social work backgrounds sometimes take them places they never would have imagined. Who knows where mine will lead next? Or yours? There is one thing that I know for certain.

I am a social worker. STILL.

Think About It

1. What does it mean to be a social worker?

2. "Once a social worker, always a social worker." Do you believe this statement? Discuss.

2. How might a manager or business person who is a professional social worker act or make decisions differently from a manager or business person who is trained in business?

(Note: An earlier version of this chapter was published in More Days in the Lives of Social Workers.*)*

Appendix A—Organizations of Interest to Social Workers

This is a partial listing of professional associations and other organizations that may be useful in exploring social work in general or specific areas of practice. They provide a variety of services, including professional conferences, job listings and placement services, and publication of professional journals and other reading materials.

Alliance for Children & Families
648 N. Plankinton Ave., Suite 425
Milwaukee, WI 53203
414-359-1040
http://www.alliance1.org

Alzheimer Society of Canada
20 Eglinton Avenue W. 16th Fl.
Toronto, ON M4R 1K8
416-488-8772
Toll-free: 1-800-616-8816
Email: info@alzheimer.ca
http://alzheimer.ca/en/Home

Alzheimer's Association
225 N. Michigan Avenue, Floor 17
Chicago, IL 60601-7633
800-272-3900 – 24-hour helpline
https://www.alz.org/

American Association for Adult and Continuing Education
1827 Powers Ferry Road
Building 14, Suite 100
Atlanta, Georgia 30339
678-271-4319
Email: Office@aaace.org
https://www.aaace.org

American Association for Marriage and Family Therapy
112 South Alfred Street
Alexandria, VA 22314-3061

703-838-9808
https://www.aamft.org/

American Association of Sex Educators, Counselors, and Therapists (AASECT)
35 E. Wacker Drive
Suite 850
Chicago, IL 60601
202-449-1099
Email: info@aasect.org
https://www.aasect.org/

American Association of Suicidology
5221 Wisconsin Ave. NW
Second Floor
Washington, DC 20015
202-237-2280
http://www.suicidology.org

American Board of Examiners in Clinical Social Work
Center/ABE
241 Humphrey Street
Marblehead, MA 01945
781-639-5270
Toll-free: 800-694-5285
https://abecsw.org/

American Camping Association
5000 State Road 67 North
Martinsville, IN 46151

765-342-8456
800-428-2267
https://www.acacamps.org/

American Counseling Association
6101 Stevenson Avenue
Suite 600
Alexandria, VA 22304
800-347-6647
https://www.counseling.org/

American Family Therapy Academy
1 Barstow Road, Suite P24
Great Neck, NY 11021
910-378-4601
https://afta.org/

American Foundation for AIDS Research (AmFAR)
120 Wall Street, 13th Floor
New York, NY 10005-3908
212-806-1600
http://www.amfar.org

American Humane Association
1400 16th Street NW, Suite 360
Washington, DC 20036
800-227-4645
Email: info@americanhumane.org
http://www.americanhumane.org

American Library Association
50 E. Huron Street
Chicago IL 60611
800-545-2433
http://www.ala.org/

American Professional Society on the Abuse of Children
1706 East Broad Street
Columbus, OH 43203
614-827-1321
Toll-free: 877-402-7722
https://www.apsac.org/

American Public Health Association
800 I Street, NW
Washington, DC 20001
202-777-2742
https://www.apha.org/

American Public Human Services Association
1133 19th Street, NW, Suite 400
Washington, DC 20036
202-682-0100
https://www.aphsa.org/

American Society for Reproductive Medicine
1209 Montgomery Highway
Birmingham, AL 35216
205-978-5000
Email: asrm@asrm.org
https://www.asrm.org/

American Society of Association Executives (ASAE)
1575 I Street, NW
11th floor
Washington, DC 20005
202-371-0940
Toll-free: 888-950-2723
https://www.asaecenter.org/

American Society on Aging
575 Market St., Suite 2100
San Francisco, CA 94105-2869
415-974-9600
Toll-free: 800-537-9728
http://www.asaging.org

Association for Ambulatory Behavioral Healthcare
247 Douglas Avenue
Portsmouth, VA 23707
757-673-3741
Email: aabhorg@cox.net
https://www.aabh.org/

Association for Community Organization and Social Administration
20560 Bensley Avenue
Lynwood, IL 60411
708-757-4187
Email: office@acosa.org
http://www.acosa.org

Association for Death Education and Counseling
400 S. 4th Street, Ste. 754E
Minneapolis, MN 55415 USA
612-337-1808
Email: adec@adec.org
https://www.adec.org/

Association for Experiential Education
PO Box 13246
Denver, CO 80201-4646
303-440-8844
http://www.aee.org

Association for Play Therapy
401 Clovis Avenue, Suite 107
Clovis, CA 93612
559-298-3400
Email: info@a4pt.org
https://www.a4pt.org/default.aspx

Association for the Treatment of Sexual Abusers (ATSA)
4900 SW Griffith Drive, Suite 274
Beaverton, OR 97005
503-643-1023
Email: ATSA@tsa.com
http://www.atsa.com

Association of Baccalaureate Social Work Program Directors
1701 Duke Street
Suite 200
Alexandria, VA 22314
703-519-2043
http://www.bpdonline.org

Association of Oncology Social Work
One Parkview Plaza, Suite 800
Oakbrook Terrace, IL 60181 USA
847-686-2233
Email: info@aows.org
http://www.aosw.org

Association of Police Social Workers
Email: info@policesocialwork.org
http://www.policesocialwork.org/

Association of Reproductive Health Professionals
1300 19th Street, NW
Suite 200
Washington, DC 20036
202-466-3825
ARHP@arhp.org
http://www.arhp.org

Association of Social Work Boards
400 S. Ridge Parkway, Suite B
Culpeper, VA 22701
540-829-6880
Toll-free: 800-225-6880
Email: info@aswb.org
https://www.aswb.org/

British Association of Social Workers
37 Waterloo Street,
Birmingham, England B2 5PP
+44 (0) 121 622-3911
Email: swk@basw.co.uk
https://www.basw.co.uk/

Canadian Association of Social Workers
383 Parkdale Avenue, Suite 402
Ottawa, ON, Canada K1Y 4R4
613-729-6668
Email: casw@casw-acts.ca
https://www.casw-acts.ca/en

Center for Parent Information and Resources
35 Halsey St., 4th Floor
Newark, NJ 07102
(973) 642-8100
Toll-free: 800-695-0285
http://www.parentcenterhub.org/

Child Welfare League of America
727 15th Street, NW, 12th Floor
Washington, DC 20005
Phone: 202-688-4200
Email: cwla@cwla.org
https://www.cwla.org/

Clinical Social Work Association
P.O. Box 10
Garrisonville, VA 22463
202-599-8443
administrator@clinicalsocialwork-association.org
https://www.clinicalsocialworkas-sociation.org

Clubhouse International
483 Tenth Avenue, Suite 205
New York, NY 10018
212-582-0343
Email: info@clubhouse-intl.org
http://clubhouse-intl.org/

Council of Nephrology Social Workers
National Kidney Foundation
30 E. 33rd Street
New York, NY 10016
800-622-9010
https://www.kidney.org/professionals/CNSW

Council on Social Work Education
1701 Duke Street, Suite 200
Alexandria, VA 22314
703-683-8080
Email: info@cswe.org
https://www.cswe.org/

Employee Assistance Professionals Association
4350 N. Fairfax Drive, Suite 740
Arlington, VA 22203
703-387-1000
Email: info@eapassn.org
http://www.eapassn.org

Ernest Becker Foundation
2606 2nd Avenue, #335
Seattle, WA 98121
206-428-1964
Email: info@ernestbecker.org
http://ernestbecker.org/

Federation for Children with Special Needs
529 Main Street
Suite 1M3
Boston, MA 02129
617-236-7210
Email: fcsninfo@fcsn.org
https://fcsn.org/

Gay, Lesbian, and Straight Education Network (GLSEN)
110 William Street, 30th Floor
New York, NY 10038
info@glsen.org
212-727-0135
https://www.glsen.org/

The Gerontological Society of America
1220 L Street NW, Suite 901
Washington, DC 20005
202-842-1275
https://www.geron.org/

Health Outreach Partners
1970 Broadway, Ste. 200
Oakland, CA 94612
510-268-0091
https://outreach-partners.org/

International Association for Social Work With Groups
101 West 23rd Street, Suite 108

New York, NY 10011
718-316-0299
http://www.iaswg.org

International Bullying Prevention Association
P.O. Box 99217
Troy, MI 48099
800-929-0397
Email: info@ibpaworld.org
https://ibpaworld.org/

International Expressive Arts Therapy Association
415-489-0698
Email: info@ieata.org
https://www.ieata.org/

International Federation of Social Workers
P.O. Box 6875
Schwarztorstrasse 22
CH-3001 Berne, Switzerland
(41) 22 548 36 25
Email: global@ifsw.org
http://ifsw.org/

International Society for Traumatic Stress Studies
One Parkview Plaza, Suite 800
Oakbrook Terrace, IL 60181 USA
847-686-2234
Email: info@istss.org
http://www.istss.org

The Joint Commission
1 Renaissance Blvd.
Oakbrook Terrace, IL 60181
630-792-5000
https://www.jointcommission.org/

NAADAC—The Association for Addiction Professionals
44 Canal Center Plaza #301
Alexandria, VA 22314
800-548-0497
Email: naadac@naadac.org
https://www.naadac.org/

NALGAP Inc.—The Association of Lesbian, Gay, Bisexual and Transgender Addiction Professionals and Their Allies
P.O. Box 123
Ocean Grove NJ 07756
Email: mccabe@nalgap.org
http://www.nalgap.org

National Alliance for the Mentally Ill
3803 North Fairfax Drive, Suite 100
Arlington, VA 22203
703-524-7600
Email: info@nami.org
https://www.nami.org/

National Association for Home Care and Hospice
228 7th Street, SE
Washington, DC 20003
202-547-7424
https://www.nahc.org/

National Association of Addiction Treatment Providers
The Chancery Building
1120 Lincoln Street, Suite 1303
Denver, CO 80203
888-574-1008
Email: info@naatp.org
https://www.naatp.org/

National Association of Black Social Workers
2305 Martin Luther King Ave., SE
Washington, DC 20020
202-678-4570
Email: OfficAssistant@nabsw.org
https://nabsw.site-ym.com/

National Association of Human Rights Workers
PO Box 1062
Rocky Mount, NC 27802
https://www.nahrw.org/

National Association of Professional Geriatric Care Managers
3275 West Ina Road, Suite 130
Tucson, AZ 85741-2198
520-881-8008
http://www.caremanager.org

National Association of Social Workers
750 First Street, NE, Suite 800
Washington, DC 20002
202-408-8600
Email: membership@socialworkers.org
https://www.socialworkers.org/

National Center for Prosecution of Child Abuse
1400 Crystal Drive, Suite 330
Arlington, VA 22202
703-549-9222
http://ndaa.org/ncpca.html

National Coalition Building Institute (NCBI)
8403 Colesville Road, Suite 1100
Metro Plaza Building
Silver Spring, MD 20910
240-638-2813
Email: info@ncbi.org
http://ncbi.org/

National Coalition for the Homeless
2201 P Street, NW
Washington, DC 20037
202-462-4822
info@nationalhomeless.org
http://www.nationalhomeless.org

National Hospice and Palliative Care Organization
1731 King Street
Alexandria, VA 22314
703-837-1500
https://www.nhpco.org/

National Organization for Victim Assistance (NOVA)
510 King St., Suite 424
Alexandria, VA 22314
703-535-6682
https://www.trynova.org/

National Organization of Forensic Social Work
498 184th St.
Osceola, WI 54020
608-561-2997
http://nofsw.org/

Network for Social Work Managers
905 E. 8th St.
Los Angeles, CA 90021
213-553-1870
Email: info@socialworkmanager.org
https://socialworkmanager.org/

Network of Jewish Human Service Agencies
50 Eisenhower Drive, Suite 100
Paramus, NJ 07652
201-977-2400
Email: info@networkjhsa.org
http://www.ajfca.org

North American Association of Christians in Social Work
P.O. Box 121
Botsford, CT 06404-0121
888-426-4712
info@nacsw.org
https://www.nacsw.org/

Outward Bound
910 Jackson Street
Suite 140
Golden, CO 80401
845-424-4000
https://www.outwardbound.org/

Parents, Families and Friends of Lesbians and Gays (PFLAG)
1828 L St., NW, Suite 660
Washington, DC 20036
202-467-8180
http://www.pflag.org

Project Adventure, Inc.
719 Cabot Street
Beverly, MA 01915
800-468-8898
Email: info@pa.org
http://www.pa.org

Psychotherapy Networker
5135 MacArthur Blvd., NW
Washington, DC 20016
888-8519498
Email: info@psychnetworker.org
https://www.psychotherapynetworker.org/

RESOLVE, The National Infertility Association
7918 Jones Branch Drive, Suite 300
McLean, VA 22102
702-556-7172
Email: info@resolve.org
https://resolve.org/

School Social Work Association of America
P.O. Box 3068
London, KY 40743
800-588-4149
Email: contactus@sswaa.org
https://www.sswaa.org/

The Sentencing Project
1705 De Sales St., NW
Washington, DC, 20036
202-628-0871
Email: staff@sentencingproject.org
http://www.sentencingproject.org

Social Welfare Action Alliance
Columbus Circle Station
P.O. Box 20563
New York, NY 10023
http://www.socialwelfareaction-alliance.org

Society for Social Work Leadership in Health Care
100 N. 20th St., Suite 400
Philadelphia, PA 19103
866-237-9542
Email: info@sswlhc.org
http://sswlhc.org/

Appendix B—Web Resources

The Internet offers information on virtually any subject, including many related to social work. Listed in this Appendix are some websites related to the various topics covered in this book. There are many more, and new sites are developed every day. This list is provided as a starting point. You will find many more as you explore the Web.

Information on the Internet comes from a variety of sources. Some sites are published by well known and respected organizations. Others are published by individuals who are seeking to express a particular bias or point of view. Over the years, it has become very easy to publish on the Web, and much of the information does not go through a peer review process. For that reason, it is necessary to evaluate for yourself the information you find online, and to decide which sites are valuable to you and which ones are not. Some criteria to look at include the scope of the site, the authority of the author and/or publisher, how the information is presented, how up-to-date the site is, accuracy, and quality of the overall structure of the site.

For more information on critically evaluating Web sites, see Dalhousie University's *6 Criteria for Websites* at *https://cdn.dal.ca/content/dam/dalhousie/pdf/library/CoreSkills/6_Criteria_for_Websites.pdf.* Another helpful resource for evaluating health information online is *Evaluating Health Information* (UCSF), available at *https://www.ucsfhealth.org/education/evaluating_health_information/.*

In addition to websites, the Internet offers mailing lists (electronic discussion groups) on a variety of topics. There are many related to social work. Subscribing to most Internet mailing lists is free and open to anyone. Many of the contributors to this book heard about the opportunity to contribute through announcements on Internet mailing lists. To find LISTSERV® mailing lists on a particular topic, search the CataList site (*http://www.lsoft.com/lists/listref.html*).

To find additional websites, you can search Google (*http://www.google.com*) or other search engines. Again, the sites listed here represent a small sample of all sites available online. Also, keep in mind that this book's publication date is 2019. Internet addresses sometimes become outdated.

GENERAL SOCIAL WORK WEBSITES

Information for Practice
https://ifp.nyu.edu

MacroSW
https://www.macrosw.com

National Association of Social Workers
https://www.socialworkers.org

The New Social Worker Magazine
https://www.socialworker.com

Social Justice Solutions
http://www.socialjusticesolutions.org/

PART 1—HEALTH CARE

The Body: The Complete HIV/AIDS Resource
http://www.thebody.com

Healthfinder
https://healthfinder.gov

HealthLine
https://www.healthline.com/

HIV InSite
http://hivinsite.ucsf.edu/

Merck Manual Professional Edition
https://www.merckmanuals.com/professional

NASW Standards for Social Work Practice in Healthcare Settings
https://www.socialworkers.org/LinkClick.aspx?fileticket=fFnsRHX-4HE%3D&portalid=0

U.S. Public Health Service Commissioned Corps
http://www.usphs.gov

PART 2—SCHOOL SOCIAL WORK

NASW Standards for School Social Work Services
https://www.socialworkers.org/LinkClick.aspx?fileticket=1Ze4-9-Os7E%3D&portalid=0

Rethinking Schools
https://www.rethinkingschools.org/

Teaching Tolerance
https://www.tolerance.org/

PART 3—CHILDREN, YOUTH, AND FAMILIES

Child Trends
https://www.childtrends.org/

Children Now
https://www.childrennow.org

Children's Voice
https://www.cwla.org/childrens-voice/

Coming Up Taller
http://www.cominguptaller.org

NASW Standards for Social Work Practice in Child Welfare
*https://www.socialworkers.org/LinkClick.aspx?fileticket=_Flu_
UDcEac%3D&portalid=0*

The National Human Services Assembly
https://www.nassembly.org/

StopBullying.Gov
http://www.stopbullying.gov

PART 4—MENTAL HEALTH AND DEVELOPMENTAL DISABILITIES

American Red Cross Disaster Health and Mental Health Volunteers
*https://www.redcross.org/volunteer/volunteer-opportunities/disaster-
health-mental-health-volunteer.html*

DisabilityInfo.gov
http://www.disabilityinfo.gov

Easter Seals
http://www.easterseals.com

Eye of the Storm: Disaster Mental Health
http://www.eyeofthestorminc.com

March of Dimes
https://www.marchofdimes.com

Psychotherapy.Net
http://www.psychotherapy.net/

PART 5—SUBSTANCE USE DISORDERS

Addiction Technology Transfer Center Network
https://attcnetwork.org/

NASW Standards for Social Work Practice With Clients With Substance
Use Disorders
*https://www.socialworkers.org/LinkClick.aspx?fileticket=ICxAggMy9CU%3
D&portalid=0*

Partnership for Drug-Free Kids
https://www.drugfree.org/

PART 6—PRIVATE PRACTICE

NASW Standards for Clinical Social Work in Social Work Practice
*https://www.socialworkers.org/LinkClick.aspx?fileticket=YOg4qdefLBE%3
D&portalid=0*

Psychotherapy Finances
http://www.psyfin.com

PART 7—CRIMINAL JUSTICE

Corrections.com
http://www.corrections.com/

PART 8—OLDER ADULTS

Aging—Kaiser Health News
https://khn.org/topics/aging/

Aging Today
https://www.asaging.org/blog/content-source/13

NASW Standards for Social Work Practice With Family Caregivers of Older
Adults
*https://www.socialworkers.org/LinkClick.aspx?fileticket=aUwQL98exRM%
3d&portalid=0*

NASW Standards for Social Work Services in Long-Term Care Facilities
*https://www.socialworkers.org/LinkClick.aspx?fileticket=cwW7lzBfYxg%3
d&portalid=0*

PART 9—END OF LIFE AND LOSS

End-of-Life Care: Social Work Policy Institute
http://www.socialworkpolicy.org/research/end-of-life-care.html

NASW Standards for Palliative and End-of-Life Care
*https://www.socialworkers.org/LinkClick.aspx?fileticket=xBMd58VwEhk%
3d&portalid=0*

Pallipedia
http://pallipedia.org/

PART 10—MANAGEMENT

American Society of Association Executives: Association Career HQ
https://www.associationcareerhq.org/en

Chronicle of Philanthropy
https://www.philanthropy.com/

Nonprofit Quarterly
https://nonprofitquarterly.org/

PART 11—VETERANS AND THE MILITARY

Military Careers
https://www.careersinthemilitary.com

NASW Standards for Social Work Practice With Service Members, Veterans,
and Their Families
*https://www.socialworkers.org/LinkClick.aspx?fileticket=fg817flDop0%3d
&portalid=0*

U.S. Department of Veterans Affairs VHA Social Work Page
https://www.socialwork.va.gov

PART 12—HIGHER AND CONTINUING EDUCATION

American College Personnel Association Career Center
http://www.myacpa.org/career-central

Chronicle of Higher Education
https://www.chronicle.com

NASW Standards for Continuing Professional Education
*https://www.socialworkers.org/LinkClick.aspx?fileticket=qrXmm_
Wt7jU%3d&portalid=0*

PART 13—INTERNATIONAL SOCIAL WORK

AmeriCares Foundation
https://www.americares.org/

InterAction: A United Voice for Global Change
https://www.interaction.org/

NASW Standards and Indicators for Cultural Competence in Social Work Practice
https://www.socialworkers.org/LinkClick.aspx?fileticket=7dVckZAYUmk% 3d&portalid=0

ReliefWeb
https://reliefWeb.int/

World Health Organization
https://www.who.int/

PART 14—POLICY PRACTICE

Center for Law and Social Policy
https://www.clasp.org

Congressional Research Institute for Social Work and Policy
https://crispinc.org/

Humphreys Institute for Political Social Work
https://ssw.uconn.edu/politicalinstitute/

Social Policy Overview: Encyclopedia of Social Work
http://oxfordre.com/socialwork/view/10.1093/acre-fore/9780199975839.001.0001/acrefore-9780199975839-e-607

PART 15—WORKING IN COMMUNITIES

American Libraries
https://americanlibrariesmagazine.org/

Undoing Racism
https://www.pisab.org/

Appendix C—Useful Government Websites

This is a partial listing of U.S. government websites that address issues related to social work practice.

GENERAL GOVERNMENT SITES

211
http://www.211.org/

Agency for Healthcare Research and Quality
https://www.ahrq.gov/

Bureau of Labor Statistics (U.S. Dept. of Labor)
https://www.bls.gov/

Centers for Disease Control and Prevention
https://www.cdc.gov/

Centers for Medicare & Medicaid Services
https://www.cms.gov/

Federal Committee on Statistical Methodology
https://nces.ed.gov/FCSM/index.asp

Government Accountability Office
https://www.gao.gov/

Library of Congress
https://www.loc.gov/

National Academies of Sciences, Engineering, and Medicine
http://www.nas.edu/

Office of Management and Budget
https://www.whitehouse.gov/omb/

U.S. Census Bureau
https://www.census.gov/

U.S. Department of Health and Human Services
https//:www.hhs.gov

PART 1—HEALTH CARE

Agency for Healthcare Research and Quality
https://www.ahrq.gov/

AidsInfo (U.S Dept. of Health and Human Services)
https://aidsinfo.nih.gov/

HHS's Office of Adolescent Health
https://www.hhs.gov/ash/oah/

Indian Health Service Elder Care Initiative
https://www.ihs.gov/eldercare/

Maternal and Child Health Bureau (Health Resources & Services
Administration)
https://mchb.hrsa.gov/

National Cancer Institute (NIH)
https://www.cancer.gov/

National Center for Health Statistics (CDC)
https://www.cdc.gov/nchs/

National Center for HIV/AIDS, Viral Hepatitis, STD, and TB Prevention
https://www.cdc.gov/nchhstp/

National Center for PTSD
https://www.ptsd.va.gov/

National Institute on Aging (NIH)
https://www.nia.nih.gov/health

National Institutes of Health
https://www.nih.gov/

National Institutes of Health Alzheimer's Disease and Related Dementias
https://www.nia.nih.gov/health/alzheimers/caregiving

National Prevention Information Network (Centers for Disease Control)
https://npin.cdc.gov/

Obesity Research at the National Institutes of Health (NIH)
https://obesityresearch.nih.gov/

Surgeon General
https://www.surgeongeneral.gov/

U.S. Dept. of Health and Human Services
Office of Minority Health
https://minorityhealth.hhs.gov/

Veterans Health Administration
https://www.va.gov/health

PART 2—SCHOOL SOCIAL WORK

Digital Literacy Pages of the National Telecommunications and
Information Administration
https://digitalliteracy.gov/

National Center for Education Statistics
https://nces.ed.gov/

U.S. Department of Education
https://www.ed.gov/

PART 3—CHILDREN, YOUTH, AND FAMILIES

Administration for Native Americans (U.S. Dept. of Health & Human
Services)
https://www.acf.hhs.gov/ana

Administration on Children, Youth and Families (ACYF)
https://www.acf.hhs.gov/

Child Welfare Information Gateway (Administration for Children & Families)
https://www.childwelfare.gov/

Eating Disorders pages of the National Institute of Mental Health
https://www.nimh.nih.gov/health/publications/eating-disorders/index.shtml

Eunice Kennedy Schriver National Institute of Child Health and
Development
https://www.nichd.nih.gov/

Federal Interagency Forum on Child and Family Statistics
https://www.childstats.gov/

Interagency Working Group on Youth Programs (IWGYP)
https://youth.gov/

Intercountry Adoption information—Dept. Of State Bureau of
Consular Affairs
https://travel.state.gov/content/travel/en/Intercountry-Adoption.html

National Gang Center—Office of Juvenile Justice and Delinquency
Prevention
https://www.nationalgangcenter.gov/

Office of Adolescent Health (U.S Dept. Of Health and Human Services)
https://www.hhs.gov/ash/oah/

Office of Juvenile Justice and Delinquency Prevention (U.S. Dept. of Justice)
https://www.ojjdp.gov/

U.S. Government Interagency Anti-Bully pages
https://www.stopbullying.gov/

PART 4—MENTAL HEALTH AND DEVELOPMENTAL DISABILITIES

Administration on Developmental Disabilities
http://acf.hhs.gov/programs/add/

Agency for Healthcare Research and Quality
https://www.ahrq.gov/

Department of Justice Information and Technical Assistance,
Americans With Disabilities Act
https://www.ada.gov/

Help and Treatment Pages, National Substance Abuse and Mental Health
Services Administration
https://www.nrepp.samhsa.gov/landing.aspx

National Institute of Mental Health
https://www.nimh.nih.gov/index.shtml

National Institute on Deafness and Other Communication Disorders
https://www.nidcd.nih.gov/

Social Security Administration
https://www.ssa.gov/

Suicide Prevention Resources, Substance Abuse and Mental Health
Services Administration
*https://www.samhsa.gov/programs-campaigns/tribal-training-technical-
assistance-center/resources/suicide-prevention*

PART 5—SUBSTANCE USE DISORDERS

Alcohol Policy and Information System (National Institute on
Alcohol Abuse and Alcoholism)
https://alcoholpolicy.niaaa.nih.gov/

Centers for Disease Control and Prevention
https://www.cdc.gov/

Centers for Medicare and Medicaid Services
https://www.cms.gov/

Centers for Substance Abuse Treatment (SAMHSA)
https://www.samhsa.gov/about-us/who-we-are/offices-centers/csat

Drug Enforcement Administration's Drug Fact Sheets
https://www.dea.gov/druginfo/factsheets.shtml

National Institute on Drug Abuse
https://www.drugabuse.gov/

Office of National Drug Abuse Policy (White House)
https://www.whitehouse.gov/ondcp/

Substance Abuse and Mental Health Services Administration
https://www.samhsa.gov

PART 6—PRIVATE PRACTICE

Small Business Administration
https://www.sba.gov/

Small Business Administration's Business Planning Guides
https://www.sba.gov/business-guide/plan-your-business/write-your-business-plan

PART 7—CRIMINAL JUSTICE

Bureau of Justice Statistics
https://bjs.gov/

Federal Bureau of Prisons
https://www.bop.gov/

Office of Justice Programs
https://ojp.gov/

Office of Juvenile Justice and Delinquency Prevention, Dept. of Justice
https://www.ojjdp.gov/

U.S. Sentencing Commission
https://www.ussc.gov/

Workplace Violence pages of the Occupational Safety and Health Administration
https://www.osha.gov/SLTC/workplaceviolence/index.html

PART 8—OLDER ADULTS

Administration for Community Living
https://www.acl.gov/

Administration on Aging
https://www.acl.gov/about-acl/administration-aging

Medicare pages of the U.S. Centers for Medicare & Medicaid Services.
https://www.medicare.gov/

National Center on Elder Abuse
https://ncea.acl.gov/

National Institute on Aging
https://www.nia.nih.gov/

National Institute on Aging Alzheimer's caregiving pages
https://www.nia.nih.gov/health/alzheimers/caregiving

National Institute on Aging health information pages
https://www.nia.nih.gov/health

Social Security Administration
https://www.ssa.gov/

PART 9 —END OF LIFE AND LOSS

Benefit Finder
https://www.benefits.gov/

Medicare.gov Hospice Page
https://www.medicare.gov/coverage/hospice-care

PART 10—MANAGEMENT

Employee Benefits Security Administration
https://www.dol.gov/agencies/ebsa

Internal Revenue Service
https://www.irs.gov/

Internal Revenue Service Tax-Exempt Organization pages
https://www.irs.gov/charities-non-profits/charitable-organizations

Small Business Administration
https://www.sba.gov/

U.S. Department of Labor
https://www.dol.gov/

Veterans' Employment and Training Service
https://www.dol.gov/vets/

Women's Bureau of the U.S Department of Labor
https://www.dol.gov/wb/

PART 11—VETERANS AND THE MILITARY

After Deployment Military Resources
http://afterdeployment.dcoe.mil/

Bureau of Labor Statistics
https://www.bls.gov/

Defense Suicide Prevention Office
http://www.dspo.mil/

National Archives and Records Administration
https://www.archives.gov/

National Center for PTSD (Department of Veterans Affairs)
https://www.ptsd.va.gov/

U.S. Department of Veterans Affairs
https://www.va.gov/

Veterans' Employment and Training Service
https://www.dol.gov/vets/

PART 12—HIGHER AND CONTINUING EDUCATION

National Center for Education Research
https://ies.ed.gov/ncer/randd/

National Center for Education Statistics
https://nces.ed.gov/

Office of Career, Technical and Adult Education
https://www2.ed.gov/about/offices/list/ovae/index.html

Office of Postsecondary Education
https://www2.ed.gov/about/offices/list/ope/index.html?src=oc

U.S. Department of Education
https://www.ed.gov/

PART 13—INTERNATIONAL SOCIAL WORK

Intercountry adoption pages—U.S. Department of State
https://travel.state.gov/content/travel/en/Intercountry-Adoption.html

UNESCO
https://en.unesco.org/

United Nations Environment Programme
https://www.unenvironment.org/

United Nations International Children's Emergency Fund (UNICEF)
https://www.unicef.org/

PART 14 POLICY PRACTICE

Congress.gov
https://www.congress.gov//

Congressional Budget Office
https://www.cbo.gov/

PART 15—WORKING IN COMMUNITIES

Corporation for National & Community Service
https://www.nationalservice.gov/

Federal Emergency Management Agency
https://www.fema.gov/

National Gang Center (U.S. Department of Justice)
https://www.nationalgangcenter.gov/

U.S. Citizenship and Immigration Services (Dept. of Homeland Security)
https://www.uscis.gov/

Appendix D—Social Media, Blogs, and Podcasts, Oh My!

Gone are the days of websites as static electronic brochures or even static news sources. Internet users at every level can now contribute their own thoughts and ideas via the comment function on blogs, creating their own blogs, interacting with peers and mentors through Facebook, making professional contacts on LinkedIn, using smartphone apps, and more.

Today's children are growing up with mouse in hand and smartphone in pocket. They communicate in new ways that are changing rapidly. Information is instantly available on virtually any topic, and they are connected electronically virtually 24-7. Children are growing up technologically savvy, and this has both positive and negative implications of importance to social workers.

Social media, blogs, and podcasts have relevance to social workers clinically, professionally, and ethically. Social workers need to know about the sites and technology our clients are using. We can use these technologies ourselves to connect with like-minded professionals. We need to know how technology is being used in positive ways (such as creating support systems) and in negative ones (such as cyberbullying and sexting).

This appendix is designed to help familiarize you with this ever-changing aspect of technology and provide a sample of how new technologies are being used by social workers, agencies, and the general public. Things change quickly and constantly in the social media sphere, so use your search skills to find what is available beyond what is listed here.

General Social Media

Facebook
http://www.facebook.com
Facebook has 2.27 billion active users as of early 2019. Among these users are social workers and their clients. The National Association of Social Workers and its state chapters have an active presence on Facebook through the pages and group features, as does *The New Social Worker* magazine, most schools of social work, and any

number of other social work-related organizations. There are also Facebook pages and groups related to just about any social issue which may be of interest to you and your clients.

Instagram
http://www.instagram.com
Instagram is a social media site/app that allows sharing of photos and videos. Use the search function to find social workers and others with similar interests. It had one billion users as of June 2018.

LinkedIn
http://www.linkedin.com
Geared toward professional networking, LinkedIn had 590 million users as of December 2018. A search of LinkedIn using the term "social work" found 1,830 organized LinkedIn groups in October 2018.

Twitter
http://www.twitter.com
Follow @newsocialworker, @CSocialWorkEd, @nasw, and @aswb, among others, to find out what is happening in the world of social work in 280 characters or less. Find Twitter chats, such as #MacroSW (@OfficialMacroSW).

Social Work Blogs

You can find blogs written by individual social workers, social work students, and social work educators. There are also blogs sponsored by schools of social work and professional organizations for social workers. Here are some examples.

Clinical Intersections
https://www.socialworker.com/feature-articles/clinical-intersections

EFS Supervision Strategies Blog
http://dscreationsellenfink.homestead.com/Blog.html

Gamer Therapist
http://gamertherapist.com

NASW Social Work Blog
http://www.socialworkblog.org/

The New Social Worker Self-Care A-Z Blog
https://www.socialworker.com/feature-articles/self-care

Notes From an Aspiring Humanitarian
https://notesfromanaspiringhumanitarian.com/

The Political Social Worker Blog
http://www.politicalsocialworker.org/blog-2/

Social Work Career
http://socialwork.career

Social Work Tech
http://www.socialworktech.com

Teaching and Learning in Social Work
https://www.laureliversonhitchcock.org/

Virtual Connections
http://njsmyth.wordpress.com/

Podcasts

Melanie Sage, Ph.D., MSW, assistant professor at the University at Buffalo School of Social Work, has compiled an extensive list of social work and social work-related podcasts at: *https://www.laureliversonhitchcock.org/2019/01/30/podcasts4socialwork/*

Jonathan Singer, Ph.D., LCSW, associate professor at Loyola University Chicago School of Social Work, pioneered the podcast platform for social workers. His podcast, *The Social Work Podcast* at *http://www.socialworkpodcast.com,* is the one I recommend if you must choose only one social work podcast to listen to.

The *inSocialWork Podcast* at *https://www.insocialwork.org/* is a well-established bi-weekly podcast produced by a team at the University at Buffalo School of Social Work. I highly recommend it.

The following are some newer podcasts hosted by social workers. I crowdsourced this list on Twitter and encourage you to check them out. This, of course, is a partial list, and I hope it will inspire you to find others to add to your own professional playlist.

Bending the Arc
https://www.sp2.upenn.edu/about/actionsp2/bending-the-arc/

Building Bridges
http://bscorbettconsulting.libsyn.com/

Decolonize Social Work
http://decolonizesocialwork.org/

Doin' the Work—Frontline Stories of Social Change
https://dointhework.podbean.com/

Hip Hop Social Worker
https://anchor.fm/hip-hop-social-worker

Macro Social Work Stories
https://soundcloud.com/user-274334905/

MacroSW Podcast
https://macrosw.com/podcast/

NASW Social Work Talks
https://www.socialworkers.org/news/nasw-social-work-talks-podcast

The New Social Worker® Podast Edition
http://anchor.fm/newsocialworker

Podsocs
http://www.podsocs.com/

The Roving Social Worker
https://www.stitcher.com/podcast/anchor-podcasts/the-roving-social-worker

Social Work Discoveries
https://swdiscoveries.com/

Social Work Stories
http://socialworkstories.podbean.com/

The Social Workers Radio Talk Show
https://thesocialworkersradiotalkshow.simplecast.fm/

Therapy Chat Podcast
https://www.bahealing.com/podcast/

Social Work Titles Published by White Hat Communications/ The New Social Worker Press

- The A-to-Z Self-Care Handbook for Social Workers and Other Helping Professionals
- Beginnings, Middles, & Ends: Sideways Stories on the Art and Soul of Social Work
- Days in the Lives of Gerontological Social Workers
- Days in the Lives of Social Workers
- The Field Placement Survival Guide
- Is It Ethical?
- More Days in the Lives of Social Workers
- On Clinical Social Work: Meditations and Truths From the Field
- Real World Clinical Social Work
- Riding the Mutual Aid Bus and Other Adventures in Group Work

The New Social Worker® Magazine

Visit us online at:

The New Social Worker Online
https://www.socialworker.com

SocialWorkJobBank
http://www.socialworkjobbank.com

White Hat Communications Store
http://shop.whitehatcommunications.com

Network with us:

http://www.facebook.com/newsocialworker
http://www.facebook.com/socialworkjobbank
http://www.twitter.com/newsocialworker
https://www.linkedin.com/groups/3041069

Printed in the USA
CPSIA information can be obtained
at www.ICGtesting.com
LVHW022035100923
757782LV00003B/46

9 781929 10984